100% Complete Ecommerce VB.Net Website Template

First Edition

Michael A. Hamilton

YBDS, LLC

100% Complete Ecommerce VB.Net Website Template

by Michael A. Hamilton

Printed in the United States of America.

Published by YBDS, LLC.

ISBN 978-0-9834174-2-2

You may purchase a copy of our companion disk which contains all files for the project at http://www.amazon.com/gp/product/B00AOU76K8!

Preface

Welcome to the first edition of *100% Complete Ecommerce VB.Net Website Template.* This book offers a complete VB.net ecommerce web site solution, including:

- Database structure (a visual schema is provided so you may easily reference the design)
- SQL Server database script to create the database structure and populate type tables
- Complete web form design for each page of the site
- Complete VB.Net code behind for each page of the site
- CSS style sheets for site formatting
- Complete instructions for acquiring web hosting for the site
- Complete PayPal™ account setup instructions
- Complete PayPal™ integration into the application, allowing you to accept electronic payments via PayPal™ for your goods or services
- Complete instructions for uploading your project files to the web host

Please do not expect a complete overview of VB.Net in this book; the purpose of this book is to provide you with a complete, VB.Net ecommerce web site solution that you may use to distribute your own goods and services.

The completed product from the instructions contained in this book provides the following functionality:

- Completely data driven website
- Shopping Cart
- Checkout (using PayPal™)
- User account registration
- Login / Logout (each user session is unique)
- Search engine that searches the products in the database
- Scalable database design that allows new products and categories to be easily added
- User order history reporting (admin functionality only, not visible to registered users)
- Customer list reporting (admin functionality only, not visible to registered users)
- Automated inventory control
- FAQ
- About Us history page
- Contact Us page
- Admin tool for uploading new products (pictures are also uploaded with this tool)
- Users are automatically sent personalized email confirmation upon completion of registration
- Users are automatically sent personalized order confirmation after PayPal™ payment completes their order

You may purchase a copy of our companion disk which contains all files for the project at http://www.amazon.com/gp/product/B00AOU76K8!

Screenshots are provided as part of the step by step solution strategy in an attempt to completely illustrate how a subroutine or function will work. Screenshots also are used to display the final results of code contained herein. We would like to expressly thank the Microsoft Corporation for their generosity in allowing the use of screenshots for tutorial books; all screenshots were used with permission from Microsoft. No third party advertisement occurs in this book as a result of screenshots; for a complete review of the Microsoft policies, please visit the Microsoft Copyrighted Content Policy page.

All code examples in this book may be used for your needs. In fact, it is encouraged. We are confident that the benefits you receive from using the ecommerce web solution from this book will far exceed the cover price of the text. **You may view the site which this book was modeled from at http://www.yourbestdatasolution.com.** Additionally, you may purchase a copy of our companion disk which contains all files for the project at **http://www.yourbestdatasolution.com/ViewCategories.aspx**. Click 'View Products' link next to the **eBook Companion Disks** category in order to view and add the companion disk to your shopping cart; you will need to create a free account on our website and you must also have an active PayPal™ account in order to complete checkout for the companion disk for this book.

Finally, we welcome suggestions and comments from our readers in preparation for a second edition of this book. Please submit any ideas or problems that you would like solutions to at **http://www.yourbestdatasolution.com/BookComments.aspx**. We encourage you to review this eBook and click the Like button as well. You may also Like us on Facebook; our page is named ***100% Complete Ecommerce VB.Net Website Template*** – just follow the previous link! Use this page as a community forum for questions and comments!

How to Contact Us

mikehamilton@yourbestdatasolution.com

Contents

Required Materials .... Page 1

Web Hosting Account Setup .... Page 2

SQL Database Setup .... Page 3

PayPal™ Account Setup .... Page 21

Project Initialization .... Page 22

About Us Server Page .... Page 25

About Us Code Behind .... Page 29

Add Product Server Page .... Page 31

Add Product Code Behind .... Page 36

API Error Server Page .... Page 44

Billing Server Page .... Page 45

Billing Code Behind .... Page 49

Checkout Server Page .... Page 58

Checkout Code Behind .... Page 63

ConfirmItemAdd Server Page .... Page 71

ConfirmItemAdd Code Behind .... Page 75

Contact Us Server Page .... Page 78

Contact Us Code Behind .... Page 82

Create Account Server Page .... Page 84

Create Account Code Behind .... Page 92

Customer Details Server Page .... Page 106

Customer Details Code Behind .... Page 111

Customers Server Page .... Page 117

Customers Code Behind .... Page 121

Default Server Page .... Page 126

Default Code Behind .... Page 131

EditProduct Server Page .... Page 133

EditProduct Code Behind .... Page 138

expresscheckout Server Page .... Page 148

expresscheckout Code Behind .... Page 149

FAQ Server Page .... Page 150

FAQ Code Behind .... Page 156

Login Server Page .... Page 158

Login Code Behind .... Page 162

Logout Server Page .... Page 167

Logout Code Behind .... Page 170

OrderConfirmation Server Page .... Page 172

OrderConfirmation Code Behind .... Page 176

OrderDetails Server Page .... Page 187

OrderDetails Code Behind .... Page 191

OrderHistory Server Page .... Page 201

OrderHistory Code Behind .... Page 205

OrderReview Server Page .... Page 209

OrderReview Code Behind .... Page 214

Password Server Page .... Page 228

Password Code Behind .... Page 232

ProductDetails Server Page .... Page 235

ProductDetails Code Behind .... Page 240

You may purchase a copy of our companion disk which contains all files for the project at http://www.amazon.com/gp/product/B00AOU76K8!

SearchProducts Server Page .... Page 253

SearchProducts Code Behind .... Page 257

Shipping Server Page .... Page 262

Shipping Code Behind .... Page 266

User Message Server Page .... Page 274

User Message Code Behind .... Page 278

View Cart Server Page .... Page 280

View Cart Code Behind .... Page 284

View Categories Server Page .... Page 291

View Categories Code Behind .... Page 295

View Orders Server Page .... Page 298

View Orders Code Behind .... Page 302

View Products Server Page .... Page 308

View Products Code Behind .... Page 312

App_Code – DatabaseAccess.vb .... Page 317

App_Code – paypalfunctions.vb .... Page 321

CSS Style Sheet .... Page 332

web.config file .... Page 343

Uploading Files to Web Host .... Page 349

User Functionality .... Page 350

About the Author .... Page 367

Required Materials

In addition to the code provided by this book, the following materials are needed to successfully implement your ecommerce website solution with the instructions provided in this book:

- Microsoft Visual Studio 2008
- SQL Server Management Studio
- ASP.Net 3.5 SP1 hosting (purchased from DiscountASP.Net)
- SQL 2008 Hosting (purchased from DiscountASP.Net)
- A verified PayPal™ business account
- A PayPal™ Developer account (this is a testing environment – see PayPal™ account setup chapter)
- PayPal™ API development credentials (see PayPal™ account setup chapter)
- PayPal™ API live credentials (see PayPal™ account setup chapter)
- Your domain name for your business or organization (purchased from DiscountASP.Net)
- Computer and internet connection to upload files from your project to the web site
- Optional but recommended: *A 100% Complete Ecommerce VB.Net Website Template* companion disk available at http://www.yourbestdatasolution.com/ViewCategories.aspx. This disk contains all project files and the spacer graphics used to format each page. Click 'View Products' link next to the software category in order to add the companion disk to your shopping cart; you will need to create an account on our website and you must also have an active PayPal™ account in order to complete checkout for the companion disk for this book. This disk will save you the effort of typing the code and SQL in this eBook!

Web Hosting Account Setup

I highly recommend discountAsp.net for web hosting. Please complete the following steps to establish your web hosting account:

1. Go to http://discountasp.net.
2. Click the 'Sign Up Now' button for 3 months of free ASP.net web hosting. Unless you have thousands of products to sell, the base hosting plan should be sufficient.
3. Now, click the 'Next' button. Enter your existing domain name and click 'Use my existing domain', or enter your desired domain name in the textbox and check for availability.
4. Now, **Enter the following code for your Affiliate ID: NQDSQR -** ***Note: Setup fee for the site may be waived.***
5. Choose quarterly or annual billing period and also choose 'Windows 2008 Platform with IIS 7.0' for your Web Server. Also, select your location (US or UK).
6. Click 'Proceed to Next Step'
7. Complete your billing information. Your username will be sent to the primary email address that you list on your account. Also, the password that you create will be used to access the Control Panel provided by discountASP.net. *The Control Panel provides information that is used next to setup your SQL database, so keep the password in a safe, accessible place.*
8. Submit the order, and then check your primary email address for your username. You will return from your email to discountASP.net to set up the SQL database next.

SQL Database Setup

First, you need to setup the SQL database table structure and populate the type tables with initial values. First, you need to purchase the database from discountASP.net by doing the following:

1. Go to http://discountasp.net.
2. Using your username and password you received upon sign-up, log into the Control Panel.
3. Under Database Management, click the 'MS SQL Manager' link.
4. Click 'Order New Database'.
5. Select the version that is compatible with your SQL Server Management Studio.
6. Click 'Order New'.
7. After you have completed the order to add the database, click the 'MS SQL Manager' link again.
8. Next to your newly created database, click the 'Manage' button.
9. Here, you see the MS SQL Server information. This is critical information that you will need to connect SQL Server Management Studio to the database and also you will need the connection string to connect to the database thru the web application. Remain logged into the Control Panel to complete the next steps below.

Next, open SQL Server Management Studio and you will connect via SSMS to your database for the first time by doing the following steps:

1. The 'Connect to Server' dialog box appears upon opening SSMS.
2. Select 'Database Engine' for Server Type.
3. Enter the SQL Server Name from your MS SQL Server information in the discountASP.net Control Panel for the Server name in the SSMS dialog box.
4. Select SQL Server Authentication as the Authentication type.
5. Enter the Database Login from your MS SQL Server information in the discountASP.net Control Panel for the Login in the SSMS dialog box.
6. Enter your password for the Password in the SSMS dialog box.
7. Click 'Connect' and you are now connected to your database via SQL Server Management Studio.

You are now ready to run the SQL script that will set up your database structure. Once this script is completed, your database will be set up exactly like the schema depicted in Fig. 1 below:

Fig. 1

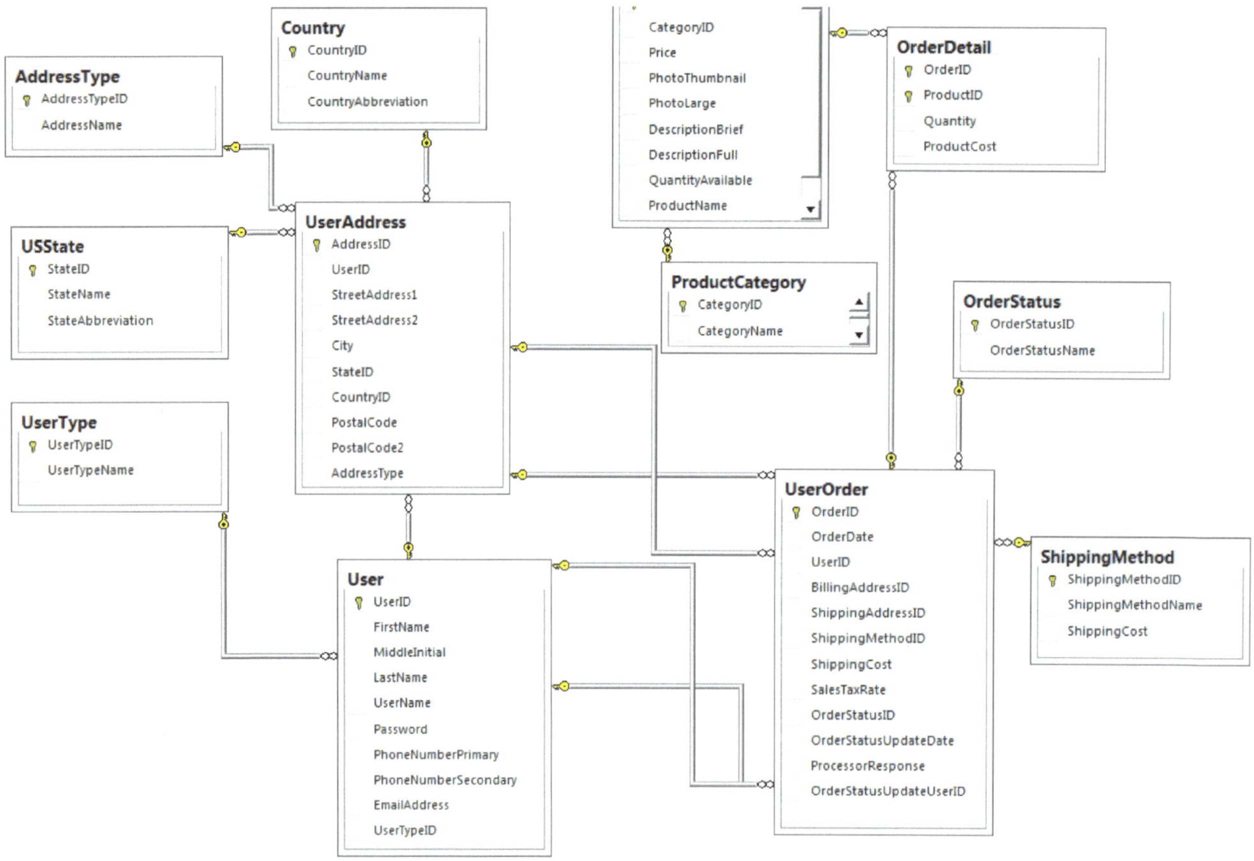

To run the SQL script, please do the following:

1. Expand the top level tree node.
2. Expand the Databases node.
3. Expand the node that is your database.
4. Open a new query window.
5. Run the SQL script that follows this list.
6. Right click your database node and Refresh.

You may purchase a copy of our companion disk which contains all files for the project at http://www.amazon.com/gp/product/B00AOU76K8!

Here is the SQL script to run in step 5; be sure to replace the Database Name highlighted in red just below this line:

```
USE [Insert your Database Name found in the Control Panel
Here]
GO

/* FIRST, THE TYPE TABLES ARE CREATED. */
/****** Object:  Table [dbo].[AddressType]    Script Date: 12/14/2011
18:18:33 ******/
SET ANSI_NULLS ON
GO

SET QUOTED_IDENTIFIER ON
GO

SET ANSI_PADDING ON
GO

CREATE TABLE [dbo].[AddressType](
	[AddressTypeID] [int] IDENTITY(1,1) NOT NULL,
	[AddressName] [varchar](255) NULL,
PRIMARY KEY CLUSTERED
(
	[AddressTypeID] ASC
)WITH (PAD_INDEX  = OFF, STATISTICS_NORECOMPUTE  = OFF, IGNORE_DUP_KEY = OFF,
ALLOW_ROW_LOCKS  = ON, ALLOW_PAGE_LOCKS  = ON) ON [PRIMARY]
) ON [PRIMARY]

GO

SET ANSI_PADDING OFF
GO

/****** Object:  Table [dbo].[USState]    Script Date: 12/14/2011 18:32:58
******/
SET ANSI_NULLS ON
GO

SET QUOTED_IDENTIFIER ON
GO

SET ANSI_PADDING ON
GO

CREATE TABLE [dbo].[USState](
	[StateID] [int] IDENTITY(1,1) NOT NULL,
	[StateName] [varchar](255) NULL,
	[StateAbbreviation] [varchar](255) NULL,
PRIMARY KEY CLUSTERED
(
	[StateID] ASC
)WITH (PAD_INDEX  = OFF, STATISTICS_NORECOMPUTE  = OFF, IGNORE_DUP_KEY = OFF,
ALLOW_ROW_LOCKS  = ON, ALLOW_PAGE_LOCKS  = ON) ON [PRIMARY]
) ON [PRIMARY]
```

```
GO

SET ANSI_PADDING OFF
GO

/****** Object:  Table [dbo].[UserType]    Script Date: 12/14/2011 18:32:23
******/
SET ANSI_NULLS ON
GO

SET QUOTED_IDENTIFIER ON
GO

SET ANSI_PADDING ON
GO

CREATE TABLE [dbo].[UserType](
	[UserTypeID] [int] IDENTITY(1,1) NOT NULL,
	[UserTypeName] [varchar](255) NULL,
PRIMARY KEY CLUSTERED
(
	[UserTypeID] ASC
)WITH (PAD_INDEX  = OFF, STATISTICS_NORECOMPUTE  = OFF, IGNORE_DUP_KEY = OFF,
ALLOW_ROW_LOCKS  = ON, ALLOW_PAGE_LOCKS  = ON) ON [PRIMARY]
) ON [PRIMARY]

GO

SET ANSI_PADDING OFF
GO

/****** Object:  Table [dbo].[ShippingMethod]    Script Date: 12/14/2011
18:31:50 ******/
SET ANSI_NULLS ON
GO

SET QUOTED_IDENTIFIER ON
GO

SET ANSI_PADDING ON
GO

CREATE TABLE [dbo].[ShippingMethod](
	[ShippingMethodID] [int] IDENTITY(1,1) NOT NULL,
	[ShippingMethodName] [varchar](255) NULL,
	[ShippingCost] [decimal](10, 2) NULL,
PRIMARY KEY CLUSTERED
(
	[ShippingMethodID] ASC
)WITH (PAD_INDEX  = OFF, STATISTICS_NORECOMPUTE  = OFF, IGNORE_DUP_KEY = OFF,
ALLOW_ROW_LOCKS  = ON, ALLOW_PAGE_LOCKS  = ON) ON [PRIMARY]
) ON [PRIMARY]

GO

SET ANSI_PADDING OFF
```

```
GO

/****** Object:  Table [dbo].[Country]    Script Date: 12/14/2011 18:20:36
******/
SET ANSI_NULLS ON
GO

SET QUOTED_IDENTIFIER ON
GO

SET ANSI_PADDING ON
GO

CREATE TABLE [dbo].[Country](
	[CountryID] [int] IDENTITY(1,1) NOT NULL,
	[CountryName] [varchar](255) NULL,
	[CountryAbbreviation] [varchar](3) NULL,
PRIMARY KEY CLUSTERED
(
	[CountryID] ASC
)WITH (PAD_INDEX  = OFF, STATISTICS_NORECOMPUTE  = OFF, IGNORE_DUP_KEY = OFF,
ALLOW_ROW_LOCKS  = ON, ALLOW_PAGE_LOCKS  = ON) ON [PRIMARY]
) ON [PRIMARY]

GO

SET ANSI_PADDING OFF
GO

/****** Object:  Table [dbo].[ProductCategory]    Script Date: 12/14/2011
18:24:51 ******/
SET ANSI_NULLS ON
GO

SET QUOTED_IDENTIFIER ON
GO

SET ANSI_PADDING ON
GO

CREATE TABLE [dbo].[ProductCategory](
	[CategoryID] [int] IDENTITY(1,1) NOT NULL,
	[CategoryName] [varchar](255) NULL,
PRIMARY KEY CLUSTERED
(
	[CategoryID] ASC
)WITH (PAD_INDEX  = OFF, STATISTICS_NORECOMPUTE  = OFF, IGNORE_DUP_KEY = OFF,
ALLOW_ROW_LOCKS  = ON, ALLOW_PAGE_LOCKS  = ON) ON [PRIMARY]
) ON [PRIMARY]

GO

SET ANSI_PADDING OFF
GO

/****** Object:  Table [dbo].[OrderStatus]    Script Date: 12/14/2011
18:35:22 ******/
```

```
SET ANSI_NULLS ON
GO

SET QUOTED_IDENTIFIER ON
GO

SET ANSI_PADDING ON
GO

CREATE TABLE [dbo].[OrderStatus](
	[OrderStatusID] [int] IDENTITY(1,1) NOT NULL,
	[OrderStatusName] [varchar](255) NULL,
PRIMARY KEY CLUSTERED
(
	[OrderStatusID] ASC
)WITH (PAD_INDEX  = OFF, STATISTICS_NORECOMPUTE  = OFF, IGNORE_DUP_KEY = OFF,
ALLOW_ROW_LOCKS  = ON, ALLOW_PAGE_LOCKS  = ON) ON [PRIMARY]
) ON [PRIMARY]

GO

SET ANSI_PADDING OFF
GO
/* END TYPE TABLES */

/****** Object:  Table [dbo].[Product]    Script Date: 12/14/2011 18:23:20
******/
SET ANSI_NULLS ON
GO

SET QUOTED_IDENTIFIER ON
GO

SET ANSI_PADDING ON
GO

CREATE TABLE [dbo].[Product](
	[ProductID] [int] IDENTITY(1,1) NOT NULL,
	[CategoryID] [int] NULL,
	[Price] [decimal](10, 2) NULL,
	[PhotoThumbnail] [varchar](255) NULL,
	[PhotoLarge] [varchar](255) NULL,
	[DescriptionBrief] [varchar](255) NULL,
	[DescriptionFull] [varchar](255) NULL,
	[QuantityAvailable] [int] NULL,
	[ProductName] [nvarchar](80) NULL,
PRIMARY KEY CLUSTERED
(
	[ProductID] ASC
)WITH (PAD_INDEX  = OFF, STATISTICS_NORECOMPUTE  = OFF, IGNORE_DUP_KEY = OFF,
ALLOW_ROW_LOCKS  = ON, ALLOW_PAGE_LOCKS  = ON) ON [PRIMARY]
) ON [PRIMARY]

GO

SET ANSI_PADDING OFF
GO
```

```
ALTER TABLE [dbo].[Product]  WITH CHECK ADD FOREIGN KEY([CategoryID])
REFERENCES [dbo].[ProductCategory] ([CategoryID])
GO

/****** Object:  Table [dbo].[User]    Script Date: 12/14/2011 18:41:27
******/
SET ANSI_NULLS ON
GO

SET QUOTED_IDENTIFIER ON
GO

SET ANSI_PADDING ON
GO

CREATE TABLE [dbo].[User](
	[UserID] [int] IDENTITY(1,1) NOT NULL,
	[FirstName] [varchar](255) NULL,
	[MiddleInitial] [varchar](255) NULL,
	[LastName] [varchar](255) NULL,
	[UserName] [varchar](255) NULL,
	[Password] [varchar](255) NULL,
	[PhoneNumberPrimary] [varchar](255) NULL,
	[PhoneNumberSecondary] [varchar](255) NULL,
	[EmailAddress] [varchar](255) NULL,
	[UserTypeID] [int] NULL,
PRIMARY KEY CLUSTERED
(
	[UserID] ASC
)WITH (PAD_INDEX  = OFF, STATISTICS_NORECOMPUTE  = OFF, IGNORE_DUP_KEY = OFF,
ALLOW_ROW_LOCKS  = ON, ALLOW_PAGE_LOCKS  = ON) ON [PRIMARY]
) ON [PRIMARY]

GO

SET ANSI_PADDING OFF
GO

ALTER TABLE [dbo].[User]  WITH CHECK ADD FOREIGN KEY([UserTypeID])
REFERENCES [dbo].[UserType] ([UserTypeID])
GO

/****** Object:  Table [dbo].[UserAddress]    Script Date: 12/14/2011
18:44:33 ******/
SET ANSI_NULLS ON
GO

SET QUOTED_IDENTIFIER ON
GO

SET ANSI_PADDING ON
GO

CREATE TABLE [dbo].[UserAddress](
	[AddressID] [int] IDENTITY(1,1) NOT NULL,
	[UserID] [int] NULL,
```

```
	[StreetAddress1] [varchar](255) NULL,
	[StreetAddress2] [varchar](255) NULL,
	[City] [varchar](255) NULL,
	[StateID] [int] NULL,
	[CountryID] [int] NULL,
	[PostalCode] [varchar](25) NULL,
	[PostalCode2] [varchar](25) NULL,
	[AddressType] [int] NULL,
PRIMARY KEY CLUSTERED
(
	[AddressID] ASC
)WITH (PAD_INDEX  = OFF, STATISTICS_NORECOMPUTE  = OFF, IGNORE_DUP_KEY = OFF,
ALLOW_ROW_LOCKS  = ON, ALLOW_PAGE_LOCKS  = ON) ON [PRIMARY]
) ON [PRIMARY]

GO

SET ANSI_PADDING OFF
GO

ALTER TABLE [dbo].[UserAddress]  WITH CHECK ADD FOREIGN KEY([AddressType])
REFERENCES [dbo].[AddressType] ([AddressTypeID])
GO

ALTER TABLE [dbo].[UserAddress]  WITH CHECK ADD FOREIGN KEY([CountryID])
REFERENCES [dbo].[Country] ([CountryID])
GO

ALTER TABLE [dbo].[UserAddress]  WITH CHECK ADD FOREIGN KEY([StateID])
REFERENCES [dbo].[USState] ([StateID])
GO

ALTER TABLE [dbo].[UserAddress]  WITH CHECK ADD FOREIGN KEY([UserID])
REFERENCES [dbo].[User] ([UserID])
GO

/****** Object:  Table [dbo].[UserOrder]    Script Date: 12/14/2011 18:45:08
******/
SET ANSI_NULLS ON
GO

SET QUOTED_IDENTIFIER ON
GO

SET ANSI_PADDING ON
GO

CREATE TABLE [dbo].[UserOrder](
	[OrderID] [int] IDENTITY(1,1) NOT NULL,
	[OrderDate] [datetime] NULL,
	[UserID] [int] NULL,
	[BillingAddressID] [int] NULL,
	[ShippingAddressID] [int] NULL,
	[ShippingMethodID] [int] NULL,
	[ShippingCost] [decimal](10, 2) NULL,
	[SalesTaxRate] [decimal](10, 2) NULL,
	[OrderStatusID] [int] NULL,
```

```
        [OrderStatusUpdateDate] [datetime] NULL,
        [ProcessorResponse] [varchar](255) NULL,
        [OrderStatusUpdateUserID] [int] NULL,
PRIMARY KEY CLUSTERED
(
        [OrderID] ASC
)WITH (PAD_INDEX  = OFF, STATISTICS_NORECOMPUTE  = OFF, IGNORE_DUP_KEY = OFF,
ALLOW_ROW_LOCKS  = ON, ALLOW_PAGE_LOCKS  = ON) ON [PRIMARY]
) ON [PRIMARY]

GO

SET ANSI_PADDING OFF
GO

ALTER TABLE [dbo].[UserOrder]  WITH CHECK ADD FOREIGN KEY([BillingAddressID])
REFERENCES [dbo].[UserAddress] ([AddressID])
GO

ALTER TABLE [dbo].[UserOrder]  WITH CHECK ADD FOREIGN KEY([OrderStatusID])
REFERENCES [dbo].[OrderStatus] ([OrderStatusID])
GO

ALTER TABLE [dbo].[UserOrder]  WITH CHECK ADD FOREIGN
KEY([OrderStatusUpdateUserID])
REFERENCES [dbo].[User] ([UserID])
GO

ALTER TABLE [dbo].[UserOrder]  WITH CHECK ADD FOREIGN
KEY([ShippingAddressID])
REFERENCES [dbo].[UserAddress] ([AddressID])
GO

ALTER TABLE [dbo].[UserOrder]  WITH CHECK ADD FOREIGN KEY([ShippingMethodID])
REFERENCES [dbo].[ShippingMethod] ([ShippingMethodID])
GO

ALTER TABLE [dbo].[UserOrder]  WITH CHECK ADD FOREIGN KEY([UserID])
REFERENCES [dbo].[User] ([UserID])
GO

/****** Object:  Table [dbo].[OrderDetail]    Script Date: 12/14/2011
18:21:11 ******/
SET ANSI_NULLS ON
GO

SET QUOTED_IDENTIFIER ON
GO

CREATE TABLE [dbo].[OrderDetail](
        [OrderID] [int] NOT NULL,
        [ProductID] [int] NOT NULL,
        [Quantity] [int] NULL,
        [ProductCost] [decimal](10, 2) NULL,
PRIMARY KEY CLUSTERED
(
        [OrderID] ASC,
```

```
        [ProductID] ASC
)WITH (PAD_INDEX  = OFF, STATISTICS_NORECOMPUTE  = OFF, IGNORE_DUP_KEY = OFF,
ALLOW_ROW_LOCKS  = ON, ALLOW_PAGE_LOCKS  = ON) ON [PRIMARY]
) ON [PRIMARY]

GO

ALTER TABLE [dbo].[OrderDetail]  WITH CHECK ADD FOREIGN KEY([OrderID])
REFERENCES [dbo].[UserOrder] ([OrderID])
GO

ALTER TABLE [dbo].[OrderDetail]  WITH CHECK ADD FOREIGN KEY([ProductID])
REFERENCES [dbo].[Product] ([ProductID])
GO

INSERT INTO [dbo].[AddressType]
           ([AddressName])
     VALUES
           ('Billing')
GO

INSERT INTO [dbo].[AddressType]
           ([AddressName])
     VALUES
           ('Shipping')
GO

INSERT INTO [dbo].[OrderStatus]
           ([OrderStatusName])
     VALUES
           ('Paid')
GO

INSERT INTO [dbo].[OrderStatus]
           ([OrderStatusName])
     VALUES
           ('Shipped')
GO

INSERT INTO [dbo].[ProductCategory]
           ([CategoryName])
     VALUES
           ('INSERT YOUR PRODUCT CATEGORY HERE')
GO

INSERT INTO [dbo].[ShippingMethod]
           ([ShippingMethodName]
           ,[ShippingCost])
     VALUES
           ('USPS',2.50)
GO

INSERT INTO [dbo].[ShippingMethod]
           ([ShippingMethodName]
           ,[ShippingCost])
     VALUES
           ('Pickup',0.00)
```

```
GO

INSERT INTO [dbo].[Country]
           ([CountryName]
           ,[CountryAbbreviation])
     VALUES
           ('United States','US')
GO

INSERT INTO [dbo].[Country]
           ([CountryName]
           ,[CountryAbbreviation])
     VALUES
           ('Canada','CA')
GO

INSERT INTO [dbo].[UserType]
           ([UserTypeName])
     VALUES
           ('Customer')
GO

INSERT INTO [dbo].[UserType]
           ([UserTypeName])
     VALUES
           ('Administrator')
GO

INSERT INTO [dbo].[USState]
           ([StateName]
           ,[StateAbbreviation])
     VALUES
           ('Alaska', 'AK')
GO

INSERT INTO [dbo].[USState]
           ([StateName]
           ,[StateAbbreviation])
     VALUES
           ('Alabama', 'AL')
GO

INSERT INTO [dbo].[USState]
           ([StateName]
           ,[StateAbbreviation])
     VALUES
           ('Arkansas', 'AR')
GO

INSERT INTO [dbo].[USState]
           ([StateName]
           ,[StateAbbreviation])
     VALUES
           ('American Samoa', 'AS')
GO

INSERT INTO [dbo].[USState]
```

```
            ([StateName]
            ,[StateAbbreviation])
     VALUES
            ('Arizona', 'AZ')
GO

INSERT INTO [dbo].[USState]
            ([StateName]
            ,[StateAbbreviation])
     VALUES
            ('California', 'CA')
GO

INSERT INTO [dbo].[USState]
            ([StateName]
            ,[StateAbbreviation])
     VALUES
            ('Colorado', 'CO')
GO

INSERT INTO [dbo].[USState]
            ([StateName]
            ,[StateAbbreviation])
     VALUES
            ('Connecticut', 'CT')
GO

INSERT INTO [dbo].[USState]
            ([StateName]
            ,[StateAbbreviation])
     VALUES
            ('District of Columbia', 'DC')
GO

INSERT INTO [dbo].[USState]
            ([StateName]
            ,[StateAbbreviation])
     VALUES
            ('Delaware', 'DE')
GO

INSERT INTO [dbo].[USState]
            ([StateName]
            ,[StateAbbreviation])
     VALUES
            ('Florida', 'FL')
GO

INSERT INTO [dbo].[USState]
            ([StateName]
            ,[StateAbbreviation])
     VALUES
            ('Georgia', 'GA')
GO

INSERT INTO [dbo].[USState]
            ([StateName]
```

```
          ,[StateAbbreviation])
     VALUES
          ('Guam', 'GU')
GO

INSERT INTO [dbo].[USState]
          ([StateName]
          ,[StateAbbreviation])
     VALUES
          ('Hawaii', 'HI')
GO

INSERT INTO [dbo].[USState]
          ([StateName]
          ,[StateAbbreviation])
     VALUES
          ('Iowa', 'IA')
GO

INSERT INTO [dbo].[USState]
          ([StateName]
          ,[StateAbbreviation])
     VALUES
          ('Idaho', 'ID')
GO

INSERT INTO [dbo].[USState]
          ([StateName]
          ,[StateAbbreviation])
     VALUES
          ('Illinois', 'IL')
GO

INSERT INTO [dbo].[USState]
          ([StateName]
          ,[StateAbbreviation])
     VALUES
          ('Indiana', 'IN')
GO

INSERT INTO [dbo].[USState]
          ([StateName]
          ,[StateAbbreviation])
     VALUES
          ('Kansas', 'KS')
GO

INSERT INTO [dbo].[USState]
          ([StateName]
          ,[StateAbbreviation])
     VALUES
          ('Kentucky', 'KY')
GO

INSERT INTO [dbo].[USState]
          ([StateName]
          ,[StateAbbreviation])
```

```
     VALUES
           ('Louisiana', 'LA')
GO

INSERT INTO [dbo].[USState]
           ([StateName]
           ,[StateAbbreviation])
     VALUES
           ('Massachusetts', 'MA')
GO

INSERT INTO [dbo].[USState]
           ([StateName]
           ,[StateAbbreviation])
     VALUES
           ('Maryland', 'MD')
GO

INSERT INTO [dbo].[USState]
           ([StateName]
           ,[StateAbbreviation])
     VALUES
           ('Maine', 'ME')
GO

INSERT INTO [dbo].[USState]
           ([StateName]
           ,[StateAbbreviation])
     VALUES
           ('Marshall Islands', 'MH')
GO

INSERT INTO [dbo].[USState]
           ([StateName]
           ,[StateAbbreviation])
     VALUES
           ('Michigan', 'MI')
GO

INSERT INTO [dbo].[USState]
           ([StateName]
           ,[StateAbbreviation])
     VALUES
           ('Minnesota', 'MN')
GO

INSERT INTO [dbo].[USState]
           ([StateName]
           ,[StateAbbreviation])
     VALUES
           ('Missouri', 'MO')
GO

INSERT INTO [dbo].[USState]
           ([StateName]
           ,[StateAbbreviation])
     VALUES
```

```
            ('Mississippi', 'MS')
GO

INSERT INTO [dbo].[USState]
            ([StateName]
            ,[StateAbbreviation])
     VALUES
            ('Montana', 'MT')
GO

INSERT INTO [dbo].[USState]
            ([StateName]
            ,[StateAbbreviation])
     VALUES
            ('North Carolina', 'NC')
GO

INSERT INTO [dbo].[USState]
            ([StateName]
            ,[StateAbbreviation])
     VALUES
            ('North Dakota', 'ND')
GO

INSERT INTO [dbo].[USState]
            ([StateName]
            ,[StateAbbreviation])
     VALUES
            ('Nebraska', 'NE')
GO

INSERT INTO [dbo].[USState]
            ([StateName]
            ,[StateAbbreviation])
     VALUES
            ('New Hampshire', 'NH')
GO

INSERT INTO [dbo].[USState]
            ([StateName]
            ,[StateAbbreviation])
     VALUES
            ('New Jersey', 'NJ')
GO

INSERT INTO [dbo].[USState]
            ([StateName]
            ,[StateAbbreviation])
     VALUES
            ('New Mexico', 'NM')
GO

INSERT INTO [dbo].[USState]
            ([StateName]
            ,[StateAbbreviation])
     VALUES
            ('Nevada', 'NV')
```

```
GO

INSERT INTO [dbo].[USState]
           ([StateName]
           ,[StateAbbreviation])
     VALUES
           ('New York', 'NY')
GO

INSERT INTO [dbo].[USState]
           ([StateName]
           ,[StateAbbreviation])
     VALUES
           ('Ohio', 'OH')
GO

INSERT INTO [dbo].[USState]
           ([StateName]
           ,[StateAbbreviation])
     VALUES
           ('Oklahoma', 'OK')
GO

INSERT INTO [dbo].[USState]
           ([StateName]
           ,[StateAbbreviation])
     VALUES
           ('Oregon', 'OR')
GO

INSERT INTO [dbo].[USState]
           ([StateName]
           ,[StateAbbreviation])
     VALUES
           ('Pennsylvania', 'PA')
GO

INSERT INTO [dbo].[USState]
           ([StateName]
           ,[StateAbbreviation])
     VALUES
           ('Puerto Rico', 'PR')
GO

INSERT INTO [dbo].[USState]
           ([StateName]
           ,[StateAbbreviation])
     VALUES
           ('Rhode Island', 'RI')
GO

INSERT INTO [dbo].[USState]
           ([StateName]
           ,[StateAbbreviation])
     VALUES
           ('South Carolina', 'SC')
GO
```

```
INSERT INTO [dbo].[USState]
           ([StateName]
           ,[StateAbbreviation])
     VALUES
           ('South Dakota', 'SD')
GO

INSERT INTO [dbo].[USState]
           ([StateName]
           ,[StateAbbreviation])
     VALUES
           ('Tennessee', 'TN')
GO

INSERT INTO [dbo].[USState]
           ([StateName]
           ,[StateAbbreviation])
     VALUES
           ('Texas', 'TX')
GO

INSERT INTO [dbo].[USState]
           ([StateName]
           ,[StateAbbreviation])
     VALUES
           ('Utah', 'UT')
GO

INSERT INTO [dbo].[USState]
           ([StateName]
           ,[StateAbbreviation])
     VALUES
           ('Virginia', 'VA')
GO

INSERT INTO [dbo].[USState]
           ([StateName]
           ,[StateAbbreviation])
     VALUES
           ('Virgin Islands', 'VI')
GO

INSERT INTO [dbo].[USState]
           ([StateName]
           ,[StateAbbreviation])
     VALUES
           ('Vermont', 'VT')
GO

INSERT INTO [dbo].[USState]
           ([StateName]
           ,[StateAbbreviation])
     VALUES
           ('Washington', 'WA')
GO
```

```
INSERT INTO [dbo].[USState]
           ([StateName]
           ,[StateAbbreviation])
     VALUES
           ('Wisconsin', 'WI')
GO

INSERT INTO [dbo].[USState]
           ([StateName]
           ,[StateAbbreviation])
     VALUES
           ('West Virginia', 'WV')
GO

INSERT INTO [dbo].[USState]
           ([StateName]
           ,[StateAbbreviation])
     VALUES
           ('Wyoming', 'WY')
GO

INSERT INTO [dbo].[User] (FirstName, LastName, UserName, [Password],
PhoneNumberPrimary, PhoneNumberSecondary, EmailAddress, UserTypeID) VALUES
 ('Testing', 'User', 'User', 'Password', '1112223333', '1112223333',
'testing@yoursite.com', 1)
GO

INSERT INTO [dbo].[User] (FirstName, LastName, UserName, [Password],
PhoneNumberPrimary, PhoneNumberSecondary, EmailAddress, UserTypeID) VALUES
 ('Testing', 'Admin', 'Admin', 'Password', '1112223333', '1112223333',
'testing@yoursite.com', 2)
GO
```

At this point, your database structure should be completed and your "type" tables are populated with data. We will address adding products and user account creation in a later chapter.

PayPal™ Account Setup

The first thing you need to do here is set up a PayPal™ business account in order to obtain API credentials. These are the credentials that you will input into the PayPal™ code later in the application. ***These should never be shared with others; you will be responsible for securing these credentials.*** To create your business account, please do the following:

1. Go to www.paypal.com.
2. Click 'Sign Up' at the top of the web page.
3. Three options will be listed on the next page: Premier, Personal and Business. Click 'Get Started' under the Business option.
4. Complete your personal, secure account information with PayPal™ for Business sign up and submit.

At this point, you have established a Business account with PayPal™. You may now get your API credentials that are required later in creating and implementing your web solution. To create your API signature, please do the following:

1. Log in to PayPal™ using your Business username and password
2. Click 'Profile' under 'My Account'
3. Click 'My Selling Tools'
4. Click 'API Access'
5. Click 'Request API Credentials'
6. Check 'Request API signature'
7. Click 'Agree and Submit'
8. Your API credentials will be displayed. In the future, if you ever need to view these, you may do so by following the same steps here. Once PayPal™ has issued API credentials to you, the 'Request API Credentials' link mentioned in Step 5 becomes a 'View API Signature' link.

Save your API credentials for later; we will address them in the PayPal™ code.

Project Initialization

It is critical that you set up your website project to look exactly as displayed in Fig. 2 and Fig. 3 below. To do so, please execute the following steps:

1. Open Visual Studio 2008
2. Go to File\New Web Site
3. Select ASP.Net Web Site
4. Give your web site a name
5. Click OK
6. Note that web.config, Default.aspx, and a folder named App_Data are created automatically
7. Rename App_Data to App_Code
8. Go to File\Add New Item\ and add a web form named About Us
9. Go to File\Add New Item\ and add a web form named Add Product
10. Go to File\Add New Item\ and add a web form named API Error
11. Go to File\Add New Item\ and add a web form named Billing
12. Go to File\Add New Item\ and add a web form named Checkout
13. Go to File\Add New Item\ and add a web form named ConfirmItemAdd
14. Go to File\Add New Item\ and add a web form named Contact Us
15. Go to File\Add New Item\ and add a web form named Create Account
16. Go to File\Add New Item\ and add a web form named Customer Details
17. Go to File\Add New Item\ and add a web form named Customers
18. Go to File\Add New Item\ and add a web form named Default
19. Go to File\Add New Item\ and add a web form named EditProduct
20. Go to File\Add New Item\ and add a web form named expresscheckout
21. Go to File\Add New Item\ and add a web form named FAQ
22. Go to File\Add New Item\ and add a web form named Login
23. Go to File\Add New Item\ and add a web form named Logout
24. Go to File\Add New Item\ and add a web form named OrderConfirmation
25. Go to File\Add New Item\ and add a web form named OrderDetails
26. Go to File\Add New Item\ and add a web form named OrderHistory
27. Go to File\Add New Item\ and add a web form named OrderReview
28. Go to File\Add New Item\ and add a web form named Password
29. Go to File\Add New Item\ and add a web form named ProductDetails
30. Go to File\Add New Item\ and add a web form named SearchProducts
31. Go to File\Add New Item\ and add a web form named Shipping
32. Go to File\Add New Item\ and add a web form named User Message
33. Go to File\Add New Item\ and add a web form named View Cart

You may purchase a copy of our companion disk which contains all files for the project at http://www.amazon.com/gp/product/B00AOU76K8!

34. Go to File\Add New Item\ and add a web form named View Categories
35. Go to File\Add New Item\ and add a web form named View Orders
36. Go to File\Add New Item\ and add a web form named View Products
37. Go to File\Add New Item\ and IN THE APP_CODE FOLDER, add a VB class named DatabaseAccess.vb
38. Go to File\Add New Item\ and IN THE APP_CODE FOLDER, add a VB class named paypalfunctions.vb
39. Your project files should look the same as Fig. 2 & Fig. 3. (***You must have the companion disk in order to have the graphic files shown in the Pictures folder.***)

Fig. 2

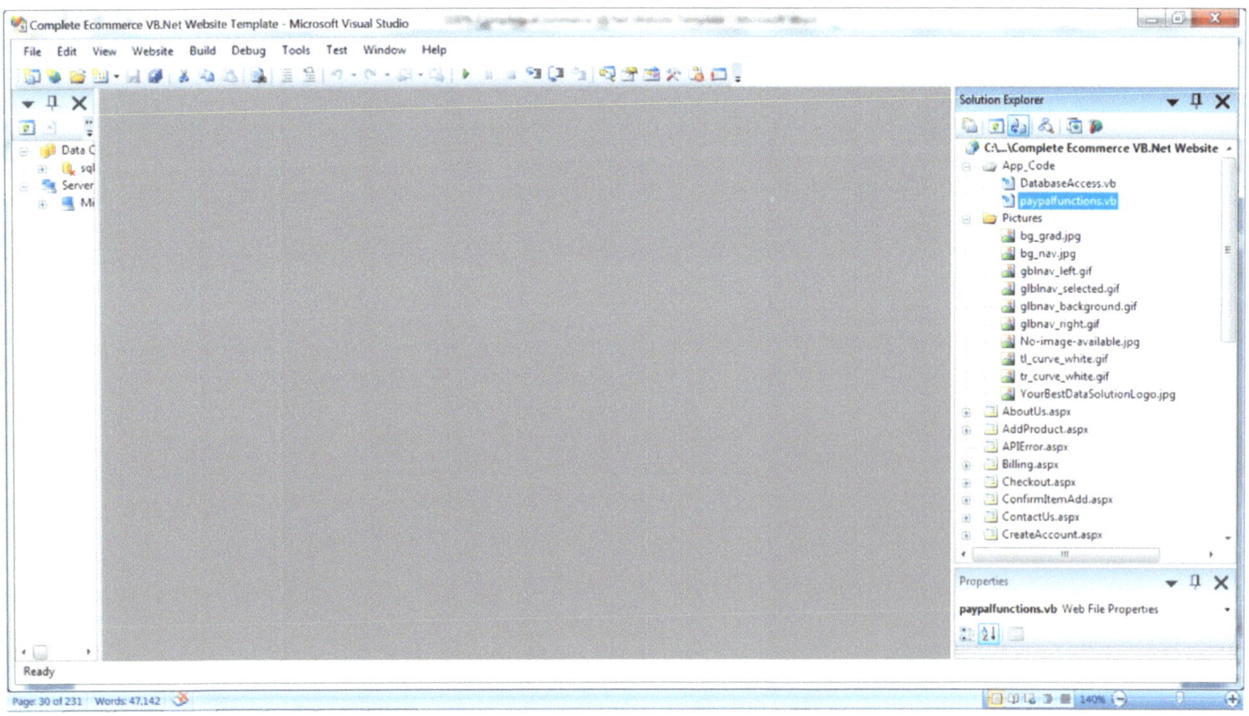

You may purchase a copy of our companion disk which contains all files for the project at http://www.amazon.com/gp/product/B00AOU76K8!

Fig. 3

You may purchase a copy of our companion disk which contains all files for the project at http://www.amazon.com/gp/product/B00AOU76K8!

About Us Server Page

Replace the existing code in the AboutUs.aspx file with the following code (***REPLACE ANY CODE IN THIS COLOR WITH YOUR OWN INFORMATION!)***:

```
<%@ Page Language="VB"
        AutoEventWireup="True"
        CodeFile="AboutUs.aspx.vb"
        Inherits="_Default" %>

<!DOCTYPE html PUBLIC "-//W3C//DTD XHTML 1.0 Transitional//EN"
"http://www.w3.org/TR/xhtml1/DTD/xhtml1-transitional.dtd">
<html xmlns="http://www.w3.org/1999/xhtml">

<head>
<meta http-equiv="Content-Type" content="text/html; charset=iso-8859-1" />
<title>About Us</title>
<link rel="stylesheet" href="emx_nav_left.css" type="text/css" />
<script type="text/javascript">

var time = 3000;
var numofitems = 7;

//menu constructor
function menu(allitems,thisitem,startstate){
  callname= "gl"+thisitem;
  divname="subglobal"+thisitem;
  this.numberofmenuitems = allitems;
  this.caller = document.getElementById(callname);
  this.thediv = document.getElementById(divname);
  this.thediv.style.visibility = startstate;
}

//menu methods
function ehandler(event,theobj){
  for (var i=1; i<= theobj.numberofmenuitems; i++){
    var shutdiv =eval( "menuitem"+i+".thediv");
    shutdiv.style.visibility="hidden";
  }
  theobj.thediv.style.visibility="visible";
}
```

You may purchase a copy of our companion disk which contains all files for the project at http://www.amazon.com/gp/product/B00AOU76K8!

```
function closesubnav(event){
 if ((event.clientY <48)||(event.clientY > 107)){
  for (var i=1; i<= numofitems; i++){
   var shutdiv =eval('menuitem'+i+'.thediv');
   shutdiv.style.visibility='hidden';
  }
 }
}
</script>
</head>
<body>

<form id="Form1" runat="server">
<div class="skipLinks">skip to: <a href="#content">page content</a> | <a
href="#pageNav">links on this page</a> | <a href="#globalNav">site navigation</a> | <a
href="#siteInfo">footer (site information)</a> </div>
<div id="masthead">
 <h1 id="siteName">Your Best Data Solution</h1>
 <div id="utility">
     <asp:LinkButton ID="lkCustomers" runat="server"
PostBackUrl="Customers.aspx">Customers</asp:LinkButton>
    |<asp:LinkButton ID="lkOrders" runat="server"
PostBackUrl="ViewOrders.aspx">Orders</asp:LinkButton>
    |<asp:LinkButton ID="lkAddProduct" PostBackUrl="AddProduct.aspx"
              runat="server">Add Product</asp:LinkButton>
    |<asp:LinkButton ID="lkEditProduct" runat="server"
PostBackUrl="ViewCategories.aspx">Edit Product</asp:LinkButton>
    |<asp:LinkButton ID="lkLogout" OnClick="logout" runat="server"
PostBackUrl="#">Logout</asp:LinkButton>
    |<asp:LinkButton ID="lkChangePassword" PostBackUrl="Password.aspx"
runat="server">Change Password</asp:LinkButton>
 </div>
 <div id="globalNav"> <img alt="" src="Pictures/gblnav_left.gif" height="32" width="4"
id="gnl" /> <img alt="" src="Pictures/glbnav_right.gif" height="32" width="4" id="gnr" />
  <div id="globalLink">
     <a href="Default.aspx" id="A1" class="glink">
     Home</a>
     <a href="ViewCategories.aspx" id="gl1" class="glink" >
     View Products</a>
     <a href="SearchProducts.aspx" id="gl2" class="glink">Search</a>
     <a href="ViewCart.aspx" id="gl3" class="glink">View Cart</a>
     <a href="Checkout.aspx" id="gl4" class="glink">Checkout</a>
     <a href="CreateAccount.aspx" id="gl5" class="glink">Create
     Account</a>
     <a href="Login.aspx" id="gl6" class="glink">Login
     </a><a href="OrderHistory.aspx" id="gl7" class="glink">Order
```

```
      History</a>
      <a href="FAQ.aspx" id="A2" class="glink">FAQ</a>
      <asp:Label ID="loginStatus" Visible="false" runat="server"></asp:Label>
      </div>
  </div>
<div id="pagecell1">
  <img alt="" src="Pictures/tl_curve_white.gif" height="6" width="6" id="tl" /> <img alt=""
src="Pictures/tr_curve_white.gif" height="6" width="6" id="tr" />

    <div id="pageName">
   <img alt="small logo" src="Pictures/YourBestDataSolutionLogo.jpg" height="50"
width="60"/> </div>
  <div id="pageNav">
    <div class="relatedLinks">
      <h3>Related Link Category</h3>
      <a href="FAQ.aspx#anchor3">Automation</a>
      <a href="FAQ.aspx#anchor1">Customized Reporting</a>
      <a href="FAQ.aspx#anchor2">Database Design</a>
      <a href="FAQ.aspx#anchor12">Data Migration</a>
      <a href="FAQ.aspx#anchor4">Data Modeling</a>
      <a href="FAQ.aspx#anchor14">Desktop Application Solutions</a>
      <a href="FAQ.aspx#anchor5">eCommerce Solutions</a>
      <a href="FAQ.aspx#anchor6">eMail Marketing</a>
      <a href="FAQ.aspx#anchor7">Mobile App Development</a>
      <a href="FAQ.aspx#anchor8">PayPal™ Integration</a>
      <a href="FAQ.aspx#anchor9">Web Design</a>
      <a href="FAQ.aspx#anchor10">Web Development</a>
    </div>
  </div>
  <div id="content">
    <div class="feature">
      <h3>Your Best Data Solution is a lasting solution!</h3>
          <p> <asp:Label ID="Label1"
                runat="server" >We think the best IT solutions are scalable solutions that last.
We do not feel that non-scalable solutions are advantageous to our company or mission.
You should only need our services again if your business rules change!</asp:Label> </p>
      <p> <asp:Label ID="paragraph1"
                runat="server" >YBDS, LLC incorporated in the state of Indiana effective
January 1, 2011.  YBDS, LLC will be actively seeking Chamber of Commerce membership
on or before 04/15/2011.</asp:Label> </p>
    </div>
    <div class="story">
  <div id="siteInfo"> <img alt="small logo" src="Pictures/YourBestDataSolutionLogo.jpg"
width="59" height="66" />
          <a href="AboutUs.aspx">About Us</a> |
          <a href="ContactUs.aspx">Contact Us</a> |
```

You may purchase a copy of our companion disk which contains all files for the project at http://www.amazon.com/gp/product/B00AOU76K8!

```
    ©2012 YBDS, LLC </div>

</div>
<br />
   </form>
</body>
</html>
```

You may purchase a copy of our companion disk which contains all files for the project at http://www.amazon.com/gp/product/B00AOU76K8!

About Us Code Behind

Replace the existing code in the AboutUs.aspx.vb file with the following code:

```
Imports System.Data
Imports System.Data.SqlClient

Partial Class _Default
   Inherits System.Web.UI.Page

   Protected Sub Page_Load(ByVal sender As Object, ByVal e As EventArgs) Handles Me.Load

      If (Session("firstName") = Nothing) Then
         'User is not logged in.  Continue.
         lkLogout.Visible = False
         lkChangePassword.Visible = False
         lkChangePassword.Enabled = False
         lkCustomers.Visible = False
         lkCustomers.Enabled = False
         lkOrders.Visible = False
         lkOrders.Enabled = False
         lkAddProduct.Visible = False
         lkAddProduct.Enabled = False
         lkEditProduct.Visible = False
         lkEditProduct.Enabled = False
      Else
         If (Session("isAdmin")) Then
            lkCustomers.Visible = True
            lkCustomers.Enabled = True
            lkOrders.Visible = True
            lkOrders.Enabled = True
            lkAddProduct.Visible = True
            lkAddProduct.Enabled = True
            lkEditProduct.Visible = True
            lkEditProduct.Enabled = True
         Else
            lkCustomers.Visible = False
            lkCustomers.Enabled = False
            lkOrders.Visible = False
            lkOrders.Enabled = False
            lkAddProduct.Visible = False
            lkAddProduct.Enabled = False
```

```
            lkEditProduct.Visible = False
            lkEditProduct.Enabled = False
        End If
        lkChangePassword.Visible = True
        lkChangePassword.Enabled = True
        loginStatus.Text = "Welcome " & Session("firstName").ToString() & "!"
        loginStatus.Visible = True
        Exit Sub
    End If

  End Sub

  Protected Sub logout()
    Session("firstName") = Nothing
    Session.Clear()
    Page.Response.Redirect("Logout.aspx")
  End Sub
End Class
```

Add Product Server Page

Replace the existing code in the AddProduct.aspx file with the following code (***REPLACE ANY CODE IN THIS COLOR WITH YOUR OWN INFORMATION!)***:

```
<%@ Page Language="VB"
      AutoEventWireup="True"
      CodeFile="AddProduct.aspx.vb"
      Inherits="_Default" %>

<!DOCTYPE html PUBLIC "-//W3C//DTD XHTML 1.0 Transitional//EN"
"http://www.w3.org/TR/xhtml1/DTD/xhtml1-transitional.dtd">
<html xmlns="http://www.w3.org/1999/xhtml">

<head>
<meta http-equiv="Content-Type" content="text/html; charset=iso-8859-1" />
<title>Add Product</title>
<link rel="stylesheet" href="emx_nav_left.css" type="text/css" />
<script type="text/javascript">

var time = 3000;
var numofitems = 7;

//menu constructor
function menu(allitems,thisitem,startstate){
  callname= "gl"+thisitem;
  divname="subglobal"+thisitem;
  this.numberofmenuitems = allitems;
  this.caller = document.getElementById(callname);
  this.thediv = document.getElementById(divname);
  this.thediv.style.visibility = startstate;
}

//menu methods
function ehandler(event,theobj){
  for (var i=1; i<= theobj.numberofmenuitems; i++){
    var shutdiv =eval( "menuitem"+i+".thediv");
    shutdiv.style.visibility="hidden";
  }
  theobj.thediv.style.visibility="visible";
}
```

You may purchase a copy of our companion disk which contains all files for the project at http://www.amazon.com/gp/product/B00AOU76K8!

```
function closesubnav(event){
  if ((event.clientY <48)||(event.clientY > 107)){
    for (var i=1; i<= numofitems; i++){
      var shutdiv =eval('menuitem'+i+'.thediv');
      shutdiv.style.visibility='hidden';
    }
  }
}
</script>
</head>
<body>

<form id="Form1" runat="server">
<div class="skipLinks">skip to: <a href="#content">page content</a> | <a
href="#pageNav">links on this page</a> | <a href="#globalNav">site navigation</a> | <a
href="#siteInfo">footer (site information)</a> </div>
<div id="masthead">
  <h1 id="siteName">Your Best Data Solution</h1>
  <div id="utility">
      <asp:LinkButton ID="lkCustomers" runat="server"
PostBackUrl="Customers.aspx">Customers</asp:LinkButton>
    | <asp:LinkButton ID="lkOrders" runat="server"
PostBackUrl="ViewOrders.aspx">Orders</asp:LinkButton>
    | <asp:LinkButton ID="lkAddProduct" PostBackUrl="AddProduct.aspx"
                  runat="server">Add Product</asp:LinkButton>
    | <asp:LinkButton ID="lkEditProduct" runat="server"
PostBackUrl="ViewCategories.aspx">Edit Product</asp:LinkButton>
    | <asp:LinkButton ID="lkLogout" OnClick="logout" runat="server"
PostBackUrl="#">Logout</asp:LinkButton>
    | <asp:LinkButton ID="lkChangePassword" PostBackUrl="Password.aspx"
runat="server">Change Password</asp:LinkButton>
  </div>
  <div id="globalNav"> <img alt="" src="Pictures/gblnav_left.gif" height="32" width="4"
id="gnl" /> <img alt="" src="Pictures/glbnav_right.gif" height="32" width="4" id="gnr" />
   <div id="globalLink">
      <a href="Default.aspx" id="A1" class="glink">
      Home</a>
      <a href="ViewCategories.aspx" id="gl1" class="glink" >
      View Products</a>
      <a href="SearchProducts.aspx" id="gl2" class="glink">Search</a>
      <a href="ViewCart.aspx" id="gl3" class="glink">View Cart</a>
      <a href="Checkout.aspx" id="gl4" class="glink">Checkout</a>
      <a href="CreateAccount.aspx" id="gl5" class="glink">Create
      Account</a>
      <a href="Login.aspx" id="gl6" class="glink">Login
      </a><a href="OrderHistory.aspx" id="gl7" class="glink">Order  History</a>
```

You may purchase a copy of our companion disk which contains all files for the project at http://www.amazon.com/gp/product/B00AOU76K8!

```
      <a href="FAQ.aspx" id="A2" class="glink">FAQ</a>
      <asp:Label ID="loginStatus" Visible="false" runat="server"></asp:Label>
    </div>
  </div>
<div id="pagecell1">
  <img alt="" src="Pictures/tl_curve_white.gif" height="6" width="6" id="tl" /> <img alt=""
src="Pictures/tr_curve_white.gif" height="6" width="6" id="tr" />

   <div id="pageName">
   <img alt="small logo" src="Pictures/YourBestDataSolutionLogo.jpg" height="50"
width="60"/> </div>
  <div id="pageNav">
   <div class="relatedLinks">
    <h3>Related Link Category</h3>
    <a href="FAQ.aspx#anchor3">Automation</a>
    <a href="FAQ.aspx#anchor1">Customized Reporting</a>
    <a href="FAQ.aspx#anchor2">Database Design</a>
    <a href="FAQ.aspx#anchor12">Data Migration</a>
    <a href="FAQ.aspx#anchor4">Data Modeling</a>
    <a href="FAQ.aspx#anchor14">Desktop Application Solutions</a>
    <a href="FAQ.aspx#anchor5">eCommerce Solutions</a>
    <a href="FAQ.aspx#anchor6">eMail Marketing</a>
    <a href="FAQ.aspx#anchor7">Mobile App Development</a>
    <a href="FAQ.aspx#anchor8">PayPal™ Integration</a>
    <a href="FAQ.aspx#anchor9">Web Design</a>
    <a href="FAQ.aspx#anchor10">Web Development</a>
   </div>
  </div>
  <div id="content">
   <div class="feature">
    <h3><asp:Label runat="server"
             ID="headerLabel" BackColor="LightGray"
             Text="Add Product ** All fields are required"></asp:Label></h3>
     <p>
        <asp:Label ID="lblProductName"
              runat="server"
              Text="Product name" BackColor="#cccccc"
              Font-Bold="true"
              Width ="300"></asp:Label>
        <asp:Label Value="   " runat="server"   />
        <asp:Label ID="lblCategory" Font-Bold="true" BackColor="#cccccc" runat="server"
Text="Product Category" Width="300"></asp:Label>
        <asp:Label ID="HiddenField1" Visible="true" Value=" " runat="server" />
        <br />
        <br />
        <asp:TextBox ID="txtProductName" runat="server" Width="300"></asp:TextBox>
```

You may purchase a copy of our companion disk which contains all files for the project at http://www.amazon.com/gp/product/B00AOU76K8!

```
        <asp:HiddenField ID="HiddenField2" Value="  " runat="server"  />
        <asp:DropDownList  ID="cboCategory" AutoPostBack="true"  runat="server"
Width="300"></asp:DropDownList>
        <asp:HiddenField ID="HiddenField3" Value="  " runat="server"  />
        <asp:Label ID="nameRequired"
                runat="server" Visible="false"></asp:Label>
        <br />
        <br />
        <asp:Label ID="lblBriefDescription" Font-Bold="true" BackColor="#cccccc"
runat="server" Width="600" Text="Brief Description"></asp:Label>
        <br />
        <br />
        <asp:TextBox ID="txtBriefDescription" runat="server" Width="600"></asp:TextBox>
        <asp:Label ID="billingAddressRequired"
                runat="server" Visible="false"></asp:Label>
        <br />
        <br />
        <asp:Label ID="lblFullDescription" Font-Bold="true" BackColor="#cccccc"
runat="server" Width="600" Text="Full Description"></asp:Label>
        <br />
        <br />
        <asp:TextBox ID="txtFullDescription" runat="server" Width="600"></asp:TextBox>
        <asp:Label ID="fullDescriptionRequired"
                runat="server" Visible="false"></asp:Label>
        <br />
        <br />
        <asp:Label ID="lblQuantityAvailable" Font-Bold="true" BackColor="#cccccc"
runat="server" Width="120" Text="Quantity Available"></asp:Label>
        <asp:Label ID="lblPrice" Font-Bold="true" BackColor="#cccccc" runat="server"
Text="Price" Width="100"></asp:Label>
        <br />
        <br />
        <asp:TextBox ID="txtQuantityAvailable" runat="server" Width="100"></asp:TextBox>
        <asp:Label ID="Label1" runat="server" Text="$" Width="5"></asp:Label>
        <asp:TextBox ID="txtPrice" runat="server" Width="100"></asp:TextBox>
        <asp:Label ID="qtyAndPriceRequired"
                runat="server" Visible="false"></asp:Label>
        <br />
        <br />
    </p>
    <div>
    <hr />
        <asp:Label ID="filePath1" runat="server"></asp:Label>
        <asp:Label ID="filePathHidden" runat="server" Visible="false" ></asp:Label>
        <asp:FileUpload ID="FileUpload1"
                  runat="server" />
```

```
        <asp:Image runat="server" ID="newPicture" Visible="true" />
      <br />
      <br />
    <p>
       <asp:Button
               runat="server"
               OnClick="cmdUploadPhoto_Click"
               ID="cmdUploadPhoto"
               Text="Upload Photo" />
       <asp:Button
               runat="server"
               OnClick="cmdRemovePhoto_Click"
               ID="cmdRemovePhoto"  Visible ="false" Enabled="false"
               Text="Remove Photo" />

    </p>
    <br />
    <br />
    <br />
    <hr />
    </div>
    <p>
       <asp:Button
               runat="server"
               OnClick="cmdAddProduct_Click"
               ID="cmdAddProduct"
               Text="Add Product" />

    </p>
    </div>
    <div class="story">
  <div id="siteInfo"> <img alt="small logo" src="Pictures/YourBestDataSolutionLogo.jpg"
width="59" height="66" />
         <a href="AboutUs.aspx">About Us</a> |
         <a href="ContactUs.aspx">Contact Us</a> |
     ©2012 YBDS, LLC </div>

</div>
<br />
   </form>
</body>
</html>
```

You may purchase a copy of our companion disk which contains all files for the project at http://www.amazon.com/gp/product/B00AOU76K8!

Add Product Code Behind

Replace the existing code in the AddProduct.aspx.vb file with the following code:

```
Imports System.Data
Imports System.Data.SqlClient

Partial Class _Default
    Inherits System.Web.UI.Page

    Protected Sub Page_Load(ByVal sender As Object, ByVal e As EventArgs) Handles Me.Load

        Dim myConnection As String
        Dim cmd As SqlCommand
        Dim myAdapter As SqlDataAdapter
        Dim myDataSet As DataSet
        Dim con As SqlConnection
        Dim myAccess As DatabaseAccess

        ' Set variables for use in binding.
        myAccess = New DatabaseAccess()
        myConnection = myAccess.getConnectionString()
        con = New SqlConnection(myConnection)

        If (Session("firstName") = Nothing) Then
            'User is not logged in.  Continue.
            lkLogout.Visible = False
            lkChangePassword.Visible = False
            lkChangePassword.Enabled = False
            Session("isAdmin") = False
            lkCustomers.Visible = False
            lkCustomers.Enabled = False
            lkOrders.Visible = False
            lkOrders.Enabled = False
            lkAddProduct.Visible = False
            lkAddProduct.Enabled = False
            lkEditProduct.Visible = False
            lkEditProduct.Enabled = False
            Page.Response.Redirect("Login.aspx")
        Else
            If (Session("isAdmin")) Then
                lkCustomers.Visible = True
```

You may purchase a copy of our companion disk which contains all files for the project at http://www.amazon.com/gp/product/B00AOU76K8!

```
            lkCustomers.Enabled = True
            lkOrders.Visible = True
            lkOrders.Enabled = True
            lkAddProduct.Visible = True
            lkAddProduct.Enabled = True
            lkEditProduct.Visible = True
            lkEditProduct.Enabled = True
        Else
            lkCustomers.Visible = False
            lkCustomers.Enabled = False
            lkOrders.Visible = False
            lkOrders.Enabled = False
            lkAddProduct.Visible = False
            lkAddProduct.Enabled = False
            lkEditProduct.Visible = False
            lkEditProduct.Enabled = False
            Exit Sub
        End If
        lkChangePassword.Visible = True
        lkChangePassword.Enabled = True
        loginStatus.Text = "Welcome " & Session("firstName").ToString() & "!"
    End If

    ''''''''''''''''''''''''''''''''''''''''''''''''''''''''''''''''''''
    ' Bind Billing State combobox.
    cmd = New SqlCommand("SELECT CategoryID, CategoryName FROM ProductCategory
ORDER BY CategoryName ASC", con)
    cmd.CommandType = CommandType.Text

    myAdapter = New SqlDataAdapter(cmd)
    myDataSet = New DataSet()

    Try

        ' Open the database connection.
        con.Open()
        myAdapter.Fill(myDataSet, "ProductCategory")
    Finally
        con.Close()
        If Not (Page.IsPostBack) Then
            cboCategory.DataSource = myDataSet
            cboCategory.DataTextField = "CategoryName"
            cboCategory.DataValueField = "CategoryID"
            cboCategory.DataBind()
        End If
    End Try
```

You may purchase a copy of our companion disk which contains all files for the project at http://www.amazon.com/gp/product/B00AOU76K8!

```
End Sub

Protected Function productExists() As Boolean
    Dim myConnection As String
    Dim cmd As SqlCommand
    Dim con As SqlConnection
    Dim myAccess As DatabaseAccess
    Dim sql As String
    Dim readData As SqlDataReader
    Dim productCount As Integer

    ' Set variables for use in binding.
    myAccess = New DatabaseAccess()
    myConnection = myAccess.getConnectionString()
    con = New SqlConnection(myConnection)

    ' Get the count of jproducts in the Product table for the ProductName in the text box.

    sql = "SELECT COUNT(ProductID) AS productCount FROM [Product] " & _
        "WHERE ProductName = '" & txtProductName.Text & "'"
    cmd = New SqlCommand(sql, con)
    cmd.CommandType = Data.CommandType.Text
    Try

        ' Open database connection.
        con.Open()

        ' Execute the INSERT and fill the data reader.
        readData = cmd.ExecuteReader(CommandBehavior.CloseConnection)

    Catch a As Exception

        Throw a
    End Try
    readData.Read()
    productCount = readData("productCount")
    con.Close()
    readData.Close()
    If productCount > 0 Then
        productExists = True
    Else
        productExists = False
    End If
End Function

Protected Function allFieldsArePopulated() As Boolean
```

```
If (txtProductName.Text = "") Then
   nameRequired.Text = "Please enter product name."
   nameRequired.Visible = True
   txtProductName.Focus()
   allFieldsArePopulated = False
   Exit Function
Else
   If Len(txtProductName.Text) > 255 Then
      nameRequired.Text = "Product name must be less than 255 characters."
      nameRequired.Visible = True
      txtProductName.Focus()
      allFieldsArePopulated = False
      Exit Function
   Else
      nameRequired.Visible = False
   End If
End If

If (cboCategory.Text = "") Then
   nameRequired.Text = "Please select category."
   nameRequired.Visible = True
   cboCategory.Focus()
   allFieldsArePopulated = False
   Exit Function
Else
   nameRequired.Visible = False
End If

If (txtBriefDescription.Text = "") Then
   billingAddressRequired.Text = "Please enter brief description."
   billingAddressRequired.Visible = True
   txtBriefDescription.Focus()
   allFieldsArePopulated = False
   Exit Function
Else
   If Len(txtBriefDescription.Text) > 255 Then
      billingAddressRequired.Text = "Brief description must be less than 255 characters."
      billingAddressRequired.Visible = True
      txtBriefDescription.Focus()
      allFieldsArePopulated = False
      Exit Function
   Else
      billingAddressRequired.Visible = False
   End If
End If
```

```
If (txtFullDescription.Text = "") Then
   fullDescriptionRequired.Text = "Please enter full description."
   fullDescriptionRequired.Visible = True
   txtFullDescription.Focus()
   allFieldsArePopulated = False
   Exit Function
Else
   If Len(txtFullDescription.Text) > 255 Then
      fullDescriptionRequired.Text = "Full description must be less than 255 characters."
      fullDescriptionRequired.Visible = True
      txtFullDescription.Focus()
      allFieldsArePopulated = False
      Exit Function
   Else
      fullDescriptionRequired.Visible = False
   End If
End If

If (txtQuantityAvailable.Text = "") Then
   qtyAndPriceRequired.Text = "Please enter quantity available."
   qtyAndPriceRequired.Visible = True
   txtQuantityAvailable.Focus()
   allFieldsArePopulated = False
   Exit Function
Else
   If IsNumeric(txtQuantityAvailable.Text) = False Then
      qtyAndPriceRequired.Text = "Please enter a whole number for the quantity."
      qtyAndPriceRequired.Visible = True
      txtQuantityAvailable.Focus()
      allFieldsArePopulated = False
      Exit Function
   Else
      qtyAndPriceRequired.Visible = False
   End If
End If

If (txtPrice.Text = "") Then
   qtyAndPriceRequired.Text = "Please enter unit price."
   qtyAndPriceRequired.Visible = True
   txtPrice.Focus()
   allFieldsArePopulated = False
   Exit Function
Else
   If IsNumeric(txtPrice.Text) = False Then
      qtyAndPriceRequired.Text = "Please enter a numeric value for the price."
      qtyAndPriceRequired.Visible = True
```

```
            txtPrice.Focus()
            allFieldsArePopulated = False
            Exit Function
        Else
            qtyAndPriceRequired.Visible = False
        End If
    End If
    allFieldsArePopulated = True
End Function

Protected Sub logout()
    Session("firstName") = Nothing
    Session.Clear()
    Page.Response.Redirect("Logout.aspx")
End Sub

Protected Sub addProduct()

    Dim myConnection As String
    Dim cmd As SqlCommand
    Dim con As SqlConnection
    Dim myAccess As DatabaseAccess
    Dim sql As String
    Dim readData As SqlDataReader
    Dim requiredFieldsArePopulated As Boolean
    Dim imageName As String

    '''''''''''''''''''''''''''''''''''''''''''''''''''''''''''''''''''''''''
    ' Confirm all required fields are populated.
    requiredFieldsArePopulated = allFieldsArePopulated()
    If Not (requiredFieldsArePopulated) Then Exit Sub
    ' Confirm product does not exist.
    If (productExists()) Then Exit Sub
    '''''''''''''''''''''''''''''''''''''''''''''''''''''''''''''''''''''''''



    ' Set variables for use in binding.
    myAccess = New DatabaseAccess()
    myConnection = myAccess.getConnectionString()
    con = New SqlConnection(myConnection)

    ''''''''''''''''''''''''''''''''''''''''''''''''''''''''''''''''''''''''''''''''''''''''


    If filePathHidden.Text <> "" Then
        imageName = filePathHidden.Text
    Else
```

You may purchase a copy of our companion disk which contains all files for the project at http://www.amazon.com/gp/product/B00AOU76K8!

```
        imageName = "No-image-available.jpg"
      End If

      Session("categoryID") = cboCategory.SelectedValue

      ' All fields have been successfully validated.  Add the new product.
      sql = "INSERT INTO [Product] (ProductName, CategoryID, " & _
      "Price, PhotoThumbnail, PhotoLarge, DescriptionBrief, " & _
      "DescriptionFull, QuantityAvailable) VALUES ('" & _
       txtProductName.Text & "', " & cboCategory.SelectedValue & _
       ", " & txtPrice.Text & ", '" & imageName & "', '" & _
       imageName & "', '" & txtBriefDescription.Text & "', '" & _
       txtFullDescription.Text & "', " & txtQuantityAvailable.Text & ")"
      cmd = New SqlCommand(sql, con)
      cmd.CommandType = Data.CommandType.Text
      Try

        ' Open database connection.
        con.Open()

        ' Execute the INSERT and fill the data reader.
        readData = cmd.ExecuteReader(CommandBehavior.CloseConnection)

      Catch a As Exception

        Throw a
      End Try

      con.Close()
      readData.Close()

      ''''''''''''''''''''''''''''''''''''''''''''''''''''''''''''''''''''''''''''''''''''''''''''''''''''''''''''''''''''''''''''''''

      Page.Response.Redirect("ViewProducts.aspx")
    End Sub


    Protected Sub cboCategory_SelectedIndexChanged(ByVal sender As Object, ByVal e As
System.EventArgs) Handles cboCategory.SelectedIndexChanged

    End Sub

    Protected Sub cmdUploadPhoto_Click(ByVal sender As Object, ByVal e As
System.EventArgs) Handles cmdUploadPhoto.Click
      If Not FileUpload1.HasFile = Nothing Then

        Dim filepath As String = FileUpload1.PostedFile.FileName
```

You may purchase a copy of our companion disk which contains all files for the project at http://www.amazon.com/gp/product/B00AOU76K8!

```
            Dim pat As String = "\\(?:.+)\\(.+)\.(.+)"
            Dim r As Regex = New Regex(pat)
            'run
            Dim m As Match = r.Match(filepath)
            Dim file_ext As String = m.Groups(2).Captures(0).ToString()
            Dim filename As String = m.Groups(1).Captures(0).ToString()
            Dim file As String = filename & "." & file_ext

            'save the file to the server
            FileUpload1.PostedFile.SaveAs(Server.MapPath(".\Pictures\") & file)
            filePathHidden.Text = file
            filePath1.Text = "File uploaded."
            newPicture.ImageUrl = "Pictures\" & file
            newPicture.Height = 30
            newPicture.Width = 20
            cmdUploadPhoto.Visible = False
            cmdUploadPhoto.Enabled = False
            cmdRemovePhoto.Visible = True
            cmdRemovePhoto.Enabled = True
        End If
    End Sub

    Protected Sub cmdRemovePhoto_Click(ByVal sender As Object, ByVal e As
System.EventArgs) Handles cmdRemovePhoto.Click
        newPicture.ImageUrl = ""
        newPicture.Dispose()
        If filePath1.Text <> "" Then
            System.IO.File.Delete(Server.MapPath(".\Pictures\") & Trim(Replace(filePath1.Text, " is
uploaded.", "")))
        End If
        filePathHidden.Text = ""
        cmdUploadPhoto.Visible = True
        cmdUploadPhoto.Enabled = True
        cmdRemovePhoto.Visible = False
        cmdRemovePhoto.Enabled = False
        filePath1.Text = ""
    End Sub

    Protected Sub cmdAddProduct_Click(ByVal sender As Object, ByVal e As
System.EventArgs) Handles cmdAddProduct.Click
        addProduct()
    End Sub
End Class
```

API Error Server Page

Replace the existing code in the APIError.aspx file with the following code *(Code Behind file is not needed for API Error; if it was created, you may delete it.)*:

```
<%@ Page Language="VB" %>

<!DOCTYPE html PUBLIC "-//W3C//DTD XHTML 1.0 Transitional//EN"
"http://www.w3.org/TR/xhtml1/DTD/xhtml1-transitional.dtd">

<script runat="server">

</script>

<html xmlns="http://www.w3.org/1999/xhtml" >
<head runat="server">
   <title>PayPal™ - Error Page</title>
</head>
<body>
   <form id="form1" runat="server">
               <table>
                     <tr>
                           <td class="field"></td>
                           <td><%=Request.QueryString.Get("ErrorCode")%></td>
                     </tr>

                     <tr>
                           <td class="field"></td>
                           <td><%=Request.QueryString.Get("Desc")%></td>
                     </tr>

                     <tr>
                           <td class="field"></td>
                           <td><%=Request.QueryString.Get("Desc2")%></td>
                     </tr>

               </table>
   </form>
</body>
</html>
```

You may purchase a copy of our companion disk which contains all files for the project at http://www.amazon.com/gp/product/B00AOU76K8!

Billing Server Page

Replace the existing code in the Billing.aspx file with the following code (***REPLACE ANY CODE IN THIS COLOR WITH YOUR OWN INFORMATION!)***:

```
<%@ Page Language="VB"
        enableEventValidation="false"
        enableViewState="false"
        enableViewStateMac="false"
        AutoEventWireup="True"
        CodeFile="Billing.aspx.vb"
        Inherits="_Default" %>

<!DOCTYPE html PUBLIC "-//W3C//DTD XHTML 1.0 Transitional//EN"
"http://www.w3.org/TR/xhtml1/DTD/xhtml1-transitional.dtd">
<html xmlns="http://www.w3.org/1999/xhtml">

<head>
<meta http-equiv="Content-Type" content="text/html; charset=iso-8859-1" />
<title>Billing</title>
<link rel="stylesheet" href="emx_nav_left.css" type="text/css" />
<script type="text/javascript">

var time = 3000;
var numofitems = 7;

//menu constructor
function menu(allitems,thisitem,startstate){
  callname= "gl"+thisitem;
  divname="subglobal"+thisitem;
  this.numberofmenuitems = allitems;
  this.caller = document.getElementById(callname);
  this.thediv = document.getElementById(divname);
  this.thediv.style.visibility = startstate;
}

//menu methods
function ehandler(event,theobj){
  for (var i=1; i<= theobj.numberofmenuitems; i++){
    var shutdiv =eval( "menuitem"+i+".thediv");
    shutdiv.style.visibility="hidden";
  }
```

You may purchase a copy of our companion disk which contains all files for the project at http://www.amazon.com/gp/product/B00AOU76K8!

```
 theobj.thediv.style.visibility="visible";
}

function closesubnav(event){
 if ((event.clientY <48)||(event.clientY > 107)){
   for (var i=1; i<= numofitems; i++){
     var shutdiv =eval('menuitem'+i+'.thediv');
     shutdiv.style.visibility='hidden';
   }
  }
}
// -->
</script>
</head>
<body>

<form id="Form1" runat="server" action='expresscheckout.aspx' METHOD='POST'>
<div class="skipLinks">skip to: <a href="#content">page content</a> | <a
href="#pageNav">links on this page</a> | <a href="#globalNav">site navigation</a> | <a
href="#siteInfo">footer (site information)</a> </div>
<div id="masthead">
  <h1 id="siteName">Your Best Data Solution</h1>
  <div id="utility">
      <asp:LinkButton ID="lkCustomers" runat="server"
PostBackUrl="Customers.aspx">Customers</asp:LinkButton>
     | <asp:LinkButton ID="lkOrders" runat="server"
PostBackUrl="ViewOrders.aspx">Orders</asp:LinkButton>
     | <asp:LinkButton ID="lkAddProduct" PostBackUrl="AddProduct.aspx"
                  runat="server">Add Product</asp:LinkButton>
     | <asp:LinkButton ID="lkEditProduct" runat="server"
PostBackUrl="ViewCategories.aspx">Edit Product</asp:LinkButton>
     | <asp:LinkButton ID="lkLogout" OnClick="logout" runat="server"
PostBackUrl="#">Logout</asp:LinkButton>
     | <asp:LinkButton ID="lkChangePassword" PostBackUrl="Password.aspx"
runat="server">Change Password</asp:LinkButton>
  </div>
  <div id="globalNav"> <img alt="" src="Pictures/gblnav_left.gif" height="32" width="4"
id="gnl" /> <img alt="" src="Pictures/glbnav_right.gif" height="32" width="4" id="gnr" />
    <div id="globalLink">
      <a href="Default.aspx" id="A1" class="glink">
      Home</a>
      <a href="ViewCategories.aspx" id="gl1" class="glink" >
      View Products</a>
      <a href="SearchProducts.aspx" id="gl2" class="glink">Search</a>
      <a href="ViewCart.aspx" id="gl3" class="glink">View Cart</a>
      <a href="Checkout.aspx" id="gl4" class="glink">Checkout</a>
```

```
<a href="CreateAccount.aspx" id="gl5" class="glink">Create
Account</a>
<a href="Login.aspx" id="gl6" class="glink">Login
</a><a href="OrderHistory.aspx" id="gl7" class="glink">Order
History</a>
<a href="FAQ.aspx" id="A2" class="glink">FAQ</a>
<asp:Label ID="loginStatus" Visible="false" runat="server"></asp:Label>
</div>
</div>
<div id="pagecell1">
<img alt="" src="Pictures/tl_curve_white.gif" height="6" width="6" id="tl" /> <img alt=""
src="Pictures/tr_curve_white.gif" height="6" width="6" id="tr" />

<div id="pageName">
<img alt="small logo" src="Pictures/YourBestDataSolutionLogo.jpg" height="50"
width="60"/> </div>
<div id="pageNav">
<div class="relatedLinks">
<h3>Related Link Category</h3>
<a href="FAQ.aspx#anchor3">Automation</a>
<a href="FAQ.aspx#anchor1">Customized Reporting</a>
<a href="FAQ.aspx#anchor2">Database Design</a>
<a href="FAQ.aspx#anchor12">Data Migration</a>
<a href="FAQ.aspx#anchor4">Data Modeling</a>
<a href="FAQ.aspx#anchor14">Desktop Application Solutions</a>
<a href="FAQ.aspx#anchor5">eCommerce Solutions</a>
<a href="FAQ.aspx#anchor6">eMail Marketing</a>
<a href="FAQ.aspx#anchor7">Mobile App Development</a>
<a href="FAQ.aspx#anchor8">PayPal™ Integration</a>
<a href="FAQ.aspx#anchor9">Web Design</a>
<a href="FAQ.aspx#anchor10">Web Development</a>
</div>
</div>
<div id="content">
<div class="feature">
<h3><asp:Label runat="server" ID="headerLabel"></asp:Label></h3>
<p>
<asp:GridView ID ="categoryFilter"
        runat="server"
        DataKeyNames="ProductID"
        OnRowCommand="categoryFilter_RowCommand"
        EditRowStyle-HorizontalAlign="Center"
        HeaderStyle-BackColor="#cccccc"
        BorderStyle="None"
        OnRowDeleted="categoryFilter_RowDeleted"
        OnRowDeleting="categoryFilter_RowDeleting"
```

```
            AutoGenerateDeleteButton="false"
            EmptyDataText="No items are currently in your cart." >
      <Columns>
        <asp:TemplateField>
        <ItemTemplate>
        <asp:LinkButton ID="productDetails"
                    runat="server"
                    CommandName="Select"
                    CommandArgument="<%# Container.DataItemIndex %>"
                    Text = "Product Details"></asp:LinkButton>
        </ItemTemplate>
        </asp:TemplateField>

      </Columns>
    </asp:GridView>
      </p>
    <p>

      <input type='image' name='submit'
src='https://www.paypal.com/en_US/i/btn/btn_xpressCheckout.gif' border='0' align='top'
alt='Check out with PayPal'/>
    </p>
    </div>
    <div class="story">
  <div id="siteInfo"> <img alt="small logo" src="Pictures/YourBestDataSolutionLogo.jpg"
width="59" height="66" />
        <a href="AboutUs.aspx">About Us</a> |
        <a href="ContactUs.aspx">Contact Us</a> |
     ©2012 YBDS, LLC </div>

</div>
<br />
    </form>
</body>
</html>
```

You may purchase a copy of our companion disk which contains all files for the project at http://www.amazon.com/gp/product/B00AOU76K8!

Billing Code Behind

Replace the existing code in the Billing.aspx.vb file with the following code:

```
Imports System.Data
Imports System.Data.SqlClient
Imports System.Net.Mail

Partial Class _Default
   Inherits System.Web.UI.Page

   Protected Sub Page_Load(ByVal sender As Object, ByVal e As EventArgs) Handles Me.Load

      Dim myAccess As DatabaseAccess
      Dim myConnection As String
      Dim con As SqlConnection
      Dim cmd As SqlCommand
      Dim adapter As SqlDataAdapter
      Dim ds As DataSet
      Dim sql As String
      Dim orderID As String
      Dim readData As SqlDataReader
      Dim itemCount As Integer
      Dim orderTotal As Decimal
      Dim shippingCost As Decimal

      If (Session("firstName") = Nothing) Then
         'User is not logged in.  Continue.
         lkLogout.Visible = False
         lkChangePassword.Visible = False
         lkChangePassword.Enabled = False
         Session("isAdmin") = False
         lkCustomers.Visible = False
         lkCustomers.Enabled = False
         lkOrders.Visible = False
         lkOrders.Enabled = False
         lkAddProduct.Visible = False
         lkAddProduct.Enabled = False
         lkEditProduct.Visible = False
         lkEditProduct.Enabled = False
      Else
         If (Session("isAdmin")) Then
```

```
            lkCustomers.Visible = True
            lkCustomers.Enabled = True
            lkOrders.Visible = True
            lkOrders.Enabled = True
            lkAddProduct.Visible = True
            lkAddProduct.Enabled = True
            lkEditProduct.Visible = True
            lkEditProduct.Enabled = True
        Else
            lkCustomers.Visible = False
            lkCustomers.Enabled = False
            lkOrders.Visible = False
            lkOrders.Enabled = False
            lkAddProduct.Visible = False
            lkAddProduct.Enabled = False
            lkEditProduct.Visible = False
            lkEditProduct.Enabled = False
        End If
        lkChangePassword.Visible = True
        lkChangePassword.Enabled = True
        loginStatus.Text = "Welcome " & Session("firstName").ToString() & "!"
        loginStatus.Visible = True
    End If

    myAccess = New DatabaseAccess()
    myConnection = myAccess.getConnectionString()
    con = New SqlConnection(myConnection)

    orderID = Session("OrderID")
    If orderID = Nothing Then
        orderID = -1
    End If

    myAccess = New DatabaseAccess()
    myConnection = myAccess.getConnectionString()

    con = New SqlConnection(myConnection)
    sql = "SELECT COUNT(OrderID) AS orderCount FROM OrderDetail " & _
        "WHERE OrderID = " & orderID
    cmd = New SqlCommand(sql, con)
    cmd.CommandType = Data.CommandType.Text
    Try

        ' Open database connection.
        con.Open()
```

```
        ' Execute the INSERT and fill the data reader.
        readData = cmd.ExecuteReader(CommandBehavior.CloseConnection)

    Catch a As Exception

        Throw a
    End Try
    readData.Read()
    itemCount = readData("orderCount")
    con.Close()
    readData.Close()

    If (Session("OrderID") = Nothing) Or (itemCount = 0) Then
        orderID = -1
        sql = "SELECT p.ProductID, p.ProductName AS Product, " & _
  "od.Quantity, '$' + Convert(varchar(12), od.ProductCost) AS [Product Cost] " & _
  "FROM Product p " & _
  "INNER JOIN OrderDetail od ON od.ProductID = p.ProductID " & _
  "WHERE od.OrderID = " & orderID & " " & _
  "ORDER BY ProductName ASC"
    Else
        orderID = Session("OrderID")
        ''''''''''''''''''''''''''''''''''''''''''''''''''''''''''''''''''''''''''''''''''
        ' Get count of records.
        sql = "SELECT COUNT(p.ProductID) AS rowQty " & _
            "FROM Product p " & _
            "INNER JOIN OrderDetail od ON od.ProductID = p.ProductID " & _
            "WHERE od.OrderID = " & orderID & " "
        cmd = New SqlCommand(sql, con)
        cmd.CommandType = Data.CommandType.Text
        Try

            ' Open database connection.
            con.Open()

            ' Execute the INSERT and fill the data reader.
            readData = cmd.ExecuteReader(CommandBehavior.CloseConnection)

        Catch a As Exception

            Throw a
        End Try
        readData.Read()
        Session("rowQty") = readData("rowQty")
        readData.Close()
        con.Close()
```

```
''''''''''''''''''''''''''''''''''''''''''''''''''''''''''''''''

''''''''''''''''''''''''''''''''''''''''''''''''''''''''''''''''
' Get order total.
sql = "SELECT SUM(od.ProductCost) AS OrderTotal" & _
    " FROM Product p " & _
    "INNER JOIN OrderDetail od ON od.ProductID = p.ProductID " & _
    "WHERE od.OrderID = " & orderID & " "
cmd = New SqlCommand(sql, con)
cmd.CommandType = Data.CommandType.Text
Try

   ' Open database connection.
   con.Open()

   ' Execute the INSERT and fill the data reader.
   readData = cmd.ExecuteReader(CommandBehavior.CloseConnection)

Catch a As Exception

   Throw a
End Try
readData.Read()
Session("orderTotal") = readData("OrderTotal")
readData.Close()
con.Close()

orderTotal = Convert.ToDecimal(Session("orderTotal").ToString())
Session("productTotal") = orderTotal
shippingCost = Convert.ToDecimal(Session("shippingCost").ToString())
orderTotal = orderTotal + shippingCost
''''''''''''''''''''''''''''''''''''''''''''''''''''''''''''''''



''''''''''''''''''''''''''''''''''''''''''''''''''''''''''''
sql = "SELECT p.ProductID, od.OrderID, p.ProductName AS Product, " & _
    "od.Quantity, '$' + Convert(varchar(12), p.Price) AS [Unit Price], '$' + 
Convert(varchar(12),  od.ProductCost) AS [Total] " & _
    "FROM Product p " & _
    "INNER JOIN OrderDetail od ON od.ProductID = p.ProductID " & _
    "WHERE od.OrderID = " & orderID & " " & _
    " UNION SELECT NULL AS ProductID, '', 'Order Sub Total', " & _
    "NULL, '', '$' + Convert(varchar(12), " & FormatNumber(Session("productTotal"), 2) 
& ") " & _
    " FROM Product p " & _
```

You may purchase a copy of our companion disk which contains all files for the project at http://www.amazon.com/gp/product/B00AOU76K8!

```
            " UNION SELECT NULL AS ProductID, ", " & Chr(39) & "Shipping method - " &
Session("shippingMethodName").ToString() & Chr(39) & " AS ProductName, NULL, ", '$ ' +
Convert(varchar(12), SUM(ShippingCost)) FROM ShippingMethod WHERE
ShippingMethodID = " & Session("shippingMethodID") & _
            " UNION SELECT NULL AS ProductID, ", " & Chr(39) & "Sales Tax Rate - " &
Session("salesTaxRate").ToString() & Chr(39) & " AS ProductName, NULL, ", '$ ' +
Convert(varchar(12), " & FormatNumber(orderTotal * Session("salesTaxRate"), 2) & ") FROM
UserOrder WHERE OrderID = " & Session("OrderID") & _
            " UNION SELECT NULL AS ProductID, ", 'Totals', " & _
            "SUM(Quantity), ", '$' + Convert(varchar(12), " & FormatNumber(orderTotal +
(orderTotal * Session("salesTaxRate")), 2) & ") " & _
            " FROM Product p " & _
            "INNER JOIN OrderDetail od ON od.ProductID = p.ProductID " & _
            "WHERE od.OrderID = " & orderID & " " & _
            "ORDER BY OrderID DESC, ProductName ASC"
    End If

    cmd = New SqlCommand(sql, con)
    cmd.CommandType = Data.CommandType.Text

    adapter = New SqlDataAdapter(cmd)

    ' Fill the DataSet.
    ds = New DataSet()

    Try
      ' Open the database connection.
      con.Open()
      adapter.Fill(ds, sql)
    Finally

      con.Close()

      ' Perform the data binding.
      categoryFilter.DataSource = ds
      categoryFilter.DataBind()
    End Try
    Session("currentOrderTotal") = FormatNumber(orderTotal + (orderTotal *
Session("salesTaxRate")), 2)
    Session("payment_amt") = Session("currentOrderTotal")
    headerLabel.Text = "Shopping Cart"
  End Sub

  Protected Sub payNow()
    'If Not (allRequiredFieldsArePopulated()) Then Exit Sub
```

```
Dim myAccess As DatabaseAccess
Dim myConnection As String
Dim con As SqlConnection
Dim cmd As SqlCommand
Dim sql As String
Dim readData As SqlDataReader
Dim shippingCost As Decimal

myAccess = New DatabaseAccess()
myConnection = myAccess.getConnectionString()
con = New SqlConnection(myConnection)

' Change the status of the order to 'Paid' in the database.
sql = "SELECT ShippingCost FROM ShippingMethod " & _
    "WHERE ShippingMethodID = " & Session("shippingMethodID") & " "
cmd = New SqlCommand(sql, con)
cmd.CommandType = Data.CommandType.Text
Try

    ' Open database connection.
    con.Open()

    ' Execute the INSERT and fill the data reader.
    readData = cmd.ExecuteReader(CommandBehavior.CloseConnection)

Catch a As Exception

    Throw a
End Try
readData.Read()
shippingCost = Convert.ToDecimal(readData("ShippingCost").ToString)
readData.Close()
con.Close()

' Change the status of the order to 'Paid' in the database.
sql = "UPDATE UserOrder SET " & _
    "UserID = " & Convert.ToInt16(Session("UserID").ToString) & ", " & _
    "OrderStatusID = 1, " & _
    "ShippingCost = " & shippingCost & ", " & _
    "OrderStatusUpdateDate = '" & Now().ToString & "', " & _
"OrderStatusUpdateUserID = " & Convert.ToInt16(Session("UserID").ToString) & ", " & _
"BillingAddressID = " & Session("BillingAddressID").ToString & ", " & _
"ShippingAddressID = " & Session("ShippingAddressID").ToString & " " & _
    " WHERE OrderID = " & Session("OrderID") & " "
cmd = New SqlCommand(sql, con)
cmd.CommandType = Data.CommandType.Text
```

You may purchase a copy of our companion disk which contains all files for the project at http://www.amazon.com/gp/product/B00AOU76K8!

```
        Try

            ' Open database connection.
            con.Open()

            ' Execute the INSERT and fill the data reader.
            readData = cmd.ExecuteReader(CommandBehavior.CloseConnection)

        Catch a As Exception

            Throw a
        End Try
        readData.Read()
        readData.Close()
        con.Close()

        ' Present the user with a final receipt / invoice.
        Page.Response.Redirect("OrderConfirmation.aspx")
    End Sub

    Protected Sub logout()
        Session("firstName") = Nothing
        Session.Clear()
        Page.Response.Redirect("Logout.aspx")
    End Sub

    Protected Sub categoryFilter_RowCommand(ByVal sender As Object, ByVal e As
System.Web.UI.WebControls.GridViewCommandEventArgs) Handles
categoryFilter.RowCommand
        Dim obj As Object
        Dim id As String
        Dim ProductID As Integer
        Dim cmdName As String

        cmdName = e.CommandName
        obj = e.CommandArgument
        id = obj.ToString
        ProductID = Convert.ToInt16(id.ToString)
        Session("ProductID") =
Convert.ToInt16(categoryFilter.DataKeys(ProductID).Value.ToString)
        ProductID = Convert.ToInt16(categoryFilter.DataKeys(ProductID).Value.ToString)

        Select Case (cmdName)
            Case "Select"
                passSessionVariable()
            Case "Delete"
```

You may purchase a copy of our companion disk which contains all files for the project at http://www.amazon.com/gp/product/B00AOU76K8!

```
    End Select
  End Sub

  Protected Sub categoryFilter_RowDataBound(ByVal sender As Object, ByVal e As
System.Web.UI.WebControls.GridViewRowEventArgs) Handles categoryFilter.RowDataBound

      Dim myAccess As DatabaseAccess
      Dim myConnection As String
      Dim con As SqlConnection
      Dim cmd As SqlCommand
      Dim sql As String
      Dim readData As SqlDataReader
      Dim itemCount As Integer
      Dim orderID As Integer

      orderID = Session("OrderID")
      If orderID = Nothing Then
        orderID = -1
      End If

      myAccess = New DatabaseAccess()
      myConnection = myAccess.getConnectionString()

      con = New SqlConnection(myConnection)
      sql = "SELECT COUNT(OrderID) AS orderCount FROM OrderDetail " & _
          "WHERE OrderID = " & orderID
      cmd = New SqlCommand(sql, con)
      cmd.CommandType = Data.CommandType.Text
      Try

        ' Open database connection.
        con.Open()

        ' Execute the INSERT and fill the data reader.
        readData = cmd.ExecuteReader(CommandBehavior.CloseConnection)

      Catch a As Exception

        Throw a
      End Try
      readData.Read()
      itemCount = readData("orderCount")
      con.Close()
      readData.Close()
```

You may purchase a copy of our companion disk which contains all files for the project at http://www.amazon.com/gp/product/B00AOU76K8!

```
        If (Session("OrderID") <> Nothing) And (itemCount > 0) Then
            e.Row.Cells(1).Visible = False
            e.Row.Cells(2).Visible = False
        End If

        If (e.Row.RowIndex = Session("rowQty")) Then
            e.Row.Cells(0).Text = ""
            e.Row.Cells(1).Text = ""
        End If

        If (e.Row.RowIndex = Session("rowQty") + 1) Then
            e.Row.Cells(0).Text = ""
            e.Row.Cells(1).Text = ""
        End If

        If (e.Row.RowIndex = Session("rowQty") + 2) Then
            e.Row.Cells(0).Text = ""
            e.Row.Cells(1).Text = ""
        End If

    End Sub

    Protected Sub passSessionVariable()
        Page.Response.Redirect("ProductDetails.aspx")
    End Sub

    Protected Sub categoryFilter_RowDeleted(ByVal sender As Object, ByVal e As
System.Web.UI.WebControls.GridViewDeletedEventArgs) Handles categoryFilter.RowDeleted

    End Sub

    Protected Sub categoryFilter_RowDeleting(ByVal sender As Object, ByVal e As
System.Web.UI.WebControls.GridViewDeleteEventArgs) Handles categoryFilter.RowDeleting

    End Sub

    Protected Sub Page_PreInit(ByVal sender As Object, ByVal e As System.EventArgs) Handles
Me.PreInit

    End Sub
End Class
```

Checkout Server Page

Replace the existing code in the Checkout.aspx file with the following code (***REPLACE ANY CODE IN THIS COLOR WITH YOUR OWN INFORMATION!)***:

```
<%@ Page Language="VB"
       AutoEventWireup="True"
       CodeFile="Checkout.aspx.vb"
       Inherits="_Default" %>

<!DOCTYPE html PUBLIC "-//W3C//DTD XHTML 1.0 Transitional//EN"
"http://www.w3.org/TR/xhtml1/DTD/xhtml1-transitional.dtd">
<html xmlns="http://www.w3.org/1999/xhtml">

<head>
<meta http-equiv="Content-Type" content="text/html; charset=iso-8859-1" />
<title>Checkout</title>
<link rel="stylesheet" href="emx_nav_left.css" type="text/css" />
<script type="text/javascript">

var time = 3000;
var numofitems = 7;

//menu constructor
function menu(allitems,thisitem,startstate){
  callname= "gl"+thisitem;
  divname="subglobal"+thisitem;
  this.numberofmenuitems = allitems;
  this.caller = document.getElementById(callname);
  this.thediv = document.getElementById(divname);
  this.thediv.style.visibility = startstate;
}

//menu methods
function ehandler(event,theobj){
  for (var i=1; i<= theobj.numberofmenuitems; i++){
    var shutdiv =eval( "menuitem"+i+".thediv");
    shutdiv.style.visibility="hidden";
  }
  theobj.thediv.style.visibility="visible";
}
```

```
function closesubnav(event){
 if ((event.clientY <48)||(event.clientY > 107)){
   for (var i=1; i<= numofitems; i++){
     var shutdiv =eval('menuitem'+i+'.thediv');
     shutdiv.style.visibility='hidden';
   }
 }
}
</script>
</head>
<body>

<form id="Form1" runat="server">
<div class="skipLinks">skip to: <a href="#content">page content</a> | <a
href="#pageNav">links on this page</a> | <a href="#globalNav">site navigation</a> | <a
href="#siteInfo">footer (site information)</a> </div>
<div id="masthead">
  <h1 id="siteName">Your Best Data Solution</h1>
  <div id="utility">
      <asp:LinkButton ID="lkCustomers" runat="server"
PostBackUrl="Customers.aspx">Customers</asp:LinkButton>
     | <asp:LinkButton ID="lkOrders" runat="server"
PostBackUrl="ViewOrders.aspx">Orders</asp:LinkButton>
     | <asp:LinkButton ID="lkAddProduct" PostBackUrl="AddProduct.aspx"
                 runat="server">Add Product</asp:LinkButton>
     | <asp:LinkButton ID="lkEditProduct" runat="server"
PostBackUrl="ViewCategories.aspx">Edit Product</asp:LinkButton>
     | <asp:LinkButton ID="lkLogout" OnClick="logout" runat="server"
PostBackUrl="#">Logout</asp:LinkButton>
     | <asp:LinkButton ID="lkChangePassword" PostBackUrl="Password.aspx"
runat="server">Change Password</asp:LinkButton>
  </div>
  <div id="globalNav"> <img alt="" src="Pictures/gblnav_left.gif" height="32" width="4"
id="gnl" /> <img alt="" src="Pictures/glbnav_right.gif" height="32" width="4" id="gnr" />
    <div id="globalLink">
      <a href="Default.aspx" id="A1" class="glink">
      Home</a>
      <a href="ViewCategories.aspx" id="gl1" class="glink" >
      View Products</a>
      <a href="SearchProducts.aspx" id="gl2" class="glink">Search</a>
      <a href="ViewCart.aspx" id="gl3" class="glink">View Cart</a>
      <a href="Checkout.aspx" id="gl4" class="glink">Checkout</a>
      <a href="CreateAccount.aspx" id="gl5" class="glink">Create
      Account</a>
      <a href="Login.aspx" id="gl6" class="glink">Login
      </a><a href="OrderHistory.aspx" id="gl7" class="glink">Order
```

```
        History</a>
        <a href="FAQ.aspx" id="A2" class="glink">FAQ</a>
        <asp:Label ID="loginStatus" Visible="false" runat="server"></asp:Label>
      </div>
    </div>
<div id="pagecell1">
  <img alt="" src="Pictures/tl_curve_white.gif" height="6" width="6" id="tl" /> <img alt=""
src="Pictures/tr_curve_white.gif" height="6" width="6" id="tr" />

    <div id="pageName">
    <img alt="small logo" src="Pictures/YourBestDataSolutionLogo.jpg" height="50"
width="60"/> </div>
  <div id="pageNav">
    <div class="relatedLinks">
      <h3>Related Link Category</h3>
      <a href="FAQ.aspx#anchor3">Automation</a>
      <a href="FAQ.aspx#anchor1">Customized Reporting</a>
      <a href="FAQ.aspx#anchor2">Database Design</a>
      <a href="FAQ.aspx#anchor12">Data Migration</a>
      <a href="FAQ.aspx#anchor4">Data Modeling</a>
      <a href="FAQ.aspx#anchor14">Desktop Application Solutions</a>
      <a href="FAQ.aspx#anchor5">eCommerce Solutions</a>
      <a href="FAQ.aspx#anchor6">eMail Marketing</a>
      <a href="FAQ.aspx#anchor7">Mobile App Development</a>
      <a href="FAQ.aspx#anchor8">PayPal™ Integration</a>
      <a href="FAQ.aspx#anchor9">Web Design</a>
      <a href="FAQ.aspx#anchor10">Web Development</a>
    </div>
  </div>
  <div id="content">
    <div class="feature">
      <h3><asp:Label runat="server" ID="headerLabel"></asp:Label></h3>
       <p>
    <asp:GridView ID ="categoryFilter"
                runat="server"
                DataKeyNames="ProductID"
                OnRowCommand="categoryFilter_RowCommand"
                EditRowStyle-HorizontalAlign="Center"
                HeaderStyle-BackColor="#cccccc"
                BorderStyle="None"
                OnRowDeleted="categoryFilter_RowDeleted"
                OnRowDeleting="categoryFilter_RowDeleting"
                AutoGenerateDeleteButton="true"
                EmptyDataText="No items are currently in your cart." >
        <Columns>
          <asp:TemplateField>
```

```
        <ItemTemplate>
        <asp:LinkButton ID="productDetails"
                    runat="server"
                    CommandName="Select"
                    CommandArgument="<%# Container.DataItemIndex %>"
                    Text = "Product Details"></asp:LinkButton>
        </ItemTemplate>
        </asp:TemplateField>
      </Columns>
    </asp:GridView>
      </p>
    <p>
      <asp:Button OnClick="login"
              runat="server"
              ID="cmdLogin"
              Text="Login" />
      <asp:HiddenField ID="HiddenField1" Value=" " runat="server" />
      <asp:Button OnClick="createAccount"
              runat="server"
              ID="cmdCreateAccount"
              Text="Create Account" />
      <asp:HiddenField ID="HiddenField3" Value=" " runat="server" />
      <asp:Button OnClick="addShipping"
              runat="server"
              ID="cmdAddShipping"
              Text="Update Shipping Method" />
      <asp:HiddenField ID="HiddenField4" Value=" " runat="server" />
      <asp:Button OnClick="payNow"
              runat="server"
              ID="cmdPay"
              Visible ="false"
              Text="Pay Now" />
      <asp:HiddenField ID="HiddenField2" Value=" " runat="server" />
      <asp:Button OnClick="continueShopping"
              runat="server"
              ID="cmdContinueShopping"
              Text="Continue Shopping" />

    </p>
    </div>
    <div class="story">
  <div id="siteInfo"> <img alt="small logo" src="Pictures/YourBestDataSolutionLogo.jpg"
width="59" height="66" />
        <a href="AboutUs.aspx">About Us</a> |
        <a href="ContactUs.aspx">Contact Us</a> |
    ©2012 YBDS, LLC </div>
```

You may purchase a copy of our companion disk which contains all files for the project at http://www.amazon.com/gp/product/B00AOU76K8!

```
</div>
<br />
   </form>
</body>
</html>
```

Checkout Code Behind

Replace the existing code in the Checkout.aspx.vb file with the following code:

```
Imports System.Data
Imports System.Data.SqlClient

Partial Class _Default
    Inherits System.Web.UI.Page

    Protected Sub Page_Load(ByVal sender As Object, ByVal e As EventArgs) Handles Me.Load

        Dim myAccess As DatabaseAccess
        Dim myConnection As String
        Dim con As SqlConnection
        Dim cmd As SqlCommand
        Dim adapter As SqlDataAdapter
        Dim ds As DataSet
        Dim sql As String
        Dim orderID As String
        Dim readData As SqlDataReader
        Dim itemCount As Integer

        myAccess = New DatabaseAccess()
        myConnection = myAccess.getConnectionString()
        con = New SqlConnection(myConnection)

        If (Session("firstName") = Nothing) Then
            'User is not logged in.  Continue.
            lkLogout.Visible = False
            cmdLogin.Visible = True
            cmdLogin.Enabled = True
            cmdAddShipping.Visible = False
            cmdAddShipping.Enabled = False
            cmdCreateAccount.Visible = True
            cmdCreateAccount.Enabled = True
            lkChangePassword.Visible = False
            lkChangePassword.Enabled = False
            Session("isAdmin") = False
            lkCustomers.Visible = False
            lkCustomers.Enabled = False
            lkOrders.Visible = False
```

```
            lkOrders.Enabled = False
            lkAddProduct.Visible = False
            lkAddProduct.Enabled = False
            lkEditProduct.Visible = False
            lkEditProduct.Enabled = False
        Else
            If (Session("isAdmin")) Then
                lkCustomers.Visible = True
                lkCustomers.Enabled = True
                lkOrders.Visible = True
                lkOrders.Enabled = True
                lkAddProduct.Visible = True
                lkAddProduct.Enabled = True
                lkEditProduct.Visible = True
                lkEditProduct.Enabled = True
            Else
                lkCustomers.Visible = False
                lkCustomers.Enabled = False
                lkOrders.Visible = False
                lkOrders.Enabled = False
                lkAddProduct.Visible = False
                lkAddProduct.Enabled = False
                lkEditProduct.Visible = False
                lkEditProduct.Enabled = False
            End If
            lkChangePassword.Visible = True
            lkChangePassword.Enabled = True
            cmdLogin.Visible = False
            cmdLogin.Enabled = False
            cmdAddShipping.Visible = True
            cmdAddShipping.Enabled = True
            If (Session("shippingMethodID") = Nothing) Then
                cmdAddShipping.Text = "Add shipping method"
            Else
                cmdPay.Visible = True
                cmdAddShipping.Text = "Update shipping method"
            End If
            cmdCreateAccount.Visible = False
            cmdCreateAccount.Enabled = False
            loginStatus.Text = "Welcome " & Session("firstName").ToString() & "!"
            loginStatus.Visible = True
        End If

        orderID = Session("OrderID")
        If orderID = Nothing Then
            orderID = -1
```

You may purchase a copy of our companion disk which contains all files for the project at http://www.amazon.com/gp/product/B00AOU76K8!

```
End If

myAccess = New DatabaseAccess()
myConnection = myAccess.getConnectionString()

con = New SqlConnection(myConnection)
sql = "SELECT COUNT(OrderID) AS orderCount FROM OrderDetail " & _
    "WHERE OrderID = " & orderID
cmd = New SqlCommand(sql, con)
cmd.CommandType = Data.CommandType.Text
Try

   ' Open database connection.
   con.Open()

   ' Execute the INSERT and fill the data reader.
   readData = cmd.ExecuteReader(CommandBehavior.CloseConnection)

Catch a As Exception

   Throw a
End Try
readData.Read()
itemCount = readData("orderCount")
con.Close()
readData.Close()

If (Session("OrderID") = Nothing) Or (itemCount = 0) Then
   orderID = -1
   sql = "SELECT p.ProductID, p.ProductName AS Product, " & _
"od.Quantity, '$' + Convert(varchar(12), od.ProductCost) AS [Product Cost] " & _
"FROM Product p " & _
"INNER JOIN OrderDetail od ON od.ProductID = p.ProductID " & _
"WHERE od.OrderID = " & orderID & " " & _
"ORDER BY ProductName ASC"
Else
   orderID = Session("OrderID")
   ''''''''''''''''''''''''''''''''''''''''''''''''''''''''''''''''''

   ' Get count of records.
   sql = "SELECT COUNT(p.ProductID) AS rowQty " & _
       "FROM Product p " & _
       "INNER JOIN OrderDetail od ON od.ProductID = p.ProductID " & _
       "WHERE od.OrderID = " & orderID & " "
   cmd = New SqlCommand(sql, con)
   cmd.CommandType = Data.CommandType.Text
   Try
```

```
            ' Open database connection.
            con.Open()

            ' Execute the INSERT and fill the data reader.
            readData = cmd.ExecuteReader(CommandBehavior.CloseConnection)

        Catch a As Exception

            Throw a
        End Try
        readData.Read()
        Session("rowQty") = readData("rowQty")
        readData.Close()
        con.Close()
        ''''''''''''''''''''''''''''''''''''''''''''''''''''''''''''''
        sql = "SELECT p.ProductID, od.OrderID, p.ProductName AS Product, " & _
            "od.Quantity, '$' + Convert(varchar(12), p.Price) AS [Unit Price], '$' +
Convert(varchar(12), od.ProductCost) AS [Total] " & _
            "FROM Product p " & _
            "INNER JOIN OrderDetail od ON od.ProductID = p.ProductID " & _
            "WHERE od.OrderID = " & orderID & " " & _
            "UNION SELECT NULL, '', 'Totals', " & _
            "SUM(Quantity), '', '$' + Convert(varchar(12), SUM(od.ProductCost)) " & _
            "FROM Product p " & _
            "INNER JOIN OrderDetail od ON od.ProductID = p.ProductID " & _
            "WHERE od.OrderID = " & orderID & " " & _
            "ORDER BY OrderID DESC, ProductName ASC"
    End If

    cmd = New SqlCommand(sql, con)
    cmd.CommandType = Data.CommandType.Text

    adapter = New SqlDataAdapter(cmd)

    ' Fill the DataSet.
    ds = New DataSet()

    Try
        ' Open the database connection.
        con.Open()
        adapter.Fill(ds, sql)
    Finally

        con.Close()
```

You may purchase a copy of our companion disk which contains all files for the project at http://www.amazon.com/gp/product/B00AOU76K8!

```
            ' Perform the data binding.
            categoryFilter.DataSource = ds
            categoryFilter.DataBind()
        End Try
        'End If
        headerLabel.Text = "Checkout"

    End Sub

    Protected Sub payNow()
        Page.Response.Redirect("Billing.aspx")
    End Sub

    Protected Sub logout()
        Session("firstName") = Nothing
        Session.Clear()
        Page.Response.Redirect("Logout.aspx")
    End Sub
    Protected Sub categoryFilter_RowCommand(ByVal sender As Object, ByVal e As
System.Web.UI.WebControls.GridViewCommandEventArgs) Handles
categoryFilter.RowCommand
        Dim obj As Object
        Dim id As String
        Dim ProductID As Integer
        Dim cmdName As String
        Dim myAccess As DatabaseAccess
        Dim myConnection As String
        Dim con As SqlConnection
        Dim cmd As SqlCommand
        Dim sql As String
        Dim readData As SqlDataReader

        cmdName = e.CommandName
        obj = e.CommandArgument
        id = obj.ToString
        ProductID = Convert.ToInt16(id.ToString)
        Session("ProductID") =
Convert.ToInt16(categoryFilter.DataKeys(ProductID).Value.ToString)
        ProductID = Convert.ToInt16(categoryFilter.DataKeys(ProductID).Value.ToString)

        Select Case (cmdName)
            Case "Select"
                passSessionVariable()
            Case "Delete"
                myAccess = New DatabaseAccess()
                myConnection = myAccess.getConnectionString()
```

```
            con = New SqlConnection(myConnection)
            sql = "DELETE FROM OrderDetail WHERE " & _
                "OrderID = " & Session("OrderID") & _
                " AND ProductID = " & ProductID & " "
            cmd = New SqlCommand(sql, con)
            cmd.CommandType = Data.CommandType.Text
            Try

                ' Open database connection.
                con.Open()

                ' Execute the INSERT and fill the data reader.
                readData = cmd.ExecuteReader(CommandBehavior.CloseConnection)

            Catch a As Exception

                Throw a
            End Try
            con.Close()
            readData.Close()
            Page.Response.Redirect("ViewCart.aspx")
        End Select
    End Sub

    Protected Sub categoryFilter_RowDataBound(ByVal sender As Object, ByVal e As
System.Web.UI.WebControls.GridViewRowEventArgs) Handles categoryFilter.RowDataBound

        Dim myAccess As DatabaseAccess
        Dim myConnection As String
        Dim con As SqlConnection
        Dim cmd As SqlCommand
        Dim sql As String
        Dim readData As SqlDataReader
        Dim itemCount As Integer
        Dim orderID As Integer

        orderID = Session("OrderID")
        If orderID = Nothing Then
            orderID = -1
        End If

        myAccess = New DatabaseAccess()
        myConnection = myAccess.getConnectionString()

        con = New SqlConnection(myConnection)
```

```
    sql = "SELECT COUNT(OrderID) AS orderCount FROM OrderDetail " & _
        "WHERE OrderID = " & orderID
    cmd = New SqlCommand(sql, con)
    cmd.CommandType = Data.CommandType.Text
    Try

        ' Open database connection.
        con.Open()

        ' Execute the INSERT and fill the data reader.
        readData = cmd.ExecuteReader(CommandBehavior.CloseConnection)

    Catch a As Exception

        Throw a
    End Try
    readData.Read()
    itemCount = readData("orderCount")
    con.Close()
    readData.Close()

    If (Session("OrderID") <> Nothing) And (itemCount > 0) Then
        e.Row.Cells(2).Visible = False
        e.Row.Cells(3).Visible = False
    End If


    If (e.Row.RowIndex = Session("rowQty")) Then
        e.Row.Cells(0).Text = ""
        e.Row.Cells(1).Text = ""
    End If

    If (e.Row.RowIndex = Session("rowQty") + 1) Then
        e.Row.Cells(0).Text = ""
        e.Row.Cells(1).Text = ""
    End If
End Sub

Protected Sub passSessionVariable()
    Page.Response.Redirect("ProductDetails.aspx")
End Sub

Protected Sub addShipping()
    Page.Response.Redirect("Shipping.aspx")
End Sub
```

You may purchase a copy of our companion disk which contains all files for the project at http://www.amazon.com/gp/product/B00AOU76K8!

```
    Protected Sub login()
        Page.Response.Redirect("Login.aspx")
    End Sub

    Protected Sub continueShopping()
        Page.Response.Redirect("ViewCategories.aspx")
    End Sub

    Protected Sub createAccount()
        Page.Response.Redirect("CreateAccount.aspx")
    End Sub

    Protected Sub categoryFilter_RowDeleted(ByVal sender As Object, ByVal e As
System.Web.UI.WebControls.GridViewDeletedEventArgs) Handles categoryFilter.RowDeleted

    End Sub

    Protected Sub categoryFilter_RowDeleting(ByVal sender As Object, ByVal e As
System.Web.UI.WebControls.GridViewDeleteEventArgs) Handles categoryFilter.RowDeleting

    End Sub
End Class
```

ConfirmItemAdd Server Page

Replace the existing code in the ConfirmItemAdd.aspx file with the following code (*REPLACE ANY CODE IN THIS COLOR WITH YOUR OWN INFORMATION!)*:

```
<%@ Page Language="VB"
      AutoEventWireup="True"
      CodeFile="ConfirmItemAdd.aspx.vb"
      Inherits="_Default" %>

<!DOCTYPE html PUBLIC "-//W3C//DTD XHTML 1.0 Transitional//EN"
"http://www.w3.org/TR/xhtml1/DTD/xhtml1-transitional.dtd">
<html xmlns="http://www.w3.org/1999/xhtml">

<head>
<meta http-equiv="Content-Type" content="text/html; charset=iso-8859-1" />
<title>ConfirmItemAdd</title>
<link rel="stylesheet" href="emx_nav_left.css" type="text/css" />
<script type="text/javascript">

var time = 3000;
var numofitems = 7;

//menu constructor
function menu(allitems,thisitem,startstate){
  callname= "gl"+thisitem;
  divname="subglobal"+thisitem;
  this.numberofmenuitems = allitems;
  this.caller = document.getElementById(callname);
  this.thediv = document.getElementById(divname);
  this.thediv.style.visibility = startstate;
}

//menu methods
function ehandler(event,theobj){
  for (var i=1; i<= theobj.numberofmenuitems; i++){
    var shutdiv =eval( "menuitem"+i+".thediv");
    shutdiv.style.visibility="hidden";
  }
  theobj.thediv.style.visibility="visible";
}
```

You may purchase a copy of our companion disk which contains all files for the project at http://www.amazon.com/gp/product/B00AOU76K8!

```
function closesubnav(event){
  if ((event.clientY <48)||(event.clientY > 107)){
    for (var i=1; i<= numofitems; i++){
      var shutdiv =eval('menuitem'+i+'.thediv');
      shutdiv.style.visibility='hidden';
    }
  }
}
// -->
</script>
</head>
<body>

<form id="Form1" runat="server">
<div class="skipLinks">skip to: <a href="#content">page content</a> | <a
href="#pageNav">links on this page</a> | <a href="#globalNav">site navigation</a> | <a
href="#siteInfo">footer (site information)</a> </div>
<div id="masthead">
  <h1 id="siteName">Your Best Data Solution</h1>
  <div id="utility">
      <asp:LinkButton ID="lkCustomers" runat="server"
PostBackUrl="Customers.aspx">Customers</asp:LinkButton>
    | <asp:LinkButton ID="lkOrders" runat="server"
PostBackUrl="ViewOrders.aspx">Orders</asp:LinkButton>
    | <asp:LinkButton ID="lkAddProduct" PostBackUrl="AddProduct.aspx"
            runat="server">Add Product</asp:LinkButton>
    | <asp:LinkButton ID="lkEditProduct" runat="server"
PostBackUrl="ViewCategories.aspx">Edit Product</asp:LinkButton>
    | <asp:LinkButton ID="lkLogout" OnClick="logout" runat="server"
PostBackUrl="#">Logout</asp:LinkButton>
    | <asp:LinkButton ID="lkChangePassword" PostBackUrl="Password.aspx"
runat="server">Change Password</asp:LinkButton>
  </div>
  <div id="globalNav"> <img alt="" src="Pictures/gblnav_left.gif" height="32" width="4"
id="gnl" /> <img alt="" src="Pictures/glbnav_right.gif" height="32" width="4" id="gnr" />
    <div id="globalLink">
      <a href="Default.aspx" id="A1" class="glink">
      Home</a>
      <a href="ViewCategories.aspx" id="gl1" class="glink" >
      View Products</a>
      <a href="SearchProducts.aspx" id="gl2" class="glink">Search</a>
      <a href="ViewCart.aspx" id="gl3" class="glink">View Cart</a>
      <a href="Checkout.aspx" id="gl4" class="glink">Checkout</a>
      <a href="CreateAccount.aspx" id="gl5" class="glink">Create
      Account</a>
      <a href="Login.aspx" id="gl6" class="glink">Login
```

```
    </a><a href="OrderHistory.aspx" id="gl7" class="glink">Order
    History</a>
    <a href="FAQ.aspx" id="A2" class="glink">FAQ</a>
    <asp:Label ID="loginStatus" Visible="false" runat="server"></asp:Label>
  </div>
 </div>
<div id="pagecell1">
 <img alt="" src="Pictures/tl_curve_white.gif" height="6" width="6" id="tl" /> <img alt=""
src="Pictures/tr_curve_white.gif" height="6" width="6" id="tr" />

  <div id="pageName">
  <img alt="small logo" src="Pictures/YourBestDataSolutionLogo.jpg" height="50"
width="60"/> </div>
 <div id="pageNav">
  <div class="relatedLinks">
   <h3>Related Link Category</h3>
   <a href="FAQ.aspx#anchor3">Automation</a>
   <a href="FAQ.aspx#anchor1">Customized Reporting</a>
   <a href="FAQ.aspx#anchor2">Database Design</a>
   <a href="FAQ.aspx#anchor12">Data Migration</a>
   <a href="FAQ.aspx#anchor4">Data Modeling</a>
   <a href="FAQ.aspx#anchor14">Desktop Application Solutions</a>
   <a href="FAQ.aspx#anchor5">eCommerce Solutions</a>
   <a href="FAQ.aspx#anchor6">eMail Marketing</a>
   <a href="FAQ.aspx#anchor7">Mobile App Development</a>
   <a href="FAQ.aspx#anchor8">PayPal™ Integration</a>
   <a href="FAQ.aspx#anchor9">Web Design</a>
   <a href="FAQ.aspx#anchor10">Web Development</a>
  </div>
 </div>
 <div id="content">
  <div class="storyCentered">
  <br /><br /><br /><br /><br /><br /><br /><br />
   <h3><asp:Label runat="server" ID="headerLabel"></asp:Label></h3>
   <p>
     <asp:LinkButton ID="continueShopping"
                runat="server"
                PostBackUrl="~/ViewCategories.aspx"
                Text="Continue Shopping"></asp:LinkButton>
     <br />
     <asp:LinkButton ID="viewMyCart"
                runat="server"
                PostBackUrl="~/ViewCart.aspx"
                Text="View Entire Cart"></asp:LinkButton>
   </p>
  </div>
```

You may purchase a copy of our companion disk which contains all files for the project at http://www.amazon.com/gp/product/B00AOU76K8!

```
 <div id="siteInfo"> <img alt="small logo" src="Pictures/YourBestDataSolutionLogo.jpg"
width="59" height="66" />
        <a href="AboutUs.aspx">About Us</a> |
        <a href="ContactUs.aspx">Contact Us</a> |
    ©2012 YBDS, LLC </div>

<br />
   </form>
</body>
</html>
```

ConfirmItemAdd Code Behind

Replace the existing code in the ConfirmItemAdd.aspx.vb file with the following code:

```
Imports System.Data
Imports DatabaseAccess
Imports System.Data.SqlClient

Partial Class _Default
   Inherits System.Web.UI.Page

   Protected Sub Page_Load(ByVal sender As Object, ByVal e As EventArgs) Handles Me.Load

      Dim myAccess As DatabaseAccess
      Dim myConnection As String
      Dim con As SqlConnection
      Dim cmd As SqlCommand
      Dim sql As String


      myAccess = New DatabaseAccess()
      myConnection = myAccess.getConnectionString()

      con = New SqlConnection(myConnection)

      If (Session("firstName") = Nothing) Then
         'User is not logged in.  Continue.
         lkLogout.Visible = False
         lkChangePassword.Visible = False
         lkChangePassword.Enabled = False
         Session("isAdmin") = False
         lkCustomers.Visible = False
         lkCustomers.Enabled = False
         lkOrders.Visible = False
         lkOrders.Enabled = False
         lkAddProduct.Visible = False
         lkAddProduct.Enabled = False
         lkEditProduct.Visible = False
         lkEditProduct.Enabled = False
      Else
         If (Session("isAdmin")) Then
            lkCustomers.Visible = True
```

```
        lkCustomers.Enabled = True
        lkOrders.Visible = True
        lkOrders.Enabled = True
        lkAddProduct.Visible = True
        lkAddProduct.Enabled = True
        lkEditProduct.Visible = True
        lkEditProduct.Enabled = True
    Else
        lkCustomers.Visible = False
        lkCustomers.Enabled = False
        lkOrders.Visible = False
        lkOrders.Enabled = False
        lkAddProduct.Visible = False
        lkAddProduct.Enabled = False
        lkEditProduct.Visible = False
        lkEditProduct.Enabled = False
    End If
    lkChangePassword.Visible = True
    lkChangePassword.Enabled = True
    loginStatus.Text = "Welcome " & Session("firstName").ToString() & "!"
    loginStatus.Visible = True
End If

''''''''''''''''''''''''''''''''''''''''''''''''''''''''''''''''''''''''''
' Set Header label text.
Dim readData As SqlDataReader
Dim val As String
Dim lpi As String
Dim sess As String

lpi = Session("lastProductID").ToString
sess = Session("orderID").ToString

sql = "SELECT ProductName, Quantity FROM Product p " & _
    "INNER JOIN OrderDetail od ON od.ProductID = p.ProductID " & _
    "WHERE p.ProductID = " & Session("lastProductID") & " " & _
    " AND od.OrderID = " & Session("orderID") & " "



cmd = New SqlCommand(sql, con)
cmd.CommandType = Data.CommandType.Text

Try

    ' Open database connection.
```

You may purchase a copy of our companion disk which contains all files for the project at http://www.amazon.com/gp/product/B00AOU76K8!

```
            con.Open()

            ' Execute the stored procedure and fill the data reader.
            readData = cmd.ExecuteReader(CommandBehavior.CloseConnection)

        Catch a As Exception

            Throw a
        End Try

        readData.Read()
        val = Session("qty").ToString
        headerLabel.Text = val
        headerLabel.Text = headerLabel.Text & " " & readData("ProductName")
        headerLabel.Text = headerLabel.Text & " have been added to your cart."
        con.Close()
        '''''''''''''''''''''''''''''''''''''''''''''''''''''''''''''''''''

    End Sub

    Protected Sub logout()
        Session("firstName") = Nothing
        Session.Clear()
        Page.Response.Redirect("Logout.aspx")
    End Sub
End Class
```

Contact Us Server Page

Replace the existing code in the ContactUs.aspx file with the following code (***REPLACE ANY CODE IN THIS COLOR WITH YOUR OWN INFORMATION!)***:

```
<%@ Page Language="VB"
        AutoEventWireup="True"
        CodeFile="ContactUs.aspx.vb"
        Inherits="_Default" %>

<!DOCTYPE html PUBLIC "-//W3C//DTD XHTML 1.0 Transitional//EN"
"http://www.w3.org/TR/xhtml1/DTD/xhtml1-transitional.dtd">
<html xmlns="http://www.w3.org/1999/xhtml">

<head>
<meta http-equiv="Content-Type" content="text/html; charset=iso-8859-1" />
<title>Contact Us</title>
<link rel="stylesheet" href="emx_nav_left.css" type="text/css" />
<script type="text/javascript">

var time = 3000;
var numofitems = 7;

//menu constructor
function menu(allitems,thisitem,startstate){
  callname= "gl"+thisitem;
  divname="subglobal"+thisitem;
  this.numberofmenuitems = allitems;
  this.caller = document.getElementById(callname);
  this.thediv = document.getElementById(divname);
  this.thediv.style.visibility = startstate;
}

//menu methods
function ehandler(event,theobj){
  for (var i=1; i<= theobj.numberofmenuitems; i++){
    var shutdiv =eval( "menuitem"+i+".thediv");
    shutdiv.style.visibility="hidden";
  }
  theobj.thediv.style.visibility="visible";
}

function closesubnav(event){
  if ((event.clientY <48)||(event.clientY > 107)){
```

```
  for (var i=1; i<= numofitems; i++){
   var shutdiv =eval('menuitem'+i+'.thediv');
   shutdiv.style.visibility='hidden';
  }
 }
}
</script>
</head>
<body>

<form id="Form1" runat="server">
<div class="skipLinks">skip to: <a href="#content">page content</a> | <a
href="#pageNav">links on this page</a> | <a href="#globalNav">site navigation</a> | <a
href="#siteInfo">footer (site information)</a> </div>
<div id="masthead">
 <h1 id="siteName">Your Best Data Solution</h1>
 <div id="utility">
    <asp:LinkButton ID="lkCustomers" runat="server"
PostBackUrl="Customers.aspx">Customers</asp:LinkButton>
   | <asp:LinkButton ID="lkOrders" runat="server"
PostBackUrl="ViewOrders.aspx">Orders</asp:LinkButton>
   | <asp:LinkButton ID="lkAddProduct" PostBackUrl="AddProduct.aspx"
             runat="server">Add Product</asp:LinkButton>
   | <asp:LinkButton ID="lkEditProduct" runat="server"
PostBackUrl="ViewCategories.aspx">Edit Product</asp:LinkButton>
   | <asp:LinkButton ID="lkLogout" OnClick="logout" runat="server"
PostBackUrl="#">Logout</asp:LinkButton>
   | <asp:LinkButton ID="lkChangePassword" PostBackUrl="Password.aspx"
runat="server">Change Password</asp:LinkButton>
 </div>
 <div id="globalNav"> <img alt="" src="Pictures/gblnav_left.gif" height="32" width="4"
id="gnl" /> <img alt="" src="Pictures/glbnav_right.gif" height="32" width="4" id="gnr" />
  <div id="globalLink">
    <a href="Default.aspx" id="A1" class="glink">
    Home</a>
    <a href="ViewCategories.aspx" id="gl1" class="glink" >
    View Products</a>
    <a href="SearchProducts.aspx" id="gl2" class="glink">Search</a>
    <a href="ViewCart.aspx" id="gl3" class="glink">View Cart</a>
    <a href="Checkout.aspx" id="gl4" class="glink">Checkout</a>
    <a href="CreateAccount.aspx" id="gl5" class="glink">Create
    Account</a>
    <a href="Login.aspx" id="gl6" class="glink">Login
    </a><a href="OrderHistory.aspx" id="gl7" class="glink">Order
    History</a>
    <a href="FAQ.aspx" id="A2" class="glink">FAQ</a>
```

```
      <asp:Label ID="loginStatus" Visible="false" runat="server"></asp:Label>
    </div>
  </div>
<div id="pagecell1">
  <img alt="" src="Pictures/tl_curve_white.gif" height="6" width="6" id="tl" /> <img alt=""
src="Pictures/tr_curve_white.gif" height="6" width="6" id="tr" />

    <div id="pageName">
    <img alt="small logo" src="Pictures/YourBestDataSolutionLogo.jpg" height="50"
width="60"/> </div>
  <div id="pageNav">
    <div class="relatedLinks">
      <h3>Data Services Links</h3>
      <a href="FAQ.aspx#anchor3">Automation</a>
      <a href="FAQ.aspx#anchor1">Customized Reporting</a>
      <a href="FAQ.aspx#anchor2">Database Design</a>
      <a href="FAQ.aspx#anchor12">Data Migration</a>
      <a href="FAQ.aspx#anchor4">Data Modeling</a>
      <a href="FAQ.aspx#anchor14">Desktop Application Solutions</a>
      <a href="FAQ.aspx#anchor5">eCommerce Solutions</a>
      <a href="FAQ.aspx#anchor6">eMail Marketing</a>
      <a href="FAQ.aspx#anchor7">Mobile App Development</a>
      <a href="FAQ.aspx#anchor8">PayPal™ Integration</a>
      <a href="FAQ.aspx#anchor9">Web Design</a>
      <a href="FAQ.aspx#anchor10">Web Development</a>
    </div>
  </div>
  <div id="content">
    <div class="feature">
      <h3>Contact Us</h3>
      <p> <asp:Label ID="paragraph1" runat="server" >
      Your Best Data Solution<br />
      2680 E. Main St<br />
      Suite 319<br />
      Plainfield, IN 46168<br />
      Phone: (317)839-4759<br />
      Web: www.yourbestdatasolution.com<br />
        </asp:Label> </p>
    </div>
    <div class="story">
  <div id="siteInfo"> <img alt="small logo" src="Pictures/YourBestDataSolutionLogo.jpg"
width="59" height="66" />
          <a href="AboutUs.aspx">About Us</a> |
          <a href="ContactUs.aspx">Contact Us</a> |
      ©2012 YBDS, LLC </div>
```

You may purchase a copy of our companion disk which contains all files for the project at http://www.amazon.com/gp/product/B00AOU76K8!

```
</div>
<br />
   </form>
</body>
</html>
```

You may purchase a copy of our companion disk which contains all files for the project at http://www.amazon.com/gp/product/B00AOU76K8!

Contact Us Code Behind

Replace the existing code in the ContactUs.aspx.vb file with the following code:

```
Imports System.Data
Imports System.Data.SqlClient

Partial Class _Default
    Inherits System.Web.UI.Page

    Protected Sub Page_Load(ByVal sender As Object, ByVal e As EventArgs) Handles Me.Load

        If (Session("firstName") = Nothing) Then
            'User is not logged in.  Continue.
            lkLogout.Visible = False
            lkChangePassword.Visible = False
            lkChangePassword.Enabled = False
            Session("isAdmin") = False
            lkCustomers.Visible = False
            lkCustomers.Enabled = False
            lkOrders.Visible = False
            lkOrders.Enabled = False
            lkAddProduct.Visible = False
            lkAddProduct.Enabled = False
            lkEditProduct.Visible = False
            lkEditProduct.Enabled = False
        Else
            If (Session("isAdmin")) Then
                lkCustomers.Visible = True
                lkCustomers.Enabled = True
                lkOrders.Visible = True
                lkOrders.Enabled = True
                lkAddProduct.Visible = True
                lkAddProduct.Enabled = True
                lkEditProduct.Visible = True
                lkEditProduct.Enabled = True
            Else
                lkCustomers.Visible = False
                lkCustomers.Enabled = False
                lkOrders.Visible = False
                lkOrders.Enabled = False
                lkAddProduct.Visible = False
                lkAddProduct.Enabled = False
                lkEditProduct.Visible = False
```

```
            lkEditProduct.Enabled = False
          End If
          lkChangePassword.Visible = False
          lkChangePassword.Enabled = False
          loginStatus.Text = "Welcome " & Session("firstName").ToString() & "!"
          loginStatus.Visible = True
       End If

    End Sub

    Protected Sub logout()
       Session("firstName") = Nothing
       Session.Clear()
       Page.Response.Redirect("Logout.aspx")
    End Sub
End Class
```

Create Account Server Page

Replace the existing code in the CreateAccount.aspx file with the following code (***REPLACE ANY CODE IN THIS COLOR WITH YOUR OWN INFORMATION!)***:

```
<%@ Page Language="VB"
     AutoEventWireup="True"
     CodeFile="CreateAccount.aspx.vb"
     Inherits="_Default" %>

<!DOCTYPE html PUBLIC "-//W3C//DTD XHTML 1.0 Transitional//EN"
"http://www.w3.org/TR/xhtml1/DTD/xhtml1-transitional.dtd">
<html xmlns="http://www.w3.org/1999/xhtml">

<head>
<meta http-equiv="Content-Type" content="text/html; charset=iso-8859-1" />
<title>Create Account</title>
<link rel="stylesheet" href="emx_nav_left.css" type="text/css" />
<script type="text/javascript">

var time = 3000;
var numofitems = 7;

//menu constructor
function menu(allitems,thisitem,startstate){
 callname= "gl"+thisitem;
 divname="subglobal"+thisitem;
 this.numberofmenuitems = allitems;
 this.caller = document.getElementById(callname);
 this.thediv = document.getElementById(divname);
 this.thediv.style.visibility = startstate;
}

//menu methods
function ehandler(event,theobj){
 for (var i=1; i<= theobj.numberofmenuitems; i++){
  var shutdiv =eval( "menuitem"+i+".thediv");
  shutdiv.style.visibility="hidden";
 }
 theobj.thediv.style.visibility="visible";
}

function closesubnav(event){
 if ((event.clientY <48)||(event.clientY > 107)){
```

You may purchase a copy of our companion disk which contains all files for the project at http://www.amazon.com/gp/product/B00AOU76K8!

```
   for (var i=1; i<= numofitems; i++){
     var shutdiv =eval('menuitem'+i+'.thediv');
     shutdiv.style.visibility='hidden';
   }
  }
}
</script>
</head>
<body>

<form id="Form1" runat="server">
<div class="skipLinks">skip to: <a href="#content">page content</a> | <a
href="#pageNav">links on this page</a> | <a href="#globalNav">site navigation</a> | <a
href="#siteInfo">footer (site information)</a> </div>
<div id="masthead">
 <h1 id="siteName">Your Best Data Solution</h1>
 <div id="utility">
     <asp:LinkButton ID="lkCustomers" runat="server"
PostBackUrl="Customers.aspx">Customers</asp:LinkButton>
    | <asp:LinkButton ID="lkOrders" runat="server"
PostBackUrl="ViewOrders.aspx">Orders</asp:LinkButton>
    | <asp:LinkButton ID="lkAddProduct" PostBackUrl="AddProduct.aspx"
                runat="server">Add Product</asp:LinkButton>
    | <asp:LinkButton ID="lkEditProduct" runat="server"
PostBackUrl="ViewCategories.aspx">Edit Product</asp:LinkButton>
    | <asp:LinkButton ID="lkLogout" OnClick="logout" runat="server"
PostBackUrl="#">Logout</asp:LinkButton>
    | <asp:LinkButton ID="lkChangePassword" PostBackUrl="Password.aspx"
runat="server">Change Password</asp:LinkButton>
 </div>
 <div id="globalNav"> <img alt="" src="Pictures/gblnav_left.gif" height="32" width="4"
id="gnl" /> <img alt="" src="Pictures/glbnav_right.gif" height="32" width="4" id="gnr" />
  <div id="globalLink">
     <a href="Default.aspx" id="A1" class="glink">
     Home</a>
     <a href="ViewCategories.aspx" id="gl1" class="glink" >
     View Products</a>
     <a href="SearchProducts.aspx" id="gl2" class="glink">Search</a>
     <a href="ViewCart.aspx" id="gl3" class="glink">View Cart</a>
     <a href="Checkout.aspx" id="gl4" class="glink">Checkout</a>
     <a href="CreateAccount.aspx" id="gl5" class="glink">Create
     Account</a>
     <a href="Login.aspx" id="gl6" class="glink">Login
     </a><a href="OrderHistory.aspx" id="gl7" class="glink">Order
     History</a>
     <a href="FAQ.aspx" id="A2" class="glink">FAQ</a>
```

```
      <asp:Label ID="loginStatus" Visible="false" runat="server"></asp:Label>
    </div>
  </div>
<div id="pagecell1">
  <img alt="" src="Pictures/tl_curve_white.gif" height="6" width="6" id="tl" /> <img alt=""
src="Pictures/tr_curve_white.gif" height="6" width="6" id="tr" />

   <div id="pageName">
   <img alt="small logo" src="Pictures/YourBestDataSolutionLogo.jpg" height="50"
width="60"/> </div>
  <div id="pageNav">
   <div class="relatedLinks">
     <h3>Related Link Category</h3>
     <a href="FAQ.aspx#anchor3">Automation</a>
     <a href="FAQ.aspx#anchor1">Customized Reporting</a>
     <a href="FAQ.aspx#anchor2">Database Design</a>
     <a href="FAQ.aspx#anchor12">Data Migration</a>
     <a href="FAQ.aspx#anchor4">Data Modeling</a>
     <a href="FAQ.aspx#anchor14">Desktop Application Solutions</a>
     <a href="FAQ.aspx#anchor5">eCommerce Solutions</a>
     <a href="FAQ.aspx#anchor6">eMail Marketing</a>
     <a href="FAQ.aspx#anchor7">Mobile App Development</a>
     <a href="FAQ.aspx#anchor8">PayPal™ Integration</a>
     <a href="FAQ.aspx#anchor9">Web Design</a>
     <a href="FAQ.aspx#anchor10">Web Development</a>
   </div>
  </div>
  <div id="content">
   <div class="feature">
     <h3><asp:Label runat="server"
              ID="headerLabel" BackColor="LightGray"
              Text="Tell Us About Yourself <font color='red'>* fields are
required</font>"></asp:Label></h3>
      <p>
         <asp:Label ID="lblFirstName"
               runat="server"
               Text="<font color='red'>* </font>First name                         "
               Width ="200"></asp:Label>
         <asp:Label Value="   " runat="server"   />
         <asp:Label ID="lblMiddleInitial"
               runat="server"
               Text="<font color='red'>* </font>Middle initial"
               Width="100"></asp:Label>
         <asp:Label ID="HiddenField1" Visible="true" Value=" " runat="server" />
         <asp:Label ID="lblLastName"
               runat="server"
```

You may purchase a copy of our companion disk which contains all files for the project at http://www.amazon.com/gp/product/B00AOU76K8!

```
            Text="<font color='red'>* </font>Last name"
            Width="200"></asp:Label>
        <br />
        <br />
        <asp:TextBox ID="txtFirstName" runat="server" Width="195"></asp:TextBox>
        <asp:HiddenField ID="HiddenField2" Value="  " runat="server"  />
        <asp:TextBox ID="txtMiddleInitial" runat="server" Width="90"></asp:TextBox>
        <asp:HiddenField ID="HiddenField3" Value="  " runat="server"  />
        <asp:TextBox ID="txtLastName" runat="server" Width="200"></asp:TextBox>
        <asp:Label ID="nameRequired"
            runat="server" Visible="false"></asp:Label>
        <br />
        <br />
        <asp:Label ID="lblBillingAddress"
            runat="server"
            Text="<font color='red'>* </font>Billing address"></asp:Label>
        <br />
        <br />
        <asp:TextBox ID="txtBillingAddress" runat="server" Width="250"></asp:TextBox>
        <asp:Label ID="billingAddressRequired"
            runat="server" Visible="false"></asp:Label>
        <br />
        <br />
        <asp:Label ID="Label1"
            runat="server"
            Text="Billing address 2"></asp:Label>
        <br />
        <br />
        <asp:TextBox ID="txtBillingAddress2" runat="server" Width="250"></asp:TextBox>
        <asp:Label ID="billingAddressRequired2"
            runat="server" Visible="false"></asp:Label>
        <br />
        <br />

        <asp:Label ID="lblBillingCity"
            runat="server"
            Text="<font color='red'>* </font>City
"
            Width ="200"></asp:Label>
        <asp:Label ID="Label2" Value="   " runat="server"   />
        <asp:Label ID="Label3"
            runat="server"
            Text="<font color='red'>* </font>State"
            Width="150"></asp:Label>
        <asp:Label ID="Label4" Visible="true" Value=" " runat="server" />
        <asp:Label ID="Label5"
```

You may purchase a copy of our companion disk which contains all files for the project at http://www.amazon.com/gp/product/B00AOU76K8!

```
            runat="server"
            Text="<font color='red'>* </font>Country"
            Width="200"></asp:Label>
        <br />
        <br />
        <asp:TextBox ID="txtBillingCity"
                runat="server"
                Width="195"></asp:TextBox>
        <asp:HiddenField ID="hiddenField4" Value="  " runat="server"  />
        <asp:DropDownList ID="cboBillingState"
                AutoPostBack="true"
                OnSelectedIndexChanged="cboBillingState_SelectedIndexChanged"
                runat="server"
                Width="140"></asp:DropDownList>
        <asp:HiddenField ID="HiddenField5" Value="  " runat="server"  />
        <asp:DropDownList ID="cboBillingCountry"
                OnSelectedIndexChanged="cboBillingCountry_SelectedIndexChanged"
                AutoPostBack="true"
                runat="server" Width="200"></asp:DropDownList>
        <asp:Label ID="cityStateCountryRequired"
            runat="server" Visible="false"></asp:Label>
        <br />
        <br />
        <asp:Label ID="lblPostalCode"
            runat="server"
            Text="<font color='red'>* </font>ZIP/Postal Code"
            Width ="135"></asp:Label>
        <asp:Label ID="lblPostalCode2"
            runat="server"
            Text="ZIP/Postal Code 2"
            Width ="135"></asp:Label>
        <br />
        <br />
        <asp:TextBox ID="txtPostalCode" runat="server" Width="125"></asp:TextBox>
        <asp:TextBox ID="txtPostalCode2" runat="server" Width="125"></asp:TextBox>
        <asp:Label ID="postalCodeRequired"
            runat="server" Visible="false"></asp:Label>
        <br />
        <br />
        <asp:Label ID="lblPrimaryPhoneNumber"
            runat="server"
            Text="<font color='red'>* </font>Primary Phone Number"></asp:Label>
        <asp:Label ID="lblSecondaryPhoneNumber"
            runat="server"
            Text="Secondary Phone Number"></asp:Label>
        <br />
```

```
        <br />
        <asp:TextBox ID="txtPrimaryPhoneNumber"
                 runat="server"
                 Width="155"></asp:TextBox>
        <asp:TextBox ID="txtSecondaryPhoneNumber"
                 runat="server"
                 Width="155"></asp:TextBox>
        <asp:Label ID="phoneNumberRequired"
               runat="server" Visible="false"></asp:Label>
        <br />
        <br />
        <asp:Label ID="lblEmailAddress"
               runat="server"
               Text="<font color='red'>* </font>Email address"></asp:Label>
        <br />
        <br />
        <asp:TextBox ID="txtEmailAddress"
                 runat="server"
                 Width="200"></asp:TextBox>
        <asp:Label ID="emailAddressRequired"
               runat="server" Visible="false"></asp:Label>
        <br />
        <br />
        <asp:Label runat="server"
               ID="Label6"
               BackColor="LightGray"
               Font-Bold="true"
               Font-Size="Medium"
               Text="Choose your user ID and password - <font color='red'>All fields are
required</font>"></asp:Label>
        <br />
        <br />
        <asp:Label ID="lblUsername"
               runat="server"
               Text="Create your user ID <font color='red'>* must be 8-20 characters
long</font>"></asp:Label>
        <br />
        <br />
        <asp:TextBox ID="txtUserID"
                 runat="server"
                 Width="200"></asp:TextBox>
        <asp:Button
             runat="server" OnClick="checkUserNameAvailability"
             ID="checkAvailability"
             Text="Check user name availability" />
        <asp:Label ID="lblAvailability"
```

```
              runat="server" Visible="false"></asp:Label>
        <br />
        <br />
        <asp:Label ID="lblPassword"
              runat="server"
              Text="<font color='red'>* </font>Create your password"></asp:Label>
        <br />
        <br />
        <asp:TextBox ID="txtPassword"
               TextMode="Password"
               runat="server"
               Width="200"></asp:TextBox>
        <asp:Label ID="passwordRequired"
              runat="server" Visible="false"></asp:Label>
        <br />
        <br />
        <asp:Label ID="lblConfirmPassword"
              runat="server"
              Text="<font color='red'>* </font>Confirm your password"></asp:Label>
        <br />
        <br />
        <asp:TextBox ID="txtConfirmPassword"
               TextMode="Password"
               runat="server"
               Width="200"></asp:TextBox>
        <asp:Label ID="confirmPasswordRequired"
              runat="server" Visible="false"></asp:Label>
     </p>
   <p>
     <asp:Button
            runat="server"
            OnClick="insertAccount"
            ID="Button1"
            Text="Create Account" />
   </p>
   </div>
   <div class="story">
  <div id="siteInfo"> <img alt="small logo" src="Pictures/YourBestDataSolutionLogo.jpg"
width="59" height="66" />
        <a href="AboutUs.aspx">About Us</a> |
        <a href="ContactUs.aspx">Contact Us</a> |
    ©2012 YBDS, LLC </div>

</div>
<br />
   </form>
```

You may purchase a copy of our companion disk which contains all files for the project at http://www.amazon.com/gp/product/B00AOU76K8!

```
</body>
</html>
```

Create Account Code Behind

Replace the existing code in the CreateAccount.aspx.vb file with the following code (*REPLACE ANY CODE IN THIS COLOR WITH YOUR OWN INFORMATION!)*:

```
Imports System.Data
Imports System.Data.SqlClient
Imports System.Net.Mail
Imports System.Net

Partial Class _Default
    Inherits System.Web.UI.Page

    Protected Sub Page_Load(ByVal sender As Object, ByVal e As EventArgs) Handles Me.Load

        Dim myConnection As String
        Dim cmd As SqlCommand
        Dim myAdapter As SqlDataAdapter
        Dim myDataSet As DataSet
        Dim con As SqlConnection
        Dim myAccess As DatabaseAccess

        ' Set variables for use in binding.
        myAccess = New DatabaseAccess()
        myConnection = myAccess.getConnectionString()
        con = New SqlConnection(myConnection)

        If (Session("firstName") = Nothing) Then
            'User is not logged in.  Continue.
            lkLogout.Visible = False
            lkChangePassword.Visible = False
            lkChangePassword.Enabled = False
            Session("isAdmin") = False
            lkCustomers.Visible = False
            lkCustomers.Enabled = False
            lkOrders.Visible = False
            lkOrders.Enabled = False
            lkAddProduct.Visible = False
            lkAddProduct.Enabled = False
            lkEditProduct.Visible = False
            lkEditProduct.Enabled = False
        Else
            If (Session("isAdmin")) Then
                lkCustomers.Visible = True
```

You may purchase a copy of our companion disk which contains all files for the project at http://www.amazon.com/gp/product/B00AOU76K8!

```
            lkCustomers.Enabled = True
            lkOrders.Visible = True
            lkOrders.Enabled = True
            lkAddProduct.Visible = True
            lkAddProduct.Enabled = True
            lkEditProduct.Visible = True
            lkEditProduct.Enabled = True
        Else
            lkCustomers.Visible = False
            lkCustomers.Enabled = False
            lkOrders.Visible = False
            lkOrders.Enabled = False
            lkAddProduct.Visible = False
            lkAddProduct.Enabled = False
            lkEditProduct.Visible = False
            lkEditProduct.Enabled = False
        End If
        lkChangePassword.Visible = True
        lkChangePassword.Enabled = True
        loginStatus.Text = "Welcome " & Session("firstName").ToString() & "!"
        Page.Response.Redirect("UserMessage.aspx")
        Exit Sub
    End If

    ''''''''''''''''''''''''''''''''''''''''''''''''''''''

    ' Bind Billing State combobox.
    cmd = New SqlCommand("SELECT StateID, StateName FROM USState ORDER BY
StateName ASC", con)
    cmd.CommandType = CommandType.Text

    myAdapter = New SqlDataAdapter(cmd)
    myDataSet = New DataSet()

    Try

        ' Open the database connection.
        con.Open()
        myAdapter.Fill(myDataSet, "USState")
    Finally
        con.Close()
        If Not (Page.IsPostBack) Then
            cboBillingState.DataSource = myDataSet
            cboBillingState.DataSource = myDataSet.Tables(0)
            cboBillingState.DataTextField =
myDataSet.Tables(0).Columns("StateName").ColumnName.ToString()
```

```
            cboBillingState.DataValueField =
myDataSet.Tables(0).Columns("StateId").ColumnName.ToString()
            cboBillingState.DataBind()
         End If
      End Try

      ''''''''''''''''''''''''''''''''''''''''''''''''''''''''''''''''''
      ' Bind Billing Country combobox.
      cmd = New SqlCommand("SELECT CountryID, CountryName FROM Country ORDER
BY CountryID ASC", con)
      cmd.CommandType = CommandType.Text

      myAdapter = New SqlDataAdapter(cmd)
      myDataSet = New DataSet()

      Try

         ' Open the database connection.
         con.Open()
         myAdapter.Fill(myDataSet, "Country")
      Finally
         con.Close()
         If Not (Page.IsPostBack) Then
            cboBillingCountry.DataSource = myDataSet
            cboBillingCountry.DataSource = myDataSet.Tables(0)
            cboBillingCountry.DataTextField =
myDataSet.Tables(0).Columns("CountryName").ColumnName.ToString()
            cboBillingCountry.DataValueField =
myDataSet.Tables(0).Columns("CountryId").ColumnName.ToString()
            cboBillingCountry.DataBind()
         End If
      End Try
   End Sub

   Protected Sub checkUserNameAvailability()
      Dim nameExists As Boolean
      nameExists = usernameExists()
   End Sub

   Protected Function usernameExists() As Boolean
      Dim myConnection As String
      Dim cmd As SqlCommand
      Dim con As SqlConnection
      Dim myAccess As DatabaseAccess
      Dim sql As String
      Dim readData As SqlDataReader
```

```
Dim itemCount As Integer

' Set variables for use in binding.
myAccess = New DatabaseAccess()
myConnection = myAccess.getConnectionString()
con = New SqlConnection(myConnection)

' Get the count of records in the User table for the user Name in the text box.

sql = "SELECT COUNT(UserID) AS userCount FROM [User] " & _
    "WHERE Username = '" & txtUserID.Text & "'"
cmd = New SqlCommand(sql, con)
cmd.CommandType = Data.CommandType.Text
Try

   ' Open database connection.
   con.Open()

   ' Execute the INSERT and fill the data reader.
   readData = cmd.ExecuteReader(CommandBehavior.CloseConnection)

Catch a As Exception

   Throw a
End Try
readData.Read()
itemCount = readData("userCount")
con.Close()
readData.Close()

If (itemCount > 0) Then
   lblAvailability.Text = "This user name is not available."
   lblAvailability.ForeColor = Drawing.Color.DarkRed
   lblAvailability.Visible = True
   usernameExists = False
   Exit Function
Else
   If (txtUserID.Text <> "") And (Len(txtUserID.Text) >= 8) And (Len(txtUserID.Text) <=
20) Then
      lblAvailability.Text = "This user name is available."
      lblAvailability.ForeColor = Drawing.Color.DarkGreen
      lblAvailability.Visible = True
      usernameExists = True
      Exit Function
   Else
      lblAvailability.Text = "Please enter a username 8-20 characters long."
```

You may purchase a copy of our companion disk which contains all files for the project at http://www.amazon.com/gp/product/B00AOU76K8!

```
            lblAvailability.ForeColor = Drawing.Color.DarkRed
            lblAvailability.Visible = True
            usernameExists = False
            Exit Function
        End If
    End If

End Function

Protected Function allFieldsArePopulated() As Boolean
    If (txtFirstName.Text = "") Then
        nameRequired.Text = "Please enter first name."
        nameRequired.Visible = True
        txtFirstName.Focus()
        allFieldsArePopulated = False
        Exit Function
    Else
        nameRequired.Visible = False
    End If

    If (txtMiddleInitial.Text = "") Then
        nameRequired.Text = "Please enter middle initial."
        nameRequired.Visible = True
        txtMiddleInitial.Focus()
        allFieldsArePopulated = False
        Exit Function
    Else
        nameRequired.Visible = False
    End If

    If (txtLastName.Text = "") Then
        nameRequired.Text = "Please enter last name."
        nameRequired.Visible = True
        txtLastName.Focus()
        allFieldsArePopulated = False
        Exit Function
    Else
        nameRequired.Visible = False
    End If


    If (txtBillingAddress.Text = "") Then
        billingAddressRequired.Text = "Please enter billing address."
        billingAddressRequired.Visible = True
        txtBillingAddress.Focus()
        allFieldsArePopulated = False
```

```
        Exit Function
    Else
        billingAddressRequired.Visible = False
    End If

    If (txtBillingCity.Text = "") Then
        cityStateCountryRequired.Text = "Please enter city."
        cityStateCountryRequired.Visible = True
        txtBillingCity.Focus()
        allFieldsArePopulated = False
        Exit Function
    Else
        cityStateCountryRequired.Visible = False
    End If

    If (cboBillingState.Text = "") Then
        cityStateCountryRequired.Text = "Please enter state."
        cityStateCountryRequired.Visible = True
        cboBillingState.Focus()
        allFieldsArePopulated = False
        Exit Function
    Else
        cityStateCountryRequired.Visible = False
    End If

    If (cboBillingCountry.Text = "") Then
        cityStateCountryRequired.Text = "Please enter country."
        cityStateCountryRequired.Visible = True
        cboBillingCountry.Focus()
        allFieldsArePopulated = False
        Exit Function
    Else
        cityStateCountryRequired.Visible = False
    End If

    If (txtPostalCode.Text = "") Then
        postalCodeRequired.Text = "Please enter postal code."
        postalCodeRequired.Visible = True
        txtPostalCode.Focus()
        allFieldsArePopulated = False
        Exit Function
    Else
        postalCodeRequired.Visible = False
    End If

    If (txtPrimaryPhoneNumber.Text = "") Then
```

```
        phoneNumberRequired.Text = "Please enter primary phone number."
        phoneNumberRequired.Visible = True
        txtPrimaryPhoneNumber.Focus()
        allFieldsArePopulated = False
        Exit Function
    Else
        postalCodeRequired.Visible = False
    End If

    If (txtEmailAddress.Text = "") Then
        emailAddressRequired.Text = "Please enter email address."
        emailAddressRequired.Visible = True
        txtEmailAddress.Focus()
        allFieldsArePopulated = False
        Exit Function
    Else
        emailAddressRequired.Visible = False
    End If

    If (txtPassword.Text <> txtConfirmPassword.Text) Then
        passwordRequired.Text = "Please confirm your password."
        passwordRequired.Visible = True
        txtConfirmPassword.Focus()
        allFieldsArePopulated = False
        Exit Function
    Else
        passwordRequired.Visible = False
    End If

    If (txtPassword.Text = "") Then
        passwordRequired.Text = "Please enter password."
        passwordRequired.Visible = True
        txtPassword.Focus()
        allFieldsArePopulated = False
        Exit Function
    Else
        passwordRequired.Visible = False
    End If

    If (txtConfirmPassword.Text = "") Then
        passwordRequired.Text = "Please confirm your password."
        passwordRequired.Visible = True
        txtConfirmPassword.Focus()
        allFieldsArePopulated = False
        Exit Function
    Else
```

```
            passwordRequired.Visible = False
        End If
        allFieldsArePopulated = True

    End Function

    Protected Sub logout()
        Session("firstName") = Nothing
        Session.Clear()
        Page.Response.Redirect("Logout.aspx")
    End Sub

    Protected Sub insertAccount()

        Dim myConnection As String
        Dim cmd As SqlCommand
        Dim con As SqlConnection
        Dim myAccess As DatabaseAccess
        Dim sql As String
        Dim readData As SqlDataReader
        Dim nameExists As Boolean
        Dim requiredFieldsArePopulated As Boolean
        Dim variableLength As String

        variableLength = Session("firstName")
        If (variableLength = Nothing) Then
            'User is not logged in.  Continue.
            lkLogout.Visible = False
        Else
            loginStatus.Text = "Welcome " & Session("firstName").ToString() & "!"
            Page.Response.Redirect("UserMessage.aspx")
            Exit Sub
        End If
        ''''''''''''''''''''''''''''''''''''''''''''''''''''''''''''''''''
        ' Confirm all required fields are populated.
        requiredFieldsArePopulated = allFieldsArePopulated()
        If Not (requiredFieldsArePopulated) Then Exit Sub
        ''''''''''''''''''''''''''''''''''''''''''''''''''''''''''''''''''


        ' Check to see if a user exists with the current user name.
        nameExists = usernameExists()
        If Not (nameExists) Then Exit Sub

        ' Set variables for use in binding.
        myAccess = New DatabaseAccess()
        myConnection = myAccess.getConnectionString()
```

```
con = New SqlConnection(myConnection)

''''''''''''''''''''''''''''''''''''''''''''''''''''''''''''''''
' All fields have been successfully validated.  Add the user account.
sql = "INSERT INTO [User] (FirstName, MiddleInitial, LastName, " & _
"Username, Password, PhoneNumberPrimary, PhoneNumberSecondary, " & _
"EmailAddress, UserTypeID) VALUES ('" & txtFirstName.Text & "', '" & _
txtMiddleInitial.Text & "', '" & txtLastName.Text & "', '" & txtUserID.Text & "', '" &
txtPassword.Text & "', '" & txtPrimaryPhoneNumber.Text & "', '" &
txtSecondaryPhoneNumber.Text & "', '" & txtEmailAddress.Text & "', 1)"
cmd = New SqlCommand(sql, con)
cmd.CommandType = Data.CommandType.Text
Try

   ' Open database connection.
   con.Open()

   ' Execute the INSERT and fill the data reader.
   readData = cmd.ExecuteReader(CommandBehavior.CloseConnection)

Catch a As Exception

   Throw a
End Try

con.Close()
readData.Close()

''''''''''''''''''''''''''''''''''''''''''''''''''''''''''''''''
' Get the newly created user ID.
sql = "SELECT UserID FROM [User] WHERE " & _
      "Username = '" & txtUserID.Text & "'"
cmd = New SqlCommand(sql, con)
cmd.CommandType = Data.CommandType.Text
Try

   ' Open database connection.
   con.Open()

   ' Execute the INSERT and fill the data reader.
   readData = cmd.ExecuteReader(CommandBehavior.CloseConnection)

Catch a As Exception

   Throw a
End Try
```

You may purchase a copy of our companion disk which contains all files for the project at http://www.amazon.com/gp/product/B00AOU76K8!

```
readData.Read()
Session("UserID") = readData("UserID")
readData.Close()
con.Close()
Session("firstName") = txtFirstName.Text

''''''''''''''''''''''''''''''''''''''''''''''''''''''''''''''''''''
' Add the user address.
sql = "INSERT INTO UserAddress (UserID, StreetAddress1, StreetAddress2, " & _
"City, StateID, CountryID, PostalCode, " & _
"PostalCode2, AddressType) VALUES (" & Session("UserID") & ", '" & _
txtBillingAddress.Text & "', '" & txtBillingAddress2.Text & "', '" & txtBillingCity.Text &
"', " & Session("billingState") & ", " & IIf(IsNothing(Session("billingCountry")), 1,
Session("billingCountry")) & ", '" & txtPostalCode.Text & "', '" & txtPostalCode2.Text & "',1)"
cmd = New SqlCommand(sql, con)
cmd.CommandType = Data.CommandType.Text
Try

    ' Open database connection.
    con.Open()

    ' Execute the INSERT and fill the data reader.
    readData = cmd.ExecuteReader(CommandBehavior.CloseConnection)

Catch a As Exception

    Throw a
End Try

con.Close()
readData.Close()

''''''''''''''''''''''''''''''''''''''''''''''''''''''''''''''''''''
' Get the newly created user billing address ID.
sql = "SELECT AddressID FROM UserAddress WHERE " & _
      "UserID = " & Session("UserID") & " "
cmd = New SqlCommand(sql, con)
cmd.CommandType = Data.CommandType.Text
Try

    ' Open database connection.
    con.Open()

    ' Execute the INSERT and fill the data reader.
    readData = cmd.ExecuteReader(CommandBehavior.CloseConnection)
```

You may purchase a copy of our companion disk which contains all files for the project at http://www.amazon.com/gp/product/B00AOU76K8!

```
Catch a As Exception

    Throw a
End Try
readData.Read()
Session("billingAddressID") = readData("AddressID")
readData.Close()
con.Close()

If (Not (Session("OrderID") = Nothing)) Then
    ''''''''''''''''''''''''''''''''''''''''''''''''''''''''''''''''''''''''''''''''

    ' Update the UserOrder table with the UserID & BillingAddressID.
    sql = "UPDATE UserOrder SET " & _
    "UserID = " & Session("UserID") & ", " & _
    "BillingAddressID = " & Session("billingAddressID") & " " & _
    " WHERE OrderID = " & Session("OrderID") & " "
    cmd = New SqlCommand(sql, con)
    cmd.CommandType = Data.CommandType.Text
    Try

        ' Open database connection.
        con.Open()

        ' Execute the INSERT and fill the data reader.
        readData = cmd.ExecuteReader(CommandBehavior.CloseConnection)

    Catch a As Exception

        Throw a
    End Try
    readData.Close()
    con.Close()

    ' Send the confirmation email
    ' Get the newly created user billing address ID.
    sql = "SELECT FirstName, LastName, EmailAddress FROM [User] WHERE " & _
            "UserID = " & Session("UserID") & " "
    cmd = New SqlCommand(sql, con)
    cmd.CommandType = Data.CommandType.Text
    Try

        ' Open database connection.
        con.Open()

        ' Execute the INSERT and fill the data reader.
        readData = cmd.ExecuteReader(CommandBehavior.CloseConnection)
```

```
        Catch a As Exception

            Throw a
        End Try
        readData.Read()
        Session("emailFirstName") = readData("FirstName")
        Session("emailLastName") = readData("LastName")
        Session("confirmationEmailAddress") = readData("EmailAddress")
        readData.Close()
        con.Close()

        'TODO TODO TODO TODO TODO TODO TODO TODO TODO TODO TODO
        'Programmatically create a random password key to confirm
        'user account.
        'Add isActive boolean to User table.
        'Update the user record in the table with the password key.
        'The user will be made active after confirming the account via
        'the confirmation Email.
        'TODO TODO TODO TODO TODO TODO TODO TODO TODO TODO TODO

        Dim mm As MailMessage = New
MailMessage("postmaster@yourbestdatasolution.com",
Session("confirmationEmailAddress").ToString)
        Dim ssmtp As SmtpClient = New SmtpClient("localhost")
        mm.Subject = "Welcome to YourBestDataSolution!"
        mm.Body = txtFirstName.Text.ToString & ",<br/><br/>" & _
                "Thank you for registering " & _
                "ENTER YOUR BUSINESS NAME HERE!" & _
                "<br/><br/>Thank you,<br/><br/>" & _
                "ENTER YOUR NAME OR BUSINESS NAME HERE<br/>ENTER YOUR
RETURN EMAIL ADDRESS HERE"
        mm.IsBodyHtml = True
        ssmtp.Send(mm)

        Page.Response.Redirect("Shipping.aspx")
    Else
        ' Send the confirmation email
        ' Get the newly created user billing address ID.
        sql = "SELECT FirstName, LastName, EmailAddress FROM [User] WHERE " & _
                "UserID = " & Session("UserID") & " "
        cmd = New SqlCommand(sql, con)
        cmd.CommandType = Data.CommandType.Text
        Try

            ' Open database connection.
```

You may purchase a copy of our companion disk which contains all files for the project at http://www.amazon.com/gp/product/B00AOU76K8!

```
            con.Open()

            ' Execute the INSERT and fill the data reader.
            readData = cmd.ExecuteReader(CommandBehavior.CloseConnection)

        Catch a As Exception

            Throw a
        End Try
        readData.Read()
        Session("emailFirstName") = readData("FirstName")
        Session("emailLastName") = readData("LastName")
        Session("confirmationEmailAddress") = readData("EmailAddress")
        readData.Close()
        con.Close()

        'TODO TODO TODO TODO TODO TODO TODO TODO TODO TODO TODO
        'Programmatically create a random password key to confirm
        'user account.
        'Add isActive boolean to User table.
        'Update the user record in the table with the password key.
        'The user will be made active after confirming the account via
        'the confirmation Email.
        'TODO TODO TODO TODO TODO TODO TODO TODO TODO TODO TODO

        Dim mm As MailMessage = New
MailMessage("mikehamilton@yourbestdatasolution.com",
Session("confirmationEmailAddress").ToString)
        Dim ssmtp As SmtpClient = New SmtpClient("localhost")
        mm.Subject = "Welcome to YourBestDataSolution!"
        mm.Body = txtFirstName.Text.ToString & ",<br/><br/>" & _
            "Thank you for registering " & _
            "ENTER YOUR BUSINESS NAME HERE!" & _
            "<br/><br/>Thank you,<br/><br/>" & _
            "ENTER YOUR NAME OR BUSINESS NAME HERE<br/>ENTER YOUR
RETURN EMAIL ADDRESS HERE"
        mm.IsBodyHtml = True
        ssmtp.Send(mm)


        ''''''''''''''''''''''''''''''''''''''''''

        Page.Response.Redirect("ViewCategories.aspx")
      End If
    End Sub
```

You may purchase a copy of our companion disk which contains all files for the project at http://www.amazon.com/gp/product/B00AOU76K8!

```
    Protected Sub cboBillingCountry_SelectedIndexChanged(ByVal sender As Object, ByVal e
As System.EventArgs) Handles cboBillingCountry.SelectedIndexChanged
        Session("billingCountry") = cboBillingCountry.SelectedItem.Value
    End Sub

    Protected Sub cboBillingState_SelectedIndexChanged(ByVal sender As Object, ByVal e As
System.EventArgs) Handles cboBillingState.SelectedIndexChanged
        Session("billingState") = cboBillingState.SelectedItem.Value
    End Sub
End Class
```

Customer Details Server Page

Replace the existing code in the CustomerDetails.aspx file with the following code (***REPLACE ANY CODE IN THIS COLOR WITH YOUR OWN INFORMATION!***):

```
<%@ Page Language="VB"
        AutoEventWireup="True"
        CodeFile="CustomerDetails.aspx.vb"
        Inherits="_Default" %>

<!DOCTYPE html PUBLIC "-//W3C//DTD XHTML 1.0 Transitional//EN"
"http://www.w3.org/TR/xhtml1/DTD/xhtml1-transitional.dtd">
<html xmlns="http://www.w3.org/1999/xhtml">

<head>
<meta http-equiv="Content-Type" content="text/html; charset=iso-8859-1" />
<title>Customer Details</title>
<link rel="stylesheet" href="emx_nav_left.css" type="text/css" />
<script type="text/javascript">

var time = 3000;
var numofitems = 7;

//menu constructor
function menu(allitems,thisitem,startstate){
  callname= "gl"+thisitem;
  divname="subglobal"+thisitem;
  this.numberofmenuitems = allitems;
  this.caller = document.getElementById(callname);
  this.thediv = document.getElementById(divname);
  this.thediv.style.visibility = startstate;
}

//menu methods
function ehandler(event,theobj){
  for (var i=1; i<= theobj.numberofmenuitems; i++){
    var shutdiv =eval( "menuitem"+i+".thediv");
    shutdiv.style.visibility="hidden";
  }
  theobj.thediv.style.visibility="visible";
}

function closesubnav(event){
  if ((event.clientY <48)||(event.clientY > 107)){
```

You may purchase a copy of our companion disk which contains all files for the project at http://www.amazon.com/gp/product/B00AOU76K8!

```
    for (var i=1; i<= numofitems; i++){
      var shutdiv =eval('menuitem'+i+'.thediv');
      shutdiv.style.visibility='hidden';
    }
  }
}
</script>
</head>
<body>

<form id="Form1" runat="server">
<div class="skipLinks">skip to: <a href="#content">page content</a> | <a
href="#pageNav">links on this page</a> | <a href="#globalNav">site navigation</a> | <a
href="#siteInfo">footer (site information)</a> </div>
<div id="masthead">
  <h1 id="siteName">Your Best Data Solution</h1>
  <div id="utility">
        <asp:LinkButton ID="lkCustomers" runat="server"
PostBackUrl="Customers.aspx">Customers</asp:LinkButton>
      | <asp:LinkButton ID="lkOrders" runat="server"
PostBackUrl="ViewOrders.aspx">Orders</asp:LinkButton>
      | <asp:LinkButton ID="lkAddProduct" PostBackUrl="AddProduct.aspx"
                  runat="server">Add Product</asp:LinkButton>
      | <asp:LinkButton ID="lkEditProduct" runat="server"
PostBackUrl="ViewCategories.aspx">Edit Product</asp:LinkButton>
      | <asp:LinkButton ID="lkLogout" OnClick="logout" runat="server"
PostBackUrl="#">Logout</asp:LinkButton>
      | <asp:LinkButton ID="lkChangePassword" PostBackUrl="Password.aspx"
runat="server">Change Password</asp:LinkButton>
  </div>
  <div id="globalNav"> <img alt="" src="Pictures/gblnav_left.gif" height="32" width="4"
id="gnl" /> <img alt="" src="Pictures/glbnav_right.gif" height="32" width="4" id="gnr" />
    <div id="globalLink">
        <a href="Default.aspx" id="A1" class="glink">
        Home</a>
        <a href="ViewCategories.aspx" id="gl1" class="glink" >
        View Products</a>
        <a href="SearchProducts.aspx" id="gl2" class="glink">Search</a>
        <a href="ViewCart.aspx" id="gl3" class="glink">View Cart</a>
        <a href="Checkout.aspx" id="gl4" class="glink">Checkout</a>
        <a href="CreateAccount.aspx" id="gl5" class="glink">Create
        Account</a>
        <a href="Login.aspx" id="gl6" class="glink">Login
        </a><a href="OrderHistory.aspx" id="gl7" class="glink">Order
        History</a>
        <a href="FAQ.aspx" id="A2" class="glink">FAQ</a>
```

```
      <asp:Label ID="loginStatus" Visible="false" runat="server"></asp:Label>
    </div>
  </div>
<div id="pagecell1">
  <img alt="" src="Pictures/tl_curve_white.gif" height="6" width="6" id="tl" /> <img alt=""
src="Pictures/tr_curve_white.gif" height="6" width="6" id="tr" />

    <div id="pageName">
    <img alt="small logo" src="Pictures/YourBestDataSolutionLogo.jpg" height="50"
width="60"/> </div>
  <div id="pageNav">
    <div class="relatedLinks">
      <h3>Related Link Category</h3>
      <a href="FAQ.aspx#anchor3">Automation</a>
      <a href="FAQ.aspx#anchor1">Customized Reporting</a>
      <a href="FAQ.aspx#anchor2">Database Design</a>
      <a href="FAQ.aspx#anchor12">Data Migration</a>
      <a href="FAQ.aspx#anchor4">Data Modeling</a>
      <a href="FAQ.aspx#anchor14">Desktop Application Solutions</a>
      <a href="FAQ.aspx#anchor5">eCommerce Solutions</a>
      <a href="FAQ.aspx#anchor6">eMail Marketing</a>
      <a href="FAQ.aspx#anchor7">Mobile App Development</a>
      <a href="FAQ.aspx#anchor8">PayPal™ Integration</a>
      <a href="FAQ.aspx#anchor9">Web Design</a>
      <a href="FAQ.aspx#anchor10">Web Development</a>
    </div>
  </div>
  <div id="content">
    <div class="feature">
      <h3>
      <asp:Label runat="server" ID="headerLabel" BackColor="#cccccc" Text
="Customers"></asp:Label></h3>
       <p>
          <asp:Label runat="server" Width="200" ID="firstNameLabel" BackColor="#cccccc"
Font-Bold="true" Text ="First Name"></asp:Label>
           <asp:Label runat="server" Width="200" ID="middleInitialLabel" BackColor="#cccccc"
Font-Bold="true" Text ="Middle Initial"></asp:Label>
          <asp:Label runat="server" Width="200" ID="lastNameLabel" BackColor="#cccccc"
Font-Bold="true" Text ="Last Name"></asp:Label>
          <br />
          <br />
          <asp:Label runat="server" Width="200" ID="firstName" Text ="First
Name"></asp:Label>
           <asp:Label runat="server" Width="200" ID="middleInitial" Text ="Middle
Initial"></asp:Label>
```

```
        <asp:Label runat="server" Width="200" ID="lastName" Text ="Last
Name"></asp:Label>
        <br />
        <br />
        <asp:Label runat="server" Width="200" ID="userNameLabel" BackColor="#cccccc"
Font-Bold="true" Text ="User Name"></asp:Label>
        <asp:Label runat="server" Width="200" ID="primaryPhoneLabel" BackColor="#cccccc"
Font-Bold="true" Text ="Primary Phone Number"></asp:Label>
        <asp:Label runat="server" Width="200" ID="secondaryPhoneLabel"
BackColor="#cccccc" Font-Bold="true" Text ="Secondary Phone Number"></asp:Label>
        <br />
        <br />
        <asp:Label runat="server" Width="200" ID="userName" Text ="First
Name"></asp:Label>
        <asp:Label runat="server" Width="200" ID="primaryPhone" Text ="First
Name"></asp:Label>
        <asp:Label runat="server" Width="200" ID="secondaryPhone" Text ="Middle
Initial"></asp:Label>
        <br />
        <br />
        <asp:Label runat="server" Width="200" ID="emailAddressLabel" BackColor="#cccccc"
Font-Bold="true" Text ="Email Address"></asp:Label>
        <br />
        <br />
        <asp:Label runat="server" Width="200" ID="emailAddress" Text ="Last
Name"></asp:Label>
        <br />
        <br />
        <asp:Label runat="server" Width="150" ID="Label1" BackColor="#cccccc" Font-
Bold="true" Text ="Shipping Address"></asp:Label>
        <br />
        <br />
        <asp:ListBox ID ="shippingAddresses"
                Width="600"
                AutoPostBack="true"
                DataTextField="shippingAddress"
                runat="server"></asp:ListBox>
        <br />
        <br />
        <asp:Label runat="server" Width="150" ID="Label2" BackColor="#cccccc" Font-
Bold="true" Text ="Billing Address"></asp:Label>
        <br />
         <br />
        <asp:ListBox ID ="billingAddresses"
                Width="600"
                AutoPostBack="true"
```

You may purchase a copy of our companion disk which contains all files for the project at http://www.amazon.com/gp/product/B00AOU76K8!

```
                DataTextField="billingAddress"
                runat="server"></asp:ListBox>
    </p>
    <p>
        <asp:GridView ID ="categoryFilter"
                runat="server"
                DataKeyNames="Order #"
                OnRowCommand="categoryFilter_RowCommand"
                EditRowStyle-HorizontalAlign="Center"
                HeaderStyle-BackColor="#cccccc"
                BorderStyle="None"
                EmptyDataText="No details available." >
          <Columns>
            <asp:TemplateField>
            <ItemTemplate>
            <asp:LinkButton ID="viewOrder"
                    runat="server"
                    CommandName="Select"
                    CommandArgument="<%# Container.DataItemIndex %>"
                    Text = "View Order Detail"></asp:LinkButton>
            </ItemTemplate>
            </asp:TemplateField>
          </Columns>
        </asp:GridView>
    </p>
   </div>
   <div class="story">
  <div id="siteInfo"> <img alt="small logo" src="Pictures/YourBestDataSolutionLogo.jpg"
width="59" height="66" />
        <a href="AboutUs.aspx">About Us</a> |
        <a href="ContactUs.aspx">Contact Us</a> |
    ©2012 YBDS, LLC </div>

</div>
<br />
   </form>
</body>
</html>
```

You may purchase a copy of our companion disk which contains all files for the project at http://www.amazon.com/gp/product/B00AOU76K8!

Customer Details Code Behind

Replace the existing code in the CustomerDetails.aspx.vb file with the following code:

```
Imports System.Data
Imports System.IO
Imports System.Data.SqlClient

Partial Class _Default
    Inherits System.Web.UI.Page

    Protected Sub Page_Load(ByVal sender As Object, ByVal e As EventArgs) Handles Me.Load

        If (Session("firstName") = Nothing) Then
            'User is not logged in.  Continue.
            lkLogout.Visible = False
            lkChangePassword.Visible = False
            lkChangePassword.Enabled = False
            headerLabel.Text = "Please login to view your past orders."
            Session("isAdmin") = False
            lkCustomers.Visible = False
            lkCustomers.Enabled = False
            lkOrders.Visible = False
            lkOrders.Enabled = False
            lkAddProduct.Visible = False
            lkAddProduct.Enabled = False
            lkEditProduct.Visible = False
            lkEditProduct.Enabled = False
            Page.Response.Redirect("Login.aspx")
        Else
            If (Session("isAdmin")) Then
                lkCustomers.Visible = True
                lkCustomers.Enabled = True
                lkOrders.Visible = True
                lkOrders.Enabled = True
                lkAddProduct.Visible = True
                lkAddProduct.Enabled = True
                lkEditProduct.Visible = True
                lkEditProduct.Enabled = True
            Else
                lkCustomers.Visible = False
                lkCustomers.Enabled = False
                lkOrders.Visible = False
                lkOrders.Enabled = False
```

```
        lkAddProduct.Visible = False
        lkAddProduct.Enabled = False
        lkEditProduct.Visible = False
        lkEditProduct.Enabled = False
    End If
    lkChangePassword.Visible = True
    lkChangePassword.Enabled = True
    loginStatus.Text = "Welcome " & Session("firstName").ToString() & "!"
    loginStatus.Visible = True
    ''''''''''''''''''''''''''''''''''''''''''''
    ' Show the previous orders for the current user.
    Dim myAccess As DatabaseAccess
    Dim myConnection As String
    Dim con As SqlConnection
    Dim cmd As SqlCommand
    Dim adapter As SqlDataAdapter
    Dim ds As DataSet
    Dim sql As String
    Dim readData As SqlDataReader

    ' Fill database connection variables.
    myAccess = New DatabaseAccess()
    myConnection = myAccess.getConnectionString()
    con = New SqlConnection(myConnection)

    ''''''''''''''''''''''''''''''''''''''''''''''''''
    ' Get Shipping Address.
    sql = "SELECT DISTINCT StreetAddress1 + ' ' + [StreetAddress2] + ', ' +
[StreetAddress2] + ', ' + City + ', ' + StateAbbreviation + ' ' + PostalCode + ' - ' + PostalCode2 +
CountryName AS shippingAddress FROM " & _
  "UserAddress ua INNER JOIN Country c ON c.CountryID = ua.CountryID " & _
  "INNER JOIN USState st ON st.StateID = ua.StateID " & _
  "INNER JOIN UserOrder uo " & _
  "ON uo.ShippingAddressID = ua.AddressID " & _
  "WHERE uo.UserID = " & Session("customerID") & " " & _
  " AND AddressType = 2"
    cmd = New SqlCommand(sql, con)
    cmd.CommandType = Data.CommandType.Text
    adapter = New SqlDataAdapter(cmd)

    ' Fill the DataSet.
    ds = New DataSet()

    Try
        ' Open the database connection.
        con.Open()
```

You may purchase a copy of our companion disk which contains all files for the project at http://www.amazon.com/gp/product/B00AOU76K8!

```
        adapter.Fill(ds, sql)
    Finally

        con.Close()

        ' Perform the data binding.
        shippingAddresses.Items.Clear()
        shippingAddresses.DataSource = ds
        shippingAddresses.DataBind()
        shippingAddresses.SelectedIndex = 0
    End Try

    ''''''''''''''''''''''''''''''''''''''''''''''''''''''''''
    ' Get Billing Address.
    sql = "SELECT DISTINCT StreetAddress1 + ' ' + [StreetAddress2] + ', ' +
[StreetAddress2] + ', ' + City + ', ' + StateAbbreviation + ' ' + PostalCode + ' ' + CountryName AS
billingAddress FROM " & _
  "UserAddress ua INNER JOIN Country c " & _
  "ON c.CountryID = ua.CountryID " & _
  "INNER JOIN USState st ON st.StateID = ua.StateID " & _
  "INNER JOIN UserOrder uo " & _
  "ON uo.ShippingAddressID = ua.AddressID " & _
  "WHERE uo.UserID = " & Session("customerID") & " " & _
  " AND AddressType = 1"
    cmd = New SqlCommand(sql, con)
    cmd.CommandType = Data.CommandType.Text
    adapter = New SqlDataAdapter(cmd)

    ' Fill the DataSet.
    ds = New DataSet()

    Try
        ' Open the database connection.
        con.Open()
        adapter.Fill(ds, sql)
    Finally

        con.Close()

        ' Perform the data binding.
        billingAddresses.Items.Clear()
        billingAddresses.DataSource = ds
        billingAddresses.DataBind()
        billingAddresses.SelectedIndex = 0
    End Try
```

You may purchase a copy of our companion disk which contains all files for the project at http://www.amazon.com/gp/product/B00AOU76K8!

```
''''''''''''''''''''''''''''''''''''''''''''''''
sql = "SELECT uo.OrderID AS [Order #], " & _
    "uo.OrderDate AS [Order Date], " & _
    "os.OrderStatusName AS [Order Status] " & _
    "FROM UserOrder uo " & _
    "INNER JOIN OrderStatus os " & _
    "ON os.OrderStatusID = uo.OrderStatusID " & _
    "WHERE uo.UserID = " & Session("customerID") & " " & _
    "AND uo.OrderID IN (SELECT OrderID FROM OrderDetail)"
cmd = New SqlCommand(sql, con)
cmd.CommandType = Data.CommandType.Text
adapter = New SqlDataAdapter(cmd)

' Fill the DataSet.
ds = New DataSet()

Try
   ' Open the database connection.
   con.Open()
   adapter.Fill(ds, sql)
Finally

   con.Close()

   ' Perform the data binding.
   categoryFilter.DataSource = ds
   categoryFilter.DataBind()
End Try

''''''''''''''''''''''''''''''''''''''''''''''''''''''

' Get user data.
sql = "SELECT * FROM [User] " & _
    "WHERE UserID = " & Session("customerID") & " "
cmd = New SqlCommand(sql, con)
cmd.CommandType = Data.CommandType.Text
Try

   ' Open database connection.
   con.Open()

   ' Execute the INSERT and fill the data reader.
   readData = cmd.ExecuteReader(CommandBehavior.CloseConnection)

Catch a As Exception
```

You may purchase a copy of our companion disk which contains all files for the project at http://www.amazon.com/gp/product/B00AOU76K8!

```
        Throw a
      End Try
      readData.Read()
      firstName.Text = IIf(IsDBNull(readData("FirstName")), "", readData("FirstName"))
      middleInitial.Text = IIf(IsDBNull(readData("MiddleInitial")), "",
readData("MiddleInitial"))
      lastName.Text = IIf(IsDBNull(readData("LastName")), "", readData("LastName"))
      userName.Text = readData("UserName")
      primaryPhone.Text = readData("PhoneNumberPrimary")
      secondaryPhone.Text = IIf(IsDBNull(readData("PhoneNumberSecondary")), "",
readData("PhoneNumberSecondary"))
      emailAddress.Text = readData("EmailAddress")
      headerLabel.Text = "Customer Details for " + readData("FirstName") + " " +
readData("MiddleInitial") + " " + readData("LastName")
      readData.Close()
      con.Close()

    End If

  End Sub

  Protected Sub logout()
    Session("firstName") = Nothing
    Session.Clear()
    Page.Response.Redirect("Logout.aspx")
  End Sub

  Protected Sub passSessionVariable()
    ''''''''''''''''''''''''''''''''''''''''''''''''''''''''''''''''''''''''''''''
    ' Open Order details page.
    Page.Response.Redirect("OrderDetails.aspx")
  End Sub

  Protected Sub categoryFilter_RowCommand(ByVal sender As Object, ByVal e As
System.Web.UI.WebControls.GridViewCommandEventArgs) Handles
categoryFilter.RowCommand
    Dim obj As Object
    Dim id As String
    Dim orderID As Integer
    Dim cmdName As String

    cmdName = e.CommandName
    obj = e.CommandArgument
    id = obj.ToString
    orderID = Convert.ToInt16(id.ToString)
```

```
        Session("viewOrderID") =
Convert.ToInt16(categoryFilter.DataKeys(orderID).Value.ToString)
        orderID = Convert.ToInt16(categoryFilter.DataKeys(orderID).Value.ToString)

        Select Case (cmdName)
            Case "Select"
                passSessionVariable()
        End Select
    End Sub

    Protected Sub categoryFilter_RowDataBound(ByVal sender As Object, ByVal e As
System.Web.UI.WebControls.GridViewRowEventArgs) Handles categoryFilter.RowDataBound
        'e.Row.Cells(0).Visible = False
        'e.Row.Cells(1).Visible = False
    End Sub
End Class
```

You may purchase a copy of our companion disk which contains all files for the project at http://www.amazon.com/gp/product/B00AOU76K8!

Customers Server Page

Replace the existing code in the Customers.aspx file with the following code (***REPLACE ANY CODE IN THIS COLOR WITH YOUR OWN INFORMATION!)***:

```
<%@ Page Language="VB"
        AutoEventWireup="True"
        CodeFile="Customers.aspx.vb"
        Inherits="_Default" %>

<!DOCTYPE html PUBLIC "-//W3C//DTD XHTML 1.0 Transitional//EN"
"http://www.w3.org/TR/xhtml1/DTD/xhtml1-transitional.dtd">
<html xmlns="http://www.w3.org/1999/xhtml">

<head>
<meta http-equiv="Content-Type" content="text/html; charset=iso-8859-1" />
<title>Customers</title>
<link rel="stylesheet" href="emx_nav_left.css" type="text/css" />
<script type="text/javascript">

var time = 3000;
var numofitems = 7;

//menu constructor
function menu(allitems,thisitem,startstate){
  callname= "gl"+thisitem;
  divname="subglobal"+thisitem;
  this.numberofmenuitems = allitems;
  this.caller = document.getElementById(callname);
  this.thediv = document.getElementById(divname);
  this.thediv.style.visibility = startstate;
}

//menu methods
function ehandler(event,theobj){
  for (var i=1; i<= theobj.numberofmenuitems; i++){
    var shutdiv =eval( "menuitem"+i+".thediv");
    shutdiv.style.visibility="hidden";
  }
  theobj.thediv.style.visibility="visible";
}

function closesubnav(event){
  if ((event.clientY <48)||(event.clientY > 107)){
```

You may purchase a copy of our companion disk which contains all files for the project at http://www.amazon.com/gp/product/B00AOU76K8!

```
  for (var i=1; i<= numofitems; i++){
    var shutdiv =eval('menuitem'+i+'.thediv');
    shutdiv.style.visibility='hidden';
   }
  }
}
</script>
</head>
<body>

<form id="Form1" runat="server">
<div class="skipLinks">skip to: <a href="#content">page content</a> | <a
href="#pageNav">links on this page</a> | <a href="#globalNav">site navigation</a> | <a
href="#siteInfo">footer (site information)</a> </div>
<div id="masthead">
  <h1 id="siteName">Your Best Data Solution</h1>
  <div id="utility">
      <asp:LinkButton ID="lkCustomers" runat="server"
PostBackUrl="Customers.aspx">Customers</asp:LinkButton>
     | <asp:LinkButton ID="lkOrders" runat="server"
PostBackUrl="ViewOrders.aspx">Orders</asp:LinkButton>
     | <asp:LinkButton ID="lkAddProduct" PostBackUrl="AddProduct.aspx"
                   runat="server">Add Product</asp:LinkButton>
     | <asp:LinkButton ID="lkEditProduct" runat="server"
PostBackUrl="ViewCategories.aspx">Edit Product</asp:LinkButton>
     | <asp:LinkButton ID="lkLogout" OnClick="logout" runat="server"
PostBackUrl="#">Logout</asp:LinkButton>
     | <asp:LinkButton ID="lkChangePassword" PostBackUrl="Password.aspx"
runat="server">Change Password</asp:LinkButton>
  </div>
  <div id="globalNav"> <img alt="" src="Pictures/gblnav_left.gif" height="32" width="4"
id="gnl" /> <img alt="" src="Pictures/glbnav_right.gif" height="32" width="4" id="gnr" />
    <div id="globalLink">
        <a href="Default.aspx" id="A1" class="glink">
        Home</a>
        <a href="ViewCategories.aspx" id="gl1" class="glink" >
        View Products</a>
        <a href="SearchProducts.aspx" id="gl2" class="glink">Search</a>
        <a href="ViewCart.aspx" id="gl3" class="glink">View Cart</a>
        <a href="Checkout.aspx" id="gl4" class="glink">Checkout</a>
        <a href="CreateAccount.aspx" id="gl5" class="glink">Create
        Account</a>
        <a href="Login.aspx" id="gl6" class="glink">Login
        </a><a href="OrderHistory.aspx" id="gl7" class="glink">Order
        History</a>
        <a href="FAQ.aspx" id="A2" class="glink">FAQ</a>
```

```
      <asp:Label ID="loginStatus" Visible="false" runat="server"></asp:Label>
    </div>
  </div>
<div id="pagecell1">
  <img alt="" src="Pictures/tl_curve_white.gif" height="6" width="6" id="tl" /> <img alt=""
src="Pictures/tr_curve_white.gif" height="6" width="6" id="tr" />

    <div id="pageName">
    <img alt="small logo" src="Pictures/YourBestDataSolutionLogo.jpg" height="50"
width="60"/> </div>
   <div id="pageNav">
    <div class="relatedLinks">
      <h3>Related Link Category</h3>
      <a href="FAQ.aspx#anchor3">Automation</a>
      <a href="FAQ.aspx#anchor1">Customized Reporting</a>
      <a href="FAQ.aspx#anchor2">Database Design</a>
      <a href="FAQ.aspx#anchor12">Data Migration</a>
      <a href="FAQ.aspx#anchor4">Data Modeling</a>
      <a href="FAQ.aspx#anchor14">Desktop Application Solutions</a>
      <a href="FAQ.aspx#anchor5">eCommerce Solutions</a>
      <a href="FAQ.aspx#anchor6">eMail Marketing</a>
      <a href="FAQ.aspx#anchor7">Mobile App Development</a>
      <a href="FAQ.aspx#anchor8">PayPal™ Integration</a>
      <a href="FAQ.aspx#anchor9">Web Design</a>
      <a href="FAQ.aspx#anchor10">Web Development</a>
    </div>
   </div>
   <div id="content">
    <div class="feature">
      <h3>
      <asp:Label runat="server" ID="headerLabel" Text ="Customers"></asp:Label></h3>
       <p>
           <asp:GridView ID ="categoryFilter"
                       runat="server"
                       DataKeyNames="UserID"
                       OnRowCommand="categoryFilter_RowCommand"
                       EditRowStyle-HorizontalAlign="Center"
                       HeaderStyle-BackColor="#cccccc"
                       BorderStyle="None"
                       EmptyDataText="You have no customers." >
              <Columns>
                 <asp:TemplateField>
                 <ItemTemplate>
                 <asp:LinkButton ID="viewOrder"
                           runat="server"
                           CommandName="Select"
```

You may purchase a copy of our companion disk which contains all files for the project at http://www.amazon.com/gp/product/B00AOU76K8!

```
                        CommandArgument="<%# Container.DataItemIndex %>"
                        Text = "View Customer Detail"></asp:LinkButton>
                </ItemTemplate>
                </asp:TemplateField>
              </Columns>
            </asp:GridView>
        </p>

    </div>
    <div class="story">
  <div id="siteInfo"> <img alt="small logo" src="Pictures/YourBestDataSolutionLogo.jpg"
width="59" height="66" />
            <a href="AboutUs.aspx">About Us</a> |
            <a href="ContactUs.aspx">Contact Us</a> |
      ©2012 YBDS, LLC </div>

</div>
<br />
    </form>
</body>
</html>
```

You may purchase a copy of our companion disk which contains all files for the project at http://www.amazon.com/gp/product/B00AOU76K8!

Customers Code Behind

Replace the existing code in the Customers.aspx.vb file with the following code:

```
Imports System.Data
Imports System.Data.SqlClient

Partial Class _Default
   Inherits System.Web.UI.Page

   Protected Sub Page_Load(ByVal sender As Object, ByVal e As EventArgs) Handles Me.Load

      If (Session("firstName") = Nothing) Then
         'User is not logged in.  Continue.
         lkLogout.Visible = False
         lkChangePassword.Visible = False
         lkChangePassword.Enabled = False
         categoryFilter.EmptyDataText = "Please log in to view your past orders."
         categoryFilter.Visible = True
         Session("isAdmin") = False
         lkCustomers.Visible = False
         lkCustomers.Enabled = False
         lkOrders.Visible = False
         lkOrders.Enabled = False
         lkAddProduct.Visible = False
         lkAddProduct.Enabled = False
         lkEditProduct.Visible = False
         lkEditProduct.Enabled = False
         Page.Response.Redirect("Login.aspx")
      Else
         If (Session("isAdmin")) Then
            lkCustomers.Visible = True
            lkCustomers.Enabled = True
            lkOrders.Visible = True
            lkOrders.Enabled = True
            lkAddProduct.Visible = True
            lkAddProduct.Enabled = True
            lkEditProduct.Visible = True
            lkEditProduct.Enabled = True
         Else
            lkCustomers.Visible = False
            lkCustomers.Enabled = False
            lkOrders.Visible = False
            lkOrders.Enabled = False
```

```
    lkAddProduct.Visible = False
    lkAddProduct.Enabled = False
    lkEditProduct.Visible = False
    lkEditProduct.Enabled = False
End If
lkChangePassword.Visible = True
lkChangePassword.Enabled = True
loginStatus.Text = "Welcome " & Session("firstName").ToString() & "!"
loginStatus.Visible = True
''''''''''''''''''''''''''''''''''''''''''''''''''

' Show the previous orders for the current user.
Dim myAccess As DatabaseAccess
Dim myConnection As String
Dim con As SqlConnection
Dim cmd As SqlCommand
Dim adapter As SqlDataAdapter
Dim ds As DataSet
Dim sql As String
Dim userID As String
'Dim readData As SqlDataReader
'Dim itemCount As Integer

' Fill database connection variables.
myAccess = New DatabaseAccess()
myConnection = myAccess.getConnectionString()
con = New SqlConnection(myConnection)

userID = Session("UserID")
If userID = Nothing Then
    userID = -1
End If

myAccess = New DatabaseAccess()
myConnection = myAccess.getConnectionString()

con = New SqlConnection(myConnection)
sql = "SELECT UserID, " & _
 "LastName AS [Last Name], " & _
 "FirstName AS [First Name], " & _
 "MiddleInitial AS [Middle Initial] " & _
     "FROM [User] ORDER BY LastName"
cmd = New SqlCommand(sql, con)
cmd.CommandType = Data.CommandType.Text
adapter = New SqlDataAdapter(cmd)

' Fill the DataSet.
```

```
        ds = New DataSet()

        Try
           ' Open the database connection.
           con.Open()
           adapter.Fill(ds, sql)
        Finally

           con.Close()

           ' Perform the data binding.
           categoryFilter.DataSource = ds
           categoryFilter.DataBind()
        End Try
        'End If
        headerLabel.Text = "Customers"
     End If

  End Sub

  Protected Sub logout()
     Session("firstName") = Nothing
     Session.Clear()
     Page.Response.Redirect("Logout.aspx")
  End Sub

  Protected Sub passSessionVariable()
     ''''''''''''''''''''''''''''''''''''''''''''

     ' Open order details page for selected order.
     Page.Response.Redirect("CustomerDetails.aspx")
  End Sub

  Protected Sub categoryFilter_RowCommand(ByVal sender As Object, ByVal e As
System.Web.UI.WebControls.GridViewCommandEventArgs) Handles
categoryFilter.RowCommand
     Dim obj As Object
     Dim id As String
     Dim customerID As Integer
     Dim cmdName As String

     cmdName = e.CommandName
     obj = e.CommandArgument
     id = obj.ToString
     customerID = Convert.ToInt16(id.ToString)
     Session("customerID") =
Convert.ToInt16(categoryFilter.DataKeys(customerID).Value.ToString)
```

You may purchase a copy of our companion disk which contains all files for the project at http://www.amazon.com/gp/product/B00AOU76K8!

```
    customerID = Convert.ToInt16(categoryFilter.DataKeys(customerID).Value.ToString)

    Select Case (cmdName)
      Case "Select"
        passSessionVariable()
    End Select
  End Sub

  Protected Sub categoryFilter_RowDataBound(ByVal sender As Object, ByVal e As
System.Web.UI.WebControls.GridViewRowEventArgs) Handles categoryFilter.RowDataBound
    Dim myAccess As DatabaseAccess
    Dim myConnection As String
    Dim con As SqlConnection
    Dim cmd As SqlCommand
    Dim sql As String
    Dim readData As SqlDataReader
    Dim userCount As Integer
    Dim userID As Integer

    userID = Session("UserID")
    If userID = Nothing Then
      userID = -1
    End If

    myAccess = New DatabaseAccess()
    myConnection = myAccess.getConnectionString()

    con = New SqlConnection(myConnection)
    sql = "SELECT COUNT(UserID) AS users FROM [User]"
    cmd = New SqlCommand(sql, con)
    cmd.CommandType = Data.CommandType.Text
    Try

      ' Open database connection.
      con.Open()

      ' Execute the INSERT and fill the data reader.
      readData = cmd.ExecuteReader(CommandBehavior.CloseConnection)

    Catch a As Exception

      Throw a
    End Try
    readData.Read()
    userCount = readData("users")
    con.Close()
```

```
        readData.Close()

        If (Session("UserID") <> Nothing) And (userCount > 0) Then
            e.Row.Cells(1).Visible = False
        End If

    End Sub
End Class
```

You may purchase a copy of our companion disk which contains all files for the project at http://www.amazon.com/gp/product/B00AOU76K8!

Default Server Page

Replace the existing code in the Default.aspx file with the following code (***REPLACE ANY CODE IN THIS COLOR WITH YOUR OWN INFORMATION!)***:

```
<%@ Page Language="VB"
        AutoEventWireup="True"
        CodeFile="Default.aspx.vb"
        Inherits="_Default" %>

<!DOCTYPE html PUBLIC "-//W3C//DTD XHTML 1.0 Transitional//EN"
"http://www.w3.org/TR/xhtml1/DTD/xhtml1-transitional.dtd">
<html xmlns="http://www.w3.org/1999/xhtml">

<head>
<meta http-equiv="Content-Type" content="text/html; charset=iso-8859-1" />
<title>Welcome Page</title>
<link rel="stylesheet" href="emx_nav_left.css" type="text/css" />
<script type="text/javascript">

var time = 3000;
var numofitems = 7;

//menu constructor
function menu(allitems,thisitem,startstate){
  callname= "gl"+thisitem;
  divname="subglobal"+thisitem;
  this.numberofmenuitems = allitems;
  this.caller = document.getElementById(callname);
  this.thediv = document.getElementById(divname);
  this.thediv.style.visibility = startstate;
}

//menu methods
function ehandler(event,theobj){
  for (var i=1; i<= theobj.numberofmenuitems; i++){
    var shutdiv =eval( "menuitem"+i+".thediv");
    shutdiv.style.visibility="hidden";
  }
  theobj.thediv.style.visibility="visible";
}

function closesubnav(event){
  if ((event.clientY <48)||(event.clientY > 107)){
```

You may purchase a copy of our companion disk which contains all files for the project at http://www.amazon.com/gp/product/B00AOU76K8!

```
  for (var i=1; i<= numofitems; i++){
   var shutdiv =eval('menuitem'+i+'.thediv');
   shutdiv.style.visibility='hidden';
  }
 }
}
</script>
</head>
<body>

<form id="Form1" runat="server">
<div class="skipLinks">skip to: <a href="#content">page content</a> | <a
href="#pageNav">links on this page</a> | <a href="#globalNav">site navigation</a> | <a
href="#siteInfo">footer (site information)</a> </div>
<div id="masthead">
 <h1 id="siteName">Your Best Data Solution</h1>
 <div id="utility">
     <asp:LinkButton ID="lkCustomers" runat="server"
PostBackUrl="Customers.aspx">Customers</asp:LinkButton>
   | <asp:LinkButton ID="lkOrders" runat="server"
PostBackUrl="ViewOrders.aspx">Orders</asp:LinkButton>
   | <asp:LinkButton ID="lkAddProduct" PostBackUrl="AddProduct.aspx"
            runat="server">Add Product</asp:LinkButton>
   | <asp:LinkButton ID="lkEditProduct" runat="server"
PostBackUrl="ViewCategories.aspx">Edit Product</asp:LinkButton>
   | <asp:LinkButton ID="lkLogout" OnClick="logout" runat="server"
PostBackUrl="#">Logout</asp:LinkButton>
   | <asp:LinkButton ID="lkChangePassword" PostBackUrl="Password.aspx"
runat="server">Change Password</asp:LinkButton>
 </div>
 <div id="globalNav"> <img alt="" src="Pictures/gblnav_left.gif" height="32" width="4"
id="gnl" /> <img alt="" src="Pictures/glbnav_right.gif" height="32" width="4" id="gnr" />
  <div id="globalLink">
     <a href="Default.aspx" id="A1" class="glink">
     Home</a>
     <a href="ViewCategories.aspx" id="gl1" class="glink" >
     View Products</a>
     <a href="SearchProducts.aspx" id="gl2" class="glink">Search</a>
     <a href="ViewCart.aspx" id="gl3" class="glink">View Cart</a>
     <a href="Checkout.aspx" id="gl4" class="glink">Checkout</a>
     <a href="CreateAccount.aspx" id="gl5" class="glink">Create
     Account</a>
     <a href="Login.aspx" id="gl6" class="glink">Login
     </a><a href="OrderHistory.aspx" id="gl7" class="glink">Order
     History</a>
     <a href="FAQ.aspx" id="A2" class="glink">FAQ</a>
```

```
      <asp:Label ID="loginStatus" Visible="false" runat="server"></asp:Label>
    </div>
  </div>
<div id="pagecell1">
  <img alt="" src="Pictures/tl_curve_white.gif" height="6" width="6" id="tl" /> <img alt=""
src="Pictures/tr_curve_white.gif" height="6" width="6" id="tr" />

   <div id="pageName">
   <img alt="small logo" src="Pictures/YourBestDataSolutionLogo.jpg" height="50"
width="60"/> </div>
  <div id="pageNav">
   <div class="relatedLinks">
    <h3>Data Services Links</h3>
    <a href="FAQ.aspx#anchor3">Automation</a>
    <a href="FAQ.aspx#anchor1">Customized Reporting</a>
    <a href="FAQ.aspx#anchor2">Database Design</a>
    <a href="FAQ.aspx#anchor12">Data Migration</a>
    <a href="FAQ.aspx#anchor4">Data Modeling</a>
    <a href="FAQ.aspx#anchor14">Desktop Application Solutions</a>
    <a href="FAQ.aspx#anchor5">eCommerce Solutions</a>
    <a href="FAQ.aspx#anchor6">eMail Marketing</a>
    <a href="FAQ.aspx#anchor7">Mobile App Development</a>
    <a href="FAQ.aspx#anchor8">PayPal™ Integration</a>
    <a href="FAQ.aspx#anchor9">Web Design</a>
    <a href="FAQ.aspx#anchor10">Web Development</a>
   </div>
  </div>
  <div id="content">
   <div class="feature"> <img src="Pictures/VBA Cookbook Cover.jpg" alt="" width="400"
height="400" />
    <h3>Welcome to Your Best Data Solution! </h3>
     <p>We have over 8 years of experience in modelling and developing scalable,
        extensible data solutions for our clients. We provide the unique ability to
        serve as a data analyst, database developer and programmer in order to address
        and solve your most difficult business problems.   We provide
        solutions using Perl, .NET, VBA, Visual Basic, PHP and Java programming
        languages while serving your needs in MySQL, SQL Server, PostgreSQL, and
Oracle
        database platforms.</p>
        <p>The Products tab of this website provides an excellent demonstration of our data
           driven programming. All products are actually live products in our own store,
           and this site allows you to make purchases from the website using
PayPal™! 
           Permissions are enforced in the Products portion of the website; users must
           register with the site before completing checkout.  This provides vendors
```

You may purchase a copy of our companion disk which contains all files for the project at http://www.amazon.com/gp/product/B00AOU76K8!

```
            with an automatic customer list.  The shopping cart is very user-
friendly. 
            Users may view larger images of the product; while there is no limit to the
            quantity of items that may be added to the shopping cart, the user is accurately
            restricted from choosing an item quantity that is greater than the available
            inventory.  The user is given the option of shipping methods during the
            Checkout process of the shopping cart.  Additionally, inventory is
            automatically updated when purchases are made, and a confirmation email is sent
            to the customer from the site upon completion of the sale via PayPal™. 
This is a complete                              ecommerce solution that we can provide your
business!</p>
        <p>In addition, Your Best Data Solution has authored a very informative look at MS
           Access programming titled The Complete MS Access VBA Cookbook</u>.
          This book is available in our store or from Google Books (<B>ISBN 13: 978-0-
9834174-0-8</B>).  </P>

        <p><font color="red">***** REMEMBER - We provide the following high quality
data services:</font>
         <ul>
             <li>Automation</li>
             <li>Customized Reporting</li>
             <li>Database Design</li>
             <li>Data Migration</li>
             <li>Data Modelling</li>
             <li>Desktop Application Solutions</li>
             <li>eCommerce Solutions</li>
             <li>eMail Marketing</li>
             <li>Mobile App Development</li>
             <li>PayPal™ Integration</li>
             <li>Web Design</li>
             <li>Web Development</li>
         </ul>
                </p>
        <p>Contact us today for our analysis.  We guarantee that our service will provide
value above and
        beyond the cost of our service!</p>

    </div>
    <div class="story">
  <div id="siteInfo"> <img alt="small logo" src="Pictures/YourBestDataSolutionLogo.jpg"
width="59" height="66" />
          <a href="AboutUs.aspx">About Us</a> |
          <a href="ContactUs.aspx">Contact Us</a> |
      ©2012 YBDS, LLC </div>

</div>
```

You may purchase a copy of our companion disk which contains all files for the project at http://www.amazon.com/gp/product/B00AOU76K8!

```
<br />
   </form>
</body>
</html>
```

You may purchase a copy of our companion disk which contains all files for the project at http://www.amazon.com/gp/product/B00AOU76K8!

Default Code Behind

Replace the existing code in the Default.aspx.vb file with the following code:

```
Imports System.Data
Imports System.Data.SqlClient

Partial Class _Default
   Inherits System.Web.UI.Page

   Protected Sub Page_Load(ByVal sender As Object, ByVal e As EventArgs) Handles Me.Load

      If (Session("firstName") = Nothing) Then
         'User is not logged in.  Continue.
         lkLogout.Visible = False
         lkChangePassword.Visible = False
         lkChangePassword.Enabled = False
         Session("isAdmin") = False
         lkCustomers.Visible = False
         lkCustomers.Enabled = False
         lkOrders.Visible = False
         lkOrders.Enabled = False
         lkAddProduct.Visible = False
         lkAddProduct.Enabled = False
         lkEditProduct.Visible = False
         lkEditProduct.Enabled = False
      Else
         Dim myAccess As New DatabaseAccess()
         Session("isAdmin") = myAccess.isAdmin(Convert.ToInt16(Session("userID")))
         If (Session("isAdmin")) Then
            lkCustomers.Visible = True
            lkCustomers.Enabled = True
            lkOrders.Visible = True
            lkOrders.Enabled = True
            lkAddProduct.Visible = True
            lkAddProduct.Enabled = True
            lkEditProduct.Visible = True
            lkEditProduct.Enabled = True
         Else
            lkCustomers.Visible = False
            lkCustomers.Enabled = False
            lkOrders.Visible = False
            lkOrders.Enabled = False
            lkAddProduct.Visible = False
```

```
            lkAddProduct.Enabled = False
            lkEditProduct.Visible = False
            lkEditProduct.Enabled = False
        End If
        lkChangePassword.Visible = True
        lkChangePassword.Enabled = True
        loginStatus.Text = "Welcome " & Session("firstName").ToString() & "!"
        loginStatus.Visible = True
    End If

  End Sub

  Protected Sub logout()
    Session("firstName") = Nothing
    Session.Clear()
    Page.Response.Redirect("Logout.aspx")
  End Sub

End Class
```

Edit Product Server Page

Replace the existing code in the EditProducts.aspx file with the following code (***REPLACE ANY CODE IN THIS COLOR WITH YOUR OWN INFORMATION!)***:

```
<%@ Page Language="VB"
      AutoEventWireup="True"
      CodeFile="EditProduct.aspx.vb"
      Inherits="_Default" %>

<!DOCTYPE html PUBLIC "-//W3C//DTD XHTML 1.0 Transitional//EN"
"http://www.w3.org/TR/xhtml1/DTD/xhtml1-transitional.dtd">
<html xmlns="http://www.w3.org/1999/xhtml">

<head>
<meta http-equiv="Content-Type" content="text/html; charset=iso-8859-1" />
<title>Edit Products</title>
<link rel="stylesheet" href="emx_nav_left.css" type="text/css" />
<script type="text/javascript">

var time = 3000;
var numofitems = 7;

//menu constructor
function menu(allitems,thisitem,startstate){
  callname= "gl"+thisitem;
  divname="subglobal"+thisitem;
  this.numberofmenuitems = allitems;
  this.caller = document.getElementById(callname);
  this.thediv = document.getElementById(divname);
  this.thediv.style.visibility = startstate;
}

//menu methods
function ehandler(event,theobj){
  for (var i=1; i<= theobj.numberofmenuitems; i++){
    var shutdiv =eval( "menuitem"+i+".thediv");
    shutdiv.style.visibility="hidden";
  }
  theobj.thediv.style.visibility="visible";
}

function closesubnav(event){
  if ((event.clientY <48)||(event.clientY > 107)){
```

You may purchase a copy of our companion disk which contains all files for the project at http://www.amazon.com/gp/product/B00AOU76K8!

```
   for (var i=1; i<= numofitems; i++){
    var shutdiv =eval('menuitem'+i+'.thediv');
    shutdiv.style.visibility='hidden';
   }
  }
}
</script>
</head>
<body>

<form id="Form1" runat="server">
<div class="skipLinks">skip to: <a href="#content">page content</a> | <a
href="#pageNav">links on this page</a> | <a href="#globalNav">site navigation</a> | <a
href="#siteInfo">footer (site information)</a> </div>
<div id="masthead">
  <h1 id="siteName">Your Best Data Solution</h1>
  <div id="utility">
       <asp:LinkButton ID="lkCustomers" runat="server"
PostBackUrl="Customers.aspx">Customers</asp:LinkButton>
     |<asp:LinkButton ID="lkOrders" runat="server"
PostBackUrl="ViewOrders.aspx">Orders</asp:LinkButton>
     |<asp:LinkButton ID="lkAddProduct" PostBackUrl="AddProduct.aspx"
                 runat="server">Add Product</asp:LinkButton>
     |<asp:LinkButton ID="lkEditProduct" runat="server"
PostBackUrl="ViewCategories.aspx">Edit Product</asp:LinkButton>
     |<asp:LinkButton ID="lkLogout" OnClick="logout" runat="server"
PostBackUrl="#">Logout</asp:LinkButton>
     |<asp:LinkButton ID="lkChangePassword" PostBackUrl="Password.aspx"
runat="server">Change Password</asp:LinkButton>
  </div>
  <div id="globalNav"> <img alt="" src="Pictures/gblnav_left.gif" height="32" width="4"
id="gnl" /> <img alt="" src="Pictures/glbnav_right.gif" height="32" width="4" id="gnr" />
    <div id="globalLink">
       <a href="Default.aspx" id="A1" class="glink">
       Home</a>
       <a href="ViewCategories.aspx" id="gl1" class="glink" >
       View Products</a>
       <a href="SearchProducts.aspx" id="gl2" class="glink">Search</a>
       <a href="ViewCart.aspx" id="gl3" class="glink">View Cart</a>
       <a href="Checkout.aspx" id="gl4" class="glink">Checkout</a>
       <a href="CreateAccount.aspx" id="gl5" class="glink">Create
       Account</a>
       <a href="Login.aspx" id="gl6" class="glink">Login
       </a><a href="OrderHistory.aspx" id="gl7" class="glink">Order
       History</a>
       <a href="FAQ.aspx" id="A2" class="glink">FAQ</a>
```

```
      <asp:Label ID="loginStatus" Visible="false" runat="server"></asp:Label>
    </div>
  </div>
<div id="pagecell1">
  <img alt="" src="Pictures/tl_curve_white.gif" height="6" width="6" id="tl" /> <img alt=""
src="Pictures/tr_curve_white.gif" height="6" width="6" id="tr" />

   <div id="pageName">
   <img alt="small logo" src="Pictures/YourBestDataSolutionLogo.jpg" height="50"
width="60"/> </div>
  <div id="pageNav">
    <div class="relatedLinks">
      <h3>Related Link Category</h3>
      <a href="FAQ.aspx#anchor3">Automation</a>
      <a href="FAQ.aspx#anchor1">Customized Reporting</a>
      <a href="FAQ.aspx#anchor2">Database Design</a>
      <a href="FAQ.aspx#anchor12">Data Migration</a>
      <a href="FAQ.aspx#anchor4">Data Modeling</a>
      <a href="FAQ.aspx#anchor14">Desktop Application Solutions</a>
      <a href="FAQ.aspx#anchor5">eCommerce Solutions</a>
      <a href="FAQ.aspx#anchor6">eMail Marketing</a>
      <a href="FAQ.aspx#anchor7">Mobile App Development</a>
      <a href="FAQ.aspx#anchor8">PayPal™ Integration</a>
      <a href="FAQ.aspx#anchor9">Web Design</a>
      <a href="FAQ.aspx#anchor10">Web Development</a>
    </div>
  </div>
  <div id="content">
    <div class="feature">
      <h3><asp:Label runat="server"
                ID="headerLabel" BackColor="LightGray"
                Text="Edit Product ** All fields except picture are required
**"></asp:Label></h3>
        <p>
           <asp:Label ID="lblProductName"
                 runat="server"
                 Text="Product name"
                 BackColor="#cccccc"
                 Font-Bold="true"
                 Width ="300"></asp:Label>
           <asp:Label Value="   " runat="server"   />
           <asp:Label ID="lblCategory" BackColor="#cccccc" runat="server" Font-Bold="true"
 Text="Product Category" Width="300"></asp:Label>
           <asp:Label ID="HiddenField1" Visible="true" Value=" " runat="server" />
           <br />
           <br />
```

You may purchase a copy of our companion disk which contains all files for the project at http://www.amazon.com/gp/product/B00AOU76K8!

```
        <asp:TextBox ID="txtProductName" runat="server" Width="300"></asp:TextBox>
        <asp:HiddenField ID="HiddenField2" Value=" " runat="server" />
        <asp:DropDownList ID="cboCategory" AutoPostBack="true" runat="server"
Width="300"></asp:DropDownList>
        <asp:HiddenField ID="HiddenField3" Value=" " runat="server" />
        <asp:Label ID="nameRequired"
            runat="server" Visible="false"></asp:Label>
        <br />
        <br />
        <asp:Label ID="lblBriefDescription" BackColor="#cccccc" Font-Bold="true"
runat="server" Width="600" Text="Brief Description"></asp:Label>
        <br />
        <br />
        <asp:TextBox ID="txtBriefDescription" runat="server" Width="600"></asp:TextBox>
        <asp:Label ID="billingAddressRequired"
            runat="server" Visible="false"></asp:Label>
        <br />
        <br />
        <asp:Label ID="lblFullDescription" BackColor="#cccccc" Font-Bold="true"
runat="server" Width="600" Text="Full Description"></asp:Label>
        <br />
        <br />
        <asp:TextBox ID="txtFullDescription" runat="server" Width="600"></asp:TextBox>
        <asp:Label ID="fullDescriptionRequired"
            runat="server" Visible="false"></asp:Label>
        <br />
        <br />
        <asp:Label ID="lblQuantityAvailable" BackColor="#cccccc" Font-Bold="true"
runat="server" Width="120" Text="Quantity Available"></asp:Label>
        <asp:Label ID="lblPrice" BackColor="#cccccc" runat="server" Font-Bold="true"
Text="Price" Width="100"></asp:Label>
        <br />
        <br />
        <asp:TextBox ID="txtQuantityAvailable" runat="server" Width="100"></asp:TextBox>
        <asp:Label ID="Label1" runat="server" Text="$" Width="5"></asp:Label>
        <asp:TextBox ID="txtPrice" runat="server" Width="100"></asp:TextBox>
        <asp:Label ID="qtyAndPriceRequired"
            runat="server" Visible="false"></asp:Label>
        <br />
        <br />
    </p>
    <div>
    <hr />
        <asp:Label ID="filePath1" Font-Bold="true" runat="server"></asp:Label>
        <asp:Label ID="filePathHidden" runat="server" Font-Bold="true" Visible="false"
></asp:Label>
```

```
        <asp:FileUpload ID="FileUpload1"
                    runat="server" />
        <asp:Image runat="server" ID="newPicture" Visible="true" />
      <br />
      <br />
    <p>
      <asp:Button
              runat="server"
              OnClick="cmdUploadPhoto_Click"
              ID="cmdUploadPhoto"
              Text="Upload Photo" />
      <asp:Button
              runat="server"
              OnClick="cmdRemovePhoto_Click"
              ID="cmdRemovePhoto"  Visible ="false" Enabled="false"
              Text="Remove Photo" />

    </p>
    <br />
    <br />
    <br />
    <hr />
    </div>
    <p>
      <asp:Button
              runat="server"
              OnClick="cmdAddProduct_Click"
              ID="cmdAddProduct"
              Text="Save Product Revisions" />

    </p>
    </div>
    <div class="story">
  <div id="siteInfo"> <img alt="small logo" src="Pictures/YourBestDataSolutionLogo.jpg"
width="59" height="66" />
        <a href="AboutUs.aspx">About Us</a> |
        <a href="ContactUs.aspx">Contact Us</a> |
    ©2012 YBDS, LLC </div>

</div>
<br />
    </form>
</body>
</html>
```

You may purchase a copy of our companion disk which contains all files for the project at http://www.amazon.com/gp/product/B00AOU76K8!

Edit Product Code Behind

Replace the existing code in the EditProducts.aspx.vb file with the following code:

```
Imports System.Data
Imports System.Data.SqlClient

Partial Class _Default
   Inherits System.Web.UI.Page

   Protected Sub Page_Load(ByVal sender As Object, ByVal e As EventArgs) Handles Me.Load

      Dim myConnection As String
      Dim cmd As SqlCommand
      Dim myAdapter As SqlDataAdapter
      Dim myDataSet As DataSet
      Dim con As SqlConnection
      Dim myAccess As DatabaseAccess

      ' Set variables for use in binding.
      myAccess = New DatabaseAccess()
      myConnection = myAccess.getConnectionString()
      con = New SqlConnection(myConnection)

      If (Session("firstName") = Nothing) Then
         'User is not logged in.  Continue.
         lkLogout.Visible = False
         lkChangePassword.Visible = False
         lkChangePassword.Enabled = False
         Session("isAdmin") = False
         lkCustomers.Visible = False
         lkCustomers.Enabled = False
         lkOrders.Visible = False
         lkOrders.Enabled = False
         lkAddProduct.Visible = False
         lkAddProduct.Enabled = False
         lkEditProduct.Visible = False
         lkEditProduct.Enabled = False
         Page.Response.Redirect("Login.aspx")
      Else
         If (Session("isAdmin")) Then
            lkCustomers.Visible = True
            lkCustomers.Enabled = True
            lkOrders.Visible = True
```

```
            lkOrders.Enabled = True
            lkAddProduct.Visible = True
            lkAddProduct.Enabled = True
            lkEditProduct.Visible = True
            lkEditProduct.Enabled = True
        Else
            lkCustomers.Visible = False
            lkCustomers.Enabled = False
            lkOrders.Visible = False
            lkOrders.Enabled = False
            lkAddProduct.Visible = False
            lkAddProduct.Enabled = False
            lkEditProduct.Visible = False
            lkEditProduct.Enabled = False
            Exit Sub
        End If
        lkChangePassword.Visible = True
        lkChangePassword.Enabled = True
        loginStatus.Text = "Welcome " & Session("firstName").ToString() & "!"
    End If

    ''''''''''''''''''''''''''''''''''''''''''''''''''''''''''''''''

    ' Bind Billing State combobox.
    cmd = New SqlCommand("SELECT CategoryID, CategoryName FROM ProductCategory
ORDER BY CategoryName ASC", con)
    cmd.CommandType = CommandType.Text

    myAdapter = New SqlDataAdapter(cmd)
    myDataSet = New DataSet()

    Try

        ' Open the database connection.
        con.Open()
        myAdapter.Fill(myDataSet, "ProductCategory")
    Finally
        con.Close()
        If Not (Page.IsPostBack) Then
            cboCategory.DataSource = myDataSet
            cboCategory.DataTextField = "CategoryName"
            cboCategory.DataValueField = "CategoryID"
            cboCategory.DataBind()
        End If
    End Try

    ''''''''''''''''''''''''''''''''''''''''''''''''''''''''''
```

You may purchase a copy of our companion disk which contains all files for the project at http://www.amazon.com/gp/product/B00AOU76K8!

```
' Load the form.
If Not (Page.IsPostBack) Then
    Dim sql As String
    Dim readData As SqlDataReader

    ' Set variables for use in binding.
    myAccess = New DatabaseAccess()
    myConnection = myAccess.getConnectionString()
    con = New SqlConnection(myConnection)

    sql = "SELECT * FROM [Product] " & _
        "WHERE ProductID = '" & Session("productID") & "'"
    cmd = New SqlCommand(sql, con)
    cmd.CommandType = Data.CommandType.Text
    Try

        ' Open database connection.
        con.Open()

        ' Execute the INSERT and fill the data reader.
        readData = cmd.ExecuteReader(CommandBehavior.CloseConnection)

    Catch a As Exception

        Throw a
    End Try
    readData.Read()
    txtBriefDescription.Text = IIf(IsDBNull(readData("DescriptionBrief")), "",
readData("DescriptionBrief"))
    txtFullDescription.Text = IIf(IsDBNull(readData("DescriptionFull")), "",
readData("DescriptionFull"))
    txtQuantityAvailable.Text = IIf(IsDBNull(readData("QuantityAvailable")), "",
readData("QuantityAvailable"))
    txtPrice.Text = IIf(IsDBNull(readData("Price")), "", readData("Price"))
    txtProductName.Text = IIf(IsDBNull(readData("ProductName")), "",
readData("ProductName"))
    cboCategory.SelectedValue = IIf(IsDBNull(readData("CategoryID")), "",
readData("CategoryID"))
    newPicture.ImageUrl = "Pictures\" & IIf(IsDBNull(readData("PhotoThumbnail")), "",
readData("PhotoThumbnail"))
    filePathHidden.Text = IIf(IsDBNull(readData("PhotoThumbnail")), "",
readData("PhotoThumbnail"))
    If IsDBNull(readData("PhotoThumbnail")) Or readData("PhotoThumbnail") = "" Then
        cmdUploadPhoto.Visible = True
        cmdUploadPhoto.Enabled = True
        cmdRemovePhoto.Visible = False
```

```
            cmdRemovePhoto.Enabled = False
        Else
            cmdUploadPhoto.Visible = False
            cmdUploadPhoto.Enabled = False
            cmdRemovePhoto.Visible = True
            cmdRemovePhoto.Enabled = True
        End If
        newPicture.Height = 30
        newPicture.Width = 20
        con.Close()
        readData.Close()
    End If
End Sub

Protected Function productExists() As Boolean
    Dim myConnection As String
    Dim cmd As SqlCommand
    Dim con As SqlConnection
    Dim myAccess As DatabaseAccess
    Dim sql As String
    Dim readData As SqlDataReader
    Dim productCount As Integer

    ' Set variables for use in binding.
    myAccess = New DatabaseAccess()
    myConnection = myAccess.getConnectionString()
    con = New SqlConnection(myConnection)

    ' Get the count of jproducts in the Product table for the ProductName in the text box.

    sql = "SELECT COUNT(ProductID) AS productCount FROM [Product] " & _
        "WHERE ProductName = '" & txtProductName.Text & "'"
    cmd = New SqlCommand(sql, con)
    cmd.CommandType = Data.CommandType.Text
    Try

        ' Open database connection.
        con.Open()

        ' Execute the INSERT and fill the data reader.
        readData = cmd.ExecuteReader(CommandBehavior.CloseConnection)

    Catch a As Exception

        Throw a
    End Try
```

```
        readData.Read()
        productCount = readData("productCount")
        con.Close()
        readData.Close()
        If productCount > 0 Then
            productExists = True
        Else
            productExists = False
        End If
    End Function

    Protected Function allFieldsArePopulated() As Boolean
        If (txtProductName.Text = "") Then
            nameRequired.Text = "Please enter product name."
            nameRequired.Visible = True
            txtProductName.Focus()
            allFieldsArePopulated = False
            Exit Function
        Else
            If Len(txtProductName.Text) > 255 Then
                nameRequired.Text = "Product name must be less than 255 characters."
                nameRequired.Visible = True
                txtProductName.Focus()
                allFieldsArePopulated = False
                Exit Function
            Else
                nameRequired.Visible = False
            End If
        End If

        If (cboCategory.Text = "") Then
            nameRequired.Text = "Please select category."
            nameRequired.Visible = True
            cboCategory.Focus()
            allFieldsArePopulated = False
            Exit Function
        Else
            nameRequired.Visible = False
        End If

        If (txtBriefDescription.Text = "") Then
            billingAddressRequired.Text = "Please enter brief description."
            billingAddressRequired.Visible = True
            txtBriefDescription.Focus()
            allFieldsArePopulated = False
            Exit Function
```

```
Else
   If Len(txtBriefDescription.Text) > 255 Then
      billingAddressRequired.Text = "Brief description must be less than 255 characters."
      billingAddressRequired.Visible = True
      txtBriefDescription.Focus()
      allFieldsArePopulated = False
      Exit Function
   Else
      billingAddressRequired.Visible = False
   End If
End If

If (txtFullDescription.Text = "") Then
   fullDescriptionRequired.Text = "Please enter full description."
   fullDescriptionRequired.Visible = True
   txtFullDescription.Focus()
   allFieldsArePopulated = False
   Exit Function
Else
   If Len(txtFullDescription.Text) > 255 Then
      fullDescriptionRequired.Text = "Full description must be less than 255 characters."
      fullDescriptionRequired.Visible = True
      txtFullDescription.Focus()
      allFieldsArePopulated = False
      Exit Function
   Else
      fullDescriptionRequired.Visible = False
   End If
End If

If (txtQuantityAvailable.Text = "") Then
   qtyAndPriceRequired.Text = "Please enter quantity available."
   qtyAndPriceRequired.Visible = True
   txtQuantityAvailable.Focus()
   allFieldsArePopulated = False
   Exit Function
Else
   If IsNumeric(txtQuantityAvailable.Text) = False Then
      qtyAndPriceRequired.Text = "Please enter a whole number for the quantity."
      qtyAndPriceRequired.Visible = True
      txtQuantityAvailable.Focus()
      allFieldsArePopulated = False
      Exit Function
   Else
      qtyAndPriceRequired.Visible = False
   End If
```

```
    End If

    If (txtPrice.Text = "") Then
      qtyAndPriceRequired.Text = "Please enter unit price."
      qtyAndPriceRequired.Visible = True
      txtPrice.Focus()
      allFieldsArePopulated = False
      Exit Function
    Else
      If IsNumeric(txtPrice.Text) = False Then
        qtyAndPriceRequired.Text = "Please enter a numeric value for the price."
        qtyAndPriceRequired.Visible = True
        txtPrice.Focus()
        allFieldsArePopulated = False
        Exit Function
      Else
        qtyAndPriceRequired.Visible = False
      End If
    End If
    allFieldsArePopulated = True
  End Function

  Protected Sub logout()
    Session("firstName") = Nothing
    Session.Clear()
    Page.Response.Redirect("Logout.aspx")
  End Sub

  Protected Sub saveProduct()

    Dim myConnection As String
    Dim cmd As SqlCommand
    Dim con As SqlConnection
    Dim myAccess As DatabaseAccess
    Dim sql As String
    Dim readData As SqlDataReader
    Dim requiredFieldsArePopulated As Boolean
    Dim imageName As String

    ''''''''''''''''''''''''''''''''''''''''''''''''''''''''''''''''
    ' Confirm all required fields are populated.
    requiredFieldsArePopulated = allFieldsArePopulated()
    If Not (requiredFieldsArePopulated) Then Exit Sub
    ''''''''''''''''''''''''''''''''''''''''''''''''''''''''''''''''
```

```
' Set variables for use in binding.
myAccess = New DatabaseAccess()
myConnection = myAccess.getConnectionString()
con = New SqlConnection(myConnection)

''''''''''''''''''''''''''''''''''''''''''''''''''''''''''''''''''''''''''''''

If filePathHidden.Text <> "" Then
   imageName = filePathHidden.Text
Else
   imageName = "No-image-available.jpg"
End If
' All fields have been successfully validated.  Add the new product.
sql = "UPDATE [Product] " & _
      "SET ProductName = '" & txtProductName.Text & "', " & _
      "CategoryID = " & cboCategory.SelectedValue & ", " & _
      "Price = " & txtPrice.Text & ", " & _
      "PhotoThumbnail = '" & imageName & "', " & _
      "PhotoLarge = '" & imageName & "', " & _
      "DescriptionBrief = '" & txtBriefDescription.Text & "', " & _
      "DescriptionFull = '" & txtFullDescription.Text & "', " & _
      "QuantityAvailable = " & txtQuantityAvailable.Text & " " & _
      "WHERE ProductID = " & Session("productID") & " "
cmd = New SqlCommand(sql, con)
cmd.CommandType = Data.CommandType.Text
Try

   ' Open database connection.
   con.Open()

   ' Execute the INSERT and fill the data reader.
   readData = cmd.ExecuteReader(CommandBehavior.CloseConnection)

Catch a As Exception

   Throw a
End Try

con.Close()
readData.Close()
Session("CategoryID") = cboCategory.SelectedValue
''''''''''''''''''''''''''''''''''''''''''''''''''''''''''''''''''''''''''''''
Page.Response.Redirect("ViewProducts.aspx")
End Sub
```

```
    Protected Sub cboCategory_SelectedIndexChanged(ByVal sender As Object, ByVal e As
System.EventArgs) Handles cboCategory.SelectedIndexChanged

    End Sub

    Protected Sub cmdUploadPhoto_Click(ByVal sender As Object, ByVal e As
System.EventArgs) Handles cmdUploadPhoto.Click
        If Not FileUpload1.HasFile = Nothing Then

            Dim filepath As String = FileUpload1.PostedFile.FileName
            Dim pat As String = "\\(?:.+)\\(.+)\.(.+)"
            Dim r As Regex = New Regex(pat)
            'run
            Dim m As Match = r.Match(filepath)
            Dim file_ext As String = m.Groups(2).Captures(0).ToString()
            Dim filename As String = m.Groups(1).Captures(0).ToString()
            Dim file As String = filename & "." & file_ext

            'save the file to the server
            FileUpload1.PostedFile.SaveAs(Server.MapPath(".\Pictures\") & file)
            filePathHidden.Text = file
            filePath1.Text = "File uploaded."
            newPicture.ImageUrl = "Pictures\" & file
            newPicture.Height = 30
            newPicture.Width = 20
            cmdUploadPhoto.Visible = False
            cmdUploadPhoto.Enabled = False
            cmdRemovePhoto.Visible = True
            cmdRemovePhoto.Enabled = True
        End If
    End Sub

    Protected Sub cmdRemovePhoto_Click(ByVal sender As Object, ByVal e As
System.EventArgs) Handles cmdRemovePhoto.Click
        newPicture.ImageUrl = ""
        newPicture.Dispose()
        If filePath1.Text <> "" Then
            System.IO.File.Delete(Server.MapPath(".\Pictures\") & Trim(Replace(filePath1.Text, " is
uploaded.", "")))
        End If
        filePathHidden.Text = ""
        cmdUploadPhoto.Visible = True
        cmdUploadPhoto.Enabled = True
        cmdRemovePhoto.Visible = False
        cmdRemovePhoto.Enabled = False
        filePath1.Text = ""
```

You may purchase a copy of our companion disk which contains all files for the project at http://www.amazon.com/gp/product/B00AOU76K8!

```
    End Sub

    Protected Sub cmdAddProduct_Click(ByVal sender As Object, ByVal e As
System.EventArgs) Handles cmdAddProduct.Click
        saveProduct()
    End Sub
End Class
```

You may purchase a copy of our companion disk which contains all files for the project at http://www.amazon.com/gp/product/B00AOU76K8!

expresscheckout Server Page

Replace the existing code in the expresscheckout.aspx file with the following code:

```
<%@ Page Language="VB" AutoEventWireup="true" CodeFile="expresscheckout.aspx.vb"
Inherits="expresscheckout" %>

<!DOCTYPE html PUBLIC "-//W3C//DTD XHTML 1.0 Transitional//EN"
"http://www.w3.org/TR/xhtml1/DTD/xhtml1-transitional.dtd">

<html xmlns="http://www.w3.org/1999/xhtml" >
<head runat="server">
   <title></title>
</head>
<body>
</body>
</html>
```

expresscheckout Code Behind

Replace the existing code in the expresscheckout.aspx.vb file with the following code:

```
Imports System
Imports System.Web
Imports NVPAPICaller

Partial Class expresscheckout
   Inherits System.Web.UI.Page

   Private Sub expresscheckout_Load(ByVal sender As System.Object, ByVal e As
System.EventArgs) Handles MyBase.Load
      Dim test As New NVPAPICaller()
      Dim retMsg As String = ""
      Dim token As String = ""

      If Session("payment_amt") IsNot Nothing Then
         Dim amt As String = Session("payment_amt").ToString()

         Dim ret As Boolean = test.ShortcutExpressCheckout(amt, Session("OrderID"), token,
retMsg)
         If ret Then
            Session("token") = token
            Response.Redirect(retMsg)
         Else
            Response.Redirect("APIError.aspx?" & retMsg)
         End If
      Else
         Response.Redirect("APIError.aspx?ErrorCode=AmtMissing")
      End If
   End Sub
   Private Sub InitializeComponent()

   End Sub
End Class
```

You may purchase a copy of our companion disk which contains all files for the project at http://www.amazon.com/gp/product/B00AOU76K8!

FAQ Server Page

Replace the existing code in the FAQ.aspx file with the following code (***REPLACE ANY CODE IN THIS COLOR WITH YOUR OWN INFORMATION!)***:

```
<%@ Page Language="VB"
        AutoEventWireup="True"
        CodeFile="FAQ.aspx.vb"
        Inherits="_Default" %>

<!DOCTYPE html PUBLIC "-//W3C//DTD XHTML 1.0 Transitional//EN"
"http://www.w3.org/TR/xhtml1/DTD/xhtml1-transitional.dtd">
<html xmlns="http://www.w3.org/1999/xhtml">

<head>
<meta http-equiv="Content-Type" content="text/html; charset=iso-8859-1" />
<title>Frequently Asked Questions</title>
<link rel="stylesheet" href="emx_nav_left.css" type="text/css" />
<script type="text/javascript">

var time = 3000;
var numofitems = 7;

//menu constructor
function menu(allitems,thisitem,startstate){
  callname= "gl"+thisitem;
  divname="subglobal"+thisitem;
  this.numberofmenuitems = allitems;
  this.caller = document.getElementById(callname);
  this.thediv = document.getElementById(divname);
  this.thediv.style.visibility = startstate;
}

//menu methods
function ehandler(event,theobj){
  for (var i=1; i<= theobj.numberofmenuitems; i++){
    var shutdiv =eval( "menuitem"+i+".thediv");
    shutdiv.style.visibility="hidden";
  }
  theobj.thediv.style.visibility="visible";
}

function closesubnav(event){
  if ((event.clientY <48)||(event.clientY > 107)){
```

```
  for (var i=1; i<= numofitems; i++){
   var shutdiv =eval('menuitem'+i+'.thediv');
   shutdiv.style.visibility='hidden';
  }
 }
}
</script>
</head>
<body>

<form id="Form1" runat="server">
<div class="skipLinks">skip to: <a href="#content">page content</a> | <a
href="#pageNav">links on this page</a> | <a href="#globalNav">site navigation</a> | <a
href="#siteInfo">footer (site information)</a> </div>
<div id="masthead">
 <h1 id="siteName">Your Best Data Solution</h1>
 <div id="utility">
    <asp:LinkButton ID="lkCustomers" runat="server"
PostBackUrl="Customers.aspx">Customers</asp:LinkButton>
   | <asp:LinkButton ID="lkOrders" runat="server"
PostBackUrl="ViewOrders.aspx">Orders</asp:LinkButton>
   | <asp:LinkButton ID="lkAddProduct" PostBackUrl="AddProduct.aspx"
              runat="server">Add Product</asp:LinkButton>
   | <asp:LinkButton ID="lkEditProduct" runat="server"
PostBackUrl="ViewCategories.aspx">Edit Product</asp:LinkButton>
   | <asp:LinkButton ID="lkLogout" OnClick="logout" runat="server"
PostBackUrl="#">Logout</asp:LinkButton>
   | <asp:LinkButton ID="lkChangePassword" PostBackUrl="Password.aspx"
runat="server">Change Password</asp:LinkButton>
 </div>
 <div id="globalNav"> <img alt="" src="Pictures/gblnav_left.gif" height="32" width="4"
id="gnl" /> <img alt="" src="Pictures/glbnav_right.gif" height="32" width="4" id="gnr" />
  <div id="globalLink">
    <a href="Default.aspx" id="A1" class="glink">
    Home</a>
    <a href="ViewCategories.aspx" id="gl1" class="glink" >
    View Products</a>
    <a href="SearchProducts.aspx" id="gl2" class="glink">Search</a>
    <a href="ViewCart.aspx" id="gl3" class="glink">View Cart</a>
    <a href="Checkout.aspx" id="gl4" class="glink">Checkout</a>
    <a href="CreateAccount.aspx" id="gl5" class="glink">Create
    Account</a>
    <a href="Login.aspx" id="gl6" class="glink">Login
    </a><a href="OrderHistory.aspx" id="gl7" class="glink">Order
    History</a>
    <a href="FAQ.aspx" id="A2" class="glink">FAQ</a>
```

```
      <asp:Label ID="loginStatus" Visible="false" runat="server"></asp:Label>
    </div>
  </div>
<div id="pagecell1">
  <img alt="" src="Pictures/tl_curve_white.gif" height="6" width="6" id="tl" /> <img alt=""
src="Pictures/tr_curve_white.gif" height="6" width="6" id="tr" />

    <div id="pageName">
    <img alt="small logo" src="Pictures/YourBestDataSolutionLogo.jpg" height="50"
width="60"/> </div>
  <div id="pageNav">
    <div class="relatedLinks">
      <h3>Related Link Category</h3>
      <a href="FAQ.aspx#anchor3">Automation</a>
      <a href="FAQ.aspx#anchor1">Customized Reporting</a>
      <a href="FAQ.aspx#anchor2">Database Design</a>
      <a href="FAQ.aspx#anchor12">Data Migration</a>
      <a href="FAQ.aspx#anchor4">Data Modeling</a>
      <a href="FAQ.aspx#anchor14">Desktop Application Solutions</a>
      <a href="FAQ.aspx#anchor5">eCommerce Solutions</a>
      <a href="FAQ.aspx#anchor6">eMail Marketing</a>
      <a href="FAQ.aspx#anchor7">Mobile App Development</a>
      <a href="FAQ.aspx#anchor8">PayPal™ Integration</a>
      <a href="FAQ.aspx#anchor9">Web Design</a>
      <a href="FAQ.aspx#anchor10">Web Development</a>
    </div>
  </div>
  <div id="content">
    <div class="feature">
      <h3>FAQ <asp:Label ID="Label14" runat="server" ForeColor="Red" Font-Bold="true"> -
Frequently Asked Questions</asp:Label></h3>
      <p>
        <a name ="anchor3"><asp:Label ID="Label3" runat="server" ForeColor="Red" Font-
Bold="true">Automation</asp:Label><br /><br /></a>
        We can automate tedious tasks and free up your employee resources.  We can
automatically provide reliable data in the desired format to help serve your customers,
meet deadlines, communicate with suppliers, make informed decisions and generate
profits. Use our Automation services to transfer data between applications, and import or
export data from web.  We can move data from any data source and present your data in
various formats.
<br /><br />

        <a name ="anchor1"><asp:Label ID="Label1" runat="server" ForeColor="Red" Font-
Bold="true">Customized Reporting</asp:Label><br /><br /></a>
        We determine the scope of requested reports and identify the target audience.  This
allows
```

You may purchase a copy of our companion disk which contains all files for the project at http://www.amazon.com/gp/product/B00AOU76K8!

us to accurately collect the information for the report. We conclude by formatting and organizing the report so the target audience is presented with the best information for the decision making process.

<a name ="anchor2"><asp:Label ID="Label2" runat="server" ForeColor="Red" Font-Bold="true">**Database Design**</asp:Label>

</a>

Before creating a database for you, we determine the purpose of the database. We find and organize the information required, dividing the information into tables. We then turn information items into columns, specify primary keys and set up the table relationships. We then refine the design if needed and apply normalization rules.

<a name ="anchor12"><asp:Label ID="Label15" runat="server" ForeColor="Red" Font-Bold="true">**Data Migration**</asp:Label>

</a>
We perform data migration programmatically when your organization must merge, change computer systems or upgrade to new systems. We map data on the old system to the new system in order to develop a design for data extraction and data loading. Then, we perform data extraction from the old system and load the data to the new system. Data cleaning is performed as necessary. We execute extraction, cleansing, load, and verification in a development environment until the results are approved; at that point, we perform the deployment to the new system.

<a name ="anchor4"><asp:Label ID="Label4" runat="server" ForeColor="Red" Font-Bold="true">**Data Modeling**</asp:Label>

</a>

We understand the importance of consistently providing uniform definition and format of data across systems in order to achieve compatibility of data. Correct identification of entity types is critical to data modeling success. We provide an Entity/Relationship (ER) diagram as the final step of this process.

<a name ="anchor14"><asp:Label ID="Label16" runat="server" ForeColor="Red" Font-Bold="true">**Desktop Application Solutions**</asp:Label>

</a>
We develop custom desktop application solutions for organizations that offer user-friendly interfaces, multi-user capability, cost effectiveness, scalability, and reporting.

<a name ="anchor5"><asp:Label ID="Label5" runat="server" ForeColor="Red" Font-Bold="true">**eCommerce Solutions**</asp:Label>

</a>

We offer complete ecommerce solutions, including customer registration, shopping cart, checkout and PayPal™ payment integration. This site include a live example of an ecommerce solution. Click View Products to view products for sale and complete a purchase of any selected products!

<a name ="anchor6"><asp:Label ID="Label6" runat="server" ForeColor="Red" Font-Bold="true">**eMail Marketing**</asp:Label>

</a>

```
          Use this form of direct marketing as a means of communicating commercial or
fund-raising messages to your existing or prospective customer base, enhancing
relationships, encouraging customer loyalty and repeat business, acquiring new customers
or convincing current customers to purchase something immediately!  An exact return on
investment may be tracked.<br /><br />

        <a name ="anchor7"><asp:Label ID="Label7" runat="server" ForeColor="Red" Font-
Bold="true">Mobile App Development</asp:Label><br /><br /></a>

        We can develop custom application software for small low-power handheld devices
such as PDAs or mobile phones that may be downloaded by customers from various mobile
software distribution platforms.<br /><br />

        <a name ="anchor8"><asp:Label ID="Label8" runat="server" ForeColor="Red" Font-
Bold="true">PayPal™ Integration</asp:Label><br /><br /></a>

          We offer complete ecommerce solutions, including customer registration, shopping
cart, checkout and PayPal™ payment integration.  This site include a live example of an
ecommerce solution.  Click View Products to view products for sale and complete a
purchase of any selected products!<br /><br />

        <a name ="anchor9"><asp:Label ID="Label9" runat="server" ForeColor="Red" Font-
Bold="true">Web Design</asp:Label><br /><br /></a>

        We will handle all facets of your website including the information architecture, the
layout or the pages, and the conceptual design with branding.<br /><br />

        <a name ="anchor10"><asp:Label ID="Label11" runat="server" ForeColor="Red" Font-
Bold="true">Web Development</asp:Label><br /><br /></a>
        We develop a web sites for the Internet (World Wide Web) or an intranet (a private
network).  This can include web design, web content, client liaison, client-side/server-side
scripting, web server and network security configuration, and e-commerce development.
This is great for businesses that want to sell products and services or to automate business
workflow!
                  <br /><br />


</p>

   </div>
   <div class="story">
  <div id="siteInfo"> <img alt="small logo" src="Pictures/YourBestDataSolutionLogo.jpg"
width="59" height="66" />
        <a href="AboutUs.aspx">About Us</a> |
        <a href="ContactUs.aspx">Contact Us</a> |
    ©2012 YBDS, LLC </div>
```

You may purchase a copy of our companion disk which contains all files for the project at http://www.amazon.com/gp/product/B00AOU76K8!

```
</div>
<br />
   </form>
</body>
</html>
```

You may purchase a copy of our companion disk which contains all files for the project at http://www.amazon.com/gp/product/B00AOU76K8!

FAQ Code Behind

Replace the existing code in the FAQ.aspx.vb file with the following code:

```
Imports System.Data
Imports System.Data.SqlClient

Partial Class _Default
   Inherits System.Web.UI.Page

   Protected Sub Page_Load(ByVal sender As Object, ByVal e As EventArgs) Handles Me.Load

      If (Session("firstName") = Nothing) Then
         'User is not logged in.  Continue.
         lkLogout.Visible = False
         lkChangePassword.Visible = False
         lkChangePassword.Enabled = False
         Session("isAdmin") = False
         lkCustomers.Visible = False
         lkCustomers.Enabled = False
         lkOrders.Visible = False
         lkOrders.Enabled = False
         lkAddProduct.Visible = False
         lkAddProduct.Enabled = False
         lkEditProduct.Visible = False
         lkEditProduct.Enabled = False
      Else
         If (Session("isAdmin")) Then
            lkCustomers.Visible = True
            lkCustomers.Enabled = True
            lkOrders.Visible = True
            lkOrders.Enabled = True
            lkAddProduct.Visible = True
            lkAddProduct.Enabled = True
            lkEditProduct.Visible = True
            lkEditProduct.Enabled = True
         Else
            lkCustomers.Visible = False
            lkCustomers.Enabled = False
            lkOrders.Visible = False
            lkOrders.Enabled = False
            lkAddProduct.Visible = False
            lkAddProduct.Enabled = False
            lkEditProduct.Visible = False
```

```
            lkEditProduct.Enabled = False
        End If
        lkChangePassword.Visible = True
        lkChangePassword.Enabled = True
        loginStatus.Text = "Welcome " & Session("firstName").ToString() & "!"
        loginStatus.Visible = True
      End If
    End Sub

    Protected Sub logout()
      Session("firstName") = Nothing
      Session.Clear()
      Page.Response.Redirect("Logout.aspx")
    End Sub
End Class
```

Login Server Page

Replace the existing code in the Login.aspx file with the following code (***REPLACE ANY CODE IN THIS COLOR WITH YOUR OWN INFORMATION!)***:

```
<%@ Page Language="VB"
        AutoEventWireup="True"
        CodeFile="Login.aspx.vb"
        Inherits="_Default" %>

<!DOCTYPE html PUBLIC "-//W3C//DTD XHTML 1.0 Transitional//EN"
"http://www.w3.org/TR/xhtml1/DTD/xhtml1-transitional.dtd">
<html xmlns="http://www.w3.org/1999/xhtml">

<head>
<meta http-equiv="Content-Type" content="text/html; charset=iso-8859-1" />
<title>Login</title>
<link rel="stylesheet" href="emx_nav_left.css" type="text/css" />
<script type="text/javascript">

var time = 3000;
var numofitems = 7;

//menu constructor
function menu(allitems,thisitem,startstate){
  callname= "gl"+thisitem;
  divname="subglobal"+thisitem;
  this.numberofmenuitems = allitems;
  this.caller = document.getElementById(callname);
  this.thediv = document.getElementById(divname);
  this.thediv.style.visibility = startstate;
}

//menu methods
function ehandler(event,theobj){
  for (var i=1; i<= theobj.numberofmenuitems; i++){
    var shutdiv =eval( "menuitem"+i+".thediv");
    shutdiv.style.visibility="hidden";
  }
  theobj.thediv.style.visibility="visible";
}

function closesubnav(event){
  if ((event.clientY <48)||(event.clientY > 107)){
```

```
  for (var i=1; i<= numofitems; i++){
   var shutdiv =eval('menuitem'+i+'.thediv');
   shutdiv.style.visibility='hidden';
  }
 }
}
</script>
</head>
<body>

<form id="Form1" runat="server">
<div class="skipLinks">skip to: <a href="#content">page content</a> | <a
href="#pageNav">links on this page</a> | <a href="#globalNav">site navigation</a> | <a
href="#siteInfo">footer (site information)</a> </div>
<div id="masthead">
 <h1 id="siteName">Your Best Data Solution</h1>
 <div id="utility">
    <asp:LinkButton ID="lkCustomers" runat="server"
PostBackUrl="Customers.aspx">Customers</asp:LinkButton>
   | <asp:LinkButton ID="lkOrders" runat="server"
PostBackUrl="ViewOrders.aspx">Orders</asp:LinkButton>
   | <asp:LinkButton ID="lkAddProduct" PostBackUrl="AddProduct.aspx"
          runat="server">Add Product</asp:LinkButton>
   | <asp:LinkButton ID="lkEditProduct" runat="server"
PostBackUrl="ViewCategories.aspx">Edit Product</asp:LinkButton>
   | <asp:LinkButton ID="lkLogout" OnClick="logout" runat="server"
PostBackUrl="#">Logout</asp:LinkButton>
   | <asp:LinkButton ID="lkChangePassword" PostBackUrl="Password.aspx"
runat="server">Change Password</asp:LinkButton>
 </div>
 <div id="globalNav"> <img alt="" src="Pictures/gblnav_left.gif" height="32" width="4"
id="gnl" /> <img alt="" src="Pictures/glbnav_right.gif" height="32" width="4" id="gnr" />
  <div id="globalLink">
    <a href="Default.aspx" id="A1" class="glink">
    Home</a>
    <a href="ViewCategories.aspx" id="gl1" class="glink" >
    View Products</a>
    <a href="SearchProducts.aspx" id="gl2" class="glink">Search</a>
    <a href="ViewCart.aspx" id="gl3" class="glink">View Cart</a>
    <a href="Checkout.aspx" id="gl4" class="glink">Checkout</a>
    <a href="CreateAccount.aspx" id="gl5" class="glink">Create
    Account</a>
    <a href="Login.aspx" id="gl6" class="glink">Login
    </a><a href="OrderHistory.aspx" id="gl7" class="glink">Order
    History</a>
    <a href="FAQ.aspx" id="A2" class="glink">FAQ</a>
```

```
      <asp:Label ID="loginStatus" Visible="false" runat="server"></asp:Label>
    </div>
  </div>
<div id="pagecell1">
  <img alt="" src="Pictures/tl_curve_white.gif" height="6" width="6" id="tl" /> <img alt=""
src="Pictures/tr_curve_white.gif" height="6" width="6" id="tr" />

    <div id="pageName">
    <img alt="small logo" src="Pictures/YourBestDataSolutionLogo.jpg" height="50"
width="60"/> </div>
  <div id="pageNav">
    <div class="relatedLinks">
      <h3>Related Link Category</h3>
      <a href="FAQ.aspx#anchor3">Automation</a>
      <a href="FAQ.aspx#anchor1">Customized Reporting</a>
      <a href="FAQ.aspx#anchor2">Database Design</a>
      <a href="FAQ.aspx#anchor12">Data Migration</a>
      <a href="FAQ.aspx#anchor4">Data Modeling</a>
      <a href="FAQ.aspx#anchor14">Desktop Application Solutions</a>
      <a href="FAQ.aspx#anchor5">eCommerce Solutions</a>
      <a href="FAQ.aspx#anchor6">eMail Marketing</a>
      <a href="FAQ.aspx#anchor7">Mobile App Development</a>
      <a href="FAQ.aspx#anchor8">PayPal™ Integration</a>
      <a href="FAQ.aspx#anchor9">Web Design</a>
      <a href="FAQ.aspx#anchor10">Web Development</a>
    </div>
  </div>
  <div id="content">
    <div class="feature">
      <h3>Login</h3>
       <p> <asp:Label ID="paragraph1"
              runat="server" >Sign into your account </asp:Label> </p>
       <p>
       <p>
          <asp:Label ID="Label2"
              runat="server" Text="User name" Width="100"></asp:Label>
          <asp:TextBox ID="txtUserID"
                    runat="server"
                    Width="200"></asp:TextBox>
          <asp:Label ID="userIDRequired"
                  runat="server" Visible="false"></asp:Label>
          <br />
          <br />
          <asp:Label ID="lblPassword"
                  runat="server"
                  Text="Password " Width="100"></asp:Label>
```

```
        <asp:TextBox ID="txtPassword"
                TextMode="Password"
                runat="server"
                Width="200"></asp:TextBox>
        <asp:Label ID="passwordRequired"
              runat="server" Visible="false"></asp:Label>
        <br />
        <br />
        <asp:Button
            runat="server"
            OnClick="login"
            ID="cmdLogin"
            Text="Login" />
    </p>
    <p>
    <asp:Label ID="Label1"
             runat="server" Text="Don't have an account?  Create one now."></asp:Label>
    <br />
    <br />
    <asp:Button
            runat="server"
            OnClick="insertAccount"
            ID="cmdCreateAccount"
            Text="Create Account" />
    </p>
  </div>
  <div class="story">
 <div id="siteInfo"> <img alt="small logo" src="Pictures/YourBestDataSolutionLogo.jpg"
width="59" height="66" />
        <a href="AboutUs.aspx">About Us</a> |
        <a href="ContactUs.aspx">Contact Us</a> |
    ©2012 YBDS, LLC </div>

</div>
<br />
  </form>
</body>
</html>
```

You may purchase a copy of our companion disk which contains all files for the project at http://www.amazon.com/gp/product/B00AOU76K8!

Login Code Behind

Replace the existing code in the Login.aspx.vb file with the following code:

```
Imports System.Data
Imports System.Data.SqlClient

Partial Class _Default
   Inherits System.Web.UI.Page

   Protected Sub Page_Load(ByVal sender As Object, ByVal e As EventArgs) Handles Me.Load

      If (Session("firstName") = Nothing) Then
         'User is not logged in.  Continue.
         lkLogout.Visible = False
         lkLogout.Enabled = False
         Session("isAdmin") = False
         lkCustomers.Visible = False
         lkCustomers.Enabled = False
         lkOrders.Visible = False
         lkOrders.Enabled = False
         lkAddProduct.Visible = False
         lkAddProduct.Enabled = False
         lkEditProduct.Visible = False
         lkEditProduct.Enabled = False
         lkChangePassword.Visible = False
         lkChangePassword.Enabled = False
      Else
         If (Session("isAdmin")) Then
            lkCustomers.Visible = True
            lkCustomers.Enabled = True
            lkOrders.Visible = True
            lkOrders.Enabled = True
            lkAddProduct.Visible = True
            lkAddProduct.Enabled = True
            lkEditProduct.Visible = True
            lkEditProduct.Enabled = True
         Else
            lkCustomers.Visible = False
            lkCustomers.Enabled = False
            lkOrders.Visible = False
            lkOrders.Enabled = False
            lkAddProduct.Visible = False
            lkAddProduct.Enabled = False
```

```
            lkEditProduct.Visible = False
            lkEditProduct.Enabled = False
          End If
          loginStatus.Text = "Welcome " & Session("firstName").ToString() & "!"
          Page.Response.Redirect("UserMessage.aspx")
          Exit Sub
        End If

    End Sub

    Protected Sub insertAccount()
        Page.Response.Redirect("CreateAccount.aspx")
    End Sub

    Protected Sub login()
        If (Not (allFieldsArePopulated())) Then Exit Sub
        confirmLogin()
    End Sub

    Protected Sub confirmLogin()

        Dim myConnection As String
        Dim cmd As SqlCommand
        Dim con As SqlConnection
        Dim myAccess As DatabaseAccess
        Dim sql As String
        Dim readData As SqlDataReader

        ' Set variables for use in binding.
        myAccess = New DatabaseAccess()
        myConnection = myAccess.getConnectionString()
        con = New SqlConnection(myConnection)
        ''''''''''''''''''''''''''''''''''''''''''''''''''''''''''''''''''''''''

        ' Confirm the login.
        sql = "SELECT COUNT(UserID) AS userExists FROM [User] WHERE " & _
              "Username = '" & txtUserID.Text & "'" & _
              " AND Password = '" & txtPassword.Text & "'"
        cmd = New SqlCommand(sql, con)
        cmd.CommandType = Data.CommandType.Text
        Try

            ' Open database connection.
            con.Open()

            ' Execute the INSERT and fill the data reader.
            readData = cmd.ExecuteReader(CommandBehavior.CloseConnection)
```

You may purchase a copy of our companion disk which contains all files for the project at http://www.amazon.com/gp/product/B00AOU76K8!

```
Catch a As Exception
    Throw a
End Try
readData.Read()

Session("userExists") = readData("userExists")
readData.Close()
con.Close()

If (Session("userExists") > 0) Then
    ' Store the user's first name in session.
    sql = "SELECT FirstName, LastName, UserID, EmailAddress FROM [User] WHERE "
& _
            "Username = '" & txtUserID.Text & "'" & _
            " AND Password = '" & txtPassword.Text & "'" & _
            " GROUP BY UserID, FirstName, LastName, EmailAddress"
    cmd = New SqlCommand(sql, con)
    cmd.CommandType = Data.CommandType.Text
    Try

        ' Open database connection.
        con.Open()

        ' Execute the INSERT and fill the data reader.
        readData = cmd.ExecuteReader(CommandBehavior.CloseConnection)

    Catch a As Exception

        Throw a
    End Try
    readData.Read()
    Session("firstName") = readData("FirstName")
    Session("lastName") = readData("LastName")
    Session("userID") = readData("UserID")
    Session("EmailAddress") = readData("EmailAddress")
    readData.Close()
    con.Close()

    If (Session("OrderID") = Nothing) Then
        'Do nothing
    Else
        ' Update current cart with the user id
        ' if the Session order id variable is not empty.
        sql = "UPDATE UserOrder SET " & _
            "UserID = " & Session("userID") & " " & _
```

```
        " WHERE OrderID = " & Session("OrderID") & " "
    cmd = New SqlCommand(sql, con)
    cmd.CommandType = Data.CommandType.Text
    Try

      ' Open database connection.
      con.Open()

      ' Execute the INSERT and fill the data reader.
      readData = cmd.ExecuteReader(CommandBehavior.CloseConnection)

    Catch a As Exception

      Throw a
    End Try

    con.Close()
    readData.Close()
  End If
  Session("isAdmin") = myAccess.isAdmin(Convert.ToInt16(Session("userID")))
  If (Session("isAdmin")) Then
    lkCustomers.Visible = True
    lkCustomers.Enabled = True
    lkOrders.Visible = True
    lkOrders.Enabled = True
    lkAddProduct.Visible = True
    lkAddProduct.Enabled = True
    lkEditProduct.Visible = True
    lkEditProduct.Enabled = True
  Else
    lkCustomers.Visible = False
    lkCustomers.Enabled = False
    lkOrders.Visible = False
    lkOrders.Enabled = False
    lkAddProduct.Visible = False
    lkAddProduct.Enabled = False
    lkEditProduct.Visible = False
    lkEditProduct.Enabled = False
  End If
  Page.Response.Redirect("Checkout.aspx")
Else
  Session("isAdmin") = False
  userIDRequired.Text = "Your user name and/or password are invalid.  Please re-enter
your credentials and login."
  userIDRequired.Visible = True
End If
```

You may purchase a copy of our companion disk which contains all files for the project at http://www.amazon.com/gp/product/B00AOU76K8!

```
    End Sub
    Protected Sub logout()
        Session("firstName") = Nothing
        Session.Clear()
        Page.Response.Redirect("Logout.aspx")
    End Sub

    Protected Function allFieldsArePopulated() As Boolean
        If (txtUserID.Text = "") Then
            userIDRequired.Text = "Please enter user name."
            userIDRequired.Visible = True
            txtUserID.Focus()
            allFieldsArePopulated = False
            Exit Function
        Else
            userIDRequired.Visible = False
        End If
        If (txtPassword.Text = "") Then
            passwordRequired.Text = "Please enter password."
            passwordRequired.Visible = True
            txtPassword.Focus()
            allFieldsArePopulated = False
            Exit Function
        Else
            passwordRequired.Visible = False
        End If
        allFieldsArePopulated = True
    End Function


End Class
```

Logout Server Page

Replace the existing code in the Logout.aspx file with the following code (***REPLACE ANY CODE IN THIS COLOR WITH YOUR OWN INFORMATION!)***:

```
<%@ Page Language="VB"
      AutoEventWireup="True"
      CodeFile="Logout.aspx.vb"
      Inherits="_Default" %>

<!DOCTYPE html PUBLIC "-//W3C//DTD XHTML 1.0 Transitional//EN"
"http://www.w3.org/TR/xhtml1/DTD/xhtml1-transitional.dtd">
<html xmlns="http://www.w3.org/1999/xhtml">

<head>
<meta http-equiv="Content-Type" content="text/html; charset=iso-8859-1" />
<title>Logout</title>
<link rel="stylesheet" href="emx_nav_left.css" type="text/css" />
<script type="text/javascript">

var time = 3000;
var numofitems = 7;

//menu constructor
function menu(allitems,thisitem,startstate){
  callname= "gl"+thisitem;
  divname="subglobal"+thisitem;
  this.numberofmenuitems = allitems;
  this.caller = document.getElementById(callname);
  this.thediv = document.getElementById(divname);
  this.thediv.style.visibility = startstate;
}

//menu methods
function ehandler(event,theobj){
  for (var i=1; i<= theobj.numberofmenuitems; i++){
    var shutdiv =eval( "menuitem"+i+".thediv");
    shutdiv.style.visibility="hidden";
  }
  theobj.thediv.style.visibility="visible";
}

function closesubnav(event){
  if ((event.clientY <48)||(event.clientY > 107)){
```

You may purchase a copy of our companion disk which contains all files for the project at http://www.amazon.com/gp/product/B00AOU76K8!

```
   for (var i=1; i<= numofitems; i++){
    var shutdiv =eval('menuitem'+i+'.thediv');
    shutdiv.style.visibility='hidden';
   }
  }
}
</script>
</head>
<body>

<form id="Form1" runat="server">
<div class="skipLinks">skip to: <a href="#content">page content</a> | <a
href="#pageNav">links on this page</a> | <a href="#globalNav">site navigation</a> | <a
href="#siteInfo">footer (site information)</a> </div>
<div id="masthead">
  <h1 id="siteName">Your Best Data Solution</h1>
  <div id="utility">
       <asp:LinkButton ID="lkCustomers" runat="server"
PostBackUrl="Customers.aspx">Customers</asp:LinkButton>
     | <asp:LinkButton ID="lkOrders" runat="server"
PostBackUrl="ViewOrders.aspx">Orders</asp:LinkButton>
     | <asp:LinkButton ID="lkAddProduct" PostBackUrl="AddProduct.aspx"
                   runat="server">Add Product</asp:LinkButton>
     | <asp:LinkButton ID="lkEditProduct" runat="server"
PostBackUrl="ViewCategories.aspx">Edit Product</asp:LinkButton>
     | <asp:LinkButton ID="lkLogout" runat="server"
PostBackUrl="#">Logout</asp:LinkButton>
     | <asp:LinkButton ID="lkChangePassword" PostBackUrl="Password.aspx"
runat="server">Change Password</asp:LinkButton>
  </div>
  <div id="globalNav"> <img alt="" src="Pictures/gblnav_left.gif" height="32" width="4"
id="gnl" /> <img alt="" src="Pictures/glbnav_right.gif" height="32" width="4" id="gnr" />
    <div id="globalLink">
        <a href="Default.aspx" id="A1" class="glink">
        Home</a>
        <a href="ViewCategories.aspx" id="gl1" class="glink" >
        View Products</a>
        <a href="SearchProducts.aspx" id="gl2" class="glink">Search</a>
        <a href="ViewCart.aspx" id="gl3" class="glink">View Cart</a>
        <a href="Checkout.aspx" id="gl4" class="glink">Checkout</a>
        <a href="CreateAccount.aspx" id="gl5" class="glink">Create
        Account</a>
        <a href="Login.aspx" id="gl6" class="glink">Login
        </a><a href="OrderHistory.aspx" id="gl7" class="glink">Order
        History</a>
        <a href="FAQ.aspx" id="A2" class="glink">FAQ</a>
```

```
      <asp:Label ID="loginStatus" Visible="false" runat="server"></asp:Label>
    </div>
  </div>
<div id="pagecell1">
  <img alt="" src="Pictures/tl_curve_white.gif" height="6" width="6" id="tl" /> <img alt=""
src="Pictures/tr_curve_white.gif" height="6" width="6" id="tr" />

    <div id="pageName">
    <img alt="small logo" src="Pictures/YourBestDataSolutionLogo.jpg" height="50"
width="60"/> </div>
  <div id="pageNav">
    <div class="relatedLinks">
      <h3>Related Link Category</h3>
      <a href="FAQ.aspx#anchor3">Automation</a>
      <a href="FAQ.aspx#anchor1">Customized Reporting</a>
      <a href="FAQ.aspx#anchor2">Database Design</a>
      <a href="FAQ.aspx#anchor12">Data Migration</a>
      <a href="FAQ.aspx#anchor4">Data Modeling</a>
      <a href="FAQ.aspx#anchor14">Desktop Application Solutions</a>
      <a href="FAQ.aspx#anchor5">eCommerce Solutions</a>
      <a href="FAQ.aspx#anchor6">eMail Marketing</a>
      <a href="FAQ.aspx#anchor7">Mobile App Development</a>
      <a href="FAQ.aspx#anchor8">PayPal™ Integration</a>
      <a href="FAQ.aspx#anchor9">Web Design</a>
      <a href="FAQ.aspx#anchor10">Web Development</a>
    </div>
  </div>
  <div id="content">
    <div class="feature">
      <h3>You have logged out.  Thanks for visiting Your Best Data Solution!</h3>
    </div>
    <div class="story">
  <div id="siteInfo"> <img alt="small logo" src="Pictures/YourBestDataSolutionLogo.jpg"
width="59" height="66" />
          <a href="AboutUs.aspx">About Us</a> |
          <a href="ContactUs.aspx">Contact Us</a> |
     ©2012 YBDS, LLC </div>

</div>
<br />
    </form>
</body>
</html>
```

You may purchase a copy of our companion disk which contains all files for the project at http://www.amazon.com/gp/product/B00AOU76K8!

Logout Code Behind

Replace the existing code in the Logout.aspx.vb file with the following code:

```
Imports System.Data
Imports System.Data.SqlClient

Partial Class _Default
   Inherits System.Web.UI.Page

   Protected Sub Page_Load(ByVal sender As Object, ByVal e As EventArgs) Handles Me.Load

      If (Session("firstName") = Nothing) Then
         'User is not logged in.  Continue.
         '  LinkButton4.Visible = False
         Session("isAdmin") = False
         lkCustomers.Visible = False
         lkCustomers.Enabled = False
         lkOrders.Visible = False
         lkOrders.Enabled = False
         lkAddProduct.Visible = False
         lkAddProduct.Enabled = False
         lkEditProduct.Visible = False
         lkEditProduct.Enabled = False
         lkChangePassword.Visible = False
         lkChangePassword.Enabled = False
         lkLogout.Visible = False
         lkLogout.Enabled = False
      Else
         If (Session("isAdmin")) Then
            lkCustomers.Visible = True
            lkCustomers.Enabled = True
            lkOrders.Visible = True
            lkOrders.Enabled = True
            lkAddProduct.Visible = True
            lkAddProduct.Enabled = True
            lkEditProduct.Visible = True
            lkEditProduct.Enabled = True
         Else
            lkCustomers.Visible = False
            lkCustomers.Enabled = False
            lkOrders.Visible = False
            lkOrders.Enabled = False
            lkAddProduct.Visible = False
```

```
            lkAddProduct.Enabled = False
            lkEditProduct.Visible = False
            lkEditProduct.Enabled = False
        End If
        'Update the User Order with the currentUser ID.
        loginStatus.Text = "Welcome " & Session("firstName").ToString() & "!"
        loginStatus.Visible = True
    End If

  End Sub
End Class
```

You may purchase a copy of our companion disk which contains all files for the project at http://www.amazon.com/gp/product/B00AOU76K8!

Order Confirmation Server Page

Replace the existing code in the OrderConfirmation.aspx file with the following code (***REPLACE ANY CODE IN THIS COLOR WITH YOUR OWN INFORMATION!)***:

```
<%@ Page Language="VB"
        AutoEventWireup="True"
        enableEventValidation="false"
        enableViewState="false"
        enableViewStateMac="false"
        CodeFile="OrderConfirmation.aspx.vb"
        Inherits="_Default" %>

<!DOCTYPE html PUBLIC "-//W3C//DTD XHTML 1.0 Transitional//EN"
"http://www.w3.org/TR/xhtml1/DTD/xhtml1-transitional.dtd">
<html xmlns="http://www.w3.org/1999/xhtml">

<head>
<meta http-equiv="Content-Type" content="text/html; charset=iso-8859-1" />
<title>Order Confirmation</title>
<link rel="stylesheet" href="emx_nav_left.css" type="text/css" />
<script type="text/javascript">

var time = 3000;
var numofitems = 7;

//menu constructor
function menu(allitems,thisitem,startstate){
  callname= "gl"+thisitem;
  divname="subglobal"+thisitem;
  this.numberofmenuitems = allitems;
  this.caller = document.getElementById(callname);
  this.thediv = document.getElementById(divname);
  this.thediv.style.visibility = startstate;
}

//menu methods
function ehandler(event,theobj){
  for (var i=1; i<= theobj.numberofmenuitems; i++){
    var shutdiv =eval( "menuitem"+i+".thediv");
    shutdiv.style.visibility="hidden";
  }
  theobj.thediv.style.visibility="visible";
}
```

You may purchase a copy of our companion disk which contains all files for the project at http://www.amazon.com/gp/product/B00AOU76K8!

```
function closesubnav(event){
 if ((event.clientY <48)||(event.clientY > 107)){
   for (var i=1; i<= numofitems; i++){
     var shutdiv =eval('menuitem'+i+'.thediv');
     shutdiv.style.visibility='hidden';
   }
  }
}
</script>
</head>
<body>

<form id="Form1" runat="server">
<div class="skipLinks">skip to: <a href="#content">page content</a> | <a
href="#pageNav">links on this page</a> | <a href="#globalNav">site navigation</a> | <a
href="#siteInfo">footer (site information)</a> </div>
<div id="masthead">
  <h1 id="siteName">Your Best Data Solution</h1>
  <div id="utility">
      <asp:LinkButton ID="lkCustomers" runat="server"
PostBackUrl="Customers.aspx">Customers</asp:LinkButton>
     | <asp:LinkButton ID="lkOrders" runat="server"
PostBackUrl="ViewOrders.aspx">Orders</asp:LinkButton>
     | <asp:LinkButton ID="lkAddProduct" PostBackUrl="AddProduct.aspx"
                  runat="server">Add Product</asp:LinkButton>
     | <asp:LinkButton ID="lkEditProduct" runat="server"
PostBackUrl="ViewCategories.aspx">Edit Product</asp:LinkButton>
     | <asp:LinkButton ID="lkLogout" OnClick="logout" runat="server"
PostBackUrl="#">Logout</asp:LinkButton>
     | <asp:LinkButton ID="lkChangePassword" PostBackUrl="Password.aspx"
runat="server">Change Password</asp:LinkButton>
  </div>
  <div id="globalNav"> <img alt="" src="Pictures/gblnav_left.gif" height="32" width="4"
id="gnl" /> <img alt="" src="Pictures/glbnav_right.gif" height="32" width="4" id="gnr" />
    <div id="globalLink">
       <a href="Default.aspx" id="A1" class="glink">
       Home</a>
       <a href="ViewCategories.aspx" id="gl1" class="glink" >
       View Products</a>
       <a href="SearchProducts.aspx" id="gl2" class="glink">Search</a>
       <a href="ViewCart.aspx" id="gl3" class="glink">View Cart</a>
       <a href="Checkout.aspx" id="gl4" class="glink">Checkout</a>
       <a href="CreateAccount.aspx" id="gl5" class="glink">Create
       Account</a>
       <a href="Login.aspx" id="gl6" class="glink">Login
```

```
</a><a href="OrderHistory.aspx" id="gl7" class="glink">Order
History</a>
<a href="FAQ.aspx" id="A2" class="glink">FAQ</a>
<asp:Label ID="loginStatus" Visible="false" runat="server"></asp:Label>
</div>
</div>
<div id="pagecell1">
<img alt="" src="Pictures/tl_curve_white.gif" height="6" width="6" id="tl" /> <img alt=""
src="Pictures/tr_curve_white.gif" height="6" width="6" id="tr" />

<div id="pageName">
<img alt="small logo" src="Pictures/YourBestDataSolutionLogo.jpg" height="50"
width="60"/> </div>
<div id="pageNav">
<div class="relatedLinks">
<h3>Related Link Category</h3>
<a href="FAQ.aspx#anchor3">Automation</a>
<a href="FAQ.aspx#anchor1">Customized Reporting</a>
<a href="FAQ.aspx#anchor2">Database Design</a>
<a href="FAQ.aspx#anchor12">Data Migration</a>
<a href="FAQ.aspx#anchor4">Data Modeling</a>
<a href="FAQ.aspx#anchor14">Desktop Application Solutions</a>
<a href="FAQ.aspx#anchor5">eCommerce Solutions</a>
<a href="FAQ.aspx#anchor6">eMail Marketing</a>
<a href="FAQ.aspx#anchor7">Mobile App Development</a>
<a href="FAQ.aspx#anchor8">PayPal™ Integration</a>
<a href="FAQ.aspx#anchor9">Web Design</a>
<a href="FAQ.aspx#anchor10">Web Development</a>
</div>
</div>
<div id="content">
<div class="feature">
<h3>Order Confirmation</h3>
<p>
<asp:Label ID="orderDetails"
        runat="server"
        Visible="true"></asp:Label>
        <br />
        <br />
<asp:GridView ID ="categoryFilter"
        runat="server"
        DataKeyNames="Product"
        EditRowStyle-HorizontalAlign="Center"
        HeaderStyle-BackColor="#cccccc"
        BorderStyle="None">
</asp:GridView>
```

You may purchase a copy of our companion disk which contains all files for the project at http://www.amazon.com/gp/product/B00AOU76K8!

```
            <br />
            <br />
    <asp:Label ID="lblTotal"
            runat="server" Visible="true"></asp:Label>
            <br />
            <br />
    <asp:Label ID="Label1" Text = "Your order will be shipped to:"
            runat="server" Visible="true"></asp:Label>
            <br />
            <br />
    <asp:Label ID="lblName"
            runat="server" Visible="true"></asp:Label>
    <br />
    <asp:Label ID="shippingDetails"
            runat="server" Visible="true"></asp:Label>
    <br />
    <asp:Label ID="shippingDetails1"
            runat="server" Visible="true"></asp:Label>
    <br />
    <asp:Label ID="shippingDetails2"
            runat="server" c Visible="true"></asp:Label>
    <br />
    <asp:Label ID="shippingDetails5"
            runat="server" Visible="true"></asp:Label>
    <br />
    <asp:Label ID="shippingDetails6"
            runat="server" Visible="true"></asp:Label>
                <br />
    <asp:Label ID="shippingDetails7"
            runat="server" Visible="true"></asp:Label>
    </p>
   </div>
   <div class="story">
  <div id="siteInfo"> <img alt="small logo" src="Pictures/YourBestDataSolutionLogo.jpg"
width="59" height="66" />
        <a href="AboutUs.aspx">About Us</a> |
        <a href="ContactUs.aspx">Contact Us</a> |
    ©2012 YBDS, LLC </div>

</div>
<br />
  </form>
</body>
</html>
```

You may purchase a copy of our companion disk which contains all files for the project at http://www.amazon.com/gp/product/B00AOU76K8!

Order Confirmation Code Behind

Replace the existing code in the OrderConfirmation.aspx.vb file with the following code:

```
Imports System.Data
Imports System.IO
Imports System.Data.SqlClient
Imports System.Net.Mail

Partial Class _Default
   Inherits System.Web.UI.Page

   Protected Sub Page_Error(ByVal sender As Object, ByVal e As System.EventArgs) Handles
Me.Error

   End Sub

   Protected Sub Page_Load(ByVal sender As Object, ByVal e As EventArgs) Handles Me.Load

      Dim decoder As New NVPCodec()
      Dim test As New NVPAPICaller()
      Dim retMsg As String = ""
      Dim token As String
      Dim finalPaymentAmount As String = ""
      Dim payerId As String
      Dim ShippingAddress As String = ""

      token = Session("token").ToString()
      payerId = ""

      Dim ret As Boolean = test.GetShippingDetails(token, payerId, ShippingAddress, retMsg)
      If ret Then
         Session("payerId") = payerId
         ' Unique transaction ID of the payment. Note: If the PaymentAction of the request was
Authorization or Order, this value is your AuthorizationID for use with the Authorization &
Capture APIs.
         Dim transactionId As String = decoder("TRANSACTIONID")

         ' The type of transaction Possible values: l cart l express-checkout
         Dim transactionType As String = decoder("TRANSACTIONTYPE")

         ' Indicates whether the payment is instant or delayed. Possible values: l none l echeck l
instant
         Dim paymentType As String = decoder("PAYMENTTYPE")
```

You may purchase a copy of our companion disk which contains all files for the project at http://www.amazon.com/gp/product/B00AOU76K8!

```
' Time/date stamp of payment
Dim orderTime As String = decoder("ORDERTIME")

' The final amount charged, including any shipping and taxes from your Merchant Profile.
Dim amt As String = decoder("strACK")

' A three-character currency code for one of the currencies listed in PayPay-Supported
Transactional Currencies. Default: USD.
Dim currencyCode As String = decoder("CURRENCYCODE")

' PayPal™ fee amount charged for the transaction
Dim feeAmt As String = decoder("FEEAMT")

' Amount deposited in your PayPal™ account after a currency conversion.
Dim settleAmt As String = decoder("SETTLEAMT")

' Tax charged on the transaction.
Dim taxAmt As String = decoder("TAXAMT")

" Exchange rate if a currency conversion occurred. Relevant only if your are billing in
their non-primary currency. If
Dim exchangeRate As String = decoder("EXCHANGERATE")
Else
Response.Redirect("APIError.aspx?" & retMsg)
End If

''''''''''''''''''''''''''''''''''''''''''''''

'Session("orderID") = sessionID
If (Session("firstName") = Nothing) Then
    'User is not logged in.  Continue.
    lkLogout.Visible = False
    Session("isAdmin") = False
    lkCustomers.Visible = False
    lkCustomers.Enabled = False
    lkOrders.Visible = False
    lkOrders.Enabled = False
    lkAddProduct.Visible = False
    lkAddProduct.Enabled = False
    lkEditProduct.Visible = False
    lkEditProduct.Enabled = False
Else
    If (Session("isAdmin")) Then
        lkCustomers.Visible = True
        lkCustomers.Enabled = True
        lkOrders.Visible = True
```

```
            lkOrders.Enabled = True
            lkAddProduct.Visible = True
            lkAddProduct.Enabled = True
            lkEditProduct.Visible = True
            lkEditProduct.Enabled = True
        Else
            lkCustomers.Visible = False
            lkCustomers.Enabled = False
            lkOrders.Visible = False
            lkOrders.Enabled = False
            lkAddProduct.Visible = False
            lkAddProduct.Enabled = False
            lkEditProduct.Visible = False
            lkEditProduct.Enabled = False
        End If
        'Update the User Order with the currentUser ID.
        loginStatus.Text = "Welcome " & Session("firstName").ToString() & "!"
        loginStatus.Visible = True
    End If

    Dim myAccess As DatabaseAccess
    Dim myConnection As String
    Dim con As SqlConnection
    Dim cmd As SqlCommand
    Dim adapter As SqlDataAdapter
    Dim ds As DataSet
    Dim sql As String
    Dim readData As SqlDataReader
    Dim orderTotal As Decimal
    Dim shippingCost As Decimal

    If (Session("firstName") = Nothing) Then
        'User is not logged in.  Continue.
        lkLogout.Visible = False
        lkChangePassword.Visible = False
        lkChangePassword.Enabled = False
    Else
        lkChangePassword.Visible = True
        lkChangePassword.Enabled = True
        loginStatus.Text = "Welcome " & Session("firstName").ToString() & "!"
        loginStatus.Visible = True
    End If

    myAccess = New DatabaseAccess()
    myConnection = myAccess.getConnectionString()
    con = New SqlConnection(myConnection)
```

```
' Get order total.
sql = "SELECT SUM(od.ProductCost) AS OrderTotal" & _
    " FROM Product p " & _
    "INNER JOIN OrderDetail od ON od.ProductID = p.ProductID " & _
    "WHERE od.OrderID = " & Session("orderID") & " "
cmd = New SqlCommand(sql, con)
cmd.CommandType = Data.CommandType.Text
Try

  ' Open database connection.
  con.Open()

  ' Execute the INSERT and fill the data reader.
  readData = cmd.ExecuteReader(CommandBehavior.CloseConnection)

Catch a As Exception

  Throw a
End Try
readData.Read()
Session("orderTotal") = readData("OrderTotal")
readData.Close()
con.Close()

orderTotal = Convert.ToDecimal(Session("orderTotal").ToString())
Session("productTotal") = orderTotal
shippingCost = Convert.ToDecimal(Session("shippingCost").ToString())
orderTotal = orderTotal + shippingCost
''''''''''''''''''''''''''''''''''''''''''''''''''''''''''



''''''''''''''''''''''''''''''''''''''''''''''''''''''''''
sql = "SELECT p.ProductID, od.OrderId, p.ProductName AS Product, " & _
    "od.Quantity, '$' + Convert(varchar(12), p.Price) AS [Unit Price], '$' +
Convert(varchar(12), od.ProductCost) AS [Total] " & _
    "FROM Product p " & _
    "INNER JOIN OrderDetail od ON od.ProductID = p.ProductID " & _
    "WHERE od.OrderID = " & Session("orderID") & " " & _
      " UNION SELECT NULL AS ProductID, '', 'Order Sub Total', " & _
      "NULL, '', '$' + Convert(varchar(12), " & FormatNumber(Session("productTotal"), 2)
& ") " & _
    " UNION SELECT NULL, '', " & Chr(39) & "Shipping method - " &
Session("shippingMethodName").ToString() & Chr(39) & " AS ProductName, NULL, '', '$ ' +
```

You may purchase a copy of our companion disk which contains all files for the project at http://www.amazon.com/gp/product/B00AOU76K8!

```
Convert(varchar(12), SUM(ShippingCost)) FROM ShippingMethod WHERE
ShippingMethodID = " & Session("shippingMethodID") & _
        " UNION SELECT NULL, '', " & Chr(39) & "Sales Tax Rate - " &
Session("salesTaxRate").ToString() & Chr(39) & " AS ProductName, NULL, '', '$ ' +
Convert(varchar(12), " & FormatNumber(orderTotal * Session("salesTaxRate"), 2) & ") FROM
UserOrder WHERE OrderID = " & Session("OrderID") & _
        " UNION SELECT NULL, '', 'Totals', " & _
        "SUM(Quantity), '', '$' + Convert(varchar(12), " & FormatNumber(orderTotal +
(orderTotal * Session("salesTaxRate")), 2) & ") " & _
        " FROM Product p " & _
        "INNER JOIN OrderDetail od ON od.ProductID = p.ProductID " & _
        "WHERE od.OrderID = " & Session("orderID") & " " & _
        "ORDER BY OrderID DESC, ProductName ASC"

    cmd = New SqlCommand(sql, con)
    cmd.CommandType = Data.CommandType.Text

    adapter = New SqlDataAdapter(cmd)

    ' Fill the DataSet.
    ds = New DataSet()

    Try
      ' Open the database connection.
      con.Open()
      adapter.Fill(ds, sql)
    Finally
      con.Close()
      categoryFilter.DataSource = ds
      categoryFilter.DataBind()
    End Try


    ''''''''''''''''''''''''''''''''''''''''''''''''''''''
    'create the mail message
    Dim strFrom = "ENTER YOUR EMAIL ADDRESS THAT ORIGINATES ORDER
CONFIRMATION"
    Dim strTo = Session("EmailAddress")
    Dim MailMsg As New MailMessage(New MailAddress(strFrom.Trim()), New
MailAddress(strTo))
    MailMsg.BodyEncoding = Encoding.Default
    MailMsg.Subject = "Order # " & Session("OrderID")
    MailMsg.Body = Session("firstName") & ",<br/><br/>" & _
        "Your order # " & Session("OrderID") & _
        " is confirmed for the following:<br/><br/>" & _
        "<table border=""0"">" & _
```

```
            "<tr style=""background-color:Lavender"">" & _
            "<th>Product</th>" & _
            "<th>Quantity</th>" & _
            "<th>Unit Price</th>" & _
            "<th>Total</th>" & _
            "</tr>"

        Dim intcount As Integer = 0
        Dim i As Integer = 0

        For Each Row As GridViewRow In categoryFilter.Rows
          If (intcount) = categoryFilter.Rows.Count - 1 Or _
            (intcount) = categoryFilter.Rows.Count Or _
            (intcount) = categoryFilter.Rows.Count - 2 Then
             Select Case (intcount)
               ''''''''''''''SHIPPING METHOD ROW''''''''''''''''''''''''''''''''
               Case (categoryFilter.Rows.Count - 2)
                 MailMsg.Body = MailMsg.Body & _
                   "<tr style=""background-color:White"">" & _
                   "<td align=""center"">" & categoryFilter.Rows(intcount).Cells(2).Text & _
                   "</td>" & _
                   "<td>" & "" & _
                   "</td>" & _
                   "<td>" & "" & _
                   "</td>" & _
                   "<td align=""right"">" & categoryFilter.Rows(intcount).Cells(5).Text & _
                   "</td>" & _
                   "</tr>"
                 ''''''''''END SHIPPING METHOD ROW''''''''''''''''''''''''''''''''

                 ''''''''''SALES TAX ROW''''''''''''''''''''''''''''''
               Case (categoryFilter.Rows.Count - 1)
                 MailMsg.Body = MailMsg.Body & _
                   "<tr>" & _
                   "<td align=""center"">" & categoryFilter.Rows(intcount).Cells(2).Text & _
                   "</td>" & _
                   "<td align=""center"">" & categoryFilter.Rows(intcount).Cells(3).Text & _
                   "</td>" & _
                   "<td>" & "" & _
                   "</td>" & _
                   "<td align=""right"">" & categoryFilter.Rows(intcount).Cells(5).Text & _
                   "</td>" & _
                   "</tr>"
                 ''''''''END SALES TAX ROW''''''''''''''''''''''''''''''

                 ''''''''''''''''TOTALS ROW''''''''''''''''''''''''''''''''
```

You may purchase a copy of our companion disk which contains all files for the project at http://www.amazon.com/gp/product/B00AOU76K8!

```
            Case (categoryFilter.Rows.Count)
                MailMsg.Body = MailMsg.Body & _
                    "<tr>" & _
                    "<td align=""center"">" & categoryFilter.Rows(intcount).Cells(2).Text & _
                    "</td>" & _
                    "<td align=""center"">" & categoryFilter.Rows(intcount).Cells(3).Text & _
                    "</td>" & _
                    "<td>" & "" & _
                    "</td>" & _
                    "<td align=""right"">" & categoryFilter.Rows(intcount).Cells(5).Text & _
                    "</td>" & _
                    "</tr>"
                ''''''''''END TOTALS ROW''''''''''''''''''''''''''''
        End Select
        intcount = intcount + 1
    Else
        MailMsg.Body = MailMsg.Body & _
            "<tr>" & _
            IIf(categoryFilter.Rows(intcount).Cells(2).Text = "Order Sub Total" Or
(InStr(categoryFilter.Rows(intcount).Cells(2).Text, "Sales Tax Rate") > 0), "<td
align=""center"">" & categoryFilter.Rows(intcount).Cells(2).Text & _
            "</td>", "<td align=""left"">" & categoryFilter.Rows(intcount).Cells(2).Text & _
            "</td>") & _
            "<td align=""center"">" & categoryFilter.Rows(intcount).Cells(3).Text & _
            "</td>" & _
            "<td align=""center"">" & categoryFilter.Rows(intcount).Cells(4).Text & _
            "</td>" & _
            "<td align=""right"">" & categoryFilter.Rows(intcount).Cells(5).Text & _
            "</td>" & _
            "</tr>"
        intcount = intcount + 1
    End If
Next Row

MailMsg.Body = MailMsg.Body & "</table><br/><br/>" & _
 "<a href=""http://www.YOUR DOMAIN NAME GOES HERE"">View Your Order
History</a><br/>" & _
 "<br/>Thank you,<br/><br/>" & _
 "YOUR NAME<br/>YOUR EMAIL ADDRESS"

'' Get user email.
MailMsg.Priority = MailPriority.Normal
MailMsg.IsBodyHtml = True

''Smtpclient to send the mail message
Dim SmtpMail As New SmtpClient
```

You may purchase a copy of our companion disk which contains all files for the project at http://www.amazon.com/gp/product/B00AOU76K8!

```
SmtpMail.Host = "localhost"
'If (Session("firstLoad") = 1) Then

'End If
SmtpMail.Send(MailMsg)

Try

Catch ex As Exception

End Try
''''''''''''''''''''''''''''''''''''''''''''''''''

orderDetails.Text = "Your order # " & Session("orderID").ToString & " is confirmed for the
following:" & vbNewLine

lblTotal.Text = "Order Total: " & Session("currentOrderTotal")
''''''''''''''''''''''''''''''''''''''''''''''''''''''

sql = "SELECT StreetAddress1, StreetAddress2, City, " & _
    "StateName, CountryName, PostalCode, PostalCode2 " & _
    "FROM UserAddress ua " & _
    "INNER JOIN USState st ON ua.StateID = st.StateID " & _
    "INNER JOIN Country c ON c.CountryID = ua.CountryID " & _
    "INNER JOIN UserOrder od ON od.ShippingAddressID = ua.AddressID " & _
    "WHERE od.OrderID = " & Session("OrderID") & " " & _
    " AND od.ShippingAddressID = " & Session("shippingAddressID") & " "
cmd = New SqlCommand(sql, con)
cmd.CommandType = Data.CommandType.Text

Try

   ' Open database connection.
   con.Open()

   ' Execute the INSERT and fill the data reader.
   readData = cmd.ExecuteReader(CommandBehavior.CloseConnection)

Catch a As Exception

   Throw a
End Try
readData.Read()

' Set to shipping name from User Address table.
lblName.Text = Session("firstName") & " " & Session("lastName")
If (readData("StreetAddress2") <> "") Then
```

```
            shippingDetails.Text = readData("StreetAddress1") & " "
            shippingDetails1.Text = readData("StreetAddress2") & " "
            shippingDetails2.Text = readData("City") & ", " & readData("StateName") & " " &
readData("PostalCode")
            If readData("PostalCode2") <> "" Then
                shippingDetails5.Text = readData("PostalCode2") & vbNewLine
                shippingDetails6.Text = readData("CountryName") & vbNewLine
            Else
                shippingDetails5.Text = readData("CountryName") & vbNewLine
            End If
        Else
            shippingDetails.Text = readData("StreetAddress1") & " "
            shippingDetails1.Text = readData("City") & ", " & readData("StateName") & " " &
readData("PostalCode")
            If readData("PostalCode2") <> "" Then
                shippingDetails2.Text = readData("PostalCode2") & vbNewLine
                shippingDetails5.Text = readData("CountryName") & vbNewLine
            Else
                shippingDetails2.Text = readData("CountryName") & vbNewLine
            End If
        End If


        readData.Close()
        con.Close()

        '''''''UPDATE INVENTORY QUANTITY FOR EACH ITEM'''''''''''
        'If (Session("firstLoad") = 1) Then
        sql = "UPDATE Product " & _
            "SET Product.QuantityAvailable = Product.QuantityAvailable - OrderDetail.Quantity "
& _
            "FROM OrderDetail, Product " & _
            "WHERE OrderDetail.ProductID = Product.ProductID " & _
            "AND OrderDetail.OrderID = " & Session("orderID") & " "
        cmd = New SqlCommand(sql, con)
        cmd.CommandType = Data.CommandType.Text
        Try

            ' Open database connection.
            con.Open()

            ' Execute the INSERT and fill the data reader.
            readData = cmd.ExecuteReader(CommandBehavior.CloseConnection)

        Catch a As Exception
```

You may purchase a copy of our companion disk which contains all files for the project at http://www.amazon.com/gp/product/B00AOU76K8!

```
            Throw a
        End Try
        readData.Close()
        con.Close()
    End Sub

    Protected Function returnSpaces(ByVal productNameLength As Integer) As String
        Dim i As Integer = 0
        Dim spaceCount As String = ""

        For i = 0 To (80 - productNameLength)
            spaceCount = spaceCount & "_"
        Next
        returnSpaces = spaceCount
    End Function

    Protected Sub logout()
        Session("firstName") = Nothing
        Session.Clear()
        Page.Response.Redirect("Logout.aspx")
    End Sub

    Protected Sub categoryFilter_RowDataBound(ByVal sender As Object, ByVal e As
System.Web.UI.WebControls.GridViewRowEventArgs) Handles categoryFilter.RowDataBound

        Dim myAccess As DatabaseAccess
        Dim myConnection As String
        Dim con As SqlConnection
        Dim cmd As SqlCommand
        Dim sql As String
        Dim readData As SqlDataReader
        Dim itemCount As Integer
        Dim orderID As Integer

        orderID = Session("OrderID")
        If orderID = Nothing Then
            orderID = -1
        End If

        myAccess = New DatabaseAccess()
        myConnection = myAccess.getConnectionString()

        con = New SqlConnection(myConnection)
        sql = "SELECT COUNT(OrderID) AS orderCount FROM OrderDetail " & _
            "WHERE OrderID = " & orderID
        cmd = New SqlCommand(sql, con)
```

```
        cmd.CommandType = Data.CommandType.Text
        Try

            ' Open database connection.
            con.Open()

            ' Execute the INSERT and fill the data reader.
            readData = cmd.ExecuteReader(CommandBehavior.CloseConnection)

        Catch a As Exception

            Throw a
        End Try
        readData.Read()
        itemCount = readData("orderCount")
        con.Close()
        readData.Close()

        If (Session("OrderID") <> Nothing) And (itemCount > 0) Then
            e.Row.Cells(0).Visible = False
            e.Row.Cells(1).Visible = False
        End If

        If (e.Row.RowIndex = Session("rowQty")) Then
            e.Row.Cells(0).Text = ""
            ' e.Row.Cells(1).Text = ""
        End If

        If (e.Row.RowIndex = Session("rowQty") + 1) Then
            e.Row.Cells(0).Text = ""
            'e.Row.Cells(1).Text = ""
        End If

        If (e.Row.RowIndex = Session("rowQty") + 2) Then
            e.Row.Cells(0).Text = ""
            'e.Row.Cells(1).Text = ""
        End If
    End Sub
End Class
```

You may purchase a copy of our companion disk which contains all files for the project at http://www.amazon.com/gp/product/B00AOU76K8!

Order Detail Server Page

Replace the existing code in the OrderDetails.aspx file with the following code (*REPLACE ANY CODE IN THIS COLOR WITH YOUR OWN INFORMATION!*):

```
<%@ Page Language="VB"
        AutoEventWireup="True"
        CodeFile="OrderDetails.aspx.vb"
        Inherits="_Default" %>

<!DOCTYPE html PUBLIC "-//W3C//DTD XHTML 1.0 Transitional//EN"
"http://www.w3.org/TR/xhtml1/DTD/xhtml1-transitional.dtd">
<html xmlns="http://www.w3.org/1999/xhtml">

<head>
<meta http-equiv="Content-Type" content="text/html; charset=iso-8859-1" />
<title>Order Details</title>
<link rel="stylesheet" href="emx_nav_left.css" type="text/css" />
<script type="text/javascript">

var time = 3000;
var numofitems = 7;

//menu constructor
function menu(allitems,thisitem,startstate){
  callname= "gl"+thisitem;
  divname="subglobal"+thisitem;
  this.numberofmenuitems = allitems;
  this.caller = document.getElementById(callname);
  this.thediv = document.getElementById(divname);
  this.thediv.style.visibility = startstate;
}

//menu methods
function ehandler(event,theobj){
  for (var i=1; i<= theobj.numberofmenuitems; i++){
    var shutdiv =eval( "menuitem"+i+".thediv");
    shutdiv.style.visibility="hidden";
  }
  theobj.thediv.style.visibility="visible";
}

function closesubnav(event){
  if ((event.clientY <48)||(event.clientY > 107)){
```

You may purchase a copy of our companion disk which contains all files for the project at http://www.amazon.com/gp/product/B00AOU76K8!

```
    for (var i=1; i<= numofitems; i++){
     var shutdiv =eval('menuitem'+i+'.thediv');
     shutdiv.style.visibility='hidden';
    }
  }
}
</script>
</head>
<body>

<form id="Form1" runat="server">
<div class="skipLinks">skip to: <a href="#content">page content</a> | <a
href="#pageNav">links on this page</a> | <a href="#globalNav">site navigation</a> | <a
href="#siteInfo">footer (site information)</a> </div>
<div id="masthead">
  <h1 id="siteName">Your Best Data Solution</h1>
  <div id="utility">
       <asp:LinkButton ID="lkCustomers" runat="server"
PostBackUrl="Customers.aspx">Customers</asp:LinkButton>
     | <asp:LinkButton ID="lkOrders" runat="server"
PostBackUrl="ViewOrders.aspx">Orders</asp:LinkButton>
     | <asp:LinkButton ID="lkAddProduct" PostBackUrl="AddProduct.aspx"
                 runat="server">Add Product</asp:LinkButton>
     | <asp:LinkButton ID="lkEditProduct" runat="server"
PostBackUrl="ViewCategories.aspx">Edit Product</asp:LinkButton>
     | <asp:LinkButton ID="lkLogout" OnClick="logout" runat="server"
PostBackUrl="#">Logout</asp:LinkButton>
     | <asp:LinkButton ID="lkChangePassword" PostBackUrl="Password.aspx"
runat="server">Change Password</asp:LinkButton>
  </div>
  <div id="globalNav"> <img alt="" src="Pictures/gblnav_left.gif" height="32" width="4"
id="gnl" /> <img alt="" src="Pictures/glbnav_right.gif" height="32" width="4" id="gnr" />
    <div id="globalLink">
       <a href="Default.aspx" id="A1" class="glink">
       Home</a>
       <a href="ViewCategories.aspx" id="gl1" class="glink" >
       View Products</a>
       <a href="SearchProducts.aspx" id="gl2" class="glink">Search</a>
       <a href="ViewCart.aspx" id="gl3" class="glink">View Cart</a>
       <a href="Checkout.aspx" id="gl4" class="glink">Checkout</a>
       <a href="CreateAccount.aspx" id="gl5" class="glink">Create
       Account</a>
       <a href="Login.aspx" id="gl6" class="glink">Login
       </a><a href="OrderHistory.aspx" id="gl7" class="glink">Order
       History</a>
       <a href="FAQ.aspx" id="A2" class="glink">FAQ</a>
```

You may purchase a copy of our companion disk which contains all files for the project at http://www.amazon.com/gp/product/B00AOU76K8!

```
      <asp:Label ID="loginStatus" Visible="false" runat="server"></asp:Label>
    </div>
  </div>
<div id="pagecell1">
  <img alt="" src="Pictures/tl_curve_white.gif" height="6" width="6" id="tl" /> <img alt=""
src="Pictures/tr_curve_white.gif" height="6" width="6" id="tr" />

    <div id="pageName">
    <img alt="small logo" src="Pictures/YourBestDataSolutionLogo.jpg" height="50"
width="60"/> </div>
  <div id="pageNav">
    <div class="relatedLinks">
      <h3>Related Link Category</h3>
      <a href="FAQ.aspx#anchor3">Automation</a>
      <a href="FAQ.aspx#anchor1">Customized Reporting</a>
      <a href="FAQ.aspx#anchor2">Database Design</a>
      <a href="FAQ.aspx#anchor12">Data Migration</a>
      <a href="FAQ.aspx#anchor4">Data Modeling</a>
      <a href="FAQ.aspx#anchor14">Desktop Application Solutions</a>
      <a href="FAQ.aspx#anchor5">eCommerce Solutions</a>
      <a href="FAQ.aspx#anchor6">eMail Marketing</a>
      <a href="FAQ.aspx#anchor7">Mobile App Development</a>
      <a href="FAQ.aspx#anchor8">PayPal™ Integration</a>
      <a href="FAQ.aspx#anchor9">Web Design</a>
      <a href="FAQ.aspx#anchor10">Web Development</a>
    </div>
  </div>
  <div id="content">
    <div class="feature">
      <h3>
      <asp:Label runat="server" ID="headerLabel" Text ="Order History"></asp:Label></h3>
       <p>
          <asp:Label runat="server" Width="200" ID="orderStatus"
                Font-Bold="true" Text ="Update Order Status"></asp:Label>
          <asp:DropDownList runat="server" Width="150"
                    ID="cboOrderStatus"
                    AutoPostBack="true"
                    OnSelectedIndexChanged="cboOrderStatus_SelectedIndexChanged"
                    DataValueField="OrderStatusID"
                    DataTextField="OrderStatusName"></asp:DropDownList>
          <br />
          <br />
          <asp:GridView ID ="categoryFilter"
                  runat="server"
                  OnRowCommand="categoryFilter_RowCommand"
                  EditRowStyle-HorizontalAlign="Center"
```

```
                HeaderStyle-BackColor="#cccccc"
                BorderStyle="None"
                EmptyDataText="Please login to view your past orders." >
            </asp:GridView>
        </p>
        <p>
            <asp:Label runat="server" Width="150" ID="Label1" Font-Bold="true" Text ="Shipping
Address"></asp:Label>
            <asp:Label runat="server" Width="200" Visible="false" ID="Label4"></asp:Label>
            <asp:Label runat="server" Width="150" ID="Label2" Font-Bold="true" Text ="Billing
Address"></asp:Label>
            <br />

            <asp:Label runat="server" Width="150"
                ID="shippingAddress1" Text ="Shipping Address"></asp:Label>
            <asp:Label runat="server" Width="200" Visible="false" ID="Label3"></asp:Label>
            <asp:Label runat="server" Width="150"
                ID="billingAddress1" Text ="Billing Address"></asp:Label>
            <br />

            <asp:Label runat="server" Width="150"
                ID="shippingCity" Text ="City, State, Zip"></asp:Label>

            <asp:Label runat="server" Width="200" Visible="false" ID="Label12"></asp:Label>

            <asp:Label runat="server" Width="150"
                ID="billingCity" Text ="City, State, Zip"></asp:Label>
            <br />
        </p>
      </div>
      <div class="story">
    <div id="siteInfo"> <img alt="small logo" src="Pictures/YourBestDataSolutionLogo.jpg"
width="59" height="66" />
            <a href="AboutUs.aspx">About Us</a> |
            <a href="ContactUs.aspx">Contact Us</a> |
       ©2012 YBDS, LLC </div>

</div>
<br />
   </form>
</body>
</html>
```

You may purchase a copy of our companion disk which contains all files for the project at http://www.amazon.com/gp/product/B00AOU76K8!

Order Detail Code Behind

Replace the existing code in the OrderDetails.aspx.vb file with the following code:

```
Imports System.Data
Imports System.IO
Imports System.Data.SqlClient

Partial Class _Default
   Inherits System.Web.UI.Page

   Protected Sub Page_Load(ByVal sender As Object, ByVal e As EventArgs) Handles Me.Load

      Dim myAccess As DatabaseAccess
      Dim myConnection As String
      Dim con As SqlConnection
      Dim cmd As SqlCommand
      Dim adapter As SqlDataAdapter
      Dim ds As DataSet
      Dim sql As String
      Dim viewOrderID As String
      Dim orderTotal As Decimal
      Dim shippingCost As Decimal
      Dim readData As SqlDataReader

      If Not Page.IsPostBack Then
         ' Fill database connection variables.
         myAccess = New DatabaseAccess()
         myConnection = myAccess.getConnectionString()
         con = New SqlConnection(myConnection)

         ' Show the previous orders for the current user.
         viewOrderID = Session("viewOrderID")
         If viewOrderID = Nothing Then
            viewOrderID = -1
         End If

         If (Session("firstName") = Nothing) Then
            'User is not logged in.  Continue.
            lkLogout.Visible = False
            lkChangePassword.Visible = False
            lkChangePassword.Enabled = False
            headerLabel.Text = "Please login to view your past orders."
            Session("isAdmin") = False
```

```
        lkCustomers.Visible = False
        lkCustomers.Enabled = False
        lkOrders.Visible = False
        lkOrders.Enabled = False
        lkAddProduct.Visible = False
        lkAddProduct.Enabled = False
        lkEditProduct.Visible = False
        lkEditProduct.Enabled = False
        orderStatus.Visible = False
        cboOrderStatus.Visible = False
        cboOrderStatus.Enabled = False
    Else
        If (Session("isAdmin")) Then
            lkCustomers.Visible = True
            lkCustomers.Enabled = True
            lkOrders.Visible = True
            lkOrders.Enabled = True
            lkAddProduct.Visible = True
            lkAddProduct.Enabled = True
            lkEditProduct.Visible = True
            lkEditProduct.Enabled = True
            orderStatus.Visible = True
            cboOrderStatus.Visible = True
            cboOrderStatus.Enabled = True
            ' Data bind the drop down.
            sql = "SELECT OrderStatusID, OrderStatusName FROM " & _
                "OrderStatus"
            cmd = New SqlCommand(sql, con)
            cmd.CommandType = Data.CommandType.Text
            adapter = New SqlDataAdapter(cmd)

            ' Fill the DataSet.
            ds = New DataSet()

            Try
                ' Open the database connection.
                con.Open()
                adapter.Fill(ds, sql)
            Finally

                con.Close()

                ' Perform the data binding.
                cboOrderStatus.DataSource = ds
                cboOrderStatus.DataBind()
            End Try
```

You may purchase a copy of our companion disk which contains all files for the project at http://www.amazon.com/gp/product/B00AOU76K8!

```
' Get order status.
sql = "SELECT uo.OrderStatusID " & _
    " FROM UserOrder uo " & _
"INNER JOIN OrderStatus os ON os.OrderStatusID = uo.OrderStatusID " & _
    "WHERE OrderID = " & viewOrderID & " "
cmd = New SqlCommand(sql, con)
cmd.CommandType = Data.CommandType.Text
Try

    ' Open database connection.
    con.Open()

    ' Execute the INSERT and fill the data reader.
    readData = cmd.ExecuteReader(CommandBehavior.CloseConnection)

Catch a As Exception

    Throw a
End Try
readData.Read()
Session("orderStatusID") = readData("OrderStatusID")
readData.Close()
con.Close()
cboOrderStatus.SelectedValue = Session("orderStatusID")
Else
lkCustomers.Visible = False
lkCustomers.Enabled = False
lkOrders.Visible = False
lkOrders.Enabled = False
lkAddProduct.Visible = False
lkAddProduct.Enabled = False
lkEditProduct.Visible = False
lkEditProduct.Enabled = False
orderStatus.Visible = False
cboOrderStatus.Visible = False
cboOrderStatus.Enabled = False
End If
lkChangePassword.Visible = True
lkChangePassword.Enabled = True
loginStatus.Text = "Welcome " & Session("firstName").ToString() & "!"
loginStatus.Visible = True
''''''''''''''''''''''''''''''''''''''''''''''''

' Get shippingmethodID, salesTaxRate and shippingCost.
sql = "SELECT ShippingMethodID, ShippingCost, SalesTaxRate" & _
```

```
    " FROM UserOrder " & _
    "WHERE OrderID = " & viewOrderID & " "
cmd = New SqlCommand(sql, con)
cmd.CommandType = Data.CommandType.Text
Try

   ' Open database connection.
   con.Open()

   ' Execute the INSERT and fill the data reader.
   readData = cmd.ExecuteReader(CommandBehavior.CloseConnection)

Catch a As Exception

   Throw a
End Try
readData.Read()
Session("shippingMethodID") = readData("ShippingMethodID")
Session("salesTaxRate") = readData("SalesTaxRate")
Session("shippingCost") = readData("ShippingCost")
readData.Close()
con.Close()

''''''''''''''''''''''''''''''''''''''''''''''''''''''
' Get shippingMethodName.
sql = "SELECT ShippingMethodName " & _
    " FROM ShippingMethod " & _
    "WHERE ShippingMethodID = " & Session("shippingMethodID") & " "
cmd = New SqlCommand(sql, con)
cmd.CommandType = Data.CommandType.Text
Try

   ' Open database connection.
   con.Open()

   ' Execute the INSERT and fill the data reader.
   readData = cmd.ExecuteReader(CommandBehavior.CloseConnection)

Catch a As Exception

   Throw a
End Try
readData.Read()
Session("shippingMethodName") = readData("ShippingMethodName")
readData.Close()
con.Close()
```

You may purchase a copy of our companion disk which contains all files for the project at http://www.amazon.com/gp/product/B00AOU76K8!

```
        ' Get Shipping Address.
        sql = "SELECT ua.*, StateAbbreviation, CountryName FROM " & _
    "UserAddress ua INNER JOIN Country c ON c.CountryID = ua.CountryID " & _
    "INNER JOIN USState st ON st.StateID = ua.StateID " & _
    "INNER JOIN UserOrder uo ON uo.ShippingAddressID = ua.AddressID " & _
    "WHERE uo.OrderID = " & Session("viewOrderID") & " "
        cmd = New SqlCommand(sql, con)
        cmd.CommandType = Data.CommandType.Text
        Try

            ' Open database connection.
            con.Open()

            ' Execute the INSERT and fill the data reader.
            readData = cmd.ExecuteReader(CommandBehavior.CloseConnection)

        Catch a As Exception

            Throw a
        End Try
        readData.Read()
        shippingAddress1.Text = readData("StreetAddress1") & vbNewLine &
readData("StreetAddress2")
        If (readData("PostalCode2").ToString = "BillingAddress") Then
            shippingCity.Text = readData("City") & ", " & _
                        readData("StateAbbreviation") & " " & _
                        readData("PostalCode") & " " & _
                        readData("CountryName")
        Else
            shippingCity.Text = readData("City") & ", " & _
                        readData("StateAbbreviation") & " " & _
                        readData("PostalCode") & " " & _
                        readData("PostalCode2") & " " & _
                        readData("CountryName")
        End If
        readData.Close()
        con.Close()

        ''''''''''''''''''''''''''''''''''''''''''''''''''''''''''''''
        ' Get Billing Address.
        sql = "SELECT ua.*, StateAbbreviation, CountryName FROM " & _
    "UserAddress ua INNER JOIN Country c ON c.CountryID = ua.CountryID " & _
    "INNER JOIN USState st ON st.StateID = ua.StateID " & _
    "INNER JOIN UserOrder uo ON uo.BillingAddressID = ua.AddressID " & _
    "WHERE uo.OrderID = " & Session("viewOrderID") & " "
```

```
            cmd = New SqlCommand(sql, con)
            cmd.CommandType = Data.CommandType.Text
            Try

                ' Open database connection.
                con.Open()

                ' Execute the INSERT and fill the data reader.
                readData = cmd.ExecuteReader(CommandBehavior.CloseConnection)

            Catch a As Exception

                Throw a
            End Try
            readData.Read()
            billingAddress1.Text = readData("StreetAddress1") & vbNewLine &
readData("StreetAddress2")
            If (readData("PostalCode2").ToString = "BillingAddress") Then
                billingCity.Text = readData("City") & ", " & _
                                readData("StateAbbreviation") & " " & _
                                readData("PostalCode") & " " & _
                                readData("CountryName")
            Else
                billingCity.Text = readData("City") & ", " & _
                                readData("StateAbbreviation") & " " & _
                                readData("PostalCode") & " " & _
                                readData("PostalCode2") & " " & _
                                readData("CountryName")
            End If

            readData.Close()
            con.Close()


            ''''''''''''''''''''''''''''''''''''''''''''''''''''''''''
            ' Get order total.
            sql = "SELECT SUM(od.ProductCost) AS OrderTotal" & _
                " FROM Product p " & _
                "INNER JOIN OrderDetail od ON od.ProductID = p.ProductID " & _
                "WHERE od.OrderID = " & viewOrderID & " "
            cmd = New SqlCommand(sql, con)
            cmd.CommandType = Data.CommandType.Text
            Try

                ' Open database connection.
                con.Open()
```

```
        ' Execute the INSERT and fill the data reader.
        readData = cmd.ExecuteReader(CommandBehavior.CloseConnection)

    Catch a As Exception

        Throw a
    End Try
    readData.Read()
    orderTotal = readData("orderTotal")
    readData.Close()
    con.Close()
    orderTotal = Convert.ToDecimal(orderTotal)
    Session("productTotal") = orderTotal
    shippingCost = Convert.ToDecimal(Session("shippingCost").ToString())
    orderTotal = orderTotal + shippingCost
    ''''''''''''''''''''''''''''''''''''''''''''''''''''



    ''''''''''''''''''''''''''''''''''''''''''''''''''
    sql = "SELECT p.ProductID, od.OrderID, p.ProductName AS Product, " & _
        "od.Quantity, '$' + Convert(varchar(12), p.Price) AS [Unit Price], '$' +
Convert(varchar(12), od.ProductCost) AS [Total] " & _
        "FROM Product p " & _
        "INNER JOIN OrderDetail od ON od.ProductID = p.ProductID " & _
        "WHERE od.OrderID = " & viewOrderID & " " & _
        " UNION SELECT NULL AS ProductID, '', 'Order Sub Total', " & _
        "NULL, '', '$' + Convert(varchar(12), " & FormatNumber(Session("productTotal"),
2) & ") " & _
        " UNION SELECT NULL, '', " & Chr(39) & "Shipping method - " &
Session("shippingMethodName").ToString() & Chr(39) & " AS ProductName, NULL, '', '$ ' +
Convert(varchar(12), SUM(ShippingCost)) FROM ShippingMethod WHERE
ShippingMethodID = " & Session("shippingMethodID") & _
        " UNION SELECT NULL, '', " & Chr(39) & "Sales Tax Rate - " &
Session("salesTaxRate").ToString() & Chr(39) & " AS ProductName, NULL, '', '$ ' +
Convert(varchar(12), " & FormatNumber(orderTotal * Session("salesTaxRate"), 2) & ") FROM
UserOrder WHERE OrderID = " & viewOrderID & _
        " UNION SELECT NULL, '', 'Totals', " & _
        "SUM(Quantity), '', '$' + Convert(varchar(12), " & FormatNumber(orderTotal +
(orderTotal * Session("salesTaxRate")), 2) & ") " & _
        " FROM Product p " & _
        "INNER JOIN OrderDetail od ON od.ProductID = p.ProductID " & _
        "WHERE od.OrderID = " & viewOrderID & " " & _
        "ORDER BY OrderID DESC, ProductName ASC"
    cmd = New SqlCommand(sql, con)
```

```
            cmd.CommandType = Data.CommandType.Text
            adapter = New SqlDataAdapter(cmd)

            ' Fill the DataSet.
            ds = New DataSet()

            Try
                ' Open the database connection.
                con.Open()
                adapter.Fill(ds, sql)
            Finally

                con.Close()

                ' Perform the data binding.
                categoryFilter.DataSource = ds
                categoryFilter.DataBind()
            End Try

            headerLabel.Text = "Order # " & Session("viewOrderID").ToString
        End If
    End If
End Sub

Protected Sub logout()
    Session("firstName") = Nothing
    Session.Clear()
    Page.Response.Redirect("Logout.aspx")
End Sub

Protected Sub passSessionVariable()
    ''''''''''''''''''''''''''''''''''''''''''''''

    ' Open text file receipt for selected order.
End Sub

Protected Sub categoryFilter_RowCommand(ByVal sender As Object, ByVal e As
System.Web.UI.WebControls.GridViewCommandEventArgs) Handles
categoryFilter.RowCommand
    Dim obj As Object
    Dim id As String
    Dim orderID As Integer
    Dim cmdName As String

    cmdName = e.CommandName
    obj = e.CommandArgument
    id = obj.ToString
```

You may purchase a copy of our companion disk which contains all files for the project at http://www.amazon.com/gp/product/B00AOU76K8!

```
    orderID = Convert.ToInt16(id.ToString)
    Session("OrderID") = Convert.ToInt16(categoryFilter.DataKeys(orderID).Value.ToString)
    orderID = Convert.ToInt16(categoryFilter.DataKeys(orderID).Value.ToString)

    Select Case (cmdName)
      Case "Select"
        passSessionVariable()
    End Select
End Sub

Public Function GetFileContents(ByVal FullPath As String, _
  Optional ByRef ErrInfo As String = "") As String

    Dim strContents As String
    Dim objReader As StreamReader
    Try

      objReader = New StreamReader(FullPath)
      strContents = objReader.ReadToEnd()
      objReader.Close()
      Return strContents
    Catch Ex As Exception
      ErrInfo = Ex.Message
      Return ""
    End Try
End Function

Public Function SaveTextToFile(ByVal strData As String, _
 ByVal FullPath As String, _
  Optional ByVal ErrInfo As String = "") As Boolean

    ' Dim Contents As String
    Dim bAns As Boolean = False
    Dim objReader As StreamWriter
    Try


      objReader = New StreamWriter(FullPath)
      objReader.Write(strData)
      objReader.Close()
      bAns = True
    Catch Ex As Exception
      ErrInfo = Ex.Message

    End Try
    Return bAns
```

You may purchase a copy of our companion disk which contains all files for the project at http://www.amazon.com/gp/product/B00AOU76K8!

```
    End Function
    Protected Sub categoryFilter_RowDataBound(ByVal sender As Object, ByVal e As
System.Web.UI.WebControls.GridViewRowEventArgs) Handles categoryFilter.RowDataBound
        e.Row.Cells(0).Visible = False
        e.Row.Cells(1).Visible = False
    End Sub

    Protected Sub cboOrderStatus_SelectedIndexChanged(ByVal sender As Object, ByVal e As
System.EventArgs) Handles cboOrderStatus.SelectedIndexChanged

        Dim myAccess As DatabaseAccess
        Dim myConnection As String
        Dim con As SqlConnection
        Dim cmd As SqlCommand
        Dim sql As String
        Dim readData As SqlDataReader

        ' Fill database connection variables.
        myAccess = New DatabaseAccess()
        myConnection = myAccess.getConnectionString()
        con = New SqlConnection(myConnection)

        sql = "UPDATE UserOrder SET OrderStatusID = " & cboOrderStatus.SelectedItem.Value
& " " & "WHERE OrderID = " & Convert.ToInt16(Session("viewOrderID").ToString) & " "
        cmd = New SqlCommand(Sql, con)
        cmd.CommandType = Data.CommandType.Text
        Try

            ' Open database connection.
            con.Open()

            ' Execute the INSERT and fill the data reader.
            readData = cmd.ExecuteReader(CommandBehavior.CloseConnection)

        Catch a As Exception

            Throw a
        End Try

        con.Close()
        readData.Close()
    End Sub
End Class
```

You may purchase a copy of our companion disk which contains all files for the project at http://www.amazon.com/gp/product/B00AOU76K8!

Order History Server Page

Replace the existing code in the OrderHistory.aspx file with the following code (***REPLACE ANY CODE IN THIS COLOR WITH YOUR OWN INFORMATION!)***:

```
<%@ Page Language="VB"
     AutoEventWireup="True"
     CodeFile="OrderHistory.aspx.vb"
     Inherits="_Default" %>

<!DOCTYPE html PUBLIC "-//W3C//DTD XHTML 1.0 Transitional//EN"
"http://www.w3.org/TR/xhtml1/DTD/xhtml1-transitional.dtd">
<html xmlns="http://www.w3.org/1999/xhtml">

<head>
<meta http-equiv="Content-Type" content="text/html; charset=iso-8859-1" />
<title>Order History</title>
<link rel="stylesheet" href="emx_nav_left.css" type="text/css" />
<script type="text/javascript">

var time = 3000;
var numofitems = 7;

//menu constructor
function menu(allitems,thisitem,startstate){
 callname= "gl"+thisitem;
 divname="subglobal"+thisitem;
 this.numberofmenuitems = allitems;
 this.caller = document.getElementById(callname);
 this.thediv = document.getElementById(divname);
 this.thediv.style.visibility = startstate;
}

//menu methods
function ehandler(event,theobj){
 for (var i=1; i<= theobj.numberofmenuitems; i++){
  var shutdiv =eval( "menuitem"+i+".thediv");
  shutdiv.style.visibility="hidden";
 }
 theobj.thediv.style.visibility="visible";
}

function closesubnav(event){
 if ((event.clientY <48)||(event.clientY > 107)){
```

```
    for (var i=1; i<= numofitems; i++){
      var shutdiv =eval('menuitem'+i+'.thediv');
      shutdiv.style.visibility='hidden';
    }
  }
}
</script>
</head>
<body>

<form id="Form1" runat="server">
<div class="skipLinks">skip to: <a href="#content">page content</a> | <a
href="#pageNav">links on this page</a> | <a href="#globalNav">site navigation</a> | <a
href="#siteInfo">footer (site information)</a> </div>
<div id="masthead">
  <h1 id="siteName">Your Best Data Solution</h1>
  <div id="utility">
      <asp:LinkButton ID="lkCustomers" runat="server"
PostBackUrl="Customers.aspx">Customers</asp:LinkButton>
    | <asp:LinkButton ID="lkOrders" runat="server"
PostBackUrl="ViewOrders.aspx">Orders</asp:LinkButton>
    | <asp:LinkButton ID="lkAddProduct" PostBackUrl="AddProduct.aspx"
                runat="server">Add Product</asp:LinkButton>
    | <asp:LinkButton ID="lkEditProduct" runat="server"
PostBackUrl="ViewCategories.aspx">Edit Product</asp:LinkButton>
    | <asp:LinkButton ID="lkLogout" OnClick="logout" runat="server"
PostBackUrl="#">Logout</asp:LinkButton>
    | <asp:LinkButton ID="lkChangePassword" PostBackUrl="Password.aspx"
runat="server">Change Password</asp:LinkButton>
  </div>
  <div id="globalNav"> <img alt="" src="Pictures/gblnav_left.gif" height="32" width="4"
id="gnl" /> <img alt="" src="Pictures/glbnav_right.gif" height="32" width="4" id="gnr" />
    <div id="globalLink">
      <a href="Default.aspx" id="A1" class="glink">
      Home</a>
      <a href="ViewCategories.aspx" id="gl1" class="glink" >
      View Products</a>
      <a href="SearchProducts.aspx" id="gl2" class="glink">Search</a>
      <a href="ViewCart.aspx" id="gl3" class="glink">View Cart</a>
      <a href="Checkout.aspx" id="gl4" class="glink">Checkout</a>
      <a href="CreateAccount.aspx" id="gl5" class="glink">Create
      Account</a>
      <a href="Login.aspx" id="gl6" class="glink">Login
      </a><a href="OrderHistory.aspx" id="gl7" class="glink">Order
      History</a>
      <a href="FAQ.aspx" id="A2" class="glink">FAQ</a>
```

```
      <asp:Label ID="loginStatus" Visible="false" runat="server"></asp:Label>
    </div>
   </div>
<div id="pagecell1">
  <img alt="" src="Pictures/tl_curve_white.gif" height="6" width="6" id="tl" /> <img alt=""
src="Pictures/tr_curve_white.gif" height="6" width="6" id="tr" />

    <div id="pageName">
    <img alt="small logo" src="Pictures/YourBestDataSolutionLogo.jpg" height="50"
width="60"/> </div>
  <div id="pageNav">
    <div class="relatedLinks">
      <h3>Related Link Category</h3>
      <a href="FAQ.aspx#anchor3">Automation</a>
      <a href="FAQ.aspx#anchor1">Customized Reporting</a>
      <a href="FAQ.aspx#anchor2">Database Design</a>
      <a href="FAQ.aspx#anchor12">Data Migration</a>
      <a href="FAQ.aspx#anchor4">Data Modeling</a>
      <a href="FAQ.aspx#anchor14">Desktop Application Solutions</a>
      <a href="FAQ.aspx#anchor5">eCommerce Solutions</a>
      <a href="FAQ.aspx#anchor6">eMail Marketing</a>
      <a href="FAQ.aspx#anchor7">Mobile App Development</a>
      <a href="FAQ.aspx#anchor8">PayPal™ Integration</a>
      <a href="FAQ.aspx#anchor9">Web Design</a>
      <a href="FAQ.aspx#anchor10">Web Development</a>
    </div>
  </div>
  <div id="content">
    <div class="feature">
      <h3>
      <asp:Label runat="server" ID="headerLabel" Text ="Order History"></asp:Label></h3>
       <p>
          <asp:GridView ID ="categoryFilter"
                    runat="server"
                    DataKeyNames="Order #"
                    OnRowCommand="categoryFilter_RowCommand"
                    EditRowStyle-HorizontalAlign="Center"
                    HeaderStyle-BackColor="#cccccc"
                    BorderStyle="None"
                    EmptyDataText="No items are currently in your cart." >
            <Columns>
              <asp:TemplateField>
              <ItemTemplate>
              <asp:LinkButton ID="viewOrder"
                        runat="server"
                        CommandName="Select"
```

You may purchase a copy of our companion disk which contains all files for the project at http://www.amazon.com/gp/product/B00AOU76K8!

```
                        CommandArgument="<%# Container.DataItemIndex %>"
                        Text = "View Order Detail"></asp:LinkButton>
                </ItemTemplate>
                </asp:TemplateField>
              </Columns>
            </asp:GridView>
        </p>

      </div>
      <div class="story">
    <div id="siteInfo"> <img alt="small logo" src="Pictures/YourBestDataSolutionLogo.jpg"
width="59" height="66" />
            <a href="AboutUs.aspx">About Us</a> |
            <a href="ContactUs.aspx">Contact Us</a> |
        ©2012 YBDS, LLC </div>

</div>
<br />
    </form>
</body>
</html>
```

You may purchase a copy of our companion disk which contains all files for the project at http://www.amazon.com/gp/product/B00AOU76K8!

Order History Code Behind

Replace the existing code in the OrderHistory.aspx.vb file with the following code:

```
Imports System.Data
Imports System.Data.SqlClient

Partial Class _Default
    Inherits System.Web.UI.Page

    Protected Sub Page_Load(ByVal sender As Object, ByVal e As EventArgs) Handles Me.Load

        If (Session("firstName") = Nothing) Then
            'User is not logged in.  Continue.
            lkLogout.Visible = False
            lkChangePassword.Visible = False
            lkChangePassword.Enabled = False
            categoryFilter.EmptyDataText = "Please log in to view your past orders."
            categoryFilter.Visible = True
            Session("isAdmin") = False
            lkCustomers.Visible = False
            lkCustomers.Enabled = False
            lkOrders.Visible = False
            lkOrders.Enabled = False
            lkAddProduct.Visible = False
            lkAddProduct.Enabled = False
            lkEditProduct.Visible = False
            lkEditProduct.Enabled = False
        Else
            If (Session("isAdmin")) Then
                lkCustomers.Visible = True
                lkCustomers.Enabled = True
                lkOrders.Visible = True
                lkOrders.Enabled = True
                lkAddProduct.Visible = True
                lkAddProduct.Enabled = True
                lkEditProduct.Visible = True
                lkEditProduct.Enabled = True
            Else
                lkCustomers.Visible = False
                lkCustomers.Enabled = False
                lkOrders.Visible = False
                lkOrders.Enabled = False
                lkAddProduct.Visible = False
```

```
        lkAddProduct.Enabled = False
        lkEditProduct.Visible = False
        lkEditProduct.Enabled = False
    End If
    lkChangePassword.Visible = True
    lkChangePassword.Enabled = True
    loginStatus.Text = "Welcome " & Session("firstName").ToString() & "!"
    loginStatus.Visible = True
    ''''''''''''''''''''''''''''''''''''''''''''''''''''''''''''''''''''''''''''''

    ' Show the previous orders for the current user.
    Dim myAccess As DatabaseAccess
    Dim myConnection As String
    Dim con As SqlConnection
    Dim cmd As SqlCommand
    Dim adapter As SqlDataAdapter
    Dim ds As DataSet
    Dim sql As String
    Dim userID As String

    ' Fill database connection variables.
    myAccess = New DatabaseAccess()
    myConnection = myAccess.getConnectionString()
    con = New SqlConnection(myConnection)

    userID = Session("UserID")
    If userID = Nothing Then
        userID = -1
    End If

    myAccess = New DatabaseAccess()
    myConnection = myAccess.getConnectionString()

    con = New SqlConnection(myConnection)
    sql = "SELECT uo.OrderID AS [Order #], " & _
        "uo.OrderDate AS [Order Date], " & _
        "os.OrderStatusName AS [Order Status] " & _
        "FROM UserOrder uo " & _
        "INNER JOIN OrderStatus os " & _
        "ON os.OrderStatusID = uo.OrderStatusID " & _
        "WHERE uo.UserID = '" & userID & "' " & _
        "AND uo.OrderStatusID IS NOT NULL "
    cmd = New SqlCommand(sql, con)
    cmd.CommandType = Data.CommandType.Text
    adapter = New SqlDataAdapter(cmd)

    ' Fill the DataSet.
```

```
            ds = New DataSet()

            Try
                ' Open the database connection.
                con.Open()
                adapter.Fill(ds, sql)
            Finally

                con.Close()

                ' Perform the data binding.
                categoryFilter.DataSource = ds
                categoryFilter.DataBind()
            End Try
            'End If
            headerLabel.Text = "Order History"
        End If

    End Sub

    Protected Sub logout()
        Session("firstName") = Nothing
        Session.Clear()
        Page.Response.Redirect("Logout.aspx")
    End Sub

    Protected Sub passSessionVariable()
        ''''''''''''''''''''''''''''''''''''''''''''''
        ' Open order details page for selected order.
        Page.Response.Redirect("OrderDetails.aspx")
    End Sub

    Protected Sub categoryFilter_RowCommand(ByVal sender As Object, ByVal e As
System.Web.UI.WebControls.GridViewCommandEventArgs) Handles
categoryFilter.RowCommand
        Dim obj As Object
        Dim id As String
        Dim orderID As Integer
        Dim cmdName As String

        cmdName = e.CommandName
        obj = e.CommandArgument
        id = obj.ToString
        orderID = Convert.ToInt16(id.ToString)
        Session("viewOrderID") =
Convert.ToInt16(categoryFilter.DataKeys(orderID).Value.ToString)
```

You may purchase a copy of our companion disk which contains all files for the project at http://www.amazon.com/gp/product/B00AOU76K8!

```
        orderID = Convert.ToInt16(categoryFilter.DataKeys(orderID).Value.ToString)

        Select Case (cmdName)
            Case "Select"
                passSessionVariable()
        End Select
    End Sub
End Class
```

You may purchase a copy of our companion disk which contains all files for the project at http://www.amazon.com/gp/product/B00AOU76K8!

Order Review Server Page

Replace the existing code in the OrderReview.aspx file with the following code (*REPLACE ANY CODE IN THIS COLOR WITH YOUR OWN INFORMATION!*):

```
<%@ Page Language="VB"
    enableEventValidation="false"
    enableViewState="false"
    enableViewStateMac="false"
    AutoEventWireup="True"
    CodeFile="OrderReview.aspx.vb"
    Inherits="_Default" %>

<!DOCTYPE html PUBLIC "-//W3C//DTD XHTML 1.0 Transitional//EN"
"http://www.w3.org/TR/xhtml1/DTD/xhtml1-transitional.dtd">
<html xmlns="http://www.w3.org/1999/xhtml">

<head>
<meta http-equiv="Content-Type" content="text/html; charset=iso-8859-1" />
<title>Review Order</title>
<link rel="stylesheet" href="emx_nav_left.css" type="text/css" />
<script type="text/javascript">

var time = 3000;
var numofitems = 7;

//menu constructor
function menu(allitems,thisitem,startstate){
  callname= "gl"+thisitem;
  divname="subglobal"+thisitem;
  this.numberofmenuitems = allitems;
  this.caller = document.getElementById(callname);
  this.thediv = document.getElementById(divname);
  this.thediv.style.visibility = startstate;
}

//menu methods
function ehandler(event,theobj){
  for (var i=1; i<= theobj.numberofmenuitems; i++){
    var shutdiv =eval( "menuitem"+i+".thediv");
    shutdiv.style.visibility="hidden";
  }
  theobj.thediv.style.visibility="visible";
}
```

```
function closesubnav(event){
 if ((event.clientY <48)||(event.clientY > 107)){
   for (var i=1; i<= numofitems; i++){
     var shutdiv =eval('menuitem'+i+'.thediv');
     shutdiv.style.visibility='hidden';
   }
 }
}
// -->
</script>
</head>
<body>

<form id="Form1" runat="server">
<div class="skipLinks">skip to: <a href="#content">page content</a> | <a
href="#pageNav">links on this page</a> | <a href="#globalNav">site navigation</a> | <a
href="#siteInfo">footer (site information)</a> </div>
<div id="masthead">
 <h1 id="siteName">Your Best Data Solution</h1>
 <div id="utility">
      <asp:LinkButton ID="lkCustomers" runat="server"
PostBackUrl="Customers.aspx">Customers</asp:LinkButton>
    | <asp:LinkButton ID="lkOrders" runat="server"
PostBackUrl="ViewOrders.aspx">Orders</asp:LinkButton>
    | <asp:LinkButton ID="lkAddProduct" PostBackUrl="AddProduct.aspx"
                runat="server">Add Product</asp:LinkButton>
    | <asp:LinkButton ID="lkEditProduct" runat="server"
PostBackUrl="ViewCategories.aspx">Edit Product</asp:LinkButton>
    | <asp:LinkButton ID="lkLogout" OnClick="logout" runat="server"
PostBackUrl="#">Logout</asp:LinkButton>
    | <asp:LinkButton ID="lkChangePassword" PostBackUrl="Password.aspx"
runat="server">Change Password</asp:LinkButton>
 </div>
 <div id="globalNav"> <img alt="" src="Pictures/gblnav_left.gif" height="32" width="4"
id="gnl" /> <img alt="" src="Pictures/glbnav_right.gif" height="32" width="4" id="gnr" />
   <div id="globalLink">
      <a href="Default.aspx" id="A1" class="glink">
      Home</a>
      <a href="ViewCategories.aspx" id="gl1" class="glink" >
      View Products</a>
      <a href="SearchProducts.aspx" id="gl2" class="glink">Search</a>
      <a href="ViewCart.aspx" id="gl3" class="glink">View Cart</a>
      <a href="Checkout.aspx" id="gl4" class="glink">Checkout</a>
      <a href="CreateAccount.aspx" id="gl5" class="glink">Create
      Account</a>
```

```
      <a href="Login.aspx" id="gl6" class="glink">Login
      </a><a href="OrderHistory.aspx" id="gl7" class="glink">Order
      History</a>
      <a href="FAQ.aspx" id="A2" class="glink">FAQ</a>
      <asp:Label ID="loginStatus" Visible="false" runat="server"></asp:Label>
    </div>
  </div>
<div id="pagecell1">
  <img alt="" src="Pictures/tl_curve_white.gif" height="6" width="6" id="tl" /> <img alt=""
src="Pictures/tr_curve_white.gif" height="6" width="6" id="tr" />

    <div id="pageName">
    <img alt="small logo" src="Pictures/YourBestDataSolutionLogo.jpg" height="50"
width="60"/> </div>
  <div id="pageNav">
    <div class="relatedLinks">
      <h3>Related Link Category</h3>
      <a href="FAQ.aspx#anchor3">Automation</a>
      <a href="FAQ.aspx#anchor1">Customized Reporting</a>
      <a href="FAQ.aspx#anchor2">Database Design</a>
      <a href="FAQ.aspx#anchor12">Data Migration</a>
      <a href="FAQ.aspx#anchor4">Data Modeling</a>
      <a href="FAQ.aspx#anchor14">Desktop Application Solutions</a>
      <a href="FAQ.aspx#anchor5">eCommerce Solutions</a>
      <a href="FAQ.aspx#anchor6">eMail Marketing</a>
      <a href="FAQ.aspx#anchor7">Mobile App Development</a>
      <a href="FAQ.aspx#anchor8">PayPal™ Integration</a>
      <a href="FAQ.aspx#anchor9">Web Design</a>
      <a href="FAQ.aspx#anchor10">Web Development</a>
    </div>
  </div>
  <div id="content">
    <div class="feature">
      <h3><asp:Label runat="server" ID="headerLabel"></asp:Label></h3>
        <p>
    <asp:GridView ID ="categoryFilter"
              runat="server"
              DataKeyNames="ProductID"
              OnRowCommand="categoryFilter_RowCommand"
              EditRowStyle-HorizontalAlign="Center"
              HeaderStyle-BackColor="#cccccc"
              BorderStyle="None"
              OnRowDeleted="categoryFilter_RowDeleted"
              OnRowDeleting="categoryFilter_RowDeleting"
              AutoGenerateDeleteButton="false"
              EmptyDataText="No items are currently in your cart." >
```

```
<Columns>
  <asp:TemplateField>
  <ItemTemplate>
  <asp:LinkButton ID="productDetails"
            runat="server"
            CommandName="Select"
            CommandArgument="<%# Container.DataItemIndex %>"
            Text = "Product Details"></asp:LinkButton>
  </ItemTemplate>
  </asp:TemplateField>

  <asp:TemplateField>
  <ItemTemplate>
  <asp:Button CommandArgument="<%# Container.DataItemIndex %>"
          CommandName="deleteItem"
          CausesValidation="true"
          Text="Remove Item"
          runat="server"
          ID="removeItem" />
  </ItemTemplate>
  </asp:TemplateField>
</Columns>
</asp:GridView>
  </p>
<p>
  <asp:Label ID="shipTo" runat="server" Text="Ship to:" Font-
Bold="true"></asp:Label><br />
  <asp:TextBox ID="txtNamePlaceholder" runat="server" Width="100" BorderStyle="None"
Visible="true"></asp:TextBox>
  <asp:TextBox ID="txtName" runat="server" Width="400"
BorderStyle="None"></asp:TextBox><br/>
  <asp:TextBox ID="TextBox2" runat="server" Width="100" BorderStyle="None"
Visible="true"></asp:TextBox>
  <asp:TextBox ID="txtStreetAddress1" runat="server" Width="400"
BorderStyle="None"></asp:TextBox><br />
  <asp:TextBox ID="TextBox4" runat="server" Width="100" BorderStyle="None"
Visible="true"></asp:TextBox>
  <asp:TextBox ID="txtStreetAddress2" runat="server" Width="400"
BorderStyle="None"></asp:TextBox><br />
  <asp:TextBox ID="TextBox3" runat="server" Width="100" BorderStyle="None"
Visible="true"></asp:TextBox>
  <asp:TextBox ID="txtCityStateZip" runat="server" Width="400"
BorderStyle="None"></asp:TextBox>
  <br /><br />
  <asp:Button ID="cmdConfirmPayment" BackColor="SkyBlue" Text="Confirm Payment"
runat="server" OnClick="payNow" />
```

You may purchase a copy of our companion disk which contains all files for the project at http://www.amazon.com/gp/product/B00AOU76K8!

```
      <br />
    </p>
    </div>
    <div class="story">
  <div id="siteInfo"> <img alt="small logo" src="Pictures/YourBestDataSolutionLogo.jpg"
width="59" height="66" />
          <a href="AboutUs.aspx">About Us</a> |
          <a href="ContactUs.aspx">Contact Us</a> |
     ©2012 YBDS, LLC </div>

</div>
<br />
    </form>
</body>
</html>
```

You may purchase a copy of our companion disk which contains all files for the project at http://www.amazon.com/gp/product/B00AOU76K8!

Order Review Code Behind

Replace the existing code in the OrderReview.aspx.vb file with the following code:

```
Imports System.Data
Imports System.Data.SqlClient
Imports System.Net.Mail
Imports Microsoft.VisualBasic

Partial Class _Default
  Inherits System.Web.UI.Page

  Protected Sub Page_Load(ByVal sender As Object, ByVal e As EventArgs) Handles Me.Load


      ''''''''''''''''''''''''''''''''''''''''''''''
      Dim test As New NVPAPICaller()

      Dim retMsg As String = ""
      Dim token As String = Session("token").ToString()
      Dim PayerId As String = ""
      Dim shippingAddress As String = ""
      Dim ret As Boolean = test.GetShippingDetails(token, PayerId, shippingAddress, retMsg)
      Dim splitAddress() As String = Split(shippingAddress, "-")

      If ret Then
        Session("payerId") = PayerId
        ''''''''''''''''''''''''''''''''''''''''''''''''''''''''''''
        ' shippingAddress string parameter returns array of values containing the
        ' shipping address details.
        ' splitAddress(0) = First Name & Last Name
        ' splitAddress(1) = Shipping Address 1
        ' splitAddress(2) = Shipping Address 2
        ' splitAddress(3) = City
        ' splitAddress(4) = State
        ' splitAddress(5) = Zip Code
        ' These values will be used to create the Shipping Address record for the Order.
        ''''''''''''''''''''''''''''''''''''''''''''''''''''''''''''
        ' Check array length to determine if the shippingAddress2 value was passed.
        Select Case splitAddress.Length
          Case 6
            txtName.Text = splitAddress(0)
            txtStreetAddress1.Text = splitAddress(1)
            txtStreetAddress2.Text = splitAddress(2)
```

```
            txtCityStateZip.Text = splitAddress(3) & ", " & splitAddress(4) & " " &
splitAddress(5)
            Session("streetAddress1") = splitAddress(1)
            Session("streetAddress2") = splitAddress(2)
            Session("city") = splitAddress(3)
            Session("postalCode") = splitAddress(5)
          Case 5
            txtName.Text = splitAddress(0)
            txtStreetAddress1.Text = splitAddress(1)
            txtStreetAddress2.Text = splitAddress(2) & ", " & splitAddress(3) & " " &
splitAddress(4)
            ' Formatting trick.  Leave the City, State, Zip textbox
            ' empty and put the value in Street Address 2 textbox
            ' to make the address formatting look correct.
            ' Not the most advanced way to do this, but it will work
            ' for now.
            Session("streetAddress1") = splitAddress(1)
            Session("streetAddress2") = ""
            Session("city") = splitAddress(2)
            Session("postalCode") = splitAddress(4)
            Session("stateAbbreviation") = splitAddress(3).ToString
        End Select
      Else
        Response.Redirect("APIError.aspx?" & retMsg)
      End If

      Dim myAccess As DatabaseAccess
      Dim myConnection As String
      Dim con As SqlConnection
      Dim cmd As SqlCommand
      Dim adapter As SqlDataAdapter
      Dim ds As DataSet
      Dim sql As String
      Dim orderID As String
      Dim readData As SqlDataReader
      Dim itemCount As Integer
      Dim orderTotal As Decimal
      Dim shippingCost As Decimal

      If (Session("firstName") = Nothing) Then
        'User is not logged in.  Continue.
        lkLogout.Visible = False
        lkChangePassword.Visible = False
        lkChangePassword.Enabled = False
        Session("isAdmin") = False
        lkCustomers.Visible = False
```

```
    lkCustomers.Enabled = False
    lkOrders.Visible = False
    lkOrders.Enabled = False
    lkAddProduct.Visible = False
    lkAddProduct.Enabled = False
    lkEditProduct.Visible = False
    lkEditProduct.Enabled = False
Else
    If (Session("isAdmin")) Then
        lkCustomers.Visible = True
        lkCustomers.Enabled = True
        lkOrders.Visible = True
        lkOrders.Enabled = True
        lkAddProduct.Visible = True
        lkAddProduct.Enabled = True
        lkEditProduct.Visible = True
        lkEditProduct.Enabled = True
    Else
        lkCustomers.Visible = False
        lkCustomers.Enabled = False
        lkOrders.Visible = False
        lkOrders.Enabled = False
        lkAddProduct.Visible = False
        lkAddProduct.Enabled = False
        lkEditProduct.Visible = False
        lkEditProduct.Enabled = False
    End If
    lkChangePassword.Visible = True
    lkChangePassword.Enabled = True
    loginStatus.Text = "Welcome " & Session("firstName").ToString() & "!"
    loginStatus.Visible = True
End If

myAccess = New DatabaseAccess()
myConnection = myAccess.getConnectionString()
con = New SqlConnection(myConnection)

orderID = Session("OrderID")
If orderID = Nothing Then
    orderID = -1
End If

myAccess = New DatabaseAccess()
myConnection = myAccess.getConnectionString()

con = New SqlConnection(myConnection)
```

```
sql = "SELECT COUNT(OrderID) AS orderCount FROM OrderDetail " & _
    "WHERE OrderID = " & orderID
cmd = New SqlCommand(sql, con)
cmd.CommandType = Data.CommandType.Text
Try

  ' Open database connection.
  con.Open()

  ' Execute the INSERT and fill the data reader.
  readData = cmd.ExecuteReader(CommandBehavior.CloseConnection)

Catch a As Exception

  Throw a
End Try
readData.Read()
itemCount = readData("orderCount")
con.Close()
readData.Close()

If (Session("OrderID") = Nothing) Or (itemCount = 0) Then
  orderID = -1
  sql = "SELECT p.ProductID, p.ProductName AS Product, " & _
"od.Quantity, '$' + Convert(varchar(12), od.ProductCost) AS [Product Cost] " & _
"FROM Product p " & _
"INNER JOIN OrderDetail od ON od.ProductID = p.ProductID " & _
"WHERE od.OrderID = " & orderID & " " & _
"ORDER BY ProductName ASC"
Else
  orderID = Session("OrderID")
  ''''''''''''''''''''''''''''''''''''''''''''''''''''''''''''''''''''''''''''''''
  ' Get count of records.
  sql = "SELECT COUNT(p.ProductID) AS rowQty " & _
      "FROM Product p " & _
      "INNER JOIN OrderDetail od ON od.ProductID = p.ProductID " & _
      "WHERE od.OrderID = " & orderID & " "
  cmd = New SqlCommand(sql, con)
  cmd.CommandType = Data.CommandType.Text
  Try

    ' Open database connection.
    con.Open()

    ' Execute the INSERT and fill the data reader.
    readData = cmd.ExecuteReader(CommandBehavior.CloseConnection)
```

```
Catch a As Exception

    Throw a
End Try
readData.Read()
Session("rowQty") = readData("rowQty")
readData.Close()
con.Close()
''''''''''''''''''''''''''''''''''''''''''''''''''''''''''

''''''''''''''''''''''''''''''''''''''''''''''''''''''''''
' Get order total.
sql = "SELECT SUM(od.ProductCost) AS OrderTotal" & _
    " FROM Product p " & _
    "INNER JOIN OrderDetail od ON od.ProductID = p.ProductID " & _
    "WHERE od.OrderID = " & orderID & " "
cmd = New SqlCommand(sql, con)
cmd.CommandType = Data.CommandType.Text
Try

    ' Open database connection.
    con.Open()

    ' Execute the INSERT and fill the data reader.
    readData = cmd.ExecuteReader(CommandBehavior.CloseConnection)

Catch a As Exception

    Throw a
End Try
readData.Read()
Session("orderTotal") = readData("OrderTotal")
readData.Close()
con.Close()

orderTotal = Convert.ToDecimal(Session("orderTotal").ToString())
Session("productTotal") = orderTotal
shippingCost = Convert.ToDecimal(Session("shippingCost").ToString())
orderTotal = orderTotal + shippingCost
''''''''''''''''''''''''''''''''''''''''''''''''''''''''''

''''''''''''''''''''''''''''''''''''''''''''''''''''''''
sql = "SELECT p.ProductID, od.OrderID, p.ProductName AS Product, " & _
    "od.Quantity, '$' + Convert(varchar(12), p.Price) AS [Unit Price], '$' +
Convert(varchar(12),  od.ProductCost) AS [Total] " & _
```

```
                "FROM Product p " & _
                "INNER JOIN OrderDetail od ON od.ProductID = p.ProductID " & _
                "WHERE od.OrderID = " & orderID & " " & _
                " UNION SELECT NULL AS ProductID, ", 'Order Sub Total', " & _
                "NULL, ", '$' + Convert(varchar(12), " & FormatNumber(Session("productTotal"), 2)
& ") " & _
                " FROM Product p " & _
                " UNION SELECT NULL AS ProductID, ", " & Chr(39) & "Shipping method - " &
Session("shippingMethodName").ToString() & Chr(39) & " AS ProductName, NULL, ", '$ ' +
Convert(varchar(12), SUM(ShippingCost)) FROM ShippingMethod WHERE
ShippingMethodID = " & Session("shippingMethodID") & _
                " UNION SELECT NULL AS ProductID, ", " & Chr(39) & "Sales Tax Rate - " &
Session("salesTaxRate").ToString() & Chr(39) & " AS ProductName, NULL, ", '$ ' +
Convert(varchar(12), " & FormatNumber(orderTotal * Session("salesTaxRate"), 2) & ") FROM
UserOrder WHERE OrderID = " & Session("OrderID") & _
                " UNION SELECT NULL AS ProductID, ", 'Totals', " & _
                "SUM(Quantity), ", '$' + Convert(varchar(12), " & FormatNumber(orderTotal +
(orderTotal * Session("salesTaxRate")), 2) & ") " & _
                " FROM Product p " & _
                "INNER JOIN OrderDetail od ON od.ProductID = p.ProductID " & _
                "WHERE od.OrderID = " & orderID & " " & _
                "ORDER BY OrderID DESC, ProductName ASC"
    End If

    cmd = New SqlCommand(sql, con)
    cmd.CommandType = Data.CommandType.Text

    adapter = New SqlDataAdapter(cmd)

    ' Fill the DataSet.
    ds = New DataSet()

    Try
      ' Open the database connection.
      con.Open()
      adapter.Fill(ds, sql)
    Finally

      con.Close()

      ' Perform the data binding.
      categoryFilter.DataSource = ds
      categoryFilter.DataBind()
    End Try
    Session("currentOrderTotal") = FormatNumber(orderTotal + (orderTotal *
Session("salesTaxRate")), 2)
```

You may purchase a copy of our companion disk which contains all files for the project at http://www.amazon.com/gp/product/B00AOU76K8!

```
        Session("payment_amt") = Session("currentOrderTotal")
        headerLabel.Text = "Shopping Cart"
    End Sub

    Protected Sub payNow()

        Dim test As New NVPAPICaller()
        Dim retMsg As String = ""
        Dim token As String = ""
        Dim finalPaymentAmount As String = ""
        Dim payerId As String
        Dim decoder As New NVPCodec()

        token = Session("token").ToString()
        payerId = Session("payerId").ToString

        finalPaymentAmount = Session("payment_amt").ToString()

        Dim ret As Boolean = test.ConfirmPayment(finalPaymentAmount, token, payerId, decoder,
retMsg)

        If ret Then
            ' Unique transaction ID of the payment. Note: If the PaymentAction of the request was
Authorization or Order, this value is your AuthorizationID for use with the Authorization &
Capture APIs.
            Dim transactionId As String = decoder("TRANSACTIONID")

            ' The type of transaction Possible values: l cart l express-checkout
            Dim transactionType As String = decoder("TRANSACTIONTYPE")

            ' Indicates whether the payment is instant or delayed. Possible values: l none l echeck l
instant
            Dim paymentType As String = decoder("PAYMENTTYPE")

            ' Time/date stamp of payment
            Dim orderTime As String = decoder("ORDERTIME")

            ' The final amount charged, including any shipping and taxes from your Merchant Profile.
            Dim amt As String = decoder("AMT")

            ' A three-character currency code for one of the currencies listed in PayPay-Supported
Transactional Currencies. Default: USD.
            Dim currencyCode As String = decoder("CURRENCYCODE")

            ' PayPal™ fee amount charged for the transaction
            Dim feeAmt As String = decoder("FEEAMT")
```

```
' Amount deposited in your PayPal™ account after a currency conversion.
Dim settleAmt As String = decoder("SETTLEAMT")

' Tax charged on the transaction.
Dim taxAmt As String = decoder("TAXAMT")

'' Exchange rate if a currency conversion occurred. Relevant only if your are billing in
their non-primary currency. If
Dim exchangeRate As String = decoder("EXCHANGERATE")

Dim myAccess As DatabaseAccess
Dim myConnection As String
Dim con As SqlConnection
Dim cmd As SqlCommand
Dim sql As String
Dim readData As SqlDataReader
Dim shippingCost As Decimal

' Set up the database connections.
myAccess = New DatabaseAccess()
myConnection = myAccess.getConnectionString()
con = New SqlConnection(myConnection)

'''''''''''''''''GET STATE ID''''''''''''''''''''''''''''''''''''''''
sql = "SELECT StateID FROM USState " & _
    "WHERE StateAbbreviation = '" & Session("stateAbbreviation").ToString & "'"
cmd = New SqlCommand(sql, con)
cmd.CommandType = Data.CommandType.Text
Try

    ' Open database connection.
    con.Open()

    ' Execute the INSERT and fill the data reader.
    readData = cmd.ExecuteReader(CommandBehavior.CloseConnection)

Catch a As Exception

    Throw a
End Try
readData.Read()
Session("stateID") = readData("StateID").ToString
readData.Close()
con.Close()
'''''''''''''''''END GET STATE ID'''''''''''''''''''''''''''''''''''
```

You may purchase a copy of our companion disk which contains all files for the project at http://www.amazon.com/gp/product/B00AOU76K8!

```
''''''''''''''''GET COUNTRY ID''''''''''''''''''''''''''''''
' Get Country ID.   - Initially, I'll just set this at 1 for USA.

''''''''''''''''END COUNTRY ID''''''''''''''''''''''''''''''

''''''''''''''''INSERT USER SHIPPING ADDRESS''''''''''''''''
' Address Type of <shipping> = 1.
' Insert User Address.
sql = "INSERT INTO UserAddress " & _
      "(UserID, StreetAddress1, StreetAddress2, " & _
      "City, StateID, CountryID, PostalCode, " & _
      "PostalCode2, AddressType) " & _
      "VALUES (" & Session("userID") & ", '" & _
    Session("streetAddress1") & "', '" & _
    Session("streetAddress2") & "', '" & _
    Session("city") & "', " & _
    Session("stateID") & ", " & _
    1 & ", '" & _
    Session("postalCode") & "', ' ', 2)"
cmd = New SqlCommand(sql, con)
cmd.CommandType = Data.CommandType.Text
Try

    ' Open database connection.
    con.Open()

    ' Execute the INSERT and fill the data reader.
    readData = cmd.ExecuteReader(CommandBehavior.CloseConnection)

Catch a As Exception

    Throw a
End Try
readData.Close()
con.Close()
''''''''''''''''END INSERT USER SHIPPING ADDRESS''''''''''''''''

''''''''''''''''GET USER SHIPPING ADDRESS''''''''''''''''''''''
' Get User AddressID and assign it to Session("ShippingAddressID").
sql = "SELECT MAX(AddressID) AS id FROM UserAddress " & _
      "WHERE UserID = '" & Session("userID") & "' " & _
      "AND AddressType = 2"
cmd = New SqlCommand(sql, con)
cmd.CommandType = Data.CommandType.Text
Try
```

```
        ' Open database connection.
        con.Open()

        ' Execute the INSERT and fill the data reader.
        readData = cmd.ExecuteReader(CommandBehavior.CloseConnection)

    Catch a As Exception

        Throw a
    End Try
    readData.Read()
    Session("ShippingAddressID") = readData("id").ToString
    readData.Close()
    con.Close()
    '''''''''''''''''END GET USER SHIPPING ADDRESS''''''''''''''''''''


    ' Change the status of the order to 'Paid' in the database.
    sql = "SELECT ShippingCost FROM ShippingMethod " & _
        "WHERE ShippingMethodID = " & Session("shippingMethodID") & " "
    cmd = New SqlCommand(sql, con)
    cmd.CommandType = Data.CommandType.Text
    Try

        ' Open database connection.
        con.Open()

        ' Execute the INSERT and fill the data reader.
        readData = cmd.ExecuteReader(CommandBehavior.CloseConnection)

    Catch a As Exception

        Throw a
    End Try
    readData.Read()
    shippingCost = Convert.ToDecimal(readData("ShippingCost").ToString)
    readData.Close()
    con.Close()

    ' Change the status of the order to 'Paid' in the database.
    sql = "UPDATE UserOrder SET " & _
        "UserID = " & Convert.ToInt16(Session("UserID").ToString) & ", " & _
        "OrderStatusID = 1,  " & _
        "ShippingCost = " & shippingCost & ", " & _
        "OrderStatusUpdateDate = '" & Now().ToString & "', " & _
```

```
"OrderStatusUpdateUserID = " & Convert.ToInt16(Session("UserID").ToString) & ", " & _
"BillingAddressID = " & Session("BillingAddressID").ToString & ", " & _
"ShippingAddressID = " & Session("ShippingAddressID").ToString & " " & _
        " WHERE OrderID = " & Session("OrderID") & " "
    cmd = New SqlCommand(sql, con)
    cmd.CommandType = Data.CommandType.Text
    Try

        ' Open database connection.
        con.Open()

        ' Execute the INSERT and fill the data reader.
        readData = cmd.ExecuteReader(CommandBehavior.CloseConnection)

    Catch a As Exception

        Throw a
    End Try
    readData.Read()
    readData.Close()
    con.Close()

    ' Present the user with a final receipt / invoice.
    Page.Response.Redirect("OrderConfirmation.aspx")
    Session("firstLoad") = 1
  Else
    Response.Redirect("APIError.aspx?" & retMsg)
  End If
End Sub

Protected Sub logout()
  Session("firstName") = Nothing
  Session.Clear()
  Page.Response.Redirect("Logout.aspx")
End Sub

Protected Sub categoryFilter_RowCommand(ByVal sender As Object, ByVal e As
System.Web.UI.WebControls.GridViewCommandEventArgs) Handles
categoryFilter.RowCommand
    Dim obj As Object
    Dim id As String
    Dim ProductID As Integer
    Dim cmdName As String

    cmdName = e.CommandName
    obj = e.CommandArgument
```

You may purchase a copy of our companion disk which contains all files for the project at http://www.amazon.com/gp/product/B00AOU76K8!

```
        id = obj.ToString
        ProductID = Convert.ToInt16(id.ToString)
        Session("ProductID") =
Convert.ToInt16(categoryFilter.DataKeys(ProductID).Value.ToString)
        ProductID = Convert.ToInt16(categoryFilter.DataKeys(ProductID).Value.ToString)

        Select Case (cmdName)
            Case "Select"
                passSessionVariable()
            Case "Delete"
        End Select
    End Sub

    Protected Sub categoryFilter_RowDataBound(ByVal sender As Object, ByVal e As
System.Web.UI.WebControls.GridViewRowEventArgs) Handles categoryFilter.RowDataBound

        Dim myAccess As DatabaseAccess
        Dim myConnection As String
        Dim con As SqlConnection
        Dim cmd As SqlCommand
        Dim sql As String
        Dim readData As SqlDataReader
        Dim itemCount As Integer
        Dim orderID As Integer

        orderID = Session("OrderID")
        If orderID = Nothing Then
            orderID = -1
        End If

        myAccess = New DatabaseAccess()
        myConnection = myAccess.getConnectionString()

        con = New SqlConnection(myConnection)
        sql = "SELECT COUNT(OrderID) AS orderCount FROM OrderDetail " & _
            "WHERE OrderID = " & orderID
        cmd = New SqlCommand(sql, con)
        cmd.CommandType = Data.CommandType.Text
        Try

            ' Open database connection.
            con.Open()

            ' Execute the INSERT and fill the data reader.
            readData = cmd.ExecuteReader(CommandBehavior.CloseConnection)
```

```
    Catch a As Exception

        Throw a
    End Try
    readData.Read()
    itemCount = readData("orderCount")
    con.Close()
    readData.Close()

    If (Session("OrderID") <> Nothing) And (itemCount > 0) Then
        e.Row.Cells(1).Visible = False
        e.Row.Cells(2).Visible = False
    End If

    If (e.Row.RowIndex = Session("rowQty")) Then
        e.Row.Cells(0).Text = ""
        e.Row.Cells(1).Text = ""
    End If

    If (e.Row.RowIndex = Session("rowQty") + 1) Then
        e.Row.Cells(0).Text = ""
        e.Row.Cells(1).Text = ""
    End If

    If (e.Row.RowIndex = Session("rowQty") + 2) Then
        e.Row.Cells(0).Text = ""
        e.Row.Cells(1).Text = ""
    End If

  End Sub

  Protected Sub passSessionVariable()
     Page.Response.Redirect("ProductDetails.aspx")
  End Sub

  Protected Sub categoryFilter_RowDeleted(ByVal sender As Object, ByVal e As
System.Web.UI.WebControls.GridViewDeletedEventArgs) Handles categoryFilter.RowDeleted

  End Sub

  Protected Sub categoryFilter_RowDeleting(ByVal sender As Object, ByVal e As
System.Web.UI.WebControls.GridViewDeleteEventArgs) Handles categoryFilter.RowDeleting

  End Sub
```

You may purchase a copy of our companion disk which contains all files for the project at http://www.amazon.com/gp/product/B00AOU76K8!

```
End Class
```

Password Server Page

Replace the existing code in the Password.aspx file with the following code (***REPLACE ANY CODE IN THIS COLOR WITH YOUR OWN INFORMATION!)***:

```
<%@ Page Language="VB"
        AutoEventWireup="True"
        CodeFile="Password.aspx.vb"
        Inherits="_Default" %>

<!DOCTYPE html PUBLIC "-//W3C//DTD XHTML 1.0 Transitional//EN"
"http://www.w3.org/TR/xhtml1/DTD/xhtml1-transitional.dtd">
<html xmlns="http://www.w3.org/1999/xhtml">

<head>
<meta http-equiv="Content-Type" content="text/html; charset=iso-8859-1" />
<title>Password</title>
<link rel="stylesheet" href="emx_nav_left.css" type="text/css" />
<script type="text/javascript">

var time = 3000;
var numofitems = 7;

//menu constructor
function menu(allitems,thisitem,startstate){
  callname= "gl"+thisitem;
  divname="subglobal"+thisitem;
  this.numberofmenuitems = allitems;
  this.caller = document.getElementById(callname);
  this.thediv = document.getElementById(divname);
  this.thediv.style.visibility = startstate;
}

//menu methods
function ehandler(event,theobj){
  for (var i=1; i<= theobj.numberofmenuitems; i++){
    var shutdiv =eval( "menuitem"+i+".thediv");
    shutdiv.style.visibility="hidden";
  }
  theobj.thediv.style.visibility="visible";
}

function closesubnav(event){
  if ((event.clientY <48)||(event.clientY > 107)){
```

You may purchase a copy of our companion disk which contains all files for the project at http://www.amazon.com/gp/product/B00AOU76K8!

```
    for (var i=1; i<= numofitems; i++){
      var shutdiv =eval('menuitem'+i+'.thediv');
      shutdiv.style.visibility='hidden';
    }
  }
}
</script>
</head>
<body>

<form id="Form1" runat="server">
<div class="skipLinks">skip to: <a href="#content">page content</a> | <a
href="#pageNav">links on this page</a> | <a href="#globalNav">site navigation</a> | <a
href="#siteInfo">footer (site information)</a> </div>
<div id="masthead">
  <h1 id="siteName">Your Best Data Solution</h1>
  <div id="utility">
      <asp:LinkButton ID="lkCustomers" runat="server"
PostBackUrl="Customers.aspx">Customers</asp:LinkButton>
     | <asp:LinkButton ID="lkOrders" runat="server"
PostBackUrl="ViewOrders.aspx">Orders</asp:LinkButton>
     | <asp:LinkButton ID="lkAddProduct" PostBackUrl="AddProduct.aspx"
                runat="server">Add Product</asp:LinkButton>
     | <asp:LinkButton ID="lkEditProduct" runat="server"
PostBackUrl="ViewCategories.aspx">Edit Product</asp:LinkButton>
     | <asp:LinkButton ID="lkLogout" OnClick="logout" runat="server"
PostBackUrl="#">Logout</asp:LinkButton>
     | <asp:LinkButton ID="lkChangePassword" PostBackUrl="Password.aspx"
runat="server">Change Password</asp:LinkButton>
  </div>
  <div id="globalNav"> <img alt="" src="Pictures/gblnav_left.gif" height="32" width="4"
id="gnl" /> <img alt="" src="Pictures/glbnav_right.gif" height="32" width="4" id="gnr" />
    <div id="globalLink">
      <a href="Default.aspx" id="A1" class="glink">
      Home</a>
      <a href="ViewCategories.aspx" id="gl1" class="glink" >
      View Products</a>
      <a href="SearchProducts.aspx" id="gl2" class="glink">Search</a>
      <a href="ViewCart.aspx" id="gl3" class="glink">View Cart</a>
      <a href="Checkout.aspx" id="gl4" class="glink">Checkout</a>
      <a href="CreateAccount.aspx" id="gl5" class="glink">Create
      Account</a>
      <a href="Login.aspx" id="gl6" class="glink">Login
      </a><a href="OrderHistory.aspx" id="gl7" class="glink">Order
      History</a>
      <a href="FAQ.aspx" id="A2" class="glink">FAQ</a>
```

```
        <asp:Label ID="loginStatus" Visible="false" runat="server"></asp:Label>
      </div>
    </div>
  <div id="pagecell1">
    <img alt="" src="Pictures/tl_curve_white.gif" height="6" width="6" id="tl" /> <img alt=""
src="Pictures/tr_curve_white.gif" height="6" width="6" id="tr" />

      <div id="pageName">
      <img alt="small logo" src="Pictures/YourBestDataSolutionLogo.jpg" height="50"
width="60"/> </div>
    <div id="pageNav">
      <div class="relatedLinks">
        <h3>Related Link Category</h3>
        <a href="FAQ.aspx#anchor3">Automation</a>
        <a href="FAQ.aspx#anchor1">Customized Reporting</a>
        <a href="FAQ.aspx#anchor2">Database Design</a>
        <a href="FAQ.aspx#anchor12">Data Migration</a>
        <a href="FAQ.aspx#anchor4">Data Modeling</a>
        <a href="FAQ.aspx#anchor14">Desktop Application Solutions</a>
        <a href="FAQ.aspx#anchor5">eCommerce Solutions</a>
        <a href="FAQ.aspx#anchor6">eMail Marketing</a>
        <a href="FAQ.aspx#anchor7">Mobile App Development</a>
        <a href="FAQ.aspx#anchor8">PayPal™ Integration</a>
        <a href="FAQ.aspx#anchor9">Web Design</a>
        <a href="FAQ.aspx#anchor10">Web Development</a>
      </div>
    </div>
    <div id="content">
      <div class="feature">
        <h3>Login</h3>
         <p> <asp:Label ID="paragraph1"
               runat="server" >Sign into your account </asp:Label> </p>
         <p>
         <p>
            <asp:Label ID="lblPassword"
               runat="server" Text="Enter new password" Width="100"></asp:Label>
             <asp:TextBox ID="txtPassword"
                    runat="server"
                    TextMode="Password"
                    Width="200"></asp:TextBox>
             <asp:Label ID="passwordRequired"
                  runat="server" Visible="false"></asp:Label>
             <br />
             <br />
             <asp:Label ID="lblConfirmPassword"
                  runat="server"
```

You may purchase a copy of our companion disk which contains all files for the project at http://www.amazon.com/gp/product/B00AOU76K8!

```
            Text="Confirm New Password " Width="100"></asp:Label>
        <asp:TextBox ID="txtConfirmPassword"
             TextMode="Password"
             runat="server"
             Width="200"></asp:TextBox>
        <asp:Label ID="confirmPasswordRequired"
            runat="server" Visible="false"></asp:Label>
        <br />
        <br />
        <asp:Button
           runat="server"
           OnClick="updatePassword"
           ID="cmdUpdatePassword"
           Text="Update Password" />
      </p>
    </div>
    <div class="story">
  <div id="siteInfo"> <img alt="small logo" src="Pictures/YourBestDataSolutionLogo.jpg"
width="59" height="66" />
        <a href="AboutUs.aspx">About Us</a> |
        <a href="ContactUs.aspx">Contact Us</a> |
    ©2012 YBDS, LLC </div>

</div>
<br />
   </form>
</body>
</html>
```

You may purchase a copy of our companion disk which contains all files for the project at http://www.amazon.com/gp/product/B00AOU76K8!

Password Code Behind

Replace the existing code in the Password.aspx.vb file with the following code:

```
Imports System.Data
Imports System.Data.SqlClient

Partial Class _Default
   Inherits System.Web.UI.Page

   Protected Sub Page_Load(ByVal sender As Object, ByVal e As EventArgs) Handles Me.Load

      If (Session("firstName") = Nothing) Then
         'User is not logged in.  Continue.
         lkLogout.Visible = False
         lkChangePassword.Visible = False
         lkChangePassword.Enabled = False
         Session("isAdmin") = False
         lkCustomers.Visible = False
         lkCustomers.Enabled = False
         lkOrders.Visible = False
         lkOrders.Enabled = False
         lkAddProduct.Visible = False
         lkAddProduct.Enabled = False
         lkEditProduct.Visible = False
         lkEditProduct.Enabled = False
         Page.Response.Redirect("UserMessage.aspx")
      Else
         If (Session("isAdmin")) Then
            lkCustomers.Visible = True
            lkCustomers.Enabled = True
            lkOrders.Visible = True
            lkOrders.Enabled = True
            lkAddProduct.Visible = True
            lkAddProduct.Enabled = True
            lkEditProduct.Visible = True
            lkEditProduct.Enabled = True
         Else
            lkCustomers.Visible = False
            lkCustomers.Enabled = False
            lkOrders.Visible = False
            lkOrders.Enabled = False
            lkAddProduct.Visible = False
            lkAddProduct.Enabled = False
```

```
            lkEditProduct.Visible = False
            lkEditProduct.Enabled = False
        End If
        lkChangePassword.Visible = True
        lkChangePassword.Enabled = True
        loginStatus.Text = "Welcome " & Session("firstName").ToString() & "!"
        Exit Sub
    End If

End Sub

Protected Sub updatePassword()

    Dim myConnection As String
    Dim cmd As SqlCommand
    Dim con As SqlConnection
    Dim myAccess As DatabaseAccess
    Dim sql As String
    Dim readData As SqlDataReader

    ' Set variables for use in binding.
    myAccess = New DatabaseAccess()
    myConnection = myAccess.getConnectionString()
    con = New SqlConnection(myConnection)

    If Not (allFieldsArePopulated()) Then Exit Sub

    sql = "UPDATE [User] " & _
        "SET Password = '" & txtPassword.Text & "'" & _
        " WHERE UserID = '" & Session("UserID").ToString() & "'"
    cmd = New SqlCommand(sql, con)
    cmd.CommandType = Data.CommandType.Text
    Try

        ' Open database connection.
        con.Open()
        Session("passwordChanged") = False
        ' Execute the INSERT and fill the data reader.
        readData = cmd.ExecuteReader(CommandBehavior.CloseConnection)

    Catch a As Exception
        Throw a
    End Try
    readData.Read()
    Session("passwordChanged") = True
    readData.Close()
```

You may purchase a copy of our companion disk which contains all files for the project at http://www.amazon.com/gp/product/B00AOU76K8!

```
        con.Close()
        Page.Response.Redirect("UserMessage.aspx")
    End Sub

    Protected Sub logout()
        Session("firstName") = Nothing
        Session.Clear()
        Page.Response.Redirect("Logout.aspx")
    End Sub

    Protected Function allFieldsArePopulated() As Boolean
        If (txtPassword.Text = "") Then
            passwordRequired.Text = "Please enter user name."
            passwordRequired.Visible = True
            txtPassword.Focus()
            allFieldsArePopulated = False
            txtConfirmPassword.Text = ""
            Exit Function
        Else
            passwordRequired.Visible = False
        End If
        If (txtConfirmPassword.Text = "") Then
            confirmPasswordRequired.Text = "Please enter password."
            confirmPasswordRequired.Visible = True
            txtConfirmPassword.Focus()
            txtPassword.Text = ""
            allFieldsArePopulated = False
            Exit Function
        Else
            confirmPasswordRequired.Visible = False
        End If

        If (txtConfirmPassword.Text <> txtPassword.Text) Then
            passwordRequired.Text = "Passwords do not match.  Please re-type your new password
for confirmation."
            passwordRequired.Visible = True
            allFieldsArePopulated = False
            Exit Function
        End If
        allFieldsArePopulated = True
    End Function


End Class
```

You may purchase a copy of our companion disk which contains all files for the project at http://www.amazon.com/gp/product/B00AOU76K8!

Product Details Server Page

Replace the existing code in the ProductDetails.aspx file with the following code (*REPLACE ANY CODE IN THIS COLOR WITH YOUR OWN INFORMATION!*):

```
<%@ Page Language="VB"
      AutoEventWireup="True"
      CodeFile="ProductDetails.aspx.vb"
      Inherits="_Default" %>

<!DOCTYPE html PUBLIC "-//W3C//DTD XHTML 1.0 Transitional//EN"
"http://www.w3.org/TR/xhtml1/DTD/xhtml1-transitional.dtd">
<html xmlns="http://www.w3.org/1999/xhtml">

<head>
<meta http-equiv="Content-Type" content="text/html; charset=iso-8859-1" />
<title>Product Details</title>
<link rel="stylesheet" href="emx_nav_left.css" type="text/css" />
<script type="text/javascript">

var time = 3000;
var numofitems = 7;

//menu constructor
function menu(allitems,thisitem,startstate){
  callname= "gl"+thisitem;
  divname="subglobal"+thisitem;
  this.numberofmenuitems = allitems;
  this.caller = document.getElementById(callname);
  this.thediv = document.getElementById(divname);
  this.thediv.style.visibility = startstate;
}

//menu methods
function ehandler(event,theobj){
  for (var i=1; i<= theobj.numberofmenuitems; i++){
    var shutdiv =eval( "menuitem"+i+".thediv");
    shutdiv.style.visibility="hidden";
  }
  theobj.thediv.style.visibility="visible";
}

function closesubnav(event){
  if ((event.clientY <48)||(event.clientY > 107)){
```

```
    for (var i=1; i<= numofitems; i++){
     var shutdiv =eval('menuitem'+i+'.thediv');
     shutdiv.style.visibility='hidden';
    }
  }
}
// -->
</script>
</head>
<body>

<form id="Form1" runat="server">
<div class="skipLinks">skip to: <a href="#content">page content</a> | <a
href="#pageNav">links on this page</a> | <a href="#globalNav">site navigation</a> | <a
href="#siteInfo">footer (site information)</a> </div>
<div id="masthead">
  <h1 id="siteName">Your Best Data Solution</h1>
  <div id="utility">
       <asp:LinkButton ID="lkCustomers" runat="server"
PostBackUrl="Customers.aspx">Customers</asp:LinkButton>
     | <asp:LinkButton ID="lkOrders" runat="server"
PostBackUrl="ViewOrders.aspx">Orders</asp:LinkButton>
     | <asp:LinkButton ID="lkAddProduct" PostBackUrl="AddProduct.aspx"
                    runat="server">Add Product</asp:LinkButton>
     | <asp:LinkButton ID="lkEditProduct" runat="server"
PostBackUrl="ViewCategories.aspx">Edit Product</asp:LinkButton>
     | <asp:LinkButton ID="lkLogout" OnClick="logout" runat="server"
PostBackUrl="#">Logout</asp:LinkButton>
     | <asp:LinkButton ID="lkChangePassword" PostBackUrl="Password.aspx"
runat="server">Change Password</asp:LinkButton>
  </div>
  <div id="globalNav"> <img alt="" src="Pictures/gblnav_left.gif" height="32" width="4"
id="gnl" /> <img alt="" src="Pictures/glbnav_right.gif" height="32" width="4" id="gnr" />
    <div id="globalLink">
        <a href="Default.aspx" id="A1" class="glink">
        Home</a>
        <a href="ViewCategories.aspx" id="gl1" class="glink" >
        View Products</a>
        <a href="SearchProducts.aspx" id="gl2" class="glink">Search</a>
        <a href="ViewCart.aspx" id="gl3" class="glink">View Cart</a>
        <a href="Checkout.aspx" id="gl4" class="glink">Checkout</a>
        <a href="CreateAccount.aspx" id="gl5" class="glink">Create
        Account</a>
        <a href="Login.aspx" id="gl6" class="glink">Login
        </a><a href="OrderHistory.aspx" id="gl7" class="glink">Order
        History</a>
```

```
      <a href="FAQ.aspx" id="A2" class="glink">FAQ</a>
      <asp:Label ID="loginStatus" Visible="false" runat="server"></asp:Label>
    </div>
  </div>
<div id="pagecell1">
  <img alt="" src="Pictures/tl_curve_white.gif" height="6" width="6" id="tl" /> <img alt=""
src="Pictures/tr_curve_white.gif" height="6" width="6" id="tr" />

    <div id="pageName">
    <img alt="small logo" src="Pictures/YourBestDataSolutionLogo.jpg" height="50"
width="60"/> </div>
  <div id="pageNav">
    <div class="relatedLinks">
      <h3>Related Link Category</h3>
      <a href="FAQ.aspx#anchor3">Automation</a>
      <a href="FAQ.aspx#anchor1">Customized Reporting</a>
      <a href="FAQ.aspx#anchor2">Database Design</a>
      <a href="FAQ.aspx#anchor12">Data Migration</a>
      <a href="FAQ.aspx#anchor4">Data Modeling</a>
      <a href="FAQ.aspx#anchor14">Desktop Application Solutions</a>
      <a href="FAQ.aspx#anchor5">eCommerce Solutions</a>
      <a href="FAQ.aspx#anchor6">eMail Marketing</a>
      <a href="FAQ.aspx#anchor7">Mobile App Development</a>
      <a href="FAQ.aspx#anchor8">PayPal™ Integration</a>
      <a href="FAQ.aspx#anchor9">Web Design</a>
      <a href="FAQ.aspx#anchor10">Web Development</a>
    </div>
  </div>
  <div id="content">
    <div class="feature">
      <h3><asp:Label runat="server" ID="headerLabel"></asp:Label></h3>
      <p>
      <asp:Image ID ="productPicture"
              runat="server"
              Height ="330"
              Width="295" />
      </p>
    </div>
    <div class="story">
          <p>
          <asp:Label ID="qtyWarning"
                  runat="server"
                  Visible="false"></asp:Label>
    <asp:GridView ID ="categoryFilter"
              runat="server"
              DataKeyNames="ProductID"
```

You may purchase a copy of our companion disk which contains all files for the project at http://www.amazon.com/gp/product/B00AOU76K8!

```
        OnRowDataBound="categoryFilter_RowDataBound"
        OnRowCommand="categoryFilter_RowCommand"
        EditRowStyle-HorizontalAlign="Center"
        RowStyle-HorizontalAlign="Center"
        HeaderStyle-BackColor="#cccccc">
    <Columns>
      <asp:TemplateField HeaderText="Buy It Now!"
                  HeaderStyle-CssClass="storyCentered"
                  ControlStyle-CssClass="storyCentered"
                  ItemStyle-CssClass="storyCentered">
      <ItemTemplate>
      <asp:LinkButton ID="LinkButton4"
                runat="server"
                CommandName="Select"
                CommandArgument="<%# Container.DataItemIndex %>"
                Text = "Add To Cart"
                CssClass="storyCentered"></asp:LinkButton>
      </ItemTemplate>
      </asp:TemplateField>

      <asp:TemplateField HeaderText="Purchase Qty"
                  HeaderStyle-CssClass="storyCentered"
                  ControlStyle-CssClass="storyCentered"
                  ItemStyle-CssClass="storyCentered">
      <ItemTemplate>
      <asp:TextBox ID="purchaseQty"
               runat="server"
               Width="25"
               CssClass="storyCentered"></asp:TextBox>
      </ItemTemplate>
      </asp:TemplateField>
    </Columns>
  </asp:GridView>
  <br />
  <br />
  <br />
  <asp:LinkButton ID="editProduct" runat="server"
          PostBackUrl="~/EditProduct.aspx"
          Text="Edit Product" CssClass="storyCentered"
          Visible="false" ></asp:LinkButton>
    </p>
 <div id="siteInfo"> <img alt="small logo" src="Pictures/YourBestDataSolutionLogo.jpg"
width="59" height="66" />
      <a href="AboutUs.aspx">About Us</a> |
      <a href="ContactUs.aspx">Contact Us</a> |
   ©2012 YBDS, LLC </div>
```

You may purchase a copy of our companion disk which contains all files for the project at http://www.amazon.com/gp/product/B00AOU76K8!

```
</div>
<br />
   </form>
</body>
</html>
```

Product Details Code Behind

Replace the existing code in the ProductDetails.aspx.vb file with the following code:

```
Imports System.Data
Imports System.Net
Imports System.Web.HttpRequest
Imports DatabaseAccess
Imports System.Data.SqlClient

Partial Class _Default
   Inherits System.Web.UI.Page

   Protected Sub Page_Load(ByVal sender As Object, ByVal e As EventArgs) Handles Me.Load

      Dim myAccess As DatabaseAccess
      Dim myConnection As String
      Dim con As SqlConnection
      Dim cmd As SqlCommand
      Dim adapter As SqlDataAdapter
      Dim ds As DataSet
      Dim sql As String


      If (Session("firstName") = Nothing) Then
         'User is not logged in.  Continue.
         lkLogout.Visible = False
         lkChangePassword.Visible = False
         lkChangePassword.Enabled = False
         Session("isAdmin") = False
         lkCustomers.Visible = False
         lkCustomers.Enabled = False
         lkOrders.Visible = False
         lkOrders.Enabled = False
         lkAddProduct.Visible = False
         lkAddProduct.Enabled = False
         lkEditProduct.Visible = False
         lkEditProduct.Enabled = False
         editProduct.Visible = False
         editProduct.Enabled = False
      Else
         If (Session("isAdmin")) Then
            lkCustomers.Visible = True
            lkCustomers.Enabled = True
```

You may purchase a copy of our companion disk which contains all files for the project at http://www.amazon.com/gp/product/B00AOU76K8!

```
            lkOrders.Visible = True
            lkOrders.Enabled = True
            lkAddProduct.Visible = True
            lkAddProduct.Enabled = True
            lkEditProduct.Visible = True
            lkEditProduct.Enabled = True
            lkEditProduct.Visible = True
            editProduct.Visible = True
            editProduct.Enabled = True
        Else
            lkCustomers.Visible = False
            lkCustomers.Enabled = False
            lkOrders.Visible = False
            lkOrders.Enabled = False
            lkAddProduct.Visible = False
            lkAddProduct.Enabled = False
            lkEditProduct.Visible = False
            lkEditProduct.Enabled = False
            editProduct.Visible = False
            editProduct.Enabled = False
        End If
        lkChangePassword.Visible = True
        lkChangePassword.Enabled = True
        loginStatus.Text = "Welcome " & Session("firstName").ToString() & "!"
        loginStatus.Visible = True
    End If

    myAccess = New DatabaseAccess()
    myConnection = myAccess.getConnectionString()

    con = New SqlConnection(myConnection)
    sql = "SELECT ProductID, DescriptionFull AS Description,  '$' + Convert(varchar(12),
Price) AS Price, QuantityAvailable AS [Qty Available] " & _
        "FROM Product " & _
        "WHERE ProductID = " & Session("ProductID") & " "

    cmd = New SqlCommand(sql, con)
    cmd.CommandType = Data.CommandType.Text

    adapter = New SqlDataAdapter(cmd)

    ' Fill the DataSet.
    ds = New DataSet()

    Try
        ' Open the database connection.
```

You may purchase a copy of our companion disk which contains all files for the project at http://www.amazon.com/gp/product/B00AOU76K8!

```
        con.Open()
        adapter.Fill(ds, sql)
    Finally

        con.Close()

        ' Perform the data binding.
        categoryFilter.DataSource = ds
        categoryFilter.DataBind()
    End Try

    ''''''''''''''''''''''''''''''''''''''''''''''''''''''''''''''''

    ' Set Header label text.
    Dim readData As SqlDataReader
    Dim val As String
    Dim photoLarge As String

    sql = "SELECT ProductName FROM Product " & _
        "WHERE ProductID = " & Session("ProductID")


    cmd = New SqlCommand(sql, con)
    cmd.CommandType = Data.CommandType.Text

    Try

        ' Open database connection.
        con.Open()

        ' Execute the stored procedure and fill the data reader.
        readData = cmd.ExecuteReader(CommandBehavior.CloseConnection)

    Catch a As Exception

        Throw a
    End Try

    readData.Read()
    val = readData("ProductName")
    headerLabel.Text = val

    con.Close()
    ''''''''''''''''''''''''''''''''''''''''''''''''''''''''''''''''


    ''''''''''''''''''''''''''''''''''''''''''''''''''''''''''''''''
```

You may purchase a copy of our companion disk which contains all files for the project at http://www.amazon.com/gp/product/B00AOU76K8!

```
        ' Set path of the picture.
        sql = "SELECT PhotoLarge FROM Product " & _
            "WHERE ProductID = " & Session("ProductID")


        cmd = New SqlCommand(sql, con)
        cmd.CommandType = Data.CommandType.Text

        Try

            ' Open database connection.
            con.Open()

            ' Execute the stored procedure and fill the data reader.
            readData = cmd.ExecuteReader(CommandBehavior.CloseConnection)

        Catch a As Exception

            Throw a
        End Try

        readData.Read()
        photoLarge = IIf(IsDBNull(readData("PhotoLarge")), "", readData("PhotoLarge"))
        val = "Pictures/" + IIf(IsDBNull(photoLarge) Or photoLarge = "", "No-image-
available.jpg", photoLarge)
        productPicture.ImageUrl = val

        con.Close()
        '''''''''''''''''''''''''''''''''''''''''''''''''''''''''''''''''''''''''''''
    End Sub

    Protected Sub categoryFilter_RowCommand(ByVal sender As Object, ByVal e As
System.Web.UI.WebControls.GridViewCommandEventArgs) Handles
categoryFilter.RowCommand
        Dim obj As Object
        Dim id As String
        Dim prodID As Integer
        Dim qty As String

        obj = e.CommandArgument
        id = obj.ToString
        prodID = Convert.ToInt16(id.ToString)
        Session("ProductID") = Convert.ToInt16(categoryFilter.DataKeys(prodID).Value.ToString)
        prodID = Convert.ToInt16(categoryFilter.DataKeys(prodID).Value.ToString)
        qty = Request.Params("categoryFilter$ctl02$purchaseQty")
        passSessionVariable(qty)
```

```
    End Sub

    Protected Sub logout()
        Session("firstName") = Nothing
        Session.Clear()
        Page.Response.Redirect("Logout.aspx")
    End Sub

    Protected Sub categoryFilter_RowDataBound(ByVal sender As Object, ByVal e As
System.Web.UI.WebControls.GridViewRowEventArgs) Handles categoryFilter.RowDataBound
        e.Row.Cells(2).Visible = False
    End Sub

    Protected Sub passSessionVariable(ByVal qty As String)
        If (addItemToCart(qty)) Then
            ' Display page which confirms the addition to the cart and provides the user the means to
View the Entire Cart or Continue Shopping.
            Page.Response.Redirect("ConfirmItemAdd.aspx")
        End If
    End Sub
    Protected Function addItemToCart(ByVal qty As String) As Boolean
        Dim myAccess As DatabaseAccess
        Dim myConnection As String
        Dim con As SqlConnection
        Dim cmd As SqlCommand
        Dim sql As String
        Dim readData As SqlDataReader
        Dim currentDate As Date = Today
        Dim client_ip As String
        Dim client_name As String
        Dim orderID As String
        Dim productCount As Integer
        Dim unitPrice As Decimal
        Dim existingQty As Integer
        Dim qtyAvailable As Integer
        Dim exisingDetailEntry As Integer

        myAccess = New DatabaseAccess()
        myConnection = myAccess.getConnectionString()

        con = New SqlConnection(myConnection)

        ' Set time and most recently selected quantity session variables.
        Session("theTime") = Convert.ToDateTime(Now).ToString
        Session("qty") = qty
```

```
If (Session("orderID") = Nothing) Then
   orderID = ""
   ''''''''''''''''''''''''''''''''''''''''''''''''''''
   ' Confirm that quantity desired does not exceed quantity available.
   sql = "SELECT QuantityAvailable FROM Product p " & _
       "WHERE p.ProductID = " & _
       Convert.ToInt16(Session("productID").ToString)
   cmd = New SqlCommand(sql, con)
   cmd.CommandType = Data.CommandType.Text
   Try

      ' Open database connection.
      con.Open()

      ' Execute the INSERT and fill the data reader.
      readData = cmd.ExecuteReader(CommandBehavior.CloseConnection)

   Catch a As Exception

      Throw a
   End Try
   readData.Read()
   existingQty = 0
   qtyAvailable = readData("QuantityAvailable")
   readData.Close()
   con.Close()
Else
   orderID = Session("orderID").ToString
   ''''''''''''''''''''''''''''''''''''''''''''''''''''
   ' Check to see if the product has an existing entry in OrderDetail table.
   sql = "SELECT Count(OrderID) AS orderCount FROM OrderDetail " & _
       "WHERE ProductID = " & _
       Convert.ToInt16(Session("productID").ToString) & _
       " AND OrderID = " & orderID & " "
   cmd = New SqlCommand(sql, con)
   cmd.CommandType = Data.CommandType.Text
   Try

      ' Open database connection.
      con.Open()

      ' Execute the INSERT and fill the data reader.
      readData = cmd.ExecuteReader(CommandBehavior.CloseConnection)

   Catch a As Exception
```

```
        Throw a
    End Try
    readData.Read()
    exisingDetailEntry = readData("orderCount")
    readData.Close()
    con.Close()

    If (exisingDetailEntry > 0) Then
        ''''''''''''''''''''''''''''''''''''''''''''''''''''''''''''''
        ' Confirm that quantity desired does not exceed quantity available.
        sql = "SELECT QuantityAvailable, Sum(Quantity) AS qty FROM Product p " & _
            "INNER JOIN OrderDetail od ON od.ProductID = p.ProductID " & _
            "WHERE p.ProductID = " & _
            Convert.ToInt16(Session("productID").ToString) & _
            " AND od.OrderID = " & orderID & " " & _
            " GROUP BY od.Quantity, p.QuantityAvailable"
        cmd = New SqlCommand(sql, con)
        cmd.CommandType = Data.CommandType.Text
        Try

            ' Open database connection.
            con.Open()

            ' Execute the INSERT and fill the data reader.
            readData = cmd.ExecuteReader(CommandBehavior.CloseConnection)

        Catch a As Exception

            Throw a
        End Try
        readData.Read()
        existingQty = readData("qty")
        qtyAvailable = readData("QuantityAvailable")
        readData.Close()
        con.Close()
    Else
        ''''''''''''''''''''''''''''''''''''''''''''''''''''''''''''''
        ' Confirm that quantity desired does not exceed quantity available.
        sql = "SELECT QuantityAvailable FROM Product p " & _
            "WHERE p.ProductID = " & _
            Convert.ToInt16(Session("productID").ToString)
        cmd = New SqlCommand(sql, con)
        cmd.CommandType = Data.CommandType.Text
        Try

            ' Open database connection.
```

```
            con.Open()

            ' Execute the INSERT and fill the data reader.
            readData = cmd.ExecuteReader(CommandBehavior.CloseConnection)

          Catch a As Exception

            Throw a
          End Try
          readData.Read()
          existingQty = 0
          qtyAvailable = readData("QuantityAvailable")
          readData.Close()
          con.Close()
        End If
      End If

        '''''''''''''''''''''''''''''''''''''''''''''''''''''''''''''''''''''''''''''
        ''''''''''''''''''''''''''''''''''''''''''''''''''''''''''
        ''''''''''''''''''''''''''''''''''''''''''''''''''''''''''

        ' Validate the quantity input by the user.
        If IsNumeric(qty) Then
          qty = Convert.ToInt16(qty)
          qtyWarning.Visible = False
        Else
          qtyWarning.Text = "Your entry is not a valid number." & vbNewLine & "Please enter
a valid number before continuing."
          qtyWarning.Visible = True
          addItemToCart = False
          Exit Function
        End If
        If existingQty + qty > qtyAvailable Then
          qtyWarning.Text = "The quantity desired exceeds the quantity available." &
vbNewLine & "Please enter a valid quantity before continuing."
          qtyWarning.Visible = True
          addItemToCart = False
          Exit Function
        Else
          qtyWarning.Visible = False
        End If
        ''''''''''''''''''''''''''''''''''''''''''''''''''''''''''
        ''''''''''''''''''''''''''''''''''''''''''''''''''''''''''
        '''''''''''''''''''''''''''''''''''''''''''''''''''''''''''''''''''''''''''''


        'Dim salesTax As Decimal
```

```
client_ip = Request.UserHostAddress()
client_name = Request.UserHostName

''''''''''''''''''''''''''''''''''''''''''''''''''''''''''''''

' Get product unit cost.
sql = "SELECT Price FROM Product WHERE " & _
    "ProductID = " & Convert.ToInt16(Session("productID").ToString)
cmd = New SqlCommand(sql, con)
cmd.CommandType = Data.CommandType.Text
Try

   ' Open database connection.
   con.Open()

   ' Execute the INSERT and fill the data reader.
   readData = cmd.ExecuteReader(CommandBehavior.CloseConnection)

Catch a As Exception

   Throw a
End Try
readData.Read()
unitPrice = readData("Price")
readData.Close()
con.Close()

unitPrice = qty * unitPrice
'salesTax = Decimal.Round(Convert.ToDecimal(unitPrice * 0.07), 2)
''''''''''''''''''''''''''''''''''''''''''''''''''''''''''''''''


' Check to see if the user has an open order.
If (orderID = "") Then
   ' If there is not an open order, the system must first create an
   ' "empty" cart and then add the requested item(s) to it.
   sql = "INSERT INTO UserOrder (OrderDate, ProcessorResponse) VALUES ('" &
Session("theTime").ToString & "','" & "'" & client_ip & " - " & client_name & "')"
   cmd = New SqlCommand(sql, con)
   cmd.CommandType = Data.CommandType.Text
   Try

      ' Open database connection.
      con.Open()

      ' Execute the INSERT and fill the data reader.
      readData = cmd.ExecuteReader(CommandBehavior.CloseConnection)
```

You may purchase a copy of our companion disk which contains all files for the project at http://www.amazon.com/gp/product/B00AOU76K8!

```
Catch a As Exception

    Throw a
End Try
con.Close()
readData.Close()

' Get the newly created order ID.
sql = "SELECT OrderID FROM UserOrder WHERE " & _
    "ProcessorResponse = '" & client_ip & " - " & client_name & "'" & _
    " AND OrderDate = '" & Session("theTime").ToString & "'"
cmd = New SqlCommand(sql, con)
cmd.CommandType = Data.CommandType.Text
Try

    ' Open database connection.
    con.Open()

    ' Execute the INSERT and fill the data reader.
    readData = cmd.ExecuteReader(CommandBehavior.CloseConnection)

Catch a As Exception

    Throw a
End Try
readData.Read()
Session("orderID") = readData("OrderID")
readData.Close()
con.Close()

' Open order has been added.  Add the current product.
sql = "INSERT INTO OrderDetail (OrderID, ProductID, quantity, ProductCost)
VALUES " & _
"(" & Convert.ToInt16(Session("orderID").ToString) & ", " & _
Convert.ToInt16(Session("productID").ToString) & ", " & _
qty & ", " & unitPrice & ")"
cmd = New SqlCommand(sql, con)
cmd.CommandType = Data.CommandType.Text
Try

    ' Open database connection.
    con.Open()

    ' Execute the INSERT and fill the data reader.
    readData = cmd.ExecuteReader(CommandBehavior.CloseConnection)
```

```
            Catch a As Exception

                Throw a
            End Try

            readData.Read()
            Session("lastProductID") = Session("productID").ToString
            con.Close()
            readData.Close()
        Else
            ' If there is an open order and the product has not yet been added to the cart for this
order id, add the current product.
            ' Get the newly created order ID.
        sql = "SELECT Count(OrderID) AS prod FROM OrderDetail WHERE " & _
             "ProductID = " & _
             Convert.ToInt16(Session("productID").ToString) & " " & _
             " AND OrderID = " & _
             Convert.ToInt16(Session("orderID").ToString) & " "
            cmd = New SqlCommand(sql, con)
            cmd.CommandType = Data.CommandType.Text
            Try

                ' Open database connection.
                con.Open()

                ' Execute the INSERT and fill the data reader.
                readData = cmd.ExecuteReader(CommandBehavior.CloseConnection)

            Catch a As Exception

                Throw a
            End Try
            readData.Read()
            productCount = readData("prod")
            readData.Close()
            con.Close()

            If (productCount = 0) Then
                sql = "INSERT INTO OrderDetail (OrderID, ProductID, quantity, ProductCost)
VALUES " & _
                "(" & Convert.ToInt16(Session("orderID").ToString) & ", " & _
                Convert.ToInt16(Session("productID").ToString) & ", " & _
                qty & ", " & unitPrice & ")"
                cmd = New SqlCommand(sql, con)
                cmd.CommandType = Data.CommandType.Text
                Try
```

```
            ' Open database connection.
            con.Open()

            ' Execute the INSERT and fill the data reader.
            readData = cmd.ExecuteReader(CommandBehavior.CloseConnection)

        Catch a As Exception

            Throw a
        End Try

        readData.Read()
        Session("lastProductID") = Session("productID").ToString
        con.Close()
        readData.Close()
    Else
    sql = "UPDATE OrderDetail " & _
        "SET quantity = " & qty & ", " & _
        "productCost = " & unitPrice & " " & _
        "WHERE OrderID = " & _
        Convert.ToInt16(Session("orderID").ToString) & " " & _
    " AND ProductID = " & Convert.ToInt16(Session("productID").ToString) & " "
        cmd = New SqlCommand(sql, con)
        cmd.CommandType = Data.CommandType.Text
        Try

            ' Open database connection.
            con.Open()

            ' Execute the INSERT and fill the data reader.
            readData = cmd.ExecuteReader(CommandBehavior.CloseConnection)

        Catch a As Exception

            Throw a
        End Try

        readData.Read()
        Session("lastProductID") = Session("productID").ToString
        con.Close()
        readData.Close()
    End If
  End If
  addItemToCart = True
End Function
```

You may purchase a copy of our companion disk which contains all files for the project at http://www.amazon.com/gp/product/B00AOU76K8!

```
End Class
```

Search Products Server Page

Replace the existing code in the SearchProducts.aspx file with the following code (*REPLACE ANY CODE IN THIS COLOR WITH YOUR OWN INFORMATION!)*:

```
<%@ Page Language="VB"
      AutoEventWireup="True"
      CodeFile="SearchProducts.aspx.vb"
      Inherits="_Default" %>

<!DOCTYPE html PUBLIC "-//W3C//DTD XHTML 1.0 Transitional//EN"
"http://www.w3.org/TR/xhtml1/DTD/xhtml1-transitional.dtd">
<html xmlns="http://www.w3.org/1999/xhtml">

<head>
<meta http-equiv="Content-Type" content="text/html; charset=iso-8859-1" />
<title>Search Products</title>
<link rel="stylesheet" href="emx_nav_left.css" type="text/css" />
<script type="text/javascript">

var time = 3000;
var numofitems = 7;

//menu constructor
function menu(allitems,thisitem,startstate){
  callname= "gl"+thisitem;
  divname="subglobal"+thisitem;
  this.numberofmenuitems = allitems;
  this.caller = document.getElementById(callname);
  this.thediv = document.getElementById(divname);
  this.thediv.style.visibility = startstate;
}

//menu methods
function ehandler(event,theobj){
  for (var i=1; i<= theobj.numberofmenuitems; i++){
    var shutdiv =eval( "menuitem"+i+".thediv");
    shutdiv.style.visibility="hidden";
  }
  theobj.thediv.style.visibility="visible";
}

function closesubnav(event){
  if ((event.clientY <48)||(event.clientY > 107)){
```

You may purchase a copy of our companion disk which contains all files for the project at http://www.amazon.com/gp/product/B00AOU76K8!

```
    for (var i=1; i<= numofitems; i++){
     var shutdiv =eval('menuitem'+i+'.thediv');
     shutdiv.style.visibility='hidden';
    }
  }
}
// -->
</script>
</head>
<body>

<form id="Form1" runat="server">
<div class="skipLinks">skip to: <a href="#content">page content</a> | <a
href="#pageNav">links on this page</a> | <a href="#globalNav">site navigation</a> | <a
href="#siteInfo">footer (site information)</a> </div>
<div id="masthead">
  <h1 id="siteName">Your Best Data Solution</h1>
  <div id="utility">
       <asp:LinkButton ID="lkCustomers" runat="server"
PostBackUrl="Customers.aspx">Customers</asp:LinkButton>
     | <asp:LinkButton ID="lkOrders" runat="server"
PostBackUrl="ViewOrders.aspx">Orders</asp:LinkButton>
     | <asp:LinkButton ID="lkAddProduct" PostBackUrl="AddProduct.aspx"
                  runat="server">Add Product</asp:LinkButton>
     | <asp:LinkButton ID="lkEditProduct" runat="server"
PostBackUrl="ViewCategories.aspx">Edit Product</asp:LinkButton>
     | <asp:LinkButton ID="lkLogout" OnClick="logout" runat="server"
PostBackUrl="#">Logout</asp:LinkButton>
     | <asp:LinkButton ID="lkChangePassword" PostBackUrl="Password.aspx"
runat="server">Change Password</asp:LinkButton>
  </div>
  <div id="globalNav"> <img alt="" src="Pictures/gblnav_left.gif" height="32" width="4"
id="gnl" /> <img alt="" src="Pictures/glbnav_right.gif" height="32" width="4" id="gnr" />
    <div id="globalLink">
       <a href="Default.aspx" id="A1" class="glink">
       Home</a>
       <a href="ViewCategories.aspx" id="gl1" class="glink" >
       View Products</a>
       <a href="SearchProducts.aspx" id="gl2" class="glink">Search</a>
       <a href="ViewCart.aspx" id="gl3" class="glink">View Cart</a>
       <a href="Checkout.aspx" id="gl4" class="glink">Checkout</a>
       <a href="CreateAccount.aspx" id="gl5" class="glink">Create
       Account</a>
       <a href="Login.aspx" id="gl6" class="glink">Login
       </a><a href="OrderHistory.aspx" id="gl7" class="glink">Order
       History</a>
```

```
      <a href="FAQ.aspx" id="A2" class="glink">FAQ</a>
      <asp:Label ID="loginStatus" Visible="false" runat="server"></asp:Label>
    </div>
  </div>
<div id="pagecell1">
  <img alt="" src="Pictures/tl_curve_white.gif" height="6" width="6" id="tl" /> <img alt=""
src="Pictures/tr_curve_white.gif" height="6" width="6" id="tr" />

    <div id="pageName">
    <img alt="small logo" src="Pictures/YourBestDataSolutionLogo.jpg" height="50"
width="60"/> </div>
  <div id="pageNav">
    <div class="relatedLinks">
      <h3>Related Link Category</h3>
      <a href="FAQ.aspx#anchor3">Automation</a>
      <a href="FAQ.aspx#anchor1">Customized Reporting</a>
      <a href="FAQ.aspx#anchor2">Database Design</a>
      <a href="FAQ.aspx#anchor12">Data Migration</a>
      <a href="FAQ.aspx#anchor4">Data Modeling</a>
      <a href="FAQ.aspx#anchor14">Desktop Application Solutions</a>
      <a href="FAQ.aspx#anchor5">eCommerce Solutions</a>
      <a href="FAQ.aspx#anchor6">eMail Marketing</a>
      <a href="FAQ.aspx#anchor7">Mobile App Development</a>
      <a href="FAQ.aspx#anchor8">PayPal™ Integration</a>
      <a href="FAQ.aspx#anchor9">Web Design</a>
      <a href="FAQ.aspx#anchor10">Web Development</a>
    </div>
  </div>
  <div id="content">
    <div class="feature">
          <h3><asp:Label runat="server"
                    ID="headerLabel"
                    Text="Search Products"></asp:Label></h3>
                       <br />
     <asp:TextBox ID="searchText" runat="server" Width="300"></asp:TextBox>
    <asp:Label ID="Label2" runat="server" Visible="false"></asp:Label>
    <asp:Button ID="searchButton"
              runat="server"
              OnClick="returnSearchResults"
              Text="Search" />
    </div>
   <div class="story">
   <asp:GridView ID ="categoryFilter"
          runat="server"
          DataKeyNames="ProductID"
          OnRowDataBound="categoryFilter_RowDataBound"
```

You may purchase a copy of our companion disk which contains all files for the project at http://www.amazon.com/gp/product/B00AOU76K8!

```
            OnRowCommand="passSessionVariable"
            BorderStyle="None"
            CssClass="storyCentered"
            HeaderStyle-BackColor="#cccccc"
            EmptyDataText="No results match your search criteria.">
        <Columns>
          <asp:TemplateField>
          <ItemTemplate>
          <asp:LinkButton ID="productDetails"
                  runat="server"
                  CommandName="Select"
                  CommandArgument="<%# Container.DataItemIndex %>"
                  Text = "Product Details"></asp:LinkButton>
          </ItemTemplate>
          </asp:TemplateField>

          <asp:TemplateField>
          <ItemTemplate>
          <asp:Image ID="thumbnail"
                runat ="server" />
          </ItemTemplate>
          </asp:TemplateField>
        </Columns>
      </asp:GridView>
      <br /><br />
        </div>
  <div id="siteInfo"> <img alt="small logo" src="Pictures/YourBestDataSolutionLogo.jpg"
width="59" height="66" />
          <a href="AboutUs.aspx">About Us</a> |
          <a href="ContactUs.aspx">Contact Us</a> |
     ©2012 YBDS, LLC </div>

</div>
<br />
   </form>
</body>
</html>
```

You may purchase a copy of our companion disk which contains all files for the project at http://www.amazon.com/gp/product/B00AOU76K8!

Search Products Code Behind

Replace the existing code in the SearchProducts.aspx.vb file with the following code:

```
Imports System.Data
Imports DatabaseAccess
Imports System.Data.SqlClient

Partial Class _Default
    Inherits System.Web.UI.Page

    Protected Sub Page_Load(ByVal sender As Object, ByVal e As EventArgs) Handles Me.Load
        If (Session("firstName") = Nothing) Then
            'User is not logged in.  Continue.
            lkLogout.Visible = False
            lkChangePassword.Visible = False
            lkChangePassword.Enabled = False
            Session("isAdmin") = False
            lkCustomers.Visible = False
            lkCustomers.Enabled = False
            lkOrders.Visible = False
            lkOrders.Enabled = False
            lkAddProduct.Visible = False
            lkAddProduct.Enabled = False
            lkEditProduct.Visible = False
            lkEditProduct.Enabled = False
        Else
            If (Session("isAdmin")) Then
                lkCustomers.Visible = True
                lkCustomers.Enabled = True
                lkOrders.Visible = True
                lkOrders.Enabled = True
                lkAddProduct.Visible = True
                lkAddProduct.Enabled = True
                lkEditProduct.Visible = True
                lkEditProduct.Enabled = True
            Else
                lkCustomers.Visible = False
                lkCustomers.Enabled = False
                lkOrders.Visible = False
                lkOrders.Enabled = False
                lkAddProduct.Visible = False
                lkAddProduct.Enabled = False
                lkEditProduct.Visible = False
```

```
            lkEditProduct.Enabled = False
        End If
        lkChangePassword.Visible = True
        lkChangePassword.Enabled = True
        loginStatus.Text = "Welcome " & Session("firstName").ToString() & "!"
        loginStatus.Visible = True
    End If
    searchText.Focus()
End Sub

Protected Sub returnSearchResults()

    Dim myAccess As DatabaseAccess
    Dim myConnection As String
    Dim con As SqlConnection
    Dim cmd As SqlCommand
    Dim adapter As SqlDataAdapter
    Dim ds As DataSet
    Dim sql As String
    Dim whereSql As String
    Dim readData As SqlDataReader

    myAccess = New DatabaseAccess()
    myConnection = myAccess.getConnectionString()

    con = New SqlConnection(myConnection)

    whereSql = "WHERE DescriptionBrief LIKE '%" & searchText.Text & "%' OR
DescriptionFull LIKE '%" & searchText.Text & "%'"

    ''''''''''''''''''''''''''''''''''''''''''''''''''''''''''
    ' Store result count in session variable.
    sql = "SELECT COUNT(ProductID) AS results FROM Product " & whereSql
    cmd = New SqlCommand(sql, con)
    cmd.CommandType = Data.CommandType.Text
    Try

        ' Open database connection.
        con.Open()

        ' Execute the INSERT and fill the data reader.
        readData = cmd.ExecuteReader(CommandBehavior.CloseConnection)
        readData.Read()
        Session("searchResults") = readData("results")
        con.Close()
        readData.Close()
```

You may purchase a copy of our companion disk which contains all files for the project at http://www.amazon.com/gp/product/B00AOU76K8!

```
Catch a As Exception
   Session("searchResults") = 0
   con.Close()
End Try
''''''''''''''''''''''''''''''''''''''''''''''''''''

sql = "SELECT ProductID, ProductName AS [Product Name], DescriptionFull AS
Description,  '$' + Convert(varchar(12), Price) AS Price, QuantityAvailable AS [Qty Available] "
& "FROM Product " & whereSql

''' OR DescriptionFull LIKE ''' & searchText.Text & ''''

cmd = New SqlCommand(sql, con)
cmd.CommandType = Data.CommandType.Text

adapter = New SqlDataAdapter(cmd)

' Fill the DataSet.
ds = New DataSet()

Try
   ' Open the database connection.
   con.Open()
   adapter.Fill(ds, sql)
Finally

   con.Close()

   ' Perform the data binding.
   categoryFilter.DataSource = ds
   categoryFilter.DataBind()
End Try

categoryFilter.Visible = True

''''''''''''''''''''''''''''''''''''''''''''''''''''''''''

' Load the pictures.
Dim ib As Image
Dim row As GridViewRow
Dim currentRowIndex As Integer
Dim val As String

For Each row In categoryFilter.Rows
    currentRowIndex =
Convert.ToInt16(categoryFilter.DataKeys(row.RowIndex).Value.ToString)
    ib = row.FindControl("thumbnail")
```

```
            sql = "SELECT PhotoThumbnail FROM Product " & _
                "WHERE ProductID = " & currentRowIndex
            cmd = New SqlCommand(sql, con)
            cmd.CommandType = Data.CommandType.Text

            Try

                ' Open database connection.
                con.Open()

                ' Execute the stored procedure and fill the data reader.
                readData = cmd.ExecuteReader(CommandBehavior.CloseConnection)

            Catch a As Exception

                Throw a
            End Try

            readData.Read()
            val = readData("PhotoThumbnail")
            ib.ImageUrl = val
            con.Close()
        Next
        ''''''''''''''''''''''''''''''''''''''''''''''''''''''''''''''''''''

    End Sub

    Protected Sub categoryFilter_RowCommand(ByVal sender As Object, ByVal e As
System.Web.UI.WebControls.GridViewCommandEventArgs) Handles
categoryFilter.RowCommand
        Dim obj As Object
        Dim id As String
        Dim ProductID As Integer
        obj = e.CommandArgument
        id = obj.ToString
        ProductID = Convert.ToInt16(id.ToString)
        Session("ProductID") =
Convert.ToInt16(categoryFilter.DataKeys(ProductID).Value.ToString)
        ProductID = Convert.ToInt16(categoryFilter.DataKeys(ProductID).Value.ToString)
        passSessionVariable()
    End Sub

    Protected Sub categoryFilter_RowDataBound(ByVal sender As Object, ByVal e As
System.Web.UI.WebControls.GridViewRowEventArgs) Handles categoryFilter.RowDataBound
        If (Convert.ToInt16(Session("searchResults")) > 0) Then
            e.Row.Cells(2).Visible = False
```

```
      End If
    End Sub

    Protected Sub passSessionVariable()
      Page.Response.Redirect("ProductDetails.aspx")
    End Sub

    Protected Sub logout()
      Session("firstName") = Nothing
      Session.Clear()
      Page.Response.Redirect("Logout.aspx")
    End Sub
End Class
```

Shipping Server Page

Replace the existing code in the Shipping.aspx file with the following code (***REPLACE ANY CODE IN THIS COLOR WITH YOUR OWN INFORMATION!)***:

```
<%@ Page Language="VB"
        AutoEventWireup="True" Debug ="true"
        CodeFile="Shipping.aspx.vb"
        Inherits="_Default" %>

<!DOCTYPE html PUBLIC "-//W3C//DTD XHTML 1.0 Transitional//EN"
"http://www.w3.org/TR/xhtml1/DTD/xhtml1-transitional.dtd">
<html xmlns="http://www.w3.org/1999/xhtml">

<head>
<meta http-equiv="Content-Type" content="text/html; charset=iso-8859-1" />
<title>Shipping</title>
<link rel="stylesheet" href="emx_nav_left.css" type="text/css" />
<script type="text/javascript">

var time = 3000;
var numofitems = 7;

//menu constructor
function menu(allitems,thisitem,startstate){
  callname= "gl"+thisitem;
  divname="subglobal"+thisitem;
  this.numberofmenuitems = allitems;
  this.caller = document.getElementById(callname);
  this.thediv = document.getElementById(divname);
  this.thediv.style.visibility = startstate;
}

//menu methods
function ehandler(event,theobj){
  for (var i=1; i<= theobj.numberofmenuitems; i++){
    var shutdiv =eval( "menuitem"+i+".thediv");
    shutdiv.style.visibility="hidden";
  }
  theobj.thediv.style.visibility="visible";
}

function closesubnav(event){
  if ((event.clientY <48)||(event.clientY > 107)){
```

```
  for (var i=1; i<= numofitems; i++){
    var shutdiv =eval('menuitem'+i+'.thediv');
    shutdiv.style.visibility='hidden';
   }
  }
}
</script>
</head>
<body>

<form id="Form1" runat="server">
<div class="skipLinks">skip to: <a href="#content">page content</a> | <a
href="#pageNav">links on this page</a> | <a href="#globalNav">site navigation</a> | <a
href="#siteInfo">footer (site information)</a> </div>
<div id="masthead">
 <h1 id="siteName">Your Best Data Solution</h1>
 <div id="utility">
      <asp:LinkButton ID="lkCustomers" runat="server"
PostBackUrl="Customers.aspx">Customers</asp:LinkButton>
    | <asp:LinkButton ID="lkOrders" runat="server"
PostBackUrl="ViewOrders.aspx">Orders</asp:LinkButton>
    | <asp:LinkButton ID="lkAddProduct" PostBackUrl="AddProduct.aspx"
                runat="server">Add Product</asp:LinkButton>
    | <asp:LinkButton ID="lkEditProduct" runat="server"
PostBackUrl="ViewCategories.aspx">Edit Product</asp:LinkButton>
    | <asp:LinkButton ID="lkLogout" OnClick="logout" runat="server"
PostBackUrl="#">Logout</asp:LinkButton>
    | <asp:LinkButton ID="lkChangePassword" PostBackUrl="Password.aspx"
runat="server">Change Password</asp:LinkButton>
 </div>
 <div id="globalNav"> <img alt="" src="Pictures/gblnav_left.gif" height="32" width="4"
id="gnl" /> <img alt="" src="Pictures/glbnav_right.gif" height="32" width="4" id="gnr" />
   <div id="globalLink">
      <a href="Default.aspx" id="A1" class="glink">
      Home</a>
      <a href="ViewCategories.aspx" id="gl1" class="glink" >
      View Products</a>
      <a href="SearchProducts.aspx" id="gl2" class="glink">Search</a>
      <a href="ViewCart.aspx" id="gl3" class="glink">View Cart</a>
      <a href="Checkout.aspx" id="gl4" class="glink">Checkout</a>
      <a href="CreateAccount.aspx" id="gl5" class="glink">Create
      Account</a>
      <a href="Login.aspx" id="gl6" class="glink">Login
      </a><a href="OrderHistory.aspx" id="gl7" class="glink">Order
      History</a>
      <a href="FAQ.aspx" id="A2" class="glink">FAQ</a>
```

```
      <asp:Label ID="loginStatus" Visible="false" Font-Bold="true" Font-Size="Small"
runat="server"></asp:Label>
   </div>
 </div>
<div id="pagecell1">
  <img alt="" src="Pictures/tl_curve_white.gif" height="6" width="6" id="tl" /> <img alt=""
src="Pictures/tr_curve_white.gif" height="6" width="6" id="tr" />

   <div id="pageName">
   <img alt="small logo" src="Pictures/YourBestDataSolutionLogo.jpg" height="50"
width="60"/> </div>
  <div id="pageNav">
   <div class="relatedLinks">
     <h3>Related Link Category</h3>
     <a href="FAQ.aspx#anchor3">Automation</a>
     <a href="FAQ.aspx#anchor1">Customized Reporting</a>
     <a href="FAQ.aspx#anchor2">Database Design</a>
     <a href="FAQ.aspx#anchor12">Data Migration</a>
     <a href="FAQ.aspx#anchor4">Data Modeling</a>
     <a href="FAQ.aspx#anchor14">Desktop Application Solutions</a>
     <a href="FAQ.aspx#anchor5">eCommerce Solutions</a>
     <a href="FAQ.aspx#anchor6">eMail Marketing</a>
     <a href="FAQ.aspx#anchor7">Mobile App Development</a>
     <a href="FAQ.aspx#anchor8">PayPal™ Integration</a>
     <a href="FAQ.aspx#anchor9">Web Design</a>
     <a href="FAQ.aspx#anchor10">Web Development</a>
   </div>
  </div>
  <div id="content">
   <div class="feature">
     <h3><asp:Label runat="server"
              ID="headerLabel" BackColor="LightGray"
              Text="Shipping Information"></asp:Label></h3>
      <p>
         <asp:Label ID="lblShippingMethod"
                runat="server"
                Text="Shipping method" Width="150"></asp:Label>
         <asp:DropDownList ID="cboShippingMethod"
                    AutoPostBack="true" EnableViewState="true"
                    OnSelectedIndexChanged="updateShippingMethod"
                    runat="server" DataValueField="ShippingMethodID"
                    Width="200"></asp:DropDownList>
         <br />
         <br />
         <br />
      </p>
```

```
  <p>
    <asp:Button
            runat="server"
            OnClick="updateAccount"
            ID="Button1"
            Text="Continue Checkout" />
  </p>
  </div>
  <div class="story">
 <div id="siteInfo"> <img alt="small logo" src="Pictures/YourBestDataSolutionLogo.jpg"
width="59" height="66" />
        <a href="AboutUs.aspx">About Us</a> |
        <a href="ContactUs.aspx">Contact Us</a> |
    ©2012 YBDS, LLC </div>

</div>
<br />
  </form>
</body>
</html>
```

You may purchase a copy of our companion disk which contains all files for the project at http://www.amazon.com/gp/product/B00AOU76K8!

Shipping Code Behind

Replace the existing code in the Shipping.aspx.vb file with the following code:

```
Imports System.Data
Imports System.Windows.Forms
Imports System.Data.SqlClient

Partial Class _Default
   Inherits System.Web.UI.Page

   Protected Sub Page_Load(ByVal sender As Object, ByVal e As EventArgs) Handles Me.Load

      Dim myConnection As String
      Dim cmd As SqlCommand
      Dim myAdapter As SqlDataAdapter
      Dim myDataSet As DataSet
      Dim con As SqlConnection
      Dim myAccess As DatabaseAccess

      If (Session("firstName") = Nothing) Then
         'User is not logged in.  Continue.
         lkLogout.Visible = False
         lkChangePassword.Visible = False
         lkChangePassword.Enabled = False
         Session("isAdmin") = False
         lkCustomers.Visible = False
         lkCustomers.Enabled = False
         lkOrders.Visible = False
         lkOrders.Enabled = False
         lkAddProduct.Visible = False
         lkAddProduct.Enabled = False
         lkEditProduct.Visible = False
         lkEditProduct.Enabled = False
      Else
         If (Session("isAdmin")) Then
            lkCustomers.Visible = True
            lkCustomers.Enabled = True
            lkOrders.Visible = True
            lkOrders.Enabled = True
            lkAddProduct.Visible = True
            lkAddProduct.Enabled = True
            lkEditProduct.Visible = True
            lkEditProduct.Enabled = True
```

```
        Else
            lkCustomers.Visible = False
            lkCustomers.Enabled = False
            lkOrders.Visible = False
            lkOrders.Enabled = False
            lkAddProduct.Visible = False
            lkAddProduct.Enabled = False
            lkEditProduct.Visible = False
            lkEditProduct.Enabled = False
        End If
        lkChangePassword.Visible = True
        lkChangePassword.Enabled = True
        loginStatus.Text = "Welcome " & Session("firstName").ToString() & "!"
        loginStatus.Visible = True
    End If

    ' Set variables for use in binding.
    myAccess = New DatabaseAccess()
    myConnection = myAccess.getConnectionString()
    con = New SqlConnection(myConnection)

    ''''''''''''''''''''''''''''''''''''''''''''''''''''''''''''''

    ' Bind Shipping State combobox.
    cmd = New SqlCommand("SELECT StateID, StateName FROM USState ORDER BY
StateName ASC", con)
    cmd.CommandType = CommandType.Text

    myAdapter = New SqlDataAdapter(cmd)
    myDataSet = New DataSet()

    Try

        ' Open the database connection.
        con.Open()
        myAdapter.Fill(myDataSet, "USState")
    Finally
        con.Close()
        'If Not (Page.IsPostBack) Then
        '    cboBillingState.DataSource = myDataSet
        '    cboBillingState.DataSource = myDataSet.Tables(0)
        '    cboBillingState.DataTextField =
myDataSet.Tables(0).Columns("StateName").ColumnName.ToString()
        '    cboBillingState.DataValueField =
myDataSet.Tables(0).Columns("StateId").ColumnName.ToString()
        '    cboBillingState.DataBind()
        'End If
```

```
        End Try

        ''''''''''''''''''''''''''''''''''''''''''''''''''''
        ' Bind Shipping Country combobox.
        cmd = New SqlCommand("SELECT CountryID, CountryName FROM Country ORDER
BY CountryID ASC", con)
        cmd.CommandType = CommandType.Text

        myAdapter = New SqlDataAdapter(cmd)
        myDataSet = New DataSet()

        Try

            ' Open the database connection.
            con.Open()
            myAdapter.Fill(myDataSet, "Country")
        Finally
            con.Close()
            'If Not (Page.IsPostBack) Then
            '    cboBillingCountry.DataSource = myDataSet
            '    cboBillingCountry.DataSource = myDataSet.Tables(0)
            '    cboBillingCountry.DataTextField =
myDataSet.Tables(0).Columns("CountryName").ColumnName.ToString()
            '    cboBillingCountry.DataValueField =
myDataSet.Tables(0).Columns("CountryId").ColumnName.ToString()
            '    cboBillingCountry.DataBind()
            'End If
        End Try

        ''''''''''''''''''''''''''''''''''''''''''''''''''''
        ' Bind Shipping Method combobox.
        cmd = New SqlCommand("SELECT ShippingMethodID, ShippingMethodName FROM
ShippingMethod ORDER BY ShippingMethodName ASC", con)
        cmd.CommandType = CommandType.Text

        myAdapter = New SqlDataAdapter(cmd)
        myDataSet = New DataSet()

        Try

            ' Open the database connection.
            con.Open()
            myAdapter.Fill(myDataSet, "ShippingMethod")
        Finally
            If Not (Page.IsPostBack) Then
                con.Close()
```

You may purchase a copy of our companion disk which contains all files for the project at http://www.amazon.com/gp/product/B00AOU76K8!

```
            cboShippingMethod.DataSource = myDataSet
            cboShippingMethod.DataSource = myDataSet.Tables(0)
            cboShippingMethod.DataTextField =
myDataSet.Tables(0).Columns("ShippingMethodName").ColumnName.ToString()
            cboShippingMethod.DataValueField =
myDataSet.Tables(0).Columns("ShippingMethodId").ColumnName.ToString()
            cboShippingMethod.DataBind()
            cboShippingMethod.SelectedIndex = -1
         End If
      End Try
   End Sub

   Protected Sub updateShippingMethod()
      Session("tempShippingMethodID") = cboShippingMethod.SelectedItem.Value
      cboShippingMethod.EnableViewState = False
   End Sub

   Protected Sub updateAccount()

      Dim myConnection As String
      Dim cmd As SqlCommand
      Dim con As SqlConnection
      Dim myAccess As DatabaseAccess
      Dim sql As String
      Dim readData As SqlDataReader
      Dim shippingAddressID As Integer
      Dim shippingMethodID As Integer

      ' Set variables for use in binding.
      myAccess = New DatabaseAccess()
      myConnection = myAccess.getConnectionString()
      con = New SqlConnection(myConnection)

      If (Session("userID") = Nothing) Then
         headerLabel.Text = "You are not logged in.  Please log in."
         Exit Sub
      End If

      ''''''''''''''''''''''''''''''''''''''''''''''''''''''''''''''''''''

      ' Get the newly created user billing address ID.
      sql = "SELECT MAX(AddressID) AS id FROM UserAddress WHERE " & _
            "UserID = " & Session("userID") & " " & _
            " AND AddressType = 1"
      cmd = New SqlCommand(sql, con)
      cmd.CommandType = Data.CommandType.Text
      Try
```

```
    ' Open database connection.
    con.Open()

    ' Execute the INSERT and fill the data reader.
    readData = cmd.ExecuteReader(CommandBehavior.CloseConnection)

Catch a As Exception

    Throw a
End Try
readData.Read()
Session("billingAddressID") = readData("id")
Session("shippingAddressID") = readData("id")
readData.Close()
con.Close()
shippingAddressID = Session("shippingAddressID")

''''''''''''''''''''''''''''''''''''''''''''''''''''''''''''''''''''''''''''''''
' Get the newly created user shipping State ID.
sql = "SELECT StateID FROM UserAddress WHERE " & _
        "AddressID = " & Session("billingAddressID") & " "
cmd = New SqlCommand(sql, con)
cmd.CommandType = Data.CommandType.Text
Try

    ' Open database connection.
    con.Open()

    ' Execute the INSERT and fill the data reader.
    readData = cmd.ExecuteReader(CommandBehavior.CloseConnection)

Catch a As Exception

    Throw a
End Try
readData.Read()
Session("shippingStateID") = readData("StateID")
readData.Close()
con.Close()
'End If

''''''''''''''''''''''''''''''''''''''''''''''''''''''''''''''''''''''''''''''''
If (Session("tempShippingMethodID") = Nothing) Then
    shippingMethodID = cboShippingMethod.SelectedItem.Value
Else
```

```
    shippingMethodID = Session("tempShippingMethodID")
End If
Session("shippingMethodID") = shippingMethodID


' Get the tax rate.
sql = "SELECT StateAbbreviation FROM USState WHERE " & _
      "StateID = " & Session("shippingStateID") & " "
cmd = New SqlCommand(sql, con)
cmd.CommandType = Data.CommandType.Text
Try

    ' Open database connection.
    con.Open()

    ' Execute the INSERT and fill the data reader.
    readData = cmd.ExecuteReader(CommandBehavior.CloseConnection)

Catch a As Exception

    Throw a
End Try
readData.Read()
Session("stateAbbreviation") = readData("StateAbbreviation")
readData.Close()
con.Close()

If (Session("stateAbbreviation") = "IN") Then
    Session("salesTaxRate") = 0.07
    ' UPDATE the UserOrder table.
    sql = "UPDATE UserOrder SET " & _
        "UserID = " & Convert.ToInt16(Session("userID").ToString) & ", " & _
        "SalesTaxRate = 0.07, " & _
        "ShippingMethodID = " & shippingMethodID & ", " & _
        "ShippingAddressID = " & shippingAddressID & ",  " & _
        "BillingAddressID = " & Session("billingAddressID") & "  " & _
        " WHERE OrderID = " & Session("OrderID") & " "
Else
    Session("salesTaxRate") = 0.0
    ' UPDATE the UserOrder table.
    sql = "UPDATE UserOrder SET " & _
        "UserID = " & Convert.ToInt16(Session("userID").ToString) & ", " & _
        "SalesTaxRate = 0.00, " & _
        "ShippingMethodID = " & shippingMethodID & ", " & _
        "ShippingAddressID = " & shippingAddressID & ", " & _
        "BillingAddressID = " & Session("billingAddressID") & "  " & _
```

```
        " WHERE OrderID = " & Session("OrderID") & " "
    End If
    cmd = New SqlCommand(sql, con)
    cmd.CommandType = Data.CommandType.Text
    Try

        ' Open database connection.
        con.Open()

        ' Execute the INSERT and fill the data reader.
        readData = cmd.ExecuteReader(CommandBehavior.CloseConnection)

    Catch a As Exception

        Throw a
    End Try

    con.Close()
    readData.Close()

    ''''''''''''''''''''''''''''''''''''''''''''''''''''''''''''''''''''''''''''

    ''''''''''''''''''''''''''''''''''''''''''''''''''''''''''''''''
    ' Get shipping method.
    sql = "SELECT ShippingMethodName, ShippingCost " & _
        "FROM ShippingMethod " & _
        "WHERE ShippingMethodID = " & shippingMethodID & " "
    cmd = New SqlCommand(sql, con)
    cmd.CommandType = Data.CommandType.Text
    Try

        ' Open database connection.
        con.Open()

        ' Execute the INSERT and fill the data reader.
        readData = cmd.ExecuteReader(CommandBehavior.CloseConnection)

    Catch a As Exception

        Throw a
    End Try
    readData.Read()
    Session("shippingMethodName") = readData("ShippingMethodName")
    Session("shippingCost") = readData("ShippingCost")
    readData.Close()
    con.Close()
```

You may purchase a copy of our companion disk which contains all files for the project at http://www.amazon.com/gp/product/B00AOU76K8!

```
        Page.Response.Redirect("Billing.aspx")

    End Sub

    Protected Sub logout()
        Session("firstName") = Nothing
        Session.Clear()
        Page.Response.Redirect("Logout.aspx")
    End Sub

    Protected Sub cboShippingMethod_SelectedIndexChanged(ByVal sender As Object, ByVal e
As System.EventArgs) Handles cboShippingMethod.SelectedIndexChanged

        updateShippingMethod()

    End Sub
End Class
```

User Message Server Page

Replace the existing code in the UserMessage.aspx file with the following code (*REPLACE ANY CODE IN THIS COLOR WITH YOUR OWN INFORMATION!)*:

```
<%@ Page Language="VB"
        AutoEventWireup="True"
        CodeFile="UserMessage.aspx.vb"
        Inherits="_Default" %>

<!DOCTYPE html PUBLIC "-//W3C//DTD XHTML 1.0 Transitional//EN"
"http://www.w3.org/TR/xhtml1/DTD/xhtml1-transitional.dtd">
<html xmlns="http://www.w3.org/1999/xhtml">

<head>
<meta http-equiv="Content-Type" content="text/html; charset=iso-8859-1" />
<title>Alert</title>
<link rel="stylesheet" href="emx_nav_left.css" type="text/css" />
<script type="text/javascript">

var time = 3000;
var numofitems = 7;

//menu constructor
function menu(allitems,thisitem,startstate){
  callname= "gl"+thisitem;
  divname="subglobal"+thisitem;
  this.numberofmenuitems = allitems;
  this.caller = document.getElementById(callname);
  this.thediv = document.getElementById(divname);
  this.thediv.style.visibility = startstate;
}

//menu methods
function ehandler(event,theobj){
  for (var i=1; i<= theobj.numberofmenuitems; i++){
    var shutdiv =eval( "menuitem"+i+".thediv");
    shutdiv.style.visibility="hidden";
  }
  theobj.thediv.style.visibility="visible";
}

function closesubnav(event){
  if ((event.clientY <48)||(event.clientY > 107)){
```

You may purchase a copy of our companion disk which contains all files for the project at http://www.amazon.com/gp/product/B00AOU76K8!

```
  for (var i=1; i<= numofitems; i++){
   var shutdiv =eval('menuitem'+i+'.thediv');
   shutdiv.style.visibility='hidden';
  }
 }
}
</script>
</head>
<body>

<form id="Form1" runat="server">
<div class="skipLinks">skip to: <a href="#content">page content</a> | <a
href="#pageNav">links on this page</a> | <a href="#globalNav">site navigation</a> | <a
href="#siteInfo">footer (site information)</a> </div>
<div id="masthead">
 <h1 id="siteName">Your Best Data Solution</h1>
 <div id="utility">
     <asp:LinkButton ID="lkCustomers" runat="server"
PostBackUrl="Customers.aspx">Customers</asp:LinkButton>
    |<asp:LinkButton ID="lkOrders" runat="server"
PostBackUrl="ViewOrders.aspx">Orders</asp:LinkButton>
    |<asp:LinkButton ID="lkAddProduct" PostBackUrl="AddProduct.aspx"
               runat="server">Add Product</asp:LinkButton>
    |<asp:LinkButton ID="lkEditProduct" runat="server"
PostBackUrl="ViewCategories.aspx">Edit Product</asp:LinkButton>
    |<asp:LinkButton ID="lkLogout" OnClick="logout" runat="server"
PostBackUrl="#">Logout</asp:LinkButton>
    |<asp:LinkButton ID="lkChangePassword" PostBackUrl="Password.aspx"
runat="server">Change Password</asp:LinkButton>
 </div>
 <div id="globalNav"> <img alt="" src="Pictures/gblnav_left.gif" height="32" width="4"
id="gnl" /> <img alt="" src="Pictures/glbnav_right.gif" height="32" width="4" id="gnr" />
  <div id="globalLink">
     <a href="Default.aspx" id="A1" class="glink">
     Home</a>
     <a href="ViewCategories.aspx" id="gl1" class="glink" >
     View Products</a>
     <a href="SearchProducts.aspx" id="gl2" class="glink">Search</a>
     <a href="ViewCart.aspx" id="gl3" class="glink">View Cart</a>
     <a href="Checkout.aspx" id="gl4" class="glink">Checkout</a>
     <a href="CreateAccount.aspx" id="gl5" class="glink">Create
     Account</a>
     <a href="Login.aspx" id="gl6" class="glink">Login
     </a><a href="OrderHistory.aspx" id="gl7" class="glink">Order
     History</a>
     <a href="FAQ.aspx" id="A2" class="glink">FAQ</a>
```

```
      <asp:Label ID="loginStatus" Visible="false" runat="server"></asp:Label>
    </div>
  </div>
<div id="pagecell1">
  <img alt="" src="Pictures/tl_curve_white.gif" height="6" width="6" id="tl" /> <img alt=""
src="Pictures/tr_curve_white.gif" height="6" width="6" id="tr" />

    <div id="pageName">
    <img alt="small logo" src="Pictures/YourBestDataSolutionLogo.jpg" height="50"
width="60"/> </div>
  <div id="pageNav">
    <div class="relatedLinks">
      <h3>Related Link Category</h3>
      <a href="FAQ.aspx#anchor3">Automation</a>
      <a href="FAQ.aspx#anchor1">Customized Reporting</a>
      <a href="FAQ.aspx#anchor2">Database Design</a>
      <a href="FAQ.aspx#anchor12">Data Migration</a>
      <a href="FAQ.aspx#anchor4">Data Modeling</a>
      <a href="FAQ.aspx#anchor14">Desktop Application Solutions</a>
      <a href="FAQ.aspx#anchor5">eCommerce Solutions</a>
      <a href="FAQ.aspx#anchor6">eMail Marketing</a>
      <a href="FAQ.aspx#anchor7">Mobile App Development</a>
      <a href="FAQ.aspx#anchor8">PayPal™ Integration</a>
      <a href="FAQ.aspx#anchor9">Web Design</a>
      <a href="FAQ.aspx#anchor10">Web Development</a>
    </div>
  </div>
  <div id="content">
    <div class="feature">
      <h3>Important:</h3>
       <p> <asp:Label ID="userMessage"
              runat="server" ></asp:Label> </p>
       <p>

    </div>
    <div class="story">
  <div id="siteInfo"> <img alt="small logo" src="Pictures/YourBestDataSolutionLogo.jpg"
width="59" height="66" />
          <a href="AboutUs.aspx">About Us</a> |
          <a href="ContactUs.aspx">Contact Us</a> |
     ©2012 YBDS, LLC </div>

</div>
<br />
   </form>
</body>
```

You may purchase a copy of our companion disk which contains all files for the project at http://www.amazon.com/gp/product/B00AOU76K8!

```
</html>
```

User Message Code Behind

Replace the existing code in the UserMessage.aspx.vb file with the following code:

```
Imports System.Data
Imports System.Data.SqlClient

Partial Class _Default
    Inherits System.Web.UI.Page

    Protected Sub Page_Load(ByVal sender As Object, ByVal e As EventArgs) Handles Me.Load

        If (Session("firstName") = Nothing) Then
            'User is not logged in.  Continue.
            lkLogout.Visible = False
            lkChangePassword.Visible = False
            lkChangePassword.Enabled = False
            Session("isAdmin") = False
            lkCustomers.Visible = False
            lkCustomers.Enabled = False
            lkOrders.Visible = False
            lkOrders.Enabled = False
            lkAddProduct.Visible = False
            lkAddProduct.Enabled = False
            lkEditProduct.Visible = False
            lkEditProduct.Enabled = False
        Else
            If (Session("isAdmin")) Then
                lkCustomers.Visible = True
                lkCustomers.Enabled = True
                lkOrders.Visible = True
                lkOrders.Enabled = True
                lkAddProduct.Visible = True
                lkAddProduct.Enabled = True
                lkEditProduct.Visible = True
                lkEditProduct.Enabled = True
            Else
                lkCustomers.Visible = False
                lkCustomers.Enabled = False
                lkOrders.Visible = False
                lkOrders.Enabled = False
                lkAddProduct.Visible = False
                lkAddProduct.Enabled = False
                lkEditProduct.Visible = False
```

```
            lkEditProduct.Enabled = False
          End If
          lkChangePassword.Visible = True
          lkChangePassword.Enabled = True
          loginStatus.Text = "Welcome " & Session("firstName").ToString() & "!"
          If (Session("passwordChanged") = True) Then
            userMessage.Text = "Your password has been updated."
            Session("passwordChanged") = False
            Exit Sub
          Else
            userMessage.Text = "You are already logged in " & Session("firstName").ToString()
& "!  View our other great products, or Check out now to take advantage of our specials!"
            Exit Sub
          End If
        End If

    End Sub

    Protected Sub logout()
        Session("firstName") = Nothing
        Session.Clear()
        Page.Response.Redirect("Logout.aspx")
    End Sub
End Class
```

You may purchase a copy of our companion disk which contains all files for the project at http://www.amazon.com/gp/product/B00AOU76K8!

View Cart Server Page

Replace the existing code in the ViewCart.aspx file with the following code (***REPLACE ANY CODE IN THIS COLOR WITH YOUR OWN INFORMATION!)***:

```
<%@ Page Language="VB"
        AutoEventWireup="True"
        CodeFile="ViewCart.aspx.vb"
        Inherits="_Default" %>

<!DOCTYPE html PUBLIC "-//W3C//DTD XHTML 1.0 Transitional//EN"
"http://www.w3.org/TR/xhtml1/DTD/xhtml1-transitional.dtd">
<html xmlns="http://www.w3.org/1999/xhtml">

<head>
<meta http-equiv="Content-Type" content="text/html; charset=iso-8859-1" />
<title>View Cart</title>
<link rel="stylesheet" href="emx_nav_left.css" type="text/css" />
<script type="text/javascript">

var time = 3000;
var numofitems = 7;

//menu constructor
function menu(allitems,thisitem,startstate){
  callname= "gl"+thisitem;
  divname="subglobal"+thisitem;
  this.numberofmenuitems = allitems;
  this.caller = document.getElementById(callname);
  this.thediv = document.getElementById(divname);
  this.thediv.style.visibility = startstate;
}

//menu methods
function ehandler(event,theobj){
  for (var i=1; i<= theobj.numberofmenuitems; i++){
    var shutdiv =eval( "menuitem"+i+".thediv");
    shutdiv.style.visibility="hidden";
  }
  theobj.thediv.style.visibility="visible";
}

function closesubnav(event){
  if ((event.clientY <48)||(event.clientY > 107)){
```

You may purchase a copy of our companion disk which contains all files for the project at http://www.amazon.com/gp/product/B00AOU76K8!

```
    for (var i=1; i<= numofitems; i++){
      var shutdiv =eval('menuitem'+i+'.thediv');
      shutdiv.style.visibility='hidden';
    }
  }
}
// -->
</script>
</head>
<body>

<form id="Form1" runat="server">
<div class="skipLinks">skip to: <a href="#content">page content</a> | <a
href="#pageNav">links on this page</a> | <a href="#globalNav">site navigation</a> | <a
href="#siteInfo">footer (site information)</a> </div>
<div id="masthead">
  <h1 id="siteName">Your Best Data Solution</h1>
  <div id="utility">
      <asp:LinkButton ID="lkCustomers" runat="server"
PostBackUrl="Customers.aspx">Customers</asp:LinkButton>
    | <asp:LinkButton ID="lkOrders" runat="server"
PostBackUrl="ViewOrders.aspx">Orders</asp:LinkButton>
    | <asp:LinkButton ID="lkAddProduct" PostBackUrl="AddProduct.aspx"
                runat="server">Add Product</asp:LinkButton>
    | <asp:LinkButton ID="lkEditProduct" runat="server"
PostBackUrl="ViewCategories.aspx">Edit Product</asp:LinkButton>
    | <asp:LinkButton ID="lkLogout" OnClick="logout" runat="server"
PostBackUrl="#">Logout</asp:LinkButton>
    | <asp:LinkButton ID="lkChangePassword" PostBackUrl="Password.aspx"
runat="server">Change Password</asp:LinkButton>
  </div>
  <div id="globalNav"> <img alt="" src="Pictures/gblnav_left.gif" height="32" width="4"
id="gnl" /> <img alt="" src="Pictures/glbnav_right.gif" height="32" width="4" id="gnr" />
    <div id="globalLink">
      <a href="Default.aspx" id="A1" class="glink">
      Home</a>
      <a href="ViewCategories.aspx" id="gl1" class="glink" >
      View Products</a>
      <a href="SearchProducts.aspx" id="gl2" class="glink">Search</a>
      <a href="ViewCart.aspx" id="gl3" class="glink">View Cart</a>
      <a href="Checkout.aspx" id="gl4" class="glink">Checkout</a>
      <a href="CreateAccount.aspx" id="gl5" class="glink">Create
      Account</a>
      <a href="Login.aspx" id="gl6" class="glink">Login
      </a><a href="OrderHistory.aspx" id="gl7" class="glink">Order
      History</a>
```

```
      <a href="FAQ.aspx" id="A2" class="glink">FAQ</a>
      <asp:Label ID="loginStatus" Visible="false" runat="server"></asp:Label>
    </div>
  </div>
<div id="pagecell1">
  <img alt="" src="Pictures/tl_curve_white.gif" height="6" width="6" id="tl" /> <img alt=""
src="Pictures/tr_curve_white.gif" height="6" width="6" id="tr" />

    <div id="pageName">
    <img alt="small logo" src="Pictures/YourBestDataSolutionLogo.jpg" height="50"
width="60"/> </div>
  <div id="pageNav">
    <div class="relatedLinks">
      <h3>Related Link Category</h3>
      <a href="FAQ.aspx#anchor3">Automation</a>
      <a href="FAQ.aspx#anchor1">Customized Reporting</a>
      <a href="FAQ.aspx#anchor2">Database Design</a>
      <a href="FAQ.aspx#anchor12">Data Migration</a>
      <a href="FAQ.aspx#anchor4">Data Modeling</a>
      <a href="FAQ.aspx#anchor14">Desktop Application Solutions</a>
      <a href="FAQ.aspx#anchor5">eCommerce Solutions</a>
      <a href="FAQ.aspx#anchor6">eMail Marketing</a>
      <a href="FAQ.aspx#anchor7">Mobile App Development</a>
      <a href="FAQ.aspx#anchor8">PayPal™ Integration</a>
      <a href="FAQ.aspx#anchor9">Web Design</a>
      <a href="FAQ.aspx#anchor10">Web Development</a>
    </div>
  </div>
  <div id="content">
    <div class="feature">
      <h3><asp:Label runat="server" ID="headerLabel"></asp:Label></h3>
       <p>
    <asp:GridView ID ="categoryFilter"
              runat="server"
              DataKeyNames="ProductID"
              OnRowCommand="categoryFilter_RowCommand"
              EditRowStyle-HorizontalAlign="Center"
              HeaderStyle-BackColor="#cccccc"
              BorderStyle="None"
              OnRowDeleted="categoryFilter_RowDeleted"
              OnRowDeleting="categoryFilter_RowDeleting"
              AutoGenerateDeleteButton="true"
              EmptyDataText="No items are currently in your cart." >
        <Columns>
          <asp:TemplateField>
          <ItemTemplate>
```

You may purchase a copy of our companion disk which contains all files for the project at http://www.amazon.com/gp/product/B00AOU76K8!

```
        <asp:LinkButton ID="productDetails"
                    runat="server"
                    CommandName="Select"
                    CommandArgument="<%# Container.DataItemIndex %>"
                    Text = "Edit Order Qty"></asp:LinkButton>
        </ItemTemplate>
        </asp:TemplateField>
      </Columns>
    </asp:GridView>
      </p>
    <p>
      <asp:Button OnClick="continueShopping"
           runat="server"
           ID="Button2"
           Text="Continue Shopping" />
    </p>
    </div>
    <div class="story">
  <div id="siteInfo"> <img alt="small logo" src="Pictures/YourBestDataSolutionLogo.jpg"
width="59" height="66" />
        <a href="AboutUs.aspx">About Us</a> |
        <a href="ContactUs.aspx">Contact Us</a> |
     ©2012 YBDS, LLC </div>

</div>
<br />
   </form>
</body>
</html>
```

View Cart Code Behind

Replace the existing code in the ViewCart.aspx.vb file with the following code:

```
Imports System.Data
Imports System.Data.SqlClient

Partial Class _Default
    Inherits System.Web.UI.Page

    Protected Sub Page_Load(ByVal sender As Object, ByVal e As EventArgs) Handles Me.Load

        Dim myAccess As DatabaseAccess
        Dim myConnection As String
        Dim con As SqlConnection
        Dim cmd As SqlCommand
        Dim adapter As SqlDataAdapter
        Dim ds As DataSet
        Dim sql As String
        Dim orderID As String
        Dim readData As SqlDataReader
        Dim itemCount As Integer

        If (Session("firstName") = Nothing) Then
            'User is not logged in.  Continue.
            lkLogout.Visible = False
            lkChangePassword.Visible = False
            lkChangePassword.Enabled = False
            Session("isAdmin") = False
            lkCustomers.Visible = False
            lkCustomers.Enabled = False
            lkOrders.Visible = False
            lkOrders.Enabled = False
            lkAddProduct.Visible = False
            lkAddProduct.Enabled = False
            lkEditProduct.Visible = False
            lkEditProduct.Enabled = False
        Else
            If (Session("isAdmin")) Then
                lkCustomers.Visible = True
                lkCustomers.Enabled = True
                lkOrders.Visible = True
                lkOrders.Enabled = True
                lkAddProduct.Visible = True
```

```
            lkAddProduct.Enabled = True
            lkEditProduct.Visible = True
            lkEditProduct.Enabled = True
        Else
            lkCustomers.Visible = False
            lkCustomers.Enabled = False
            lkOrders.Visible = False
            lkOrders.Enabled = False
            lkAddProduct.Visible = False
            lkAddProduct.Enabled = False
            lkEditProduct.Visible = False
            lkEditProduct.Enabled = False
        End If
        lkChangePassword.Visible = True
        lkChangePassword.Enabled = True
        loginStatus.Text = "Welcome " & Session("firstName").ToString() & "!"
        loginStatus.Visible = True
    End If

    myAccess = New DatabaseAccess()
    myConnection = myAccess.getConnectionString()
    con = New SqlConnection(myConnection)

    orderID = Session("OrderID")
    If orderID = Nothing Then
        orderID = -1
    End If

    myAccess = New DatabaseAccess()
    myConnection = myAccess.getConnectionString()

    con = New SqlConnection(myConnection)
    sql = "SELECT COUNT(OrderID) AS orderCount FROM OrderDetail " & _
        "WHERE OrderID = " & orderID
    cmd = New SqlCommand(sql, con)
    cmd.CommandType = Data.CommandType.Text
    Try

        ' Open database connection.
        con.Open()

        ' Execute the INSERT and fill the data reader.
        readData = cmd.ExecuteReader(CommandBehavior.CloseConnection)

    Catch a As Exception
```

```
            Throw a
        End Try
        readData.Read()
        itemCount = readData("orderCount")
        con.Close()
        readData.Close()

        If (Session("OrderID") = Nothing) Or (itemCount = 0) Then
            orderID = -1
            sql = "SELECT p.ProductID, p.ProductName AS Product, " & _
       "od.Quantity, '$' + Convert(varchar(12), od.ProductCost) AS [Product Cost] " & _
       "FROM Product p " & _
       "INNER JOIN OrderDetail od ON od.ProductID = p.ProductID " & _
       "WHERE od.OrderID = " & orderID & " " & _
       "ORDER BY ProductName ASC"
        Else
            orderID = Session("OrderID")
            ''''''''''''''''''''''''''''''''''''''''''''''''''''''''''''''''

            ' Get count of records.
            sql = "SELECT COUNT(p.ProductID) AS rowQty " & _
                "FROM Product p " & _
                "INNER JOIN OrderDetail od ON od.ProductID = p.ProductID " & _
                "WHERE od.OrderID = " & orderID & " "
            cmd = New SqlCommand(sql, con)
            cmd.CommandType = Data.CommandType.Text
            Try

                ' Open database connection.
                con.Open()

                ' Execute the INSERT and fill the data reader.
                readData = cmd.ExecuteReader(CommandBehavior.CloseConnection)

            Catch a As Exception

                Throw a
            End Try
            readData.Read()
            Session("rowQty") = readData("rowQty")
            readData.Close()
            con.Close()
            ''''''''''''''''''''''''''''''''''''''''''''''''''''''''''''''''
            sql = "SELECT p.ProductID, od.OrderID, p.ProductName AS Product, " & _
                "od.Quantity, '$' + Convert(varchar(12), p.Price) AS [Unit Price], '$' +
Convert(varchar(12), od.ProductCost) AS [Total] " & _
                "FROM Product p " & _
```

You may purchase a copy of our companion disk which contains all files for the project at http://www.amazon.com/gp/product/B00AOU76K8!

```
            "INNER JOIN OrderDetail od ON od.ProductID = p.ProductID " & _
            "WHERE od.OrderID = " & orderID & " " & _
            "UNION SELECT NULL, '', 'Totals', " & _
            "SUM(Quantity), '', '$' + Convert(varchar(12), SUM(od.ProductCost)) " & _
            "FROM Product p " & _
            "INNER JOIN OrderDetail od ON od.ProductID = p.ProductID " & _
            "WHERE od.OrderID = " & orderID & " " & _
            "ORDER BY OrderID DESC, ProductName ASC"
    End If

    cmd = New SqlCommand(sql, con)
    cmd.CommandType = Data.CommandType.Text

    adapter = New SqlDataAdapter(cmd)

    ' Fill the DataSet.
    ds = New DataSet()

    Try
      ' Open the database connection.
      con.Open()
      adapter.Fill(ds, sql)
    Finally

      con.Close()

      ' Perform the data binding.
      categoryFilter.DataSource = ds
      categoryFilter.DataBind()
    End Try
    'End If
    headerLabel.Text = "Shopping Cart"

  End Sub

  Protected Sub continueShopping()
    Page.Response.Redirect("ViewCategories.aspx")
  End Sub

  Protected Sub categoryFilter_RowCommand(ByVal sender As Object, ByVal e As
System.Web.UI.WebControls.GridViewCommandEventArgs) Handles
categoryFilter.RowCommand
     Dim obj As Object
     Dim id As String
     Dim ProductID As Integer
     Dim cmdName As String
```

You may purchase a copy of our companion disk which contains all files for the project at http://www.amazon.com/gp/product/B00AOU76K8!

```
        Dim myAccess As DatabaseAccess
        Dim myConnection As String
        Dim con As SqlConnection
        Dim cmd As SqlCommand
        Dim sql As String
        Dim readData As SqlDataReader

        cmdName = e.CommandName
        obj = e.CommandArgument
        id = obj.ToString
        ProductID = Convert.ToInt16(id.ToString)
        Session("ProductID") =
Convert.ToInt16(categoryFilter.DataKeys(ProductID).Value.ToString)
        ProductID = Convert.ToInt16(categoryFilter.DataKeys(ProductID).Value.ToString)

        Select Case (cmdName)
            Case "Select"
                passSessionVariable()
            Case "Delete"
                myAccess = New DatabaseAccess()
                myConnection = myAccess.getConnectionString()

                con = New SqlConnection(myConnection)
                sql = "DELETE FROM OrderDetail WHERE " & _
                    "OrderID = " & Session("OrderID") & _
                    " AND ProductID = " & ProductID & " "
                cmd = New SqlCommand(sql, con)
                cmd.CommandType = Data.CommandType.Text
                Try

                    ' Open database connection.
                    con.Open()

                    ' Execute the INSERT and fill the data reader.
                    readData = cmd.ExecuteReader(CommandBehavior.CloseConnection)

                Catch a As Exception

                    Throw a
                End Try
                con.Close()
                readData.Close()
                Page.Response.Redirect("ViewCart.aspx")
        End Select
    End Sub
```

You may purchase a copy of our companion disk which contains all files for the project at http://www.amazon.com/gp/product/B00AOU76K8!

```
    Protected Sub categoryFilter_RowDataBound(ByVal sender As Object, ByVal e As
System.Web.UI.WebControls.GridViewRowEventArgs) Handles categoryFilter.RowDataBound

        Dim myAccess As DatabaseAccess
        Dim myConnection As String
        Dim con As SqlConnection
        Dim cmd As SqlCommand
        Dim sql As String
        Dim readData As SqlDataReader
        Dim itemCount As Integer
        Dim orderID As Integer

        orderID = Session("OrderID")
        If orderID = Nothing Then
            orderID = -1
        End If

        myAccess = New DatabaseAccess()
        myConnection = myAccess.getConnectionString()

        con = New SqlConnection(myConnection)
        sql = "SELECT COUNT(OrderID) AS orderCount FROM OrderDetail " & _
              "WHERE OrderID = " & orderID
        cmd = New SqlCommand(sql, con)
        cmd.CommandType = Data.CommandType.Text
        Try

            ' Open database connection.
            con.Open()

            ' Execute the INSERT and fill the data reader.
            readData = cmd.ExecuteReader(CommandBehavior.CloseConnection)

        Catch a As Exception

            Throw a
        End Try
        readData.Read()
        itemCount = readData("orderCount")
        con.Close()
        readData.Close()

        If (Session("OrderID") <> Nothing) And (itemCount > 0) Then
            e.Row.Cells(2).Visible = False
            e.Row.Cells(3).Visible = False
        End If
```

You may purchase a copy of our companion disk which contains all files for the project at http://www.amazon.com/gp/product/B00AOU76K8!

```
        If (e.Row.RowIndex = Session("rowQty")) Then 'And (itemCount > 0) Then
            e.Row.Cells(0).Text = ""
            e.Row.Cells(1).Text = ""
        End If

    End Sub

    Protected Sub passSessionVariable()
        Page.Response.Redirect("ProductDetails.aspx")
    End Sub

    Protected Sub categoryFilter_RowDeleted(ByVal sender As Object, ByVal e As
System.Web.UI.WebControls.GridViewDeletedEventArgs) Handles categoryFilter.RowDeleted

    End Sub

    Protected Sub logout()
        Session("firstName") = Nothing
        Session.Clear()
        Page.Response.Redirect("Logout.aspx")
    End Sub

    Protected Sub categoryFilter_RowDeleting(ByVal sender As Object, ByVal e As
System.Web.UI.WebControls.GridViewDeleteEventArgs) Handles categoryFilter.RowDeleting

    End Sub
End Class
```

View Categories Server Page

Replace the existing code in the ViewCategories.aspx file with the following code (*REPLACE ANY CODE IN THIS COLOR WITH YOUR OWN INFORMATION!)*:

```
<%@ Page Language="VB"
      AutoEventWireup="true" EnableEventValidation="false"
      CodeFile="ViewCategories.aspx.vb"
      Inherits="_Default" %>

<!DOCTYPE html PUBLIC "-//W3C//DTD XHTML 1.0 Transitional//EN"
"http://www.w3.org/TR/xhtml1/DTD/xhtml1-transitional.dtd">
<html xmlns="http://www.w3.org/1999/xhtml">

<head>
<meta http-equiv="Content-Type" content="text/html; charset=iso-8859-1" />
<title>View Categories</title>
<link rel="stylesheet" href="emx_nav_left.css" type="text/css" />
<script type="text/javascript">

var time = 3000;
var numofitems = 7;

//menu constructor
function menu(allitems,thisitem,startstate){
  callname= "gl"+thisitem;
  divname="subglobal"+thisitem;
  this.numberofmenuitems = allitems;
  this.caller = document.getElementById(callname);
  this.thediv = document.getElementById(divname);
  this.thediv.style.visibility = startstate;
}

//menu methods
function ehandler(event,theobj){
  for (var i=1; i<= theobj.numberofmenuitems; i++){
    var shutdiv =eval( "menuitem"+i+".thediv");
    shutdiv.style.visibility="hidden";
  }
  theobj.thediv.style.visibility="visible";
}

function closesubnav(event){
  if ((event.clientY <48)||(event.clientY > 107)){
```

You may purchase a copy of our companion disk which contains all files for the project at http://www.amazon.com/gp/product/B00AOU76K8!

```
    for (var i=1; i<= numofitems; i++){
      var shutdiv =eval('menuitem'+i+'.thediv');
      shutdiv.style.visibility='hidden';
    }
  }
}
// -->
</script>
</head>
<body>

<form id="Form1" runat="server">
<div class="skipLinks">skip to: <a href="#content">page content</a> | <a
href="#pageNav">links on this page</a> | <a href="#globalNav">site navigation</a> | <a
href="#siteInfo">footer (site information)</a> </div>
<div id="masthead">
  <h1 id="siteName">Your Best Data Solution</h1>
  <div id="utility">
      <asp:LinkButton ID="lkCustomers" runat="server"
PostBackUrl="Customers.aspx">Customers</asp:LinkButton>
    | <asp:LinkButton ID="lkOrders" runat="server"
PostBackUrl="ViewOrders.aspx">Orders</asp:LinkButton>
    | <asp:LinkButton ID="lkAddProduct" PostBackUrl="AddProduct.aspx"
                runat="server">Add Product</asp:LinkButton>
    | <asp:LinkButton ID="lkEditProduct" runat="server"
PostBackUrl="ViewCategories.aspx">Edit Product</asp:LinkButton>
    | <asp:LinkButton ID="lkLogout" OnClick="logout" runat="server"
PostBackUrl="#">Logout</asp:LinkButton>
    | <asp:LinkButton ID="lkChangePassword" PostBackUrl="Password.aspx"
runat="server">Change Password</asp:LinkButton>
  </div>
  <div id="globalNav"> <img alt="" src="Pictures/gblnav_left.gif" height="32" width="4"
id="gnl" /> <img alt="" src="Pictures/glbnav_right.gif" height="32" width="4" id="gnr" />
    <div id="globalLink">
      <a href="Default.aspx" id="A1" class="glink">
      Home</a>
      <a href="ViewCategories.aspx" id="gl1" class="glink" >
      View Products</a>
      <a href="SearchProducts.aspx" id="gl2" class="glink">Search</a>
      <a href="ViewCart.aspx" id="gl3" class="glink">View Cart</a>
      <a href="Checkout.aspx" id="gl4" class="glink">Checkout</a>
      <a href="CreateAccount.aspx" id="gl5" class="glink">Create
      Account</a>
      <a href="Login.aspx" id="gl6" class="glink">Login
      </a><a href="OrderHistory.aspx" id="gl7" class="glink">Order
      History</a>
```

```
      <a href="FAQ.aspx" id="A2" class="glink">FAQ</a>
      <asp:Label ID="loginStatus" Visible="false" runat="server"></asp:Label>
    </div>
  </div>
<div id="pagecell1">
  <img alt="" src="Pictures/tl_curve_white.gif" height="6" width="6" id="tl" /> <img alt=""
src="Pictures/tr_curve_white.gif" height="6" width="6" id="tr" />

    <div id="pageName">
    <img alt="small logo" src="Pictures/YourBestDataSolutionLogo.jpg" height="50"
width="60"/> </div>
  <div id="pageNav">
    <div class="relatedLinks">
      <h3>Related Link Category</h3>
      <a href="FAQ.aspx#anchor3">Automation</a>
      <a href="FAQ.aspx#anchor1">Customized Reporting</a>
      <a href="FAQ.aspx#anchor2">Database Design</a>
      <a href="FAQ.aspx#anchor12">Data Migration</a>
      <a href="FAQ.aspx#anchor4">Data Modeling</a>
      <a href="FAQ.aspx#anchor14">Desktop Application Solutions</a>
      <a href="FAQ.aspx#anchor5">eCommerce Solutions</a>
      <a href="FAQ.aspx#anchor6">eMail Marketing</a>
      <a href="FAQ.aspx#anchor7">Mobile App Development</a>
      <a href="FAQ.aspx#anchor8">PayPal™ Integration</a>
      <a href="FAQ.aspx#anchor9">Web Design</a>
      <a href="FAQ.aspx#anchor10">Web Development</a>
    </div>
  </div>
  <div id="content">
    <div class="feature">
      <h3>Browse By Category</h3>
        <p>
    <asp:GridView ID ="categoryFilter"
              runat="server"
              DataKeyNames="CategoryID"
              OnRowDataBound="categoryFilter_RowDataBound"
              OnRowCommand="passSessionVariable"
              HeaderStyle-BackColor="#cccccc">
        <Columns>
          <asp:TemplateField>
          <ItemTemplate>
          <asp:LinkButton runat="server"
                    CommandName="Select"
                    CommandArgument="<%# Container.DataItemIndex %>"
                    Text = "View Products"></asp:LinkButton>
          </ItemTemplate>
```

You may purchase a copy of our companion disk which contains all files for the project at http://www.amazon.com/gp/product/B00AOU76K8!

```
            </asp:TemplateField>
        </Columns>
    </asp:GridView>
       </p>

    </div>
    <div class="story">
  <div id="siteInfo"> <img alt="small logo" src="Pictures/YourBestDataSolutionLogo.jpg"
width="59" height="66" />
            <a href="AboutUs.aspx">About Us</a> |
            <a href="ContactUs.aspx">Contact Us</a> |
      ©2012 YBDS, LLC </div>

</div>
<br />
    </form>
</body>
</html>
```

You may purchase a copy of our companion disk which contains all files for the project at http://www.amazon.com/gp/product/B00AOU76K8!

View Categories Code Behind

Replace the existing code in the ViewCategories.aspx.vb file with the following code:

```
Imports System.Data
Imports System.Data.SqlClient

Partial Class _Default
    Inherits System.Web.UI.Page

    Protected Sub Page_Load(ByVal sender As Object, ByVal e As EventArgs) Handles Me.Load

        Dim myAccess As DatabaseAccess
        Dim myConnection As String
        Dim con As SqlConnection
        Dim cmd As SqlCommand
        Dim adapter As SqlDataAdapter
        Dim ds As DataSet
        Dim sql As String

        If (Session("firstName") = Nothing) Then
            'User is not logged in.  Continue.
            lkLogout.Visible = False
            lkChangePassword.Visible = False
            lkChangePassword.Enabled = False
            Session("isAdmin") = False
            lkCustomers.Visible = False
            lkCustomers.Enabled = False
            lkOrders.Visible = False
            lkOrders.Enabled = False
            lkAddProduct.Visible = False
            lkAddProduct.Enabled = False
            lkEditProduct.Visible = False
            lkEditProduct.Enabled = False
        Else
            If (Session("isAdmin")) Then
                lkCustomers.Visible = True
                lkCustomers.Enabled = True
                lkOrders.Visible = True
                lkOrders.Enabled = True
                lkAddProduct.Visible = True
                lkAddProduct.Enabled = True
                lkEditProduct.Visible = True
                lkEditProduct.Enabled = True
```

```
        Else
            lkCustomers.Visible = False
            lkCustomers.Enabled = False
            lkOrders.Visible = False
            lkOrders.Enabled = False
            lkAddProduct.Visible = False
            lkAddProduct.Enabled = False
            lkEditProduct.Visible = False
            lkEditProduct.Enabled = False
        End If
        lkChangePassword.Visible = True
        lkChangePassword.Enabled = True
        loginStatus.Text = "Welcome " & Session("firstName").ToString() & "!"
        loginStatus.Visible = True
    End If

    myAccess = New DatabaseAccess()
    myConnection = myAccess.getConnectionString()

    con = New SqlConnection(myConnection)
    sql = "SELECT CategoryID, CategoryName AS [Category Name] FROM ProductCategory
" & _
        "ORDER BY CategoryName ASC"
    cmd = New SqlCommand(sql, con)
    cmd.CommandType = Data.CommandType.Text

    adapter = New SqlDataAdapter(cmd)

    ' Fill the DataSet.
    ds = New DataSet()

    Try
        ' Open the database connection.
        con.Open()
        adapter.Fill(ds, sql)
    Finally

        con.Close()

        ' Perform the data binding.
        categoryFilter.DataSource = ds
        categoryFilter.DataBind()
    End Try
End Sub

Protected Sub logout()
```

You may purchase a copy of our companion disk which contains all files for the project at http://www.amazon.com/gp/product/B00AOU76K8!

```
        Session("firstName") = Nothing
        Session.Clear()
        Page.Response.Redirect("Logout.aspx")
    End Sub

    Public Sub passSessionVariable()
        Page.Response.Redirect("ViewProducts.aspx")
    End Sub

    Protected Sub categoryFilter_RowCommand(ByVal sender As Object, ByVal e As
System.Web.UI.WebControls.GridViewCommandEventArgs) Handles
categoryFilter.RowCommand
        Dim obj As Object
        Dim id As String
        Dim categoryID As Integer
        obj = e.CommandArgument
        id = obj.ToString
        categoryID = Convert.ToInt16(id.ToString)
        Session("categoryID") =
Convert.ToInt16(categoryFilter.DataKeys(categoryID).Value.ToString)
        categoryID = Convert.ToInt16(categoryFilter.DataKeys(categoryID).Value.ToString)
        passSessionVariable()
    End Sub

    Protected Sub categoryFilter_RowDataBound(ByVal sender As Object, ByVal e As
System.Web.UI.WebControls.GridViewRowEventArgs) Handles categoryFilter.RowDataBound
        e.Row.Cells(1).Visible = False
    End Sub
End Class
```

View Orders Server Page

Replace the existing code in the ViewOrders.aspx file with the following code (*REPLACE ANY CODE IN THIS COLOR WITH YOUR OWN INFORMATION!)*:

```
<%@ Page Language="VB"
        AutoEventWireup="True"
        CodeFile="ViewOrders.aspx.vb"
        Inherits="_Default" %>

<!DOCTYPE html PUBLIC "-//W3C//DTD XHTML 1.0 Transitional//EN"
"http://www.w3.org/TR/xhtml1/DTD/xhtml1-transitional.dtd">
<html xmlns="http://www.w3.org/1999/xhtml">

<head>
<meta http-equiv="Content-Type" content="text/html; charset=iso-8859-1" />
<title>View Orders</title>
<link rel="stylesheet" href="emx_nav_left.css" type="text/css" />
<script type="text/javascript">

var time = 3000;
var numofitems = 7;

//menu constructor
function menu(allitems,thisitem,startstate){
  callname= "gl"+thisitem;
  divname="subglobal"+thisitem;
  this.numberofmenuitems = allitems;
  this.caller = document.getElementById(callname);
  this.thediv = document.getElementById(divname);
  this.thediv.style.visibility = startstate;
}

//menu methods
function ehandler(event,theobj){
  for (var i=1; i<= theobj.numberofmenuitems; i++){
    var shutdiv =eval( "menuitem"+i+".thediv");
    shutdiv.style.visibility="hidden";
  }
  theobj.thediv.style.visibility="visible";
}

function closesubnav(event){
  if ((event.clientY <48)||(event.clientY > 107)){
```

```
    for (var i=1; i<= numofitems; i++){
      var shutdiv =eval('menuitem'+i+'.thediv');
      shutdiv.style.visibility='hidden';
    }
  }
}
</script>
</head>
<body>

<form id="Form1" runat="server">
<div class="skipLinks">skip to: <a href="#content">page content</a> | <a
href="#pageNav">links on this page</a> | <a href="#globalNav">site navigation</a> | <a
href="#siteInfo">footer (site information)</a> </div>
<div id="masthead">
  <h1 id="siteName">Your Best Data Solution</h1>
  <div id="utility">
      <asp:LinkButton ID="lkCustomers" runat="server"
PostBackUrl="Customers.aspx">Customers</asp:LinkButton>
     | <asp:LinkButton ID="lkOrders" runat="server"
PostBackUrl="ViewOrders.aspx">Orders</asp:LinkButton>
     | <asp:LinkButton ID="lkAddProduct" PostBackUrl="AddProduct.aspx"
                 runat="server">Add Product</asp:LinkButton>
     | <asp:LinkButton ID="lkEditProduct" runat="server"
PostBackUrl="ViewCategories.aspx">Edit Product</asp:LinkButton>
     | <asp:LinkButton ID="lkLogout" OnClick="logout" runat="server"
PostBackUrl="#">Logout</asp:LinkButton>
     | <asp:LinkButton ID="lkChangePassword" PostBackUrl="Password.aspx"
runat="server">Change Password</asp:LinkButton>
  </div>
  <div id="globalNav"> <img alt="" src="Pictures/gblnav_left.gif" height="32" width="4"
id="gnl" /> <img alt="" src="Pictures/glbnav_right.gif" height="32" width="4" id="gnr" />
    <div id="globalLink">
       <a href="Default.aspx" id="A1" class="glink">
       Home</a>
       <a href="ViewCategories.aspx" id="gl1" class="glink" >
       View Products</a>
       <a href="SearchProducts.aspx" id="gl2" class="glink">Search</a>
       <a href="ViewCart.aspx" id="gl3" class="glink">View Cart</a>
       <a href="Checkout.aspx" id="gl4" class="glink">Checkout</a>
       <a href="CreateAccount.aspx" id="gl5" class="glink">Create
       Account</a>
       <a href="Login.aspx" id="gl6" class="glink">Login
       </a><a href="OrderHistory.aspx" id="gl7" class="glink">Order
       History</a>
       <a href="FAQ.aspx" id="A2" class="glink">FAQ</a>
```

```
      <asp:Label ID="loginStatus" Visible="false" runat="server"></asp:Label>
    </div>
  </div>
<div id="pagecell1">
  <img alt="" src="Pictures/tl_curve_white.gif" height="6" width="6" id="tl" /> <img alt=""
src="Pictures/tr_curve_white.gif" height="6" width="6" id="tr" />

    <div id="pageName">
    <img alt="small logo" src="Pictures/YourBestDataSolutionLogo.jpg" height="50"
width="60"/> </div>
  <div id="pageNav">
    <div class="relatedLinks">
      <h3>Related Link Category</h3>
      <a href="FAQ.aspx#anchor3">Automation</a>
      <a href="FAQ.aspx#anchor1">Customized Reporting</a>
      <a href="FAQ.aspx#anchor2">Database Design</a>
      <a href="FAQ.aspx#anchor12">Data Migration</a>
      <a href="FAQ.aspx#anchor4">Data Modeling</a>
      <a href="FAQ.aspx#anchor14">Desktop Application Solutions</a>
      <a href="FAQ.aspx#anchor5">eCommerce Solutions</a>
      <a href="FAQ.aspx#anchor6">eMail Marketing</a>
      <a href="FAQ.aspx#anchor7">Mobile App Development</a>
      <a href="FAQ.aspx#anchor8">PayPal™ Integration</a>
      <a href="FAQ.aspx#anchor9">Web Design</a>
      <a href="FAQ.aspx#anchor10">Web Development</a>
    </div>
  </div>
  <div id="content">
    <div class="feature">
      <h3>
      <asp:Label runat="server" ID="headerLabel" Text ="Order History"></asp:Label></h3>
       <p>
          <asp:Label ID="dropdownLabel"
                Text="Select order status"
                runat="server"></asp:Label>
          <asp:DropDownList ID="orderType"
                    runat="server"
                    autopostback="true"
                    Width ="200"
                    OnSelectedIndexChanged="orderType_SelectedIndexChanged"
                    DataValueField="OrderStatusID"
                    DataTextField="OrderStatusName"></asp:DropDownList>
          <asp:Button ID="filterOrder"
                OnClick="filterOrder_Click"
                Text="Filter by order status"
                runat="server" />
```

```
        </br>
        <asp:GridView ID ="categoryFilter"
                runat="server"
                DataKeyNames="Order #"
                OnRowCommand="categoryFilter_RowCommand"
                EditRowStyle-HorizontalAlign="Center"
                HeaderStyle-BackColor="#cccccc"
                BorderStyle="None"
                EmptyDataText="No items are currently in your cart." >
          <Columns>
            <asp:TemplateField>
            <ItemTemplate>
            <asp:LinkButton ID="viewOrder"
                    runat="server"
                    CommandName="Select"
                    CommandArgument="<%# Container.DataItemIndex %>"
                    Text = "View Order Detail"></asp:LinkButton>
            </ItemTemplate>
            </asp:TemplateField>
          </Columns>
        </asp:GridView>
      </p>

    </div>
    <div class="story">
  <div id="siteInfo"> <img alt="small logo" src="Pictures/YourBestDataSolutionLogo.jpg"
width="59" height="66" />
        <a href="AboutUs.aspx">About Us</a> |
        <a href="ContactUs.aspx">Contact Us</a> |
    ©2012 YBDS, LLC </div>

</div>
<br />
    </form>
</body>
</html>
```

You may purchase a copy of our companion disk which contains all files for the project at http://www.amazon.com/gp/product/B00AOU76K8!

View Orders Code Behind

Replace the existing code in the ViewOrders.aspx.vb file with the following code:

```
Imports System.Data
Imports System.Data.SqlClient

Partial Class _Default
   Inherits System.Web.UI.Page

   Protected Sub Page_Load(ByVal sender As Object, ByVal e As EventArgs) Handles Me.Load

      If (Session("firstName") = Nothing) Then
         'User is not logged in.  Continue.
         lkLogout.Visible = False
         lkChangePassword.Visible = False
         lkChangePassword.Enabled = False
         categoryFilter.EmptyDataText = "Please log in to view your past orders."
         Session("isAdmin") = False
         lkCustomers.Visible = False
         lkCustomers.Enabled = False
         lkOrders.Visible = False
         lkOrders.Enabled = False
         lkAddProduct.Visible = False
         lkAddProduct.Enabled = False
         lkEditProduct.Visible = False
         lkEditProduct.Enabled = False
         categoryFilter.Visible = True
      Else
         If (Session("isAdmin")) Then
            lkCustomers.Visible = True
            lkCustomers.Enabled = True
            lkOrders.Visible = True
            lkOrders.Enabled = True
            lkAddProduct.Visible = True
            lkAddProduct.Enabled = True
            lkEditProduct.Visible = True
            lkEditProduct.Enabled = True
         Else
            lkCustomers.Visible = False
            lkCustomers.Enabled = False
            lkOrders.Visible = False
            lkOrders.Enabled = False
            lkAddProduct.Visible = False
```

```
        lkAddProduct.Enabled = False
        lkEditProduct.Visible = False
        lkEditProduct.Enabled = False
    End If
    lkChangePassword.Visible = True
    lkChangePassword.Enabled = True
    loginStatus.Text = "Welcome " & Session("firstName").ToString() & "!"
    loginStatus.Visible = True
    ''''''''''''''''''''''''''''''''''''''''''
    ' Show the previous orders for the current user.
    Dim myAccess As DatabaseAccess
    Dim myConnection As String
    Dim con As SqlConnection
    Dim cmd As SqlCommand
    Dim adapter As SqlDataAdapter
    Dim ds As DataSet
    Dim sql As String
    Dim userID As String

    ' Fill database connection variables.
    myAccess = New DatabaseAccess()
    myConnection = myAccess.getConnectionString()
    con = New SqlConnection(myConnection)

    userID = Session("UserID")
    If userID = Nothing Then
        userID = -1
    End If

    myAccess = New DatabaseAccess()
    myConnection = myAccess.getConnectionString()

    con = New SqlConnection(myConnection)
    sql = "SELECT uo.OrderID AS [Order #], " & _
        "uo.OrderDate AS [Order Date], " & _
        "os.OrderStatusName AS [Order Status] " & _
        "FROM UserOrder uo " & _
        "INNER JOIN OrderStatus os " & _
        "ON os.OrderStatusID = uo.OrderStatusID " & _
        "WHERE uo.OrderStatusID IS NOT NULL " & _
        "AND uo.OrderID IN (SELECT OrderID FROM OrderDetail)"
    cmd = New SqlCommand(sql, con)
    cmd.CommandType = Data.CommandType.Text
    adapter = New SqlDataAdapter(cmd)

    ' Fill the DataSet.
```

```
ds = New DataSet()

Try
   ' Open the database connection.
   con.Open()
   adapter.Fill(ds, sql)
Finally

   con.Close()
   Select Case (Session("orderType"))
      Case 1
         categoryFilter.EmptyDataText = "There are no paid orders to view."
      Case 2
         categoryFilter.EmptyDataText = "There are no shipped orders to view."
   End Select
   If Not (Page.IsPostBack) Then
      ' Perform the data binding.
      categoryFilter.DataSource = ds
      categoryFilter.DataBind()
   End If
End Try

' Bind the order status combo.
sql = "SELECT OrderStatusID, OrderStatusName FROM OrderStatus"
cmd = New SqlCommand(sql, con)
cmd.CommandType = Data.CommandType.Text
adapter = New SqlDataAdapter(cmd)

' Fill the DataSet.
ds = New DataSet()

Try
   ' Open the database connection.
   con.Open()
   adapter.Fill(ds, sql)
Finally

   con.Close()

   If Not (Page.IsPostBack) Then
      ' Perform the data binding.
      orderType.DataSource = ds
      orderType.DataBind()
   End If
End Try
```

```
            headerLabel.Text = "Orders"
        End If

        Session("orderType") = orderType.SelectedItem.Value
    End Sub

    Protected Sub logout()
        Session("firstName") = Nothing
        Session.Clear()
        Page.Response.Redirect("Logout.aspx")
    End Sub

    Protected Sub passSessionVariable()
        ''''''''''''''''''''''''''''''''''''''''''''''''''''''
        ' Open order details page for selected order.
        Page.Response.Redirect("OrderDetails.aspx")
    End Sub

    Protected Sub categoryFilter_RowCommand(ByVal sender As Object, ByVal e As
System.Web.UI.WebControls.GridViewCommandEventArgs) Handles
categoryFilter.RowCommand
        Dim obj As Object
        Dim id As String
        Dim orderID As Integer
        Dim cmdName As String

        cmdName = e.CommandName
        obj = e.CommandArgument
        id = obj.ToString
        orderID = Convert.ToInt16(id.ToString)
        Session("viewOrderID") =
Convert.ToInt16(categoryFilter.DataKeys(orderID).Value.ToString)
        orderID = Convert.ToInt16(categoryFilter.DataKeys(orderID).Value.ToString)

        Select Case (cmdName)
            Case "Select"
                passSessionVariable()
        End Select
    End Sub

    Protected Sub orderType_SelectedIndexChanged(ByVal sender As Object, ByVal e As
System.EventArgs) Handles orderType.SelectedIndexChanged
        Session("orderType") = orderType.SelectedItem.Value
        categoryFilter.EmptyDataText = ""
    End Sub
```

You may purchase a copy of our companion disk which contains all files for the project at http://www.amazon.com/gp/product/B00AOU76K8!

```
   Protected Sub filterOrder_Click(ByVal sender As Object, ByVal e As System.EventArgs)
Handles filterOrder.Click
      ' Show the previous orders for the current user.
      Dim myAccess As DatabaseAccess
      Dim myConnection As String
      Dim con As SqlConnection
      Dim cmd As SqlCommand
      Dim adapter As SqlDataAdapter
      Dim ds As DataSet
      Dim sql As String
      Dim userID As String
      'Dim readData As SqlDataReader
      'Dim itemCount As Integer

      ' Fill database connection variables.
      myAccess = New DatabaseAccess()
      myConnection = myAccess.getConnectionString()
      con = New SqlConnection(myConnection)

      userID = Session("UserID")
      If userID = Nothing Then
         userID = -1
      End If

      myAccess = New DatabaseAccess()
      myConnection = myAccess.getConnectionString()

      con = New SqlConnection(myConnection)
      sql = "SELECT uo.OrderID AS [Order #], " & _
          "uo.OrderDate AS [Order Date], " & _
          "os.OrderStatusName AS [Order Status] " & _
          "FROM UserOrder uo " & _
          "INNER JOIN OrderStatus os " & _
          "ON os.OrderStatusID = uo.OrderStatusID " & _
          "WHERE uo.OrderStatusID = " & Session("orderType") & " " & _
          "AND uo.OrderID IN (SELECT OrderID FROM OrderDetail)"
      cmd = New SqlCommand(sql, con)
      cmd.CommandType = Data.CommandType.Text
      adapter = New SqlDataAdapter(cmd)

      ' Fill the DataSet.
      ds = New DataSet()

      Try
         ' Open the database connection.
         con.Open()
```

```
            adapter.Fill(ds, sql)
        Finally
            con.Close()

            ' Perform the data binding.
            categoryFilter.DataSource = ds
            categoryFilter.DataBind()
        End Try
        headerLabel.Text = "Order History"
    End Sub
End Class
```

View Products Server Page

Replace the existing code in the ViewProducts.aspx file with the following code (***REPLACE ANY CODE IN THIS COLOR WITH YOUR OWN INFORMATION!)***:

```
<%@ Page Language="VB"
        AutoEventWireup="True"
        CodeFile="ViewProducts.aspx.vb"
        Inherits="_Default" %>

<!DOCTYPE html PUBLIC "-//W3C//DTD XHTML 1.0 Transitional//EN"
"http://www.w3.org/TR/xhtml1/DTD/xhtml1-transitional.dtd">
<html xmlns="http://www.w3.org/1999/xhtml">

<head>
<meta http-equiv="Content-Type" content="text/html; charset=iso-8859-1" />
<title>View Products</title>
<link rel="stylesheet" href="emx_nav_left.css" type="text/css" />
<script type="text/javascript">

var time = 3000;
var numofitems = 7;

//menu constructor
function menu(allitems,thisitem,startstate){
  callname= "gl"+thisitem;
  divname="subglobal"+thisitem;
  this.numberofmenuitems = allitems;
  this.caller = document.getElementById(callname);
  this.thediv = document.getElementById(divname);
  this.thediv.style.visibility = startstate;
}

//menu methods
function ehandler(event,theobj){
  for (var i=1; i<= theobj.numberofmenuitems; i++){
    var shutdiv =eval( "menuitem"+i+".thediv");
    shutdiv.style.visibility="hidden";
  }
  theobj.thediv.style.visibility="visible";
}

function closesubnav(event){
  if ((event.clientY <48)||(event.clientY > 107)){
    for (var i=1; i<= numofitems; i++){
      var shutdiv =eval('menuitem'+i+'.thediv');
```

You may purchase a copy of our companion disk which contains all files for the project at http://www.amazon.com/gp/product/B00AOU76K8!

```
    shutdiv.style.visibility='hidden';
   }
  }
}
// -->
</script>
</head>
<body>

<form id="Form1" runat="server">
<div class="skipLinks">skip to: <a href="#content">page content</a> | <a
href="#pageNav">links on this page</a> | <a href="#globalNav">site navigation</a> | <a
href="#siteInfo">footer (site information)</a> </div>
<div id="masthead">
  <h1 id="siteName">Your Best Data Solution</h1>
  <div id="utility">
      <asp:LinkButton ID="lkCustomers" runat="server"
PostBackUrl="Customers.aspx">Customers</asp:LinkButton>
    | <asp:LinkButton ID="lkOrders" runat="server"
PostBackUrl="ViewOrders.aspx">Orders</asp:LinkButton>
    | <asp:LinkButton ID="lkAddProduct" PostBackUrl="AddProduct.aspx"
                runat="server">Add Product</asp:LinkButton>
    | <asp:LinkButton ID="lkEditProduct" runat="server"
PostBackUrl="ViewCategories.aspx">Edit Product</asp:LinkButton>
    | <asp:LinkButton ID="lkLogout" OnClick="logout" runat="server"
PostBackUrl="#">Logout</asp:LinkButton>
    | <asp:LinkButton ID="lkChangePassword" PostBackUrl="Password.aspx"
runat="server">Change Password</asp:LinkButton>
  </div>
  <div id="globalNav"> <img alt="" src="Pictures/gblnav_left.gif" height="32" width="4"
id="gnl" /> <img alt="" src="Pictures/glbnav_right.gif" height="32" width="4" id="gnr" />
   <div id="globalLink">
      <a href="Default.aspx" id="A1" class="glink">
      Home</a>
      <a href="ViewCategories.aspx" id="gl1" class="glink" >
      View Products</a>
      <a href="SearchProducts.aspx" id="gl2" class="glink">Search</a>
      <a href="ViewCart.aspx" id="gl3" class="glink">View Cart</a>
      <a href="Checkout.aspx" id="gl4" class="glink">Checkout</a>
      <a href="CreateAccount.aspx" id="gl5" class="glink">Create
      Account</a>
      <a href="Login.aspx" id="gl6" class="glink">Login
      </a><a href="OrderHistory.aspx" id="gl7" class="glink">Order
      History</a>
      <a href="FAQ.aspx" id="A2" class="glink">FAQ</a>
      <asp:Label ID="loginStatus" Visible="false" runat="server"></asp:Label>
```

```
    </div>
  </div>
<div id="pagecell1">
  <img alt="" src="Pictures/tl_curve_white.gif" height="6" width="6" id="tl" /> <img alt=""
src="Pictures/tr_curve_white.gif" height="6" width="6" id="tr" />

    <div id="pageName">
    <img alt="small logo" src="Pictures/YourBestDataSolutionLogo.jpg" height="50"
width="60"/> </div>
  <div id="pageNav">
    <div class="relatedLinks">
      <h3>Related Link Category</h3>
      <a href="FAQ.aspx#anchor3">Automation</a>
      <a href="FAQ.aspx#anchor1">Customized Reporting</a>
      <a href="FAQ.aspx#anchor2">Database Design</a>
      <a href="FAQ.aspx#anchor12">Data Migration</a>
      <a href="FAQ.aspx#anchor4">Data Modeling</a>
      <a href="FAQ.aspx#anchor14">Desktop Application Solutions</a>
      <a href="FAQ.aspx#anchor5">eCommerce Solutions</a>
      <a href="FAQ.aspx#anchor6">eMail Marketing</a>
      <a href="FAQ.aspx#anchor7">Mobile App Development</a>
      <a href="FAQ.aspx#anchor8">PayPal™ Integration</a>
      <a href="FAQ.aspx#anchor9">Web Design</a>
      <a href="FAQ.aspx#anchor10">Web Development</a>
    </div>
  </div>
  <div id="content">
    <div class="feature">
      <h3><asp:Label runat="server" ID="headerLabel"></asp:Label></h3>
        <p>
    <asp:GridView ID ="categoryFilter"
              runat="server"
              DataKeyNames="ProductID"
              OnRowDataBound="categoryFilter_RowDataBound"
              OnRowCommand="passSessionVariable"
              HeaderStyle-BackColor="#cccccc">
        <Columns>
          <asp:TemplateField>
          <ItemTemplate>
          <asp:LinkButton ID="productDetails"
                    runat="server"
                    CommandName="Select"
                    CommandArgument="<%# Container.DataItemIndex %>"
                    Text = "Product Details"></asp:LinkButton>
          </ItemTemplate>
          </asp:TemplateField>
```

You may purchase a copy of our companion disk which contains all files for the project at http://www.amazon.com/gp/product/B00AOU76K8!

```
        <asp:TemplateField>
        <ItemTemplate>
        <asp:Image ID="thumbnail"
                Height="100" Width="100"
                runat ="server" />
        </ItemTemplate>
        </asp:TemplateField>
      </Columns>
   </asp:GridView>
     </p>

   </div>
   <div class="story">
  <div id="siteInfo"> <img alt="small logo" src="Pictures/YourBestDataSolutionLogo.jpg"
width="59" height="66" />
        <a href="AboutUs.aspx">About Us</a> |
        <a href="ContactUs.aspx">Contact Us</a> |
    ©2012 YBDS, LLC </div>

</div>
<br />
   </form>
</body>
</html>
```

View Products Code Behind

Replace the existing code in the ViewProducts.aspx.vb file with the following code:

```
Imports System.Data
Imports System.Data.SqlClient

Partial Class _Default
   Inherits System.Web.UI.Page

   Protected Sub Page_Load(ByVal sender As Object, ByVal e As EventArgs) Handles Me.Load

      Dim myAccess As DatabaseAccess
      Dim myConnection As String
      Dim con As SqlConnection
      Dim cmd As SqlCommand
      Dim adapter As SqlDataAdapter
      Dim ds As DataSet
      Dim sql As String

      If (Session("firstName") = Nothing) Then
         'User is not logged in.  Continue.
         lkLogout.Visible = False
         lkChangePassword.Visible = False
         lkChangePassword.Enabled = False
         Session("isAdmin") = False
         lkCustomers.Visible = False
         lkCustomers.Enabled = False
         lkOrders.Visible = False
         lkOrders.Enabled = False
         lkAddProduct.Visible = False
         lkAddProduct.Enabled = False
         lkEditProduct.Visible = False
         lkEditProduct.Enabled = False
      Else
         If (Session("isAdmin")) Then
            lkCustomers.Visible = True
            lkCustomers.Enabled = True
            lkOrders.Visible = True
            lkOrders.Enabled = True
            lkAddProduct.Visible = True
            lkAddProduct.Enabled = True
            lkEditProduct.Visible = True
            lkEditProduct.Enabled = True
         Else
            lkCustomers.Visible = False
```

```
            lkCustomers.Enabled = False
            lkOrders.Visible = False
            lkOrders.Enabled = False
            lkAddProduct.Visible = False
            lkAddProduct.Enabled = False
            lkEditProduct.Visible = False
            lkEditProduct.Enabled = False
        End If
        lkChangePassword.Visible = True
        lkChangePassword.Enabled = True
        loginStatus.Text = "Welcome " & Session("firstName").ToString() & "!"
        loginStatus.Visible = True
    End If

    myAccess = New DatabaseAccess()
    myConnection = myAccess.getConnectionString()

    con = New SqlConnection(myConnection)
    sql = "SELECT ProductID, ProductName AS Product FROM Product " & _
        "WHERE CategoryID = " & Session("CategoryID") & " " & _
        "ORDER BY ProductName ASC"
    cmd = New SqlCommand(sql, con)
    cmd.CommandType = Data.CommandType.Text

    adapter = New SqlDataAdapter(cmd)

    ' Fill the DataSet.
    ds = New DataSet()

    Try
        ' Open the database connection.
        con.Open()
        adapter.Fill(ds, sql)
    Finally

        con.Close()

        ' Perform the data binding.
        categoryFilter.DataSource = ds
        categoryFilter.DataBind()
    End Try

    Dim readData As SqlDataReader
    Dim val As String

    sql = "SELECT CategoryName FROM ProductCategory " & _
```

```
        "WHERE CategoryID = " & Session("categoryID")

    cmd = New SqlCommand(sql, con)
    cmd.CommandType = Data.CommandType.Text

    Try

      ' Open database connection.
      con.Open()

      ' Execute the stored procedure and fill the data reader.
      readData = cmd.ExecuteReader(CommandBehavior.CloseConnection)

    Catch a As Exception

      Throw a
    End Try

    readData.Read()
    val = readData("CategoryName")
    headerLabel.Text = val
    con.Close()

    ''''''''''''''''''''''''''''''''''''''''''''''''''''''''''''''''''''''''

    ' Load the pictures.
    Dim ib As Image
    Dim row As GridViewRow
    Dim currentRowIndex As Integer
    Dim photoThumbnail As String

    For Each row In categoryFilter.Rows
      currentRowIndex =
Convert.ToInt16(categoryFilter.DataKeys(row.RowIndex).Value.ToString)
      ib = row.FindControl("thumbnail")
      sql = "SELECT PhotoThumbnail FROM Product " & _
         "WHERE ProductID = " & currentRowIndex
      cmd = New SqlCommand(sql, con)
      cmd.CommandType = Data.CommandType.Text

      Try

        ' Open database connection.
        con.Open()

        ' Execute the stored procedure and fill the data reader.
```

You may purchase a copy of our companion disk which contains all files for the project at http://www.amazon.com/gp/product/B00AOU76K8!

```
            readData = cmd.ExecuteReader(CommandBehavior.CloseConnection)

        Catch a As Exception

            Throw a
        End Try

        readData.Read()
        photoThumbnail = IIf(IsDBNull(readData("PhotoThumbnail")), "",
readData("PhotoThumbnail"))
        val = "Pictures/" + IIf(IsDBNull(photoThumbnail) Or photoThumbnail = "", "No-image-
available.jpg", photoThumbnail)
        ib.ImageUrl = val
        con.Close()
      Next
      '''''''''''''''''''''''''''''''''''''''''''''''''''''''''''''''''''''''

   End Sub

   Protected Sub categoryFilter_RowCommand(ByVal sender As Object, ByVal e As
System.Web.UI.WebControls.GridViewCommandEventArgs) Handles
categoryFilter.RowCommand
      Dim obj As Object
      Dim id As String
      Dim ProductID As Integer
      obj = e.CommandArgument
      id = obj.ToString
      ProductID = Convert.ToInt16(id.ToString)
      Session("ProductID") =
Convert.ToInt16(categoryFilter.DataKeys(ProductID).Value.ToString)
      ProductID = Convert.ToInt16(categoryFilter.DataKeys(ProductID).Value.ToString)
      passSessionVariable()
   End Sub

   Protected Sub categoryFilter_RowDataBound(ByVal sender As Object, ByVal e As
System.Web.UI.WebControls.GridViewRowEventArgs) Handles categoryFilter.RowDataBound
      e.Row.Cells(2).Visible = False
   End Sub

   Protected Sub passSessionVariable()
      Page.Response.Redirect("ProductDetails.aspx")
   End Sub

   Protected Sub logout()
      Session("firstName") = Nothing
      Session.Clear()
      Page.Response.Redirect("Logout.aspx")
```

```
    End Sub
End Class
```

You may purchase a copy of our companion disk which contains all files for the project at http://www.amazon.com/gp/product/B00AOU76K8!

App_Code – DatabaseAccess.vb

Replace the existing code in the DatabaseAccess.vb file with the following code (*REPLACE ANY CODE IN THIS COLOR WITH YOUR OWN INFORMATION!*):

```
Imports System.Data.SqlClient
Imports System
Imports System.Data
Imports System.Configuration
Imports System.Collections
Imports System.Linq
Imports System.Web
Imports System.Web.Configuration
Imports System.Web.Security
Imports System.Web.UI
Imports System.Web.UI.HtmlControls
Imports System.Web.UI.WebControls
Imports System.Web.UI.WebControls.WebParts
Imports System.Xml.Linq
Imports Microsoft.VisualBasic

Public Class DatabaseAccess
   Public Function getConnectionString() As String
      getConnectionString = "Data Source=Enter data source from step 9 of SQL Database
Setup Chapter;" & _
      "Initial Catalog=Enter Initial Catalog from step 9 of SQL Database Setup Chapter;" &
_
      "User ID=Enter User ID from step 9 of SQL Database Setup Chapter;" & _
      "Password=Enter Password from step 9 of SQL Database Setup Chapter;"
   End Function

   Public Function isAdmin(ByVal userID As Integer) As Boolean

      ' Determine if current user is customer or admin.
      'Dim myAccess As DatabaseAccess
      Dim myConnection As String
      Dim con As SqlConnection
      Dim cmd As SqlCommand
      Dim sql As String
      Dim readData As SqlDataReader

      ' Fill database connection variables.
      myConnection = getConnectionString()
      con = New SqlConnection(myConnection)
```

You may purchase a copy of our companion disk which contains all files for the project at http://www.amazon.com/gp/product/B00AOU76K8!

```
'myAccess = New DatabaseAccess()
myConnection = getConnectionString()

con = New SqlConnection(myConnection)

' Get shippingmethodID, salesTaxRate and shippingCost.
sql = "SELECT uo.UserTypeID, UserTypeName " & _
    "FROM [User] uo " & _
    "INNER JOIN UserType ut " & _
    "ON uo.UserTypeID = ut.UserTypeID " & _
    "WHERE UserID = " & userID & " "
cmd = New SqlCommand(sql, con)
cmd.CommandType = Data.CommandType.Text
Try

  ' Open database connection.
  con.Open()

  ' Execute the INSERT and fill the data reader.
  readData = cmd.ExecuteReader(CommandBehavior.CloseConnection)

Catch a As Exception

  Throw a
End Try
readData.Read()
Select Case (readData("UserTypeName"))
  Case "Customer"
    isAdmin = False
  Case "Administrator"
    isAdmin = True
End Select
readData.Close()
con.Close()
''''''''''''''''''''''''''''''''''''''''''''''
End Function

Public Function GetDataReader(ByVal storedProcedure As String, _
                    ByVal connectionString As String, _
                    ByVal methodParameters As ArrayList) _
                    As SqlDataReader
  Dim myConnection As SqlConnection
  Dim cmd As SqlCommand
  Dim readData As SqlDataReader
```

```
        myConnection = New SqlConnection(connectionString)
        cmd = New SqlCommand(storedProcedure, myConnection)
        cmd.CommandType = Data.CommandType.Text

        Try

            ' Open database connection.
            myConnection.Open()

            ' Execute the stored procedure and fill the data reader.
            readData = cmd.ExecuteReader(CommandBehavior.CloseConnection)

            Return readData
        Catch e As Exception

            Throw e
        End Try

    End Function

    Public Function GetDataSet(ByVal storedProcedure As String, _
                    ByVal connectionString As String, _
                    ByVal methodParameters As ArrayList) As DataSet

        Dim myConnection As SqlConnection
        Dim cmd As SqlCommand
        Dim myAdapter As SqlDataAdapter
        Dim myDataSet As DataSet

        myConnection = New SqlConnection(connectionString)
        cmd = New SqlCommand(storedProcedure, myConnection)
        cmd.CommandType = CommandType.StoredProcedure

        myAdapter = New SqlDataAdapter(cmd)
        myDataSet = New DataSet()

        Try

            ' Open the database connection.
            myConnection.Open()
            myAdapter.Fill(myDataSet, "States")

        Finally
            myConnection.Close()
            GetDataSet = myDataSet
        End Try
```

```
    End Function

    Public Sub InsertUpdateDate(ByVal storedProcedure As String, _
                                ByVal connectionString As String, _
                             ByVal methodParameters As ArrayList)
        Dim myConnection As SqlConnection
        Dim cmd As SqlCommand

        myConnection = New SqlConnection(connectionString)
        cmd = New SqlCommand(storedProcedure, myConnection)
        cmd.CommandType = CommandType.StoredProcedure

        Try

            ' Open the database connection.
            myConnection.Open()

            ' Fill the data reader and close the connection.
            cmd.ExecuteNonQuery()

        Catch e As Exception

            Throw e
        End Try
    End Sub

End Class
```

App_Code – paypalfunctions.vb

Replace the existing code in the paypalfunctions.vb file with the following code (*REPLACE ANY CODE IN THIS COLOR WITH YOUR OWN INFORMATION!)*:

** This module is provided publicly by PayPal™.

```
Imports System
Imports System.Collections
Imports System.Collections.Specialized
Imports System.IO
Imports System.Net
Imports System.Text
Imports System.Data
Imports System.Configuration
Imports System.Web

Public Class NVPAPICaller

    Private pendpointurl As String = "https://api-3t.paypal.com/nvp"
    Private Const CVV2 As String = "CVV2"

    'Flag that determines the PayPal™ environment (live or sandbox)
    Private Const bSandbox As Boolean = False

    Private Const SIGNATURE As String = "SIGNATURE"
    Private Const PWD As String = "PWD"
    Private Const ACCT As String = "ACCT"

    'Replace <API_USERNAME> with your API Username
    'Replace <API_PASSWORD> with your API Password
    'Replace <API_SIGNATURE> with your Signature

    ''''''''''''''''''''''''''''''''''''''''''''''''''''''''''''''''''''''''''
    ' SANDBOX
    'Public APIUsername As String = "Enter your sandbox API Username here (see PayPal™
Account Setup Chapter)"
    'Private APIPassword As String = "Enter your sandbox API Password here (see PayPal™
Account Setup Chapter)"
    'Private APISignature As String = "Enter your sandbox API Signature here (see PayPal™
Account Setup Chapter)"
    ''''''''''''''''''''''''''''''''''''''''''''''''''''''''''''''''''''''''''

    ''''''''''''''''''''''''''''''''''''''''''''''''''''''''''''''''''''''''''
    ' PRODUCTION
```

You may purchase a copy of our companion disk which contains all files for the project at http://www.amazon.com/gp/product/B00AOU76K8!

```
    Public APIUsername As String = "Enter your API Username here (see PayPal™ Account
Setup Chapter) "
    Private APIPassword As String = " Enter your API Password here (see PayPal™ Account
Setup Chapter)"
    Private APISignature As String = " Enter your API Signature here (see PayPal™ Account
Setup Chapter)"
    ''''''''''''''''''''''''''''''''''''''''''''''''''''''''''''''

    Private Subject As String = ""
    Private BNCode As String = "PP-ECWizard"

    'HttpWebRequest Timeout specified in milliseconds
    Private Const Timeout As Integer = 5000
    Private Shared ReadOnly SECURED_NVPS As String() = New String() {ACCT, CVV2,
SIGNATURE, PWD}

    ''' <summary>
    ''' Sets the API Credentials
    ''' </summary>
    ''' <param name="Userid"></param>
    ''' <param name="Pwd"></param>
    ''' <param name="Signature"></param>
    Public Sub SetCredentials(ByVal Userid As String, ByVal Pwd As String, ByVal Signature
As String)
        APIUsername = Userid
        APIPassword = Pwd
        APISignature = Signature
    End Sub

    ''' <summary>
    ''' ShortcutExpressCheckout: The method that calls SetExpressCheckout API
    ''' </summary>
    ''' <param name="amt"></param>
    ''' <param name="token"></param>
    ''' <param name="retMsg"></param>
    ''' <returns></returns>
    Public Function ShortcutExpressCheckout(ByVal amt As String, ByVal sessionID As Long,
ByRef token As String, ByRef retMsg As String) As Boolean
        Dim host As String = "www.paypal.com"
        If bSandbox Then
            pendpointurl = "https://api-3t.sandbox.paypal.com/nvp"
            host = "www.sandbox.paypal.com"
        End If

        ' Live site
```

You may purchase a copy of our companion disk which contains all files for the project at http://www.amazon.com/gp/product/B00AOU76K8!

```
        Dim returnURL As String = "http://www.Enter your domain name
here.com/OrderReview.aspx"
        Dim cancelURL As String = "http://www.Enter your domain name
here.com/Billing.aspx"

        Dim encoder As New NVPCodec()
        encoder("METHOD") = "SetExpressCheckout"
        encoder("RETURNURL") = returnURL
        encoder("CANCELURL") = cancelURL
        encoder("AMT") = amt
        encoder("PAYMENTACTION") = "Sale"
        encoder("CURRENCYCODE") = "USD"
        encoder("PAYMENTREQUEST_0_AMT") = amt
        encoder("PAYMENTREQUEST_0_INVNUM") = sessionID

        Dim pStrrequestforNvp As String = encoder.Encode()
        Dim pStresponsenvp As String = HttpCall(pStrrequestforNvp)

        Dim decoder As New NVPCodec()
        decoder.Decode(pStresponsenvp)

        Dim strAck As String = decoder("ACK").ToLower()
        If strAck IsNot Nothing AndAlso (strAck = "success" OrElse strAck =
"successwithwarning") Then
            token = decoder("TOKEN")

            Dim ECURL As String = ("https://" & host & "/cgi-bin/webscr?cmd=_express-checkout"
& "&token=") + token

            retMsg = ECURL
            Return True
        Else
            retMsg = (("ErrorCode=" & decoder("L_ERRORCODE0") & "&" & "Desc=") +
decoder("L_SHORTMESSAGE0") & "&" & "Desc2=") + decoder("L_LONGMESSAGE0")

            Return False
        End If
    End Function

    ''' <summary>
    ''' MarkExpressCheckout: The method that calls SetExpressCheckout API, invoked from the
    ''' Billing Page EC placement
    ''' </summary>
    ''' <param name="amt"></param>
    ''' <param name="token"></param>
    ''' <param name="retMsg"></param>
```

You may purchase a copy of our companion disk which contains all files for the project at http://www.amazon.com/gp/product/B00AOU76K8!

```
''' <returns></returns>
   Public Function MarkExpressCheckout(ByVal amt As String, ByVal shipToName As String,
ByVal shipToStreet As String, ByVal shipToStreet2 As String, ByVal shipToCity As String,
ByVal shipToState As String, _
   ByVal shipToZip As String, ByVal shipToCountryCode As String, ByRef token As String,
ByRef retMsg As String) As Boolean
      Dim host As String = "www.paypal.com"
      If bSandbox Then
         pendpointurl = "https://api-3t.sandbox.paypal.com/nvp"
         host = "www.sandbox.paypal.com"
      End If

      ' Live site
      Dim returnURL As String = "http://www.Enter your domain name
here.com/OrderConfirmation.aspx"
      Dim cancelURL As String = "http://www.Enter your domain name
here.com/Billing.aspx"


      Dim encoder As New NVPCodec()
      encoder("METHOD") = "SetExpressCheckout"
      encoder("RETURNURL") = returnURL
      encoder("CANCELURL") = cancelURL
      encoder("AMT") = amt
      encoder("PAYMENTACTION") = "Sale"
      encoder("CURRENCYCODE") = "USD"

      'Optional Shipping Address entered on the merchant site
      encoder("SHIPTONAME") = shipToName
      encoder("SHIPTOSTREET") = shipToStreet
      encoder("SHIPTOSTREET2") = shipToStreet2
      encoder("SHIPTOCITY") = shipToCity
      encoder("SHIPTOSTATE") = shipToState
      encoder("SHIPTOZIP") = shipToZip
      encoder("SHIPTOCOUNTRYCODE") = shipToCountryCode


      Dim pStrrequestforNvp As String = encoder.Encode()
      Dim pStresponsenvp As String = HttpCall(pStrrequestforNvp)

      Dim decoder As New NVPCodec()
      decoder.Decode(pStresponsenvp)

      Dim strAck As String = decoder("ACK").ToLower()
      If strAck IsNot Nothing AndAlso (strAck = "success" OrElse strAck =
"successwithwarning") Then
```

```
            token = decoder("TOKEN")

            Dim ECURL As String = ("https://" & host & "/cgi-bin/webscr?cmd=_express-checkout"
& "&token=") + token

            retMsg = ECURL
            Return True
        Else
            retMsg = (("ErrorCode=" & decoder("L_ERRORCODE0") & "&" & "Desc=") +
decoder("L_SHORTMESSAGE0") & "&" & "Desc2=") + decoder("L_LONGMESSAGE0")

            Return False
        End If
    End Function

    ''' <summary>
    ''' GetShippingDetails: The method that calls SetExpressCheckout API, invoked from the
    ''' Billing Page EC placement
    ''' </summary>
    ''' <param name="token"></param>
    ''' <param name="retMsg"></param>
    ''' <returns></returns>
    Public Function GetShippingDetails(ByVal token As String, ByRef payerId As String, ByRef
ShippingAddress As String, ByRef retMsg As String) As Boolean

        If bSandbox Then
            pendpointurl = "https://api-3t.sandbox.paypal.com/nvp"
        End If

        Dim encoder As New NVPCodec()
        encoder("METHOD") = "GetExpressCheckoutDetails"
        encoder("TOKEN") = token

        Dim pStrrequestforNvp As String = encoder.Encode()
        Dim pStresponsenvp As String = HttpCall(pStrrequestforNvp)

        Dim decoder As New NVPCodec()
        decoder.Decode(pStresponsenvp)

        Dim strAck As String = decoder("ACK").ToLower()
        If strAck IsNot Nothing AndAlso (strAck = "success" OrElse strAck =
"successwithwarning") Then
            'ShippingAddress = decoder("FIRSTNAME") & "-"
            'ShippingAddress += decoder("LASTNAME") & "-"
            ShippingAddress = decoder("SHIPTONAME") & "-"
            ShippingAddress += decoder("SHIPTOSTREET") & "-"
```

You may purchase a copy of our companion disk which contains all files for the project at http://www.amazon.com/gp/product/B00AOU76K8!

```
            If decoder("SHIPTOSTREET2") <> "" Then
                ShippingAddress += decoder("SHIPTOSTREET2") & "-"
            End If
            ShippingAddress += decoder("SHIPTOCITY") & "-"
            ShippingAddress += decoder("SHIPTOSTATE") & "-"
            ShippingAddress += decoder("SHIPTOZIP") & "-"
            ShippingAddress = Left(ShippingAddress, Len(ShippingAddress) - 1)
            ''''''''BELOW IS THE DEFAULT CODE FROM PAYPAL™''''''''''''''''''''''''
            'ShippingAddress = "<table><tr>"
            'ShippingAddress += "<td> First Name </td><td>" & decoder("FIRSTNAME") &
"</td></tr>"
            'ShippingAddress += "<td> Last Name </td><td>" & decoder("LASTNAME") &
"</td></tr>"
            'ShippingAddress += "<td colspan='2'> Shipping Address</td></tr>"
            'ShippingAddress += "<td> Name </td><td>" & decoder("SHIPTONAME") &
"</td></tr>"
            'ShippingAddress += "<td> Street1 </td><td>" & decoder("SHIPTOSTREET") &
"</td></tr>"
            'ShippingAddress += "<td> Street2 </td><td>" & decoder("SHIPTOSTREET2") &
"</td></tr>"
            'ShippingAddress += "<td> City </td><td>" & decoder("SHIPTOCITY") & "</td></tr>"
            'ShippingAddress += "<td> State </td><td>" & decoder("SHIPTOSTATE") &
"</td></tr>"
            'ShippingAddress += "<td> Zip </td><td>" & decoder("SHIPTOZIP") & "</td>"
            'ShippingAddress += "</tr>"
            payerId = decoder("PAYERID")
            Return True
        Else
            retMsg = (("ErrorCode=" & decoder("L_ERRORCODE0") & "&" & "Desc=") +
decoder("L_SHORTMESSAGE0") & "&" & "Desc2=") + decoder("L_LONGMESSAGE0")

            Return False
        End If
    End Function

    ''' <summary>
    ''' ConfirmPayment: The method that calls SetExpressCheckout API, invoked from the
    ''' Billing Page EC placement
    ''' </summary>
    ''' <param name="token"></param>
    ''' <param name="retMsg"></param>
    ''' <returns></returns>
    Public Function ConfirmPayment(ByVal finalPaymentAmount As String, ByVal token As
String, ByVal PayerId As String, ByRef decoder As NVPCodec, ByRef retMsg As String) As
Boolean
        If bSandbox Then
```

You may purchase a copy of our companion disk which contains all files for the project at http://www.amazon.com/gp/product/B00AOU76K8!

```
            pendpointurl = "https://api-3t.sandbox.paypal.com/nvp"
        End If

        Dim encoder As New NVPCodec()
        encoder("METHOD") = "DoExpressCheckoutPayment"
        encoder("TOKEN") = token
        encoder("PAYMENTACTION") = "Sale"
        encoder("PAYERID") = PayerId
        encoder("AMT") = finalPaymentAmount

        Dim pStrrequestforNvp As String = encoder.Encode()
        Dim pStresponsenvp As String = HttpCall(pStrrequestforNvp)

        decoder = New NVPCodec()
        decoder.Decode(pStresponsenvp)

        Dim strAck As String = decoder("ACK").ToLower()
        If strAck IsNot Nothing AndAlso (strAck = "success" OrElse strAck =
"successwithwarning") Then
            Return True
        Else
            retMsg = (("ErrorCode=" & decoder("L_ERRORCODE0") & "&" & "Desc=") +
decoder("L_SHORTMESSAGE0") & "&" & "Desc2=") + decoder("L_LONGMESSAGE0")
            Return False
        End If
    End Function

    ''' <summary>
    ''' HttpCall: The main method that is used for all API calls
    ''' </summary>
    ''' <param name="NvpRequest"></param>
    ''' <returns></returns>
    Public Function HttpCall(ByVal NvpRequest As String) As String
        'CallNvpServer
        Dim url As String = pendpointurl

        'To Add the credentials from the profile
        Dim codec As New NVPCodec()
        Dim strPost As String = (NvpRequest & "&") + buildCredentialsNVPString()
        strPost = (strPost & "&BUTTONSOURCE=") + HttpUtility.UrlEncode(BNCode)

        Dim objRequest As HttpWebRequest = DirectCast(WebRequest.Create(url),
HttpWebRequest)
        objRequest.Timeout = Timeout
        objRequest.Method = "POST"
        objRequest.ContentLength = strPost.Length
```

```
        Try
            Using myWriter As New StreamWriter(objRequest.GetRequestStream())
                myWriter.Write(strPost)
            End Using
        Catch e As Exception
            '
            ' if (log.IsFatalEnabled)
            ' {
            ' log.Fatal(e.Message, this);
            ' }

        End Try

        'Retrieve the Response returned from the NVP API call to PayPal™
        Dim objResponse As HttpWebResponse = DirectCast(objRequest.GetResponse(),
HttpWebResponse)
        Dim result As String
        Using sr As New StreamReader(objResponse.GetResponseStream())
            result = sr.ReadToEnd()
        End Using

        'Logging the response of the transaction
        ' if (log.IsInfoEnabled)
        ' {
        ' log.Info("Result :" +
        ' " Elapsed Time : " + (DateTime.Now - startDate).Milliseconds + " ms" +
        ' result);
        ' }
        '

        Return result
    End Function

    ''' <summary>
    ''' Credentials added to the NVP string
    ''' </summary>
    ''' <returns></returns>
    Private Function buildCredentialsNVPString() As String
        Dim codec As New NVPCodec()

        If Not IsEmpty(APIUsername) Then
            codec("USER") = APIUsername
        End If

        If Not IsEmpty(APIPassword) Then
```

You may purchase a copy of our companion disk which contains all files for the project at http://www.amazon.com/gp/product/B00AOU76K8!

```
            codec(PWD) = APIPassword
        End If

        If Not IsEmpty(APISignature) Then
            codec(SIGNATURE) = APISignature
        End If

        If Not IsEmpty(Subject) Then
            codec("SUBJECT") = Subject
        End If

        codec("VERSION") = "54"

        Return codec.Encode()
    End Function

    ''' <summary>
    ''' Returns if a string is empty or null
    ''' </summary>
    ''' <param name="s">the string</param>
    ''' <returns>true if the string is not null and is not empty or just whitespace</returns>
    Public Shared Function IsEmpty(ByVal s As String) As Boolean
        Return s Is Nothing OrElse s.Trim() = String.Empty
    End Function

End Class

Public NotInheritable Class NVPCodec

    Inherits NameValueCollection
    Private Const AMPERSAND As String = "&"
    Private Const EQUALSIGN As String = "="
    Private Shared ReadOnly AMPERSAND_CHAR_ARRAY As Char() =
AMPERSAND.ToCharArray()
    Private Shared ReadOnly EQUALS_CHAR_ARRAY As Char() =
EQUALSIGN.ToCharArray()

    ''' <summary>
    ''' Returns the built NVP string of all name/value pairs in the Hashtable
    ''' </summary>
    ''' <returns></returns>
    Public Function Encode() As String
        Dim sb As New StringBuilder()
        Dim firstPair As Boolean = True
        For Each kv As String In AllKeys
            Dim name As String = UrlEncode(kv)
```

```
            Dim value As String = UrlEncode(Me(kv))
            If Not firstPair Then
                sb.Append(AMPERSAND)
            End If
            sb.Append(name).Append(EQUALSIGN).Append(value)
            firstPair = False
        Next
        Return sb.ToString()
    End Function

    ''' <summary>
    ''' Decoding the string
    ''' </summary>
    ''' <param name="nvpstring"></param>
    Public Sub Decode(ByVal nvpstring As String)
        Clear()
        For Each nvp As String In nvpstring.Split(AMPERSAND_CHAR_ARRAY)
            Dim tokens As String() = nvp.Split(EQUALS_CHAR_ARRAY)
            If tokens.Length >= 2 Then
                Dim name As String = UrlDecode(tokens(0))
                Dim value As String = UrlDecode(tokens(1))
                Add(name, value)
            End If
        Next
    End Sub

    Private Shared Function UrlDecode(ByVal s As String) As String
        Return HttpUtility.UrlDecode(s)
    End Function
    Private Shared Function UrlEncode(ByVal s As String) As String
        Return HttpUtility.UrlEncode(s)
    End Function

#Region "Array methods"
    Public Overloads Sub Add(ByVal name As String, ByVal value As String, ByVal index As
Integer)
        Me.Add(GetArrayName(index, name), value)
    End Sub

    Public Overloads Sub Remove(ByVal arrayName As String, ByVal index As Integer)
        Me.Remove(GetArrayName(index, arrayName))
    End Sub

    ''' <summary>
    '''
    ''' </summary>
```

You may purchase a copy of our companion disk which contains all files for the project at http://www.amazon.com/gp/product/B00AOU76K8!

```
  Default Public Overloads Property Item(ByVal name As String, ByVal index As Integer) As
String
      Get
        Return Me(GetArrayName(index, name))
      End Get
      Set(ByVal value As String)
        Me(GetArrayName(index, name)) = value
      End Set
  End Property

  Private Shared Function GetArrayName(ByVal index As Integer, ByVal name As String) As
String
      If index < 0 Then
        Throw New ArgumentOutOfRangeException("index", "index can not be negative : " &
index)
      End If
      Return name + index
  End Function
#End Region

End Class
```

You may purchase a copy of our companion disk which contains all files for the project at http://www.amazon.com/gp/product/B00AOU76K8!

CSS Style Sheet

Create a style sheet named ***emx_nav_left.css*** and use the following code in the newly created style sheet:

```
/***********************************************/
/* emx_nav_left.css                            */
/* Use with template Halo_leftNav.html         */
/***********************************************/

/***********************************************/
/* HTML tag styles                             */
/***********************************************/
body{
        font-family: Arial,sans-serif;
        color: #333333;
        line-height: 1.166;
        margin: 0px;
        padding: 0px;
        background: #cccccc url(Pictures/bg_grad.jpg) fixed;
}

/******* hyperlink and anchor tag styles *******/

a:link, a:visited{
        color: #005FA9;
        text-decoration: none;
}

a:hover{
        text-decoration: underline;
}

/************** header tag styles **************/

h1{
 font: bold 120% Arial,sans-serif;
 color: #334d55;
 margin: 0px;
 padding: 0px;
}

h2{
 font: bold 114% Arial,sans-serif;
```

You may purchase a copy of our companion disk which contains all files for the project at http://www.amazon.com/gp/product/B00AOU76K8!

```
 color: #006699;
 margin: 0px;
 padding: 0px;
}

h3{
 font: bold 100% Arial,sans-serif;
 color: #334d55;
 margin: 0px;
 padding: 0px;
}

h4{
 font: 100% Arial,sans-serif;
 color: #333333;
 margin: 0px;
 padding: 0px;
}

h5{
 font: 100% Arial,sans-serif;
 color: #334d55;
 margin: 0px;
 padding: 0px;
}


/*************** list tag styles ***************/

ul{
 list-style-type: square;
}

ul ul{
 list-style-type: disc;
}

ul ul ul{
 list-style-type: none;
}

/********* form and related tag styles *********/

form {
        margin: 0;
        padding: 0;
```

You may purchase a copy of our companion disk which contains all files for the project at http://www.amazon.com/gp/product/B00AOU76K8!

```
}

label{
 font: bold 1em Arial,sans-serif;
 color: #334d55;
}

input{
font-family: Arial,sans-serif;
}

/*************************************************/
/* Layout Divs.                                 */
/*************************************************/
#pagecell1{
        position:absolute;
        top: 112px;
        left: 2%;
        right: 2%;
        width:95.6%;
        background-color: #ffffff;
}

#tl {
        position:absolute;
        top: -1px;
        left: -1px;
        margin: 0px;
        padding: 0px;
        z-index: 100;
}

#tr {
        position:absolute;
        top: -1px;
        right: -1px;
        margin: 0px;
        padding: 0px;
        z-index: 100;
}

#masthead{
        position: absolute;
        top: 0px;
        left: 2%;
        right: 3%;
```

```
	width:95.6%;

}

#pageNav{
	float: left;
	width:178px;
	padding: 0px;
	background-color: #F5f7f7;
	border-right: 1px solid #cccccc;
	border-bottom: 1px solid #cccccc;
	font: small Verdana,sans-serif;
}

#content{
	padding: 0px 10px 0px 0px;
	margin:0px 0px 0px 178px;
	border-left: 1px solid #ccd2d2;
}


/************************************************/
/* Component Divs                          */
/************************************************/
#siteName{
	margin: 0px;
	padding: 16px 0px 8px 0px;
	color: #ffffff;
	font-weight: normal;
}

/************** utility styles ****************/

#utility{
	font: 75% Verdana,sans-serif;
	position: absolute;
	top: 16px;
	right: 0px;
	color: #919999;
}

#utility a{
	color: #ffffff;
}

#utility a:hover{
```

You may purchase a copy of our companion disk which contains all files for the project at http://www.amazon.com/gp/product/B00AOU76K8!

```
        text-decoration: underline;
}

/************** pageName styles ****************/

#pageName{
        padding: 0px 0px 14px 10px;
        margin: 0px;
        border-bottom:1px solid #ccd2d2;
}

#pageName h2{
        font: bold 175% Arial,sans-serif;
        color: #000000;
        margin:0px;
        padding: 0px;
}

#pageName img{
        position: absolute;
        top: 0px;
        right: 6px;
        padding: 0px;
        margin: 0px;
}

/************* globalNav styles ****************/

#globalNav{
position: relative;
width: 100%;
min-width: 640px;
height: 32px;
color: #cccccc;
padding: 0px;
margin: 0px;
background-image: url(Pictures/glbnav_background.gif);
}

#globalNav img{
        margin-bottom: -4px;

}

#gnl {
        position: absolute;
```

You may purchase a copy of our companion disk which contains all files for the project at http://www.amazon.com/gp/product/B00AOU76K8!

```
        top: 0px;
        left:0px;
}

#gnr {
        position: absolute;
        top: 0px;
        right:0px;
}

#globalLink{
        position: absolute;
        top: 6px;
        height: 22px;
        min-width: 640px;
        padding: 0px;
        margin: 0px;
        left: 10px;
        z-index: 100;
}


a.glink, a.glink:visited{
        font-size: small;
        color: #000000;
        font-weight: bold;
        margin: 0px;
        padding: 2px 5px 4px 5px;
        border-right: 1px solid #8FB8BC;
}

a.glink:hover{
        background-image: url(Pictures/glblnav_selected.gif);
        text-decoration: none;
}

.skipLinks {display: none;}

/************ subglobalNav styles **************/

.subglobalNav{
        position: absolute;
        top: 84px;
        left: 0px;
        /*width: 100%;*/
        min-width: 640px;
```

You may purchase a copy of our companion disk which contains all files for the project at http://www.amazon.com/gp/product/B00AOU76K8!

```
        height: 20px;
        padding: 0px 0px 0px 10px;
        visibility: hidden;
        color: #ffffff;
}

.subglobalNav a:link, .subglobalNav a:visited {
        font-size: 80%;
        color: #ffffff;
}

.subglobalNav a:hover{
        color: #cccccc;
}

/*************** search styles *****************/

#search{
        position: absolute;
        top: 5px;
        right: 10px;
        z-index: 101;
}

#search input{
  font-size: 70%;
  margin: 0px  0px 0px 10px;
 }

#search a:link, #search a:visited {
        font-size: 80%;
        font-weight: bold;

}

#search a:hover{
        margin: 0px;
}


/************* breadCrumb styles ***************/

#breadCrumb{
        padding: 5px 0px 5px 10px;
        font: small Verdana,sans-serif;
        color: #AAAAAA;
```

You may purchase a copy of our companion disk which contains all files for the project at http://www.amazon.com/gp/product/B00AOU76K8!

```
}

#breadCrumb a{
        color: #AAAAAA;
}

#breadCrumb a:hover{
        color: #005FA9;
        text-decoration: underline;
}


/************** feature styles *****************/

.feature{
        padding: 0px 0px 10px 10px;
        font-size: 100%;
        min-height: 200px;
        height: 200px;
}
html>body .feature {height: auto;}

.feature h3{
        font: bold 175% Arial,sans-serif;
        color: #000000;
        padding: 30px 0px 5px 0px;
}

.feature img{
        float: left;
        padding: 0px 10px 0px 0px;
}


/*************** story styles *****************/

.story {
        padding: 10px 0px 0px 10px;
        font-size: 80%;
}

.storyCentered
{ text-align: center
}

.story h3{
```

```
        font: bold 125% Arial,sans-serif;
        color: #000000;
}

.story p {
        padding: 0px 0px 10px 0px;
}

.story a.capsule{
        font: bold 1em Arial,sans-serif;
        color: #005FA9;
        display:block;
        padding-bottom: 5px;
}

.story a.capsule:hover{
        text-decoration: underline;
}

td.storyLeft{
        padding-right: 12px;
}


/************** siteInfo styles ****************/

#siteInfo{
        clear: both;
        border-top: 1px solid #cccccc;
        font-size: small;
        color: #cccccc;
        padding: 10px 10px 10px 10px;
        margin-top: 0px;
}

#siteInfo img{
        padding: 4px 4px 4px 0px;
        vertical-align: middle;
}


/************ sectionLinks styles **************/

#sectionLinks{
        margin: 0px;
        padding: 0px;
```

You may purchase a copy of our companion disk which contains all files for the project at http://www.amazon.com/gp/product/B00AOU76K8!

```
}

#sectionLinks h3{
        padding: 10px 0px 2px 10px;
        border-bottom: 1px solid #cccccc;
}

#sectionLinks a:link, #sectionLinks a:visited {
        display: block;
        border-top: 1px solid #ffffff;
        border-bottom: 1px solid #cccccc;
        background-image: url(Pictures/bg_nav.jpg);
        font-weight: bold;
        padding: 3px 0px 3px 10px;
        color: #21536A;
}

#sectionLinks a:hover{
        border-top: 1px solid #cccccc;
        background-color: #DDEEFF;
        background-image: none;
        font-weight: bold;
        text-decoration: none;
}


/************* relatedLinks styles **************/

.relatedLinks{
        margin: 0px;
        padding: 0px 0px 10px 10px;
        border-bottom: 1px solid #cccccc;
}

.relatedLinks h3{
        padding: 10px 0px 2px 0px;
}

.relatedLinks a{
        display: block;
}


/*************** advert styles ****************/
```

```
#advert{
	padding: 10px;
}

#advert img{
	display: block;
}

/********************* end *********************/
```

You may purchase a copy of our companion disk which contains all files for the project at http://www.amazon.com/gp/product/B00AOU76K8!

web.config

Your web.config file is created automatically when you create the website. Be sure the following code is included within the web.config file (***REPLACE ANY CODE IN THIS COLOR WITH YOUR OWN INFORMATION!)***:

```
<?xml version="1.0"?>
<!--
  Note: As an alternative to hand editing this file you can use the
  web admin tool to configure settings for your application. Use
  the Website->Asp.Net Configuration option in Visual Studio.
  A full list of settings and comments can be found in
  machine.config.comments usually located in
  \Windows\Microsoft.Net\Framework\v2.x\Config
-->
<configuration>
        <configSections>
                <sectionGroup name="system.web.extensions"
type="System.Web.Configuration.SystemWebExtensionsSectionGroup,
System.Web.Extensions, Version=3.5.0.0, Culture=neutral,
PublicKeyToken=31BF3856AD364E35">
                        <sectionGroup name="scripting"
type="System.Web.Configuration.ScriptingSectionGroup, System.Web.Extensions,
Version=3.5.0.0, Culture=neutral, PublicKeyToken=31BF3856AD364E35">
                                <section name="scriptResourceHandler"
type="System.Web.Configuration.ScriptingScriptResourceHandlerSection,
System.Web.Extensions, Version=3.5.0.0, Culture=neutral,
PublicKeyToken=31BF3856AD364E35" requirePermission="false"
allowDefinition="MachineToApplication"/>
                                <sectionGroup name="webServices"
type="System.Web.Configuration.ScriptingWebServicesSectionGroup, System.Web.Extensions,
Version=3.5.0.0, Culture=neutral, PublicKeyToken=31BF3856AD364E35">
                                        <section name="jsonSerialization"
type="System.Web.Configuration.ScriptingJsonSerializationSection, System.Web.Extensions,
Version=3.5.0.0, Culture=neutral, PublicKeyToken=31BF3856AD364E35"
requirePermission="false" allowDefinition="Everywhere"/>
                                        <section name="profileService"
type="System.Web.Configuration.ScriptingProfileServiceSection, System.Web.Extensions,
Version=3.5.0.0, Culture=neutral, PublicKeyToken=31BF3856AD364E35"
requirePermission="false" allowDefinition="MachineToApplication"/>
                                        <section name="authenticationService"
type="System.Web.Configuration.ScriptingAuthenticationServiceSection,
System.Web.Extensions, Version=3.5.0.0, Culture=neutral,
```

```
PublicKeyToken=31BF3856AD364E35" requirePermission="false"
allowDefinition="MachineToApplication"/>
                                                    <section name="roleService"
type="System.Web.Configuration.ScriptingRoleServiceSection, System.Web.Extensions,
Version=3.5.0.0, Culture=neutral, PublicKeyToken=31BF3856AD364E35"
requirePermission="false" allowDefinition="MachineToApplication"/>
                                          </sectionGroup>
                                </sectionGroup>
                      </sectionGroup>
          </configSections>
<appSettings></appSettings>

          <system.web>
                    <!--
          Set compilation debug="true" to insert debugging
          symbols into the compiled page. Because this
          affects performance, set this value to true only
          during development.

          Visual Basic options:
          Set strict="true" to disallow all data type conversions
          where data loss can occur.
          Set explicit="true" to force declaration of all variables.
       -->
                    <compilation debug="false" strict="false" explicit="true">
                              <assemblies>
                                        <add assembly="System.Core, Version=3.5.0.0, Culture=neutral,
PublicKeyToken=B77A5C561934E089"/>
                                        <add assembly="System.Web.Extensions, Version=3.5.0.0,
Culture=neutral, PublicKeyToken=31BF3856AD364E35"/>
                                        <add assembly="System.Data.DataSetExtensions,
Version=3.5.0.0, Culture=neutral, PublicKeyToken=B77A5C561934E089"/>
                                        <add assembly="System.Xml.Linq, Version=3.5.0.0,
Culture=neutral, PublicKeyToken=B77A5C561934E089"/>
                                        <add assembly="ADODB, Version=7.0.3300.0, Culture=neutral,
PublicKeyToken=B03F5F7F11D50A3A"/>

                                        <add assembly="Microsoft.ReportViewer.WebForms,
Version=9.0.0.0, Culture=neutral, PublicKeyToken=B03F5F7F11D50A3A"/>
                                        <add assembly="Microsoft.ReportViewer.Common,
Version=9.0.0.0, Culture=neutral, PublicKeyToken=B03F5F7F11D50A3A"/>
                                        <add assembly="System.Windows.Forms, Version=2.0.0.0,
Culture=neutral, PublicKeyToken=B77A5C561934E089"/></assemblies>
                              <buildProviders>
```

```
                    <add extension=".rdlc"
type="Microsoft.Reporting.RdlBuildProvider, Microsoft.ReportViewer.Common,
Version=9.0.0.0, Culture=neutral, PublicKeyToken=b03f5f7f11d50a3a"/>
                </buildProviders>
            </compilation>
            <pages>
                <namespaces>
                    <clear/>
                    <add namespace="System"/>
                    <add namespace="System.Collections"/>
                    <add namespace="System.Collections.Generic"/>
                    <add namespace="System.Collections.Specialized"/>
                    <add namespace="System.Configuration"/>
                    <add namespace="System.Text"/>
                    <add namespace="System.Text.RegularExpressions"/>
                    <add namespace="System.Linq"/>
                    <add namespace="System.Xml.Linq"/>
                    <add namespace="System.Web"/>
                    <add namespace="System.Web.Caching"/>
                    <add namespace="System.Web.SessionState"/>
                    <add namespace="System.Web.Security"/>
                    <add namespace="System.Web.Profile"/>
                    <add namespace="System.Web.UI"/>
                    <add namespace="System.Web.UI.WebControls"/>
                    <add namespace="System.Web.UI.WebControls.WebParts"/>
                    <add namespace="System.Web.UI.HtmlControls"/>
                </namespaces>
            </pages>
            <!--
        The <authentication> section enables configuration
        of the security authentication mode used by
        ASP.NET to identify an incoming user.
    -->
            <authentication mode="Windows"/>
            <!--
        The <customErrors> section enables configuration
        of what to do if/when an unhandled error occurs
        during the execution of a request. Specifically,
        it enables developers to configure html error pages
        to be displayed in place of a error stack trace.

    <customErrors mode="RemoteOnly" defaultRedirect="GenericErrorPage.htm">
        <error statusCode="403" redirect="NoAccess.htm" />
        <error statusCode="404" redirect="FileNotFound.htm" />
    </customErrors>
    -->
```

```
		<httpHandlers>
			<remove path="*.asmx" verb="*"/>
			<add path="*.asmx" verb="*"
type="System.Web.Script.Services.ScriptHandlerFactory, System.Web.Extensions,
Version=3.5.0.0, Culture=neutral, PublicKeyToken=31BF3856AD364E35" validate="false"/>
			<add path="*_AppService.axd" verb="*"
type="System.Web.Script.Services.ScriptHandlerFactory, System.Web.Extensions,
Version=3.5.0.0, Culture=neutral, PublicKeyToken=31BF3856AD364E35" validate="false"/>
			<add path="ScriptResource.axd" verb="GET,HEAD"
type="System.Web.Handlers.ScriptResourceHandler, System.Web.Extensions, Version=3.5.0.0,
Culture=neutral, PublicKeyToken=31BF3856AD364E35" validate="false"/>
			<add path="CrystalImageHandler.aspx" verb="GET"
type="CrystalDecisions.Web.CrystalImageHandler, CrystalDecisions.Web,
Version=10.5.3700.0, Culture=neutral, PublicKeyToken=692fbea5521e1304"/>
			<add path="Reserved.ReportViewerWebControl.axd" verb="*"
type="Microsoft.Reporting.WebForms.HttpHandler, Microsoft.ReportViewer.WebForms,
Version=9.0.0.0, Culture=neutral, PublicKeyToken=b03f5f7f11d50a3a" validate="false"/>
		</httpHandlers>
		<httpModules>
			<add name="ScriptModule" type="System.Web.Handlers.ScriptModule,
System.Web.Extensions, Version=3.5.0.0, Culture=neutral,
PublicKeyToken=31BF3856AD364E35"/>
		</httpModules>
		<identity impersonate="true"/>
	</system.web>
	<system.net>
		<mailSettings>
			<smtp deliveryMethod="Network">
				<network host="smtp.ENTER YOUR DOMAIN NAME
HERE.com" userName="ENTER YOUR ASP.NET CONTROL PANEL USERNAME
HERE" password=" ENTER YOUR ASP.NET CONTROL PANEL PASSWORD HERE "
port="25"/>
			</smtp>
		</mailSettings>
	</system.net>
	<system.codedom>
		<compilers>
			<compiler language="c#;cs;csharp" extension=".cs" warningLevel="4"
type="Microsoft.CSharp.CSharpCodeProvider, System, Version=2.0.0.0, Culture=neutral,
PublicKeyToken=b77a5c561934e089">
				<providerOption name="CompilerVersion" value="v3.5"/>
				<providerOption name="WarnAsError" value="false"/>
			</compiler>
			<compiler language="vb;vbs;visualbasic;vbscript" extension=".vb"
warningLevel="4" type="Microsoft.VisualBasic.VBCodeProvider, System, Version=2.0.0.0,
Culture=neutral, PublicKeyToken=b77a5c561934e089">
```

You may purchase a copy of our companion disk which contains all files for the project at http://www.amazon.com/gp/product/B00AOU76K8!

```
                        <providerOption name="CompilerVersion" value="v3.5"/>
                        <providerOption name="OptionInfer" value="true"/>
                        <providerOption name="WarnAsError" value="false"/>
                    </compiler>
                </compilers>
            </system.codedom>
            <!--
        The system.webServer section is required for running ASP.NET AJAX under Internet
        Information Services 7.0.  It is not necessary for previous version of IIS.
    -->
            <system.webServer>
                <validation validateIntegratedModeConfiguration="false"/>
                <modules>
                    <remove name="ScriptModule"/>
                    <add name="ScriptModule" preCondition="managedHandler"
type="System.Web.Handlers.ScriptModule, System.Web.Extensions, Version=3.5.0.0,
Culture=neutral, PublicKeyToken=31BF3856AD364E35"/>
                </modules>
                <handlers>
                    <remove name="WebServiceHandlerFactory-Integrated"/>
                    <remove name="ScriptHandlerFactory"/>
                    <remove name="ScriptHandlerFactoryAppServices"/>
                    <remove name="ScriptResource"/>
                    <add name="ScriptHandlerFactory" verb="*" path="*.asmx"
preCondition="integratedMode" type="System.Web.Script.Services.ScriptHandlerFactory,
System.Web.Extensions, Version=3.5.0.0, Culture=neutral,
PublicKeyToken=31BF3856AD364E35"/>
                    <add name="ScriptHandlerFactoryAppServices" verb="*"
path="*_AppService.axd" preCondition="integratedMode"
type="System.Web.Script.Services.ScriptHandlerFactory, System.Web.Extensions,
Version=3.5.0.0, Culture=neutral, PublicKeyToken=31BF3856AD364E35"/>
                    <add name="ScriptResource" preCondition="integratedMode"
verb="GET,HEAD" path="ScriptResource.axd"
type="System.Web.Handlers.ScriptResourceHandler, System.Web.Extensions, Version=3.5.0.0,
Culture=neutral, PublicKeyToken=31BF3856AD364E35"/>
                    <add name="CrystalImageHandler.aspx_GET" verb="GET"
path="CrystalImageHandler.aspx" type="CrystalDecisions.Web.CrystalImageHandler,
CrystalDecisions.Web, Version=10.5.3700.0, Culture=neutral,
PublicKeyToken=692fbea5521e1304" preCondition="integratedMode"/></handlers>
            </system.webServer>
            <runtime>
                <assemblyBinding xmlns="urn:schemas-microsoft-com:asm.v1">
                    <dependentAssembly>
                        <assemblyIdentity name="System.Web.Extensions"
publicKeyToken="31bf3856ad364e35"/>
```

```
                    <bindingRedirect oldVersion="1.0.0.0-1.1.0.0"
newVersion="3.5.0.0"/>
                </dependentAssembly>
                <dependentAssembly>
                    <assemblyIdentity name="System.Web.Extensions.Design"
publicKeyToken="31bf3856ad364e35"/>
                    <bindingRedirect oldVersion="1.0.0.0-1.1.0.0"
newVersion="3.5.0.0"/>
                </dependentAssembly>
            </assemblyBinding>
        </runtime>
        <businessObjects><crystalReports><rptBuildProvider><add
embedRptInResource="true"/></rptBuildProvider></crystalReports></businessObjects></confi
guration>
```

Uploading Files to Web Host

To upload your project files to the DiscountASP.Net server, perform the following steps:

1. Select WebSite from the menu, then Copy Web Site.
2. Click Connect to connect to the server.
3. For the server name, enter ftp.**YOUR DOMAIN NAME.**
4. Enter 21 for the port.
5. Check Passive Mode checkbox.
6. Enter your customer number from the DiscountASP.Net control panel, then with no spaces enter by a | and then enter your DiscountASP.Net username in the Username textbox.
7. Enter your DiscountASP.Net password in the Password textbox.
8. Click Open. The remote site now opens (provided you enter your credentials precisely)!
9. Add a folder to the Remote Web site for App_Code (Files must be organized same as your project).
10. Add a folder to the Remote Web site for Pictures (Files must be organized same as your project).
11. Click App_Code folder of the Source Web site. (The Remote Web site will automatically open the same folder so you are prepared to copy.)
12. Select each file in the Source Web site App_Code folder, then click the → arrow. This will copy the selected files from the source to the remote site.
13. Now, click Pictures folder of the Source Web site. (The Remote Web site will automatically open the same folder so you are prepared to copy.)
14. Select each file in the Source Web site Pictures folder, then click the → arrow. This will copy the selected files from the source to the remote site.
15. Finally, go back to the top level folder and select each remaining file in the Source Web site folder, then click the → arrow. This will copy the selected files from the source to the remote site.
16. You may confirm that all files were transferred correctly by viewing the status of each file in the source web site and the remote web site. The status should be 'Unchanged' on each site.
17. If Step 16 is successful, your ecommerce web site is up and running. Continue onto the next chapter and familiarize yourself with the site functionality. If you encounter any problems, it would be a typo as this site has been tested for 1 year. Direct your questions to the community forum set up on Facebook for this book if you need assistance.

User Functionality

This manual provides a thorough overview of how to use the Ecommerce VB.Net Website Template. There are two types of users that may access this system: customers and administrators. The instructions contained in this document are categorized by user functionality. Readers of these instructions are advised to follow the sequence provided as the best method to achieve comfort with the Ecommerce VB.Net Website Template.

All users will need an Internet enabled device to use the actual online ordering system. Additionally, customers will need a PayPal™ account in order to complete online ordering. Any questions about the Ecommerce VB.Net Website Template that are not addressed in this manual should be passed on to the community forum on Facebook for this book.

Home Page

The home page as shown in Fig.1a is the page that all users will see when they arrive at the www.yourbestdatasolution.com, which serves as the model for this entire book. It has the following links:

- Home
- Menu
- View Cart
- Checkout
- Create Account
- Login
- Order History
- About Us
- Contact Us

Users must be logged in with a valid username and password in order to access the View Cart, Checkout, Create Account and Order History links. The first step for a new user is to create an account. Returning users may go directly to the Login link.

Fig.1a

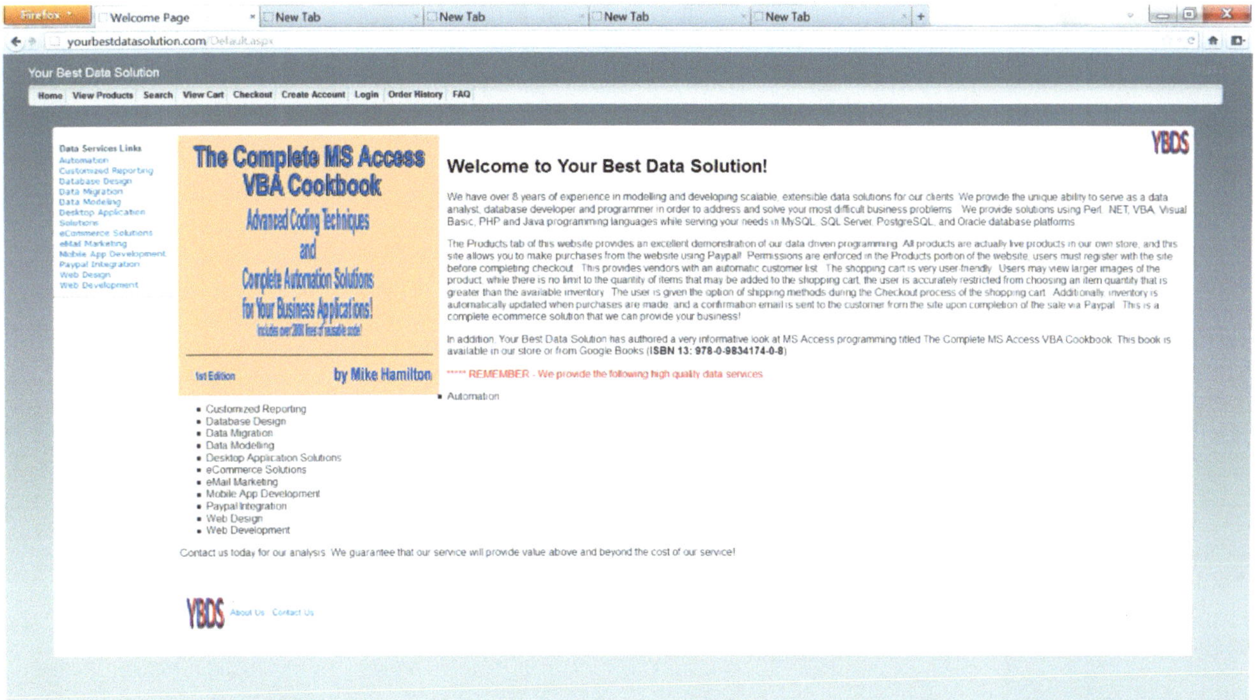

Register

All users of the Ecommerce VB.Net Website Template must have a user account before they may place an order. This user account includes basic information such as name, address, phone number, username and password. Each user will complete registration on time as shown in (Fig. 1b) and then click submit. The form depicted in this figure is reached by first clicking Login on the menu; next, click the Create Account button on the Login form to load the Create Account page. All fields on the form that are marked with a red asterisk are required before the user may submit the information on the web form.

You may purchase a copy of our companion disk which contains all files for the project at http://www.amazon.com/gp/product/B00AOU76K8!

Fig. 1b

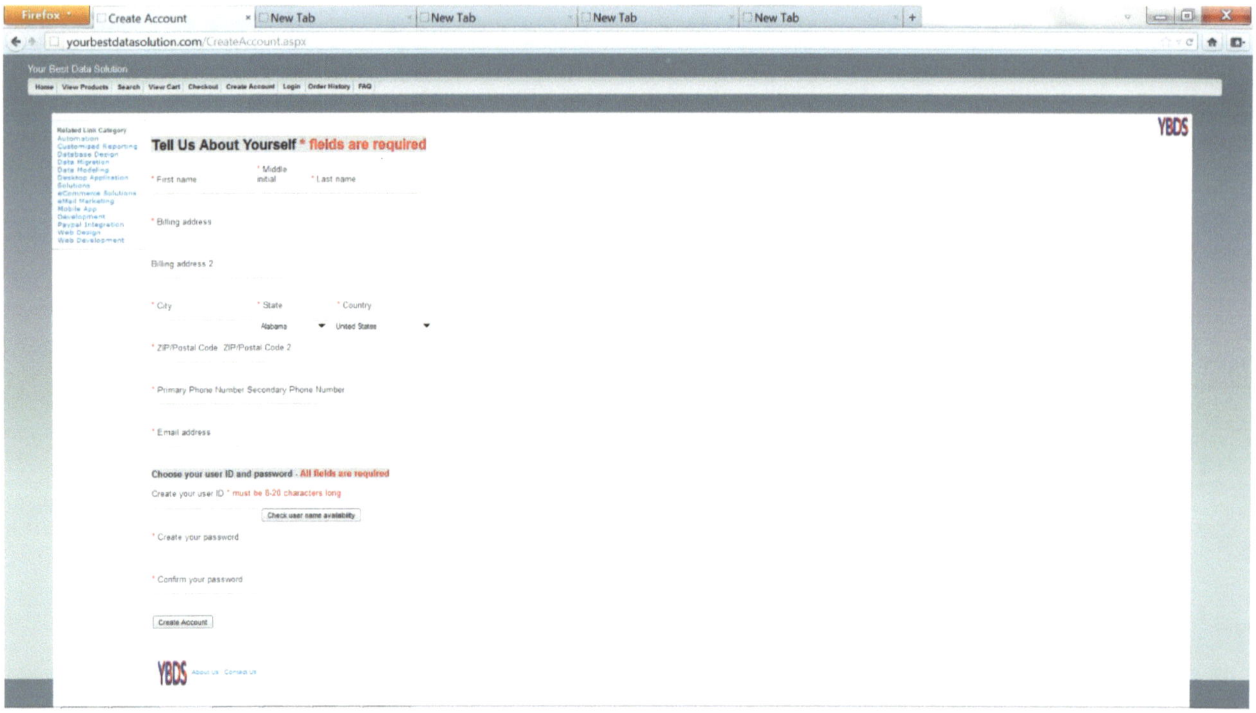

Login

The login screen is typical of any login screen you would find on the Internet. The user will enter his or her username and password, and then click the Login button as shown in Fig. 2a. If the login is successful, the user is redirected to the Menu. If not successful, the user is redirected to the Login page with an alert as seen in Fig. 3a. When you ran the SQL script to create and populate your database, two users were created by default. Those default logins are:

Username	Password	User Type
user	password	Non-admin
admin	password	Admin

Change these passwords after testing functionality or create new users as you see fit!

You may purchase a copy of our companion disk which contains all files for the project at http://www.amazon.com/gp/product/B00AOU76K8!

Fig. 2a

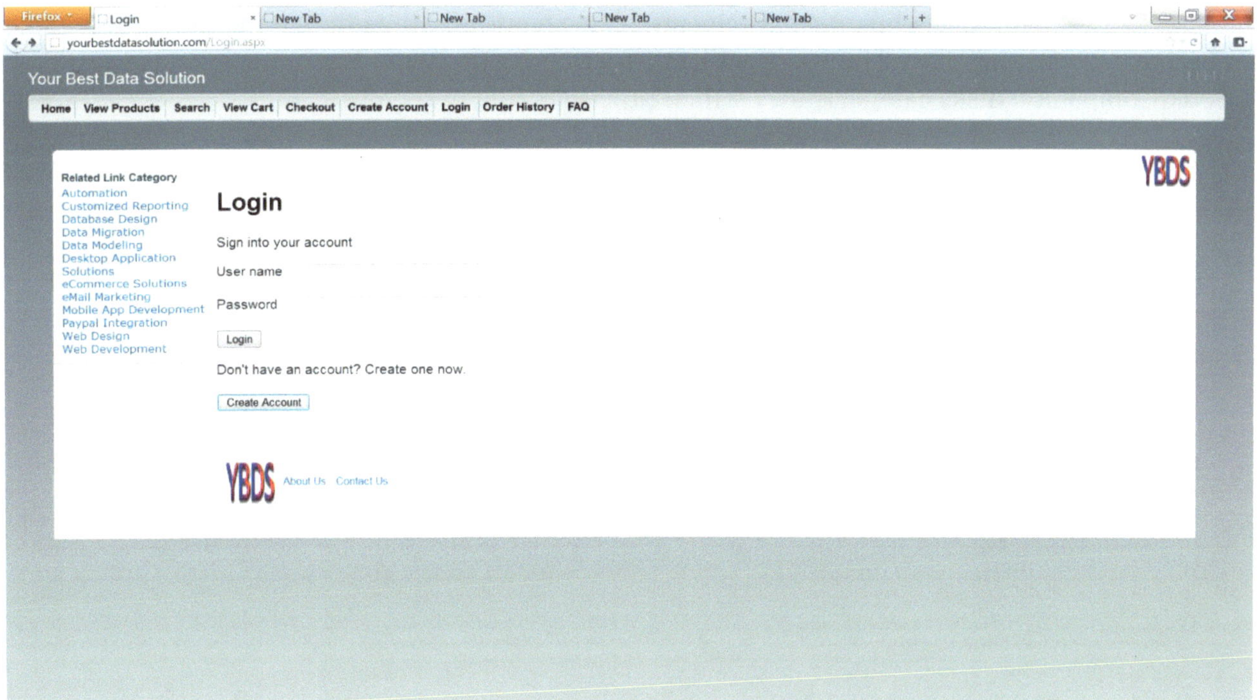

Fig. 3a

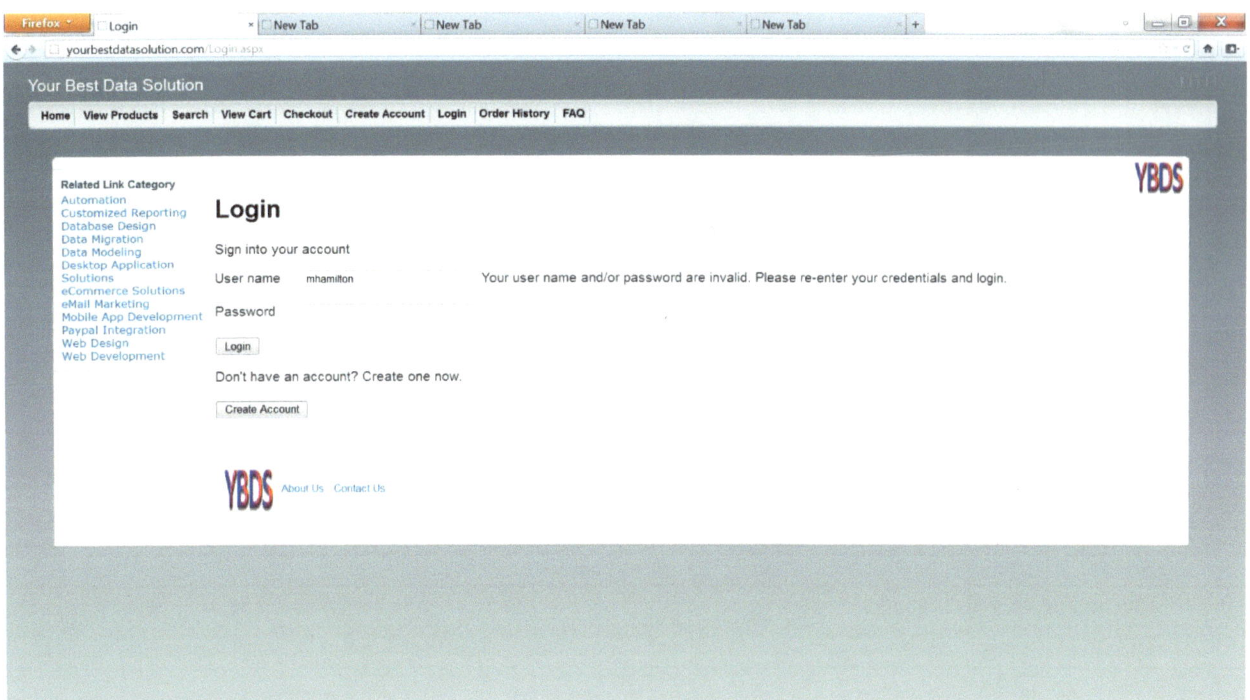

You may purchase a copy of our companion disk which contains all files for the project at http://www.amazon.com/gp/product/B00AOU76K8!

View Products

The View Products link displays the product categories with a link to the individual items of each category as displayed in Fig. 4. When a user clicks the View Products link next to the eBook Companion disks category, they will see the selection in Fig. 5 .

Fig. 4

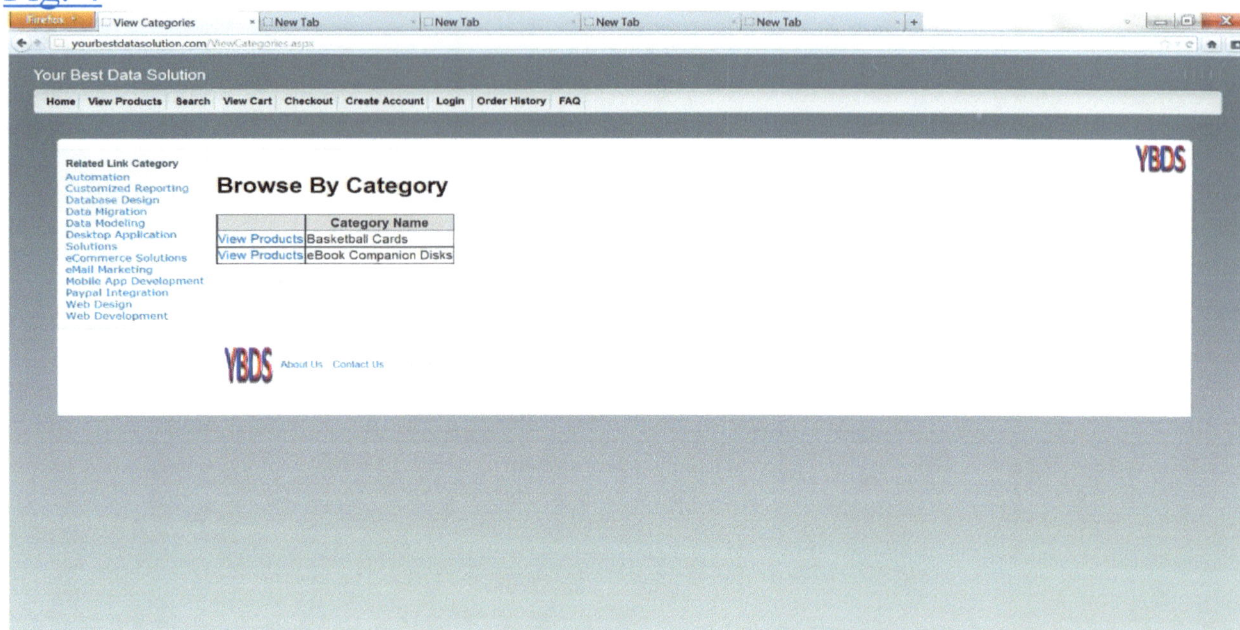

Fig. 5

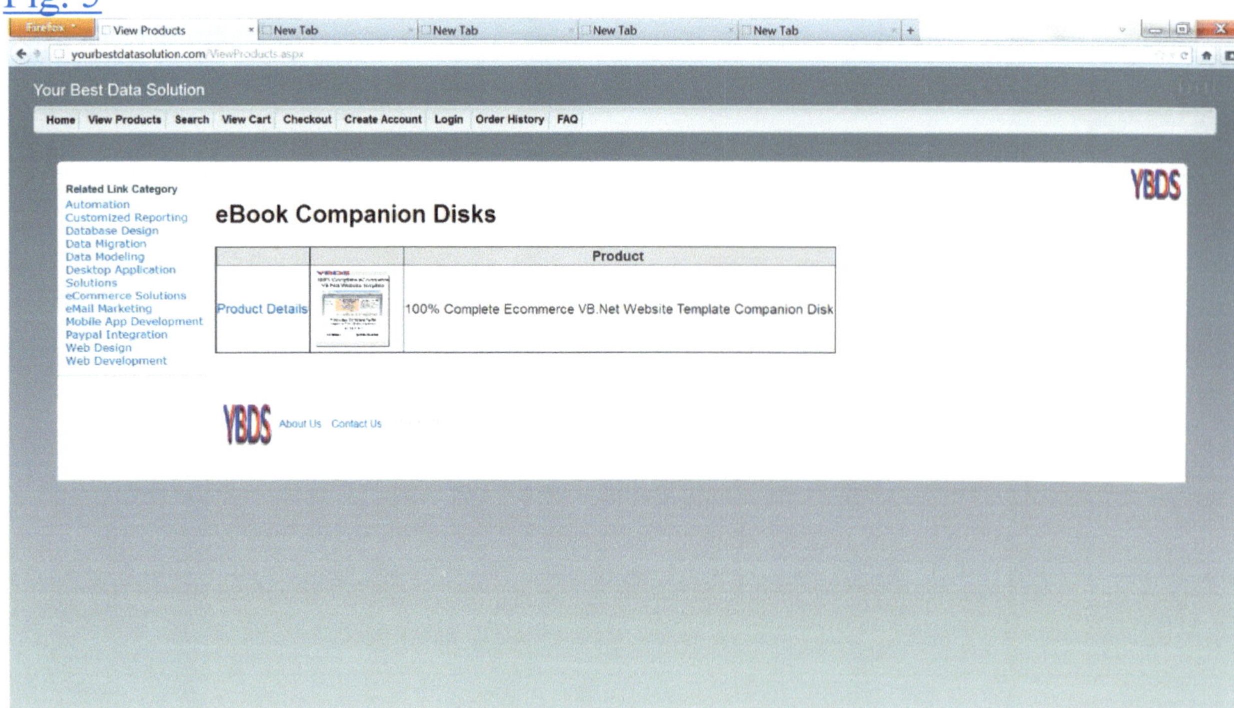

You may purchase a copy of our companion disk which contains all files for the project at http://www.amazon.com/gp/product/B00AOU76K8!

Shopping Cart

The user may then add to the shopping cart by clicking the Product Details link of the selected menu item as displayed in Fig.5. Next, the user simply enters the quantity desired, and clicks Add To Cart (see Fig. 6). The addition of the item to the shopping cart is then confirmed (see Fig. 7).

Fig. 6

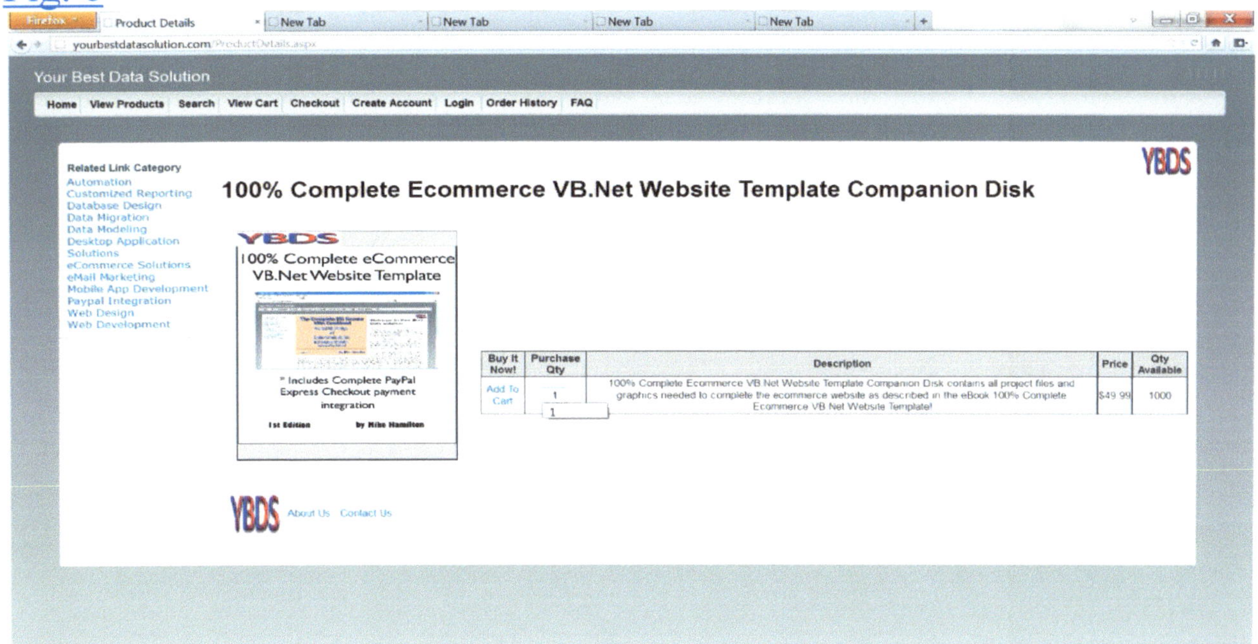

Fig. 7

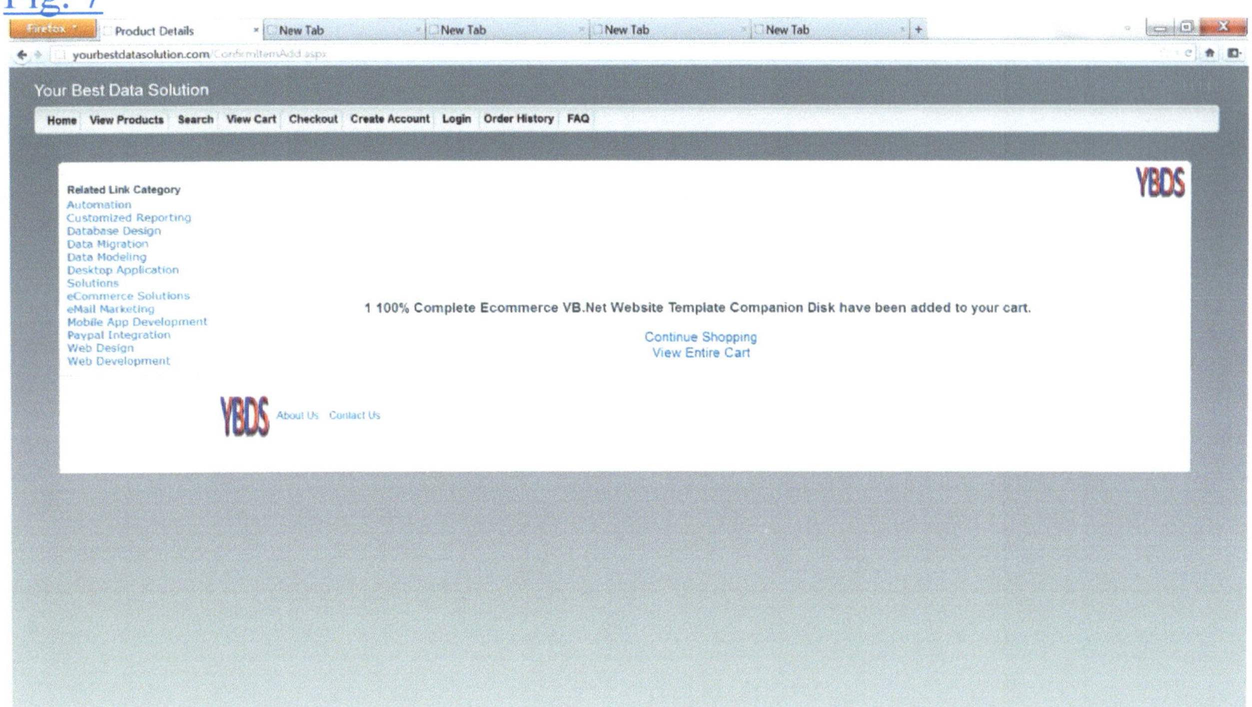

You may purchase a copy of our companion disk which contains all files for the project at http://www.amazon.com/gp/product/B00AOU76K8!

Checkout

At this point, a logged in user may go to Checkout using the menu Checkout link or continue shopping. We will go thru the Checkout process now. Fig. 8 below shows the loaded Checkout page. The user must login and add a delivery method, such as pickup or delivery, by clicking the Add delivery method button (Fig. 9 displays the Delivery Information page).

Fig. 8

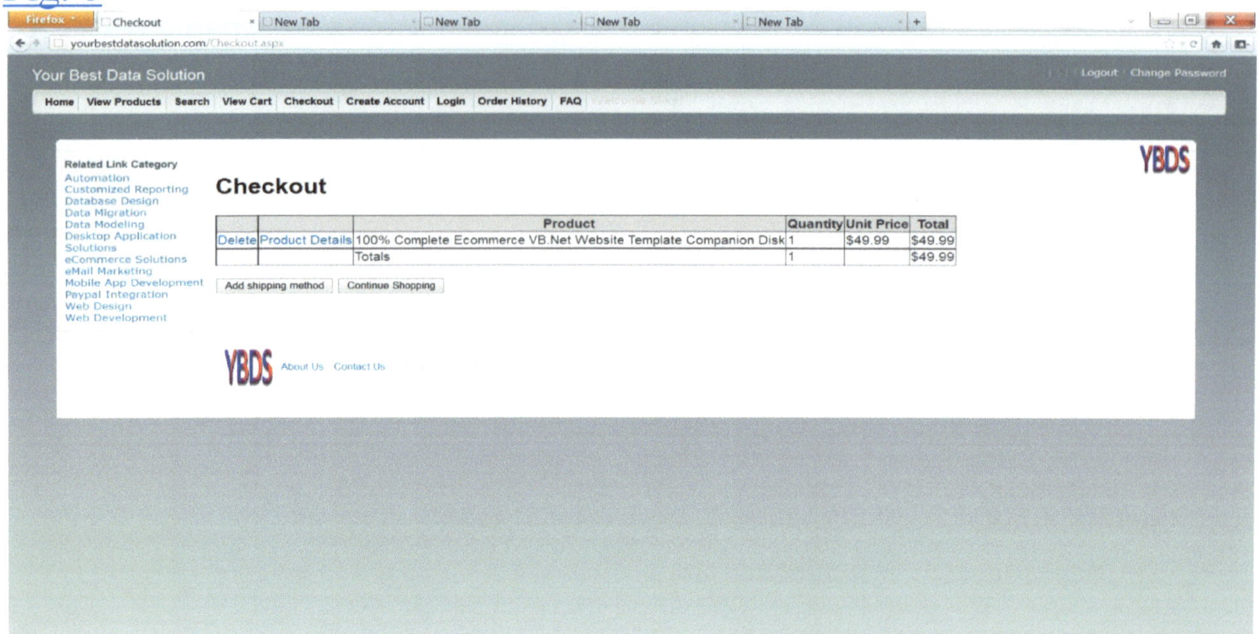

Fig. 9

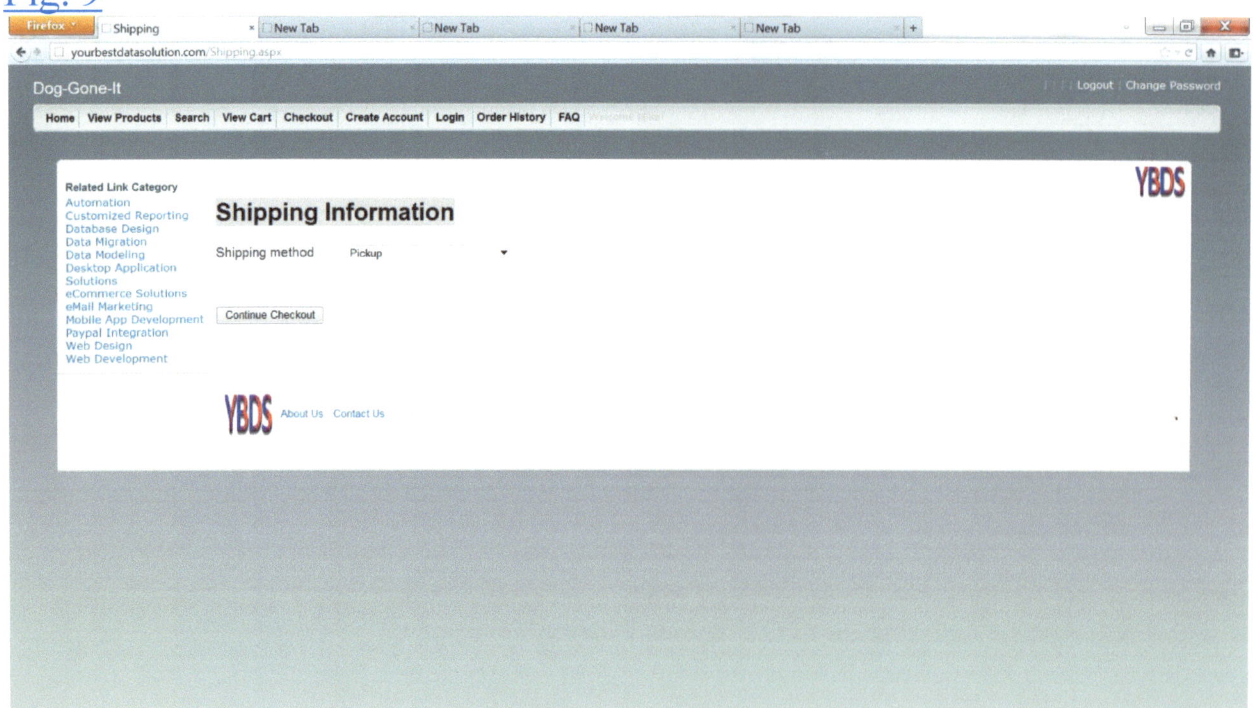

Now, when the user clicks Continue Checkout, the entire order with delivery cost and tax will be presented. Also, a PayPal™ button will now be available to complete the online payment (see Fig. 10). **THE USER MUST HAVE A VALID PayPal™ account to complete the transaction. The user will click the PayPal™ button and be redirected to the PayPal™ site, where they must enter their PayPal™ credentials (not shown).

Fig. 10

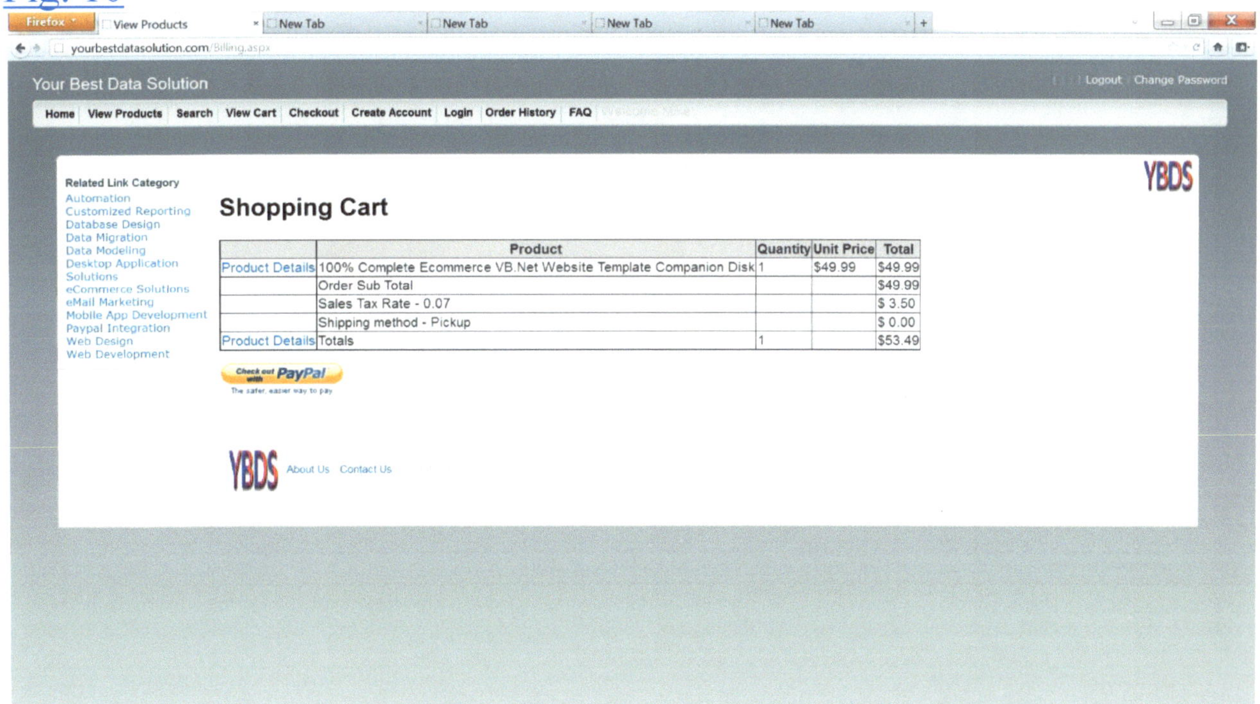

Upon login, the user will see their PayPal™ information. The user will click Confirm Payment and be redirected back to the Order Review page to finalize the order.

The order is displayed in Fig. 11. When the user clicks Confirm Payment, the PayPal™ transaction is completed, and the user is redirected to the Order Confirmation page as shown in Fig. 12. A confirmation email is sent to the email account of the buyer as well – check your email!

You may purchase a copy of our companion disk which contains all files for the project at http://www.amazon.com/gp/product/B00AOU76K8!

Fig. 11

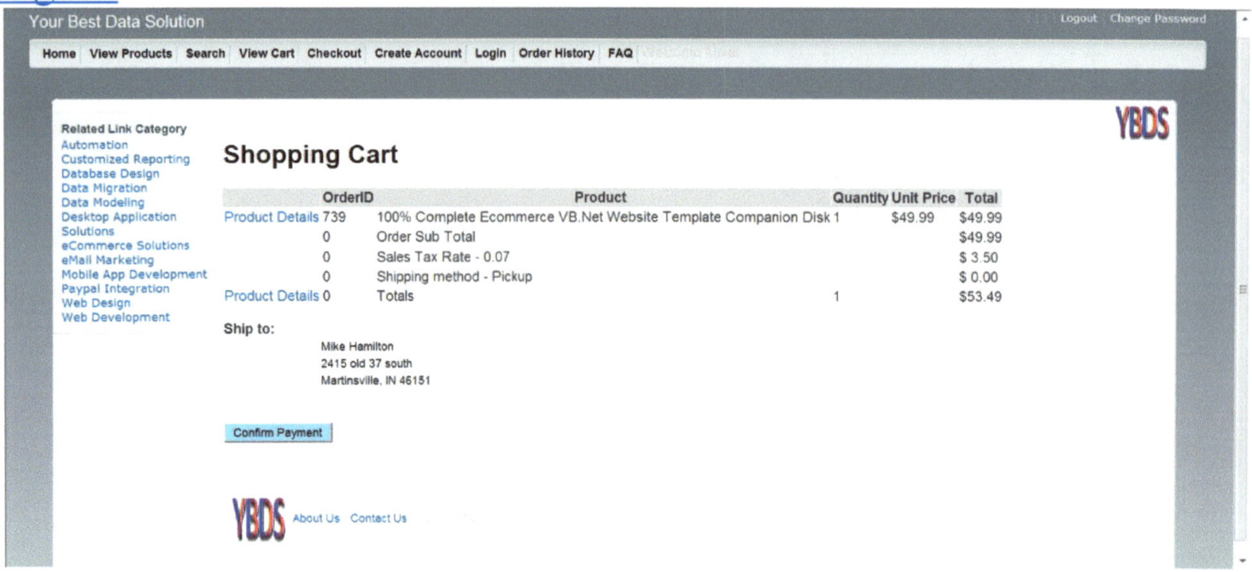

Fig. 12

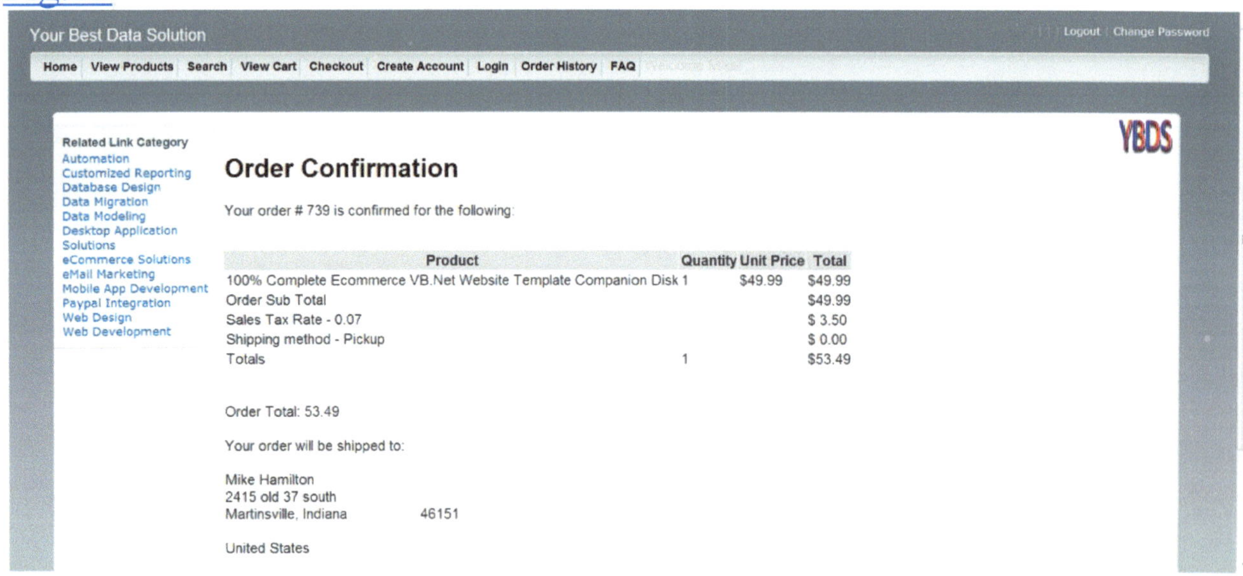

Users may view their Order History by clicking the Order History link. A list of all of the customer's orders will be displayed in chronologically descending order (Fig. 13). The user may then click the View Order Detail link to see the complete order information (Fig. 14).

You may purchase a copy of our companion disk which contains all files for the project at http://www.amazon.com/gp/product/B00AOU76K8!

Fig. 13

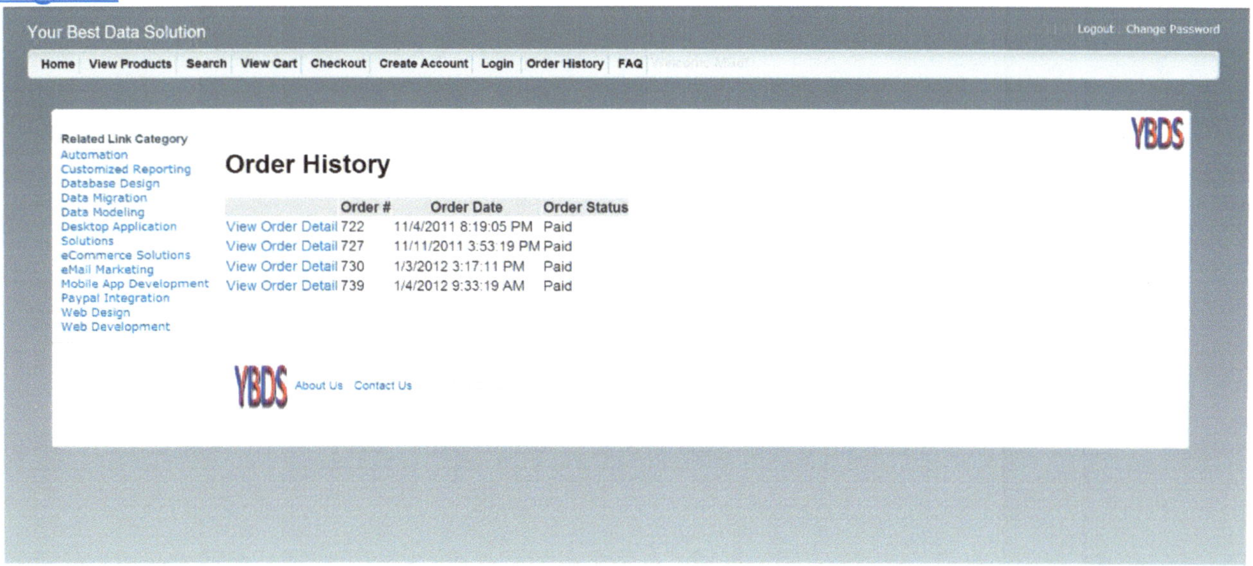

Fig. 14

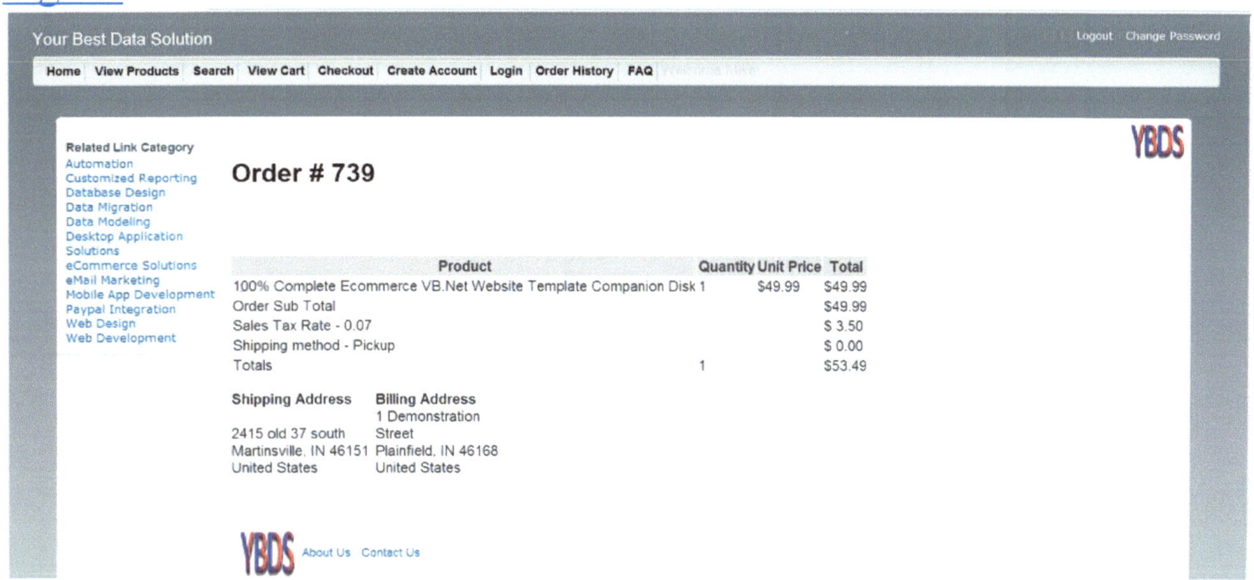

Change Password

When the user (who is logged in) clicks the Change Password link in the upper right corner, the interface shown in Fig. 15 is displayed. The user then types the new password in the top textbox, confirms the password in the second textbox, and then clicks Update Password. If the passwords do not match, an error is displayed to the user, and the user must re-enter the new password (Fig. 16). If the passwords match, the password is updated and the user must use the new password going forward. The user is redirected to a page confirming the password change (Fig. 17).

Fig. 15

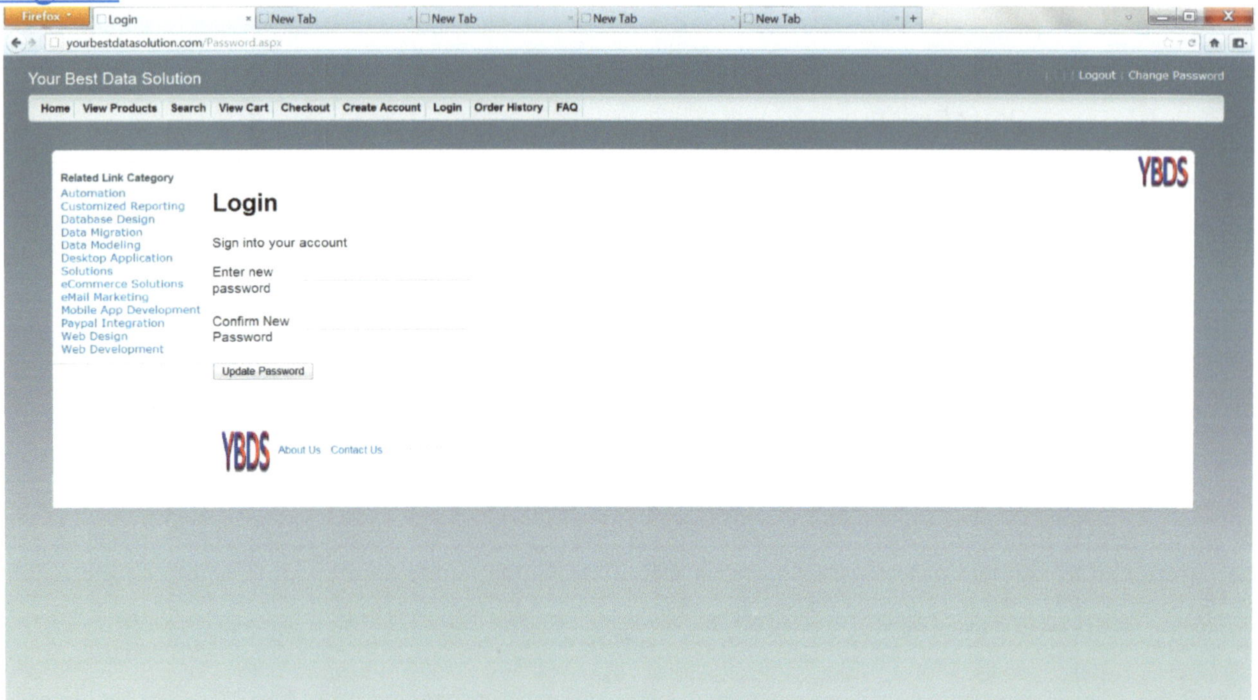

Fig. 16

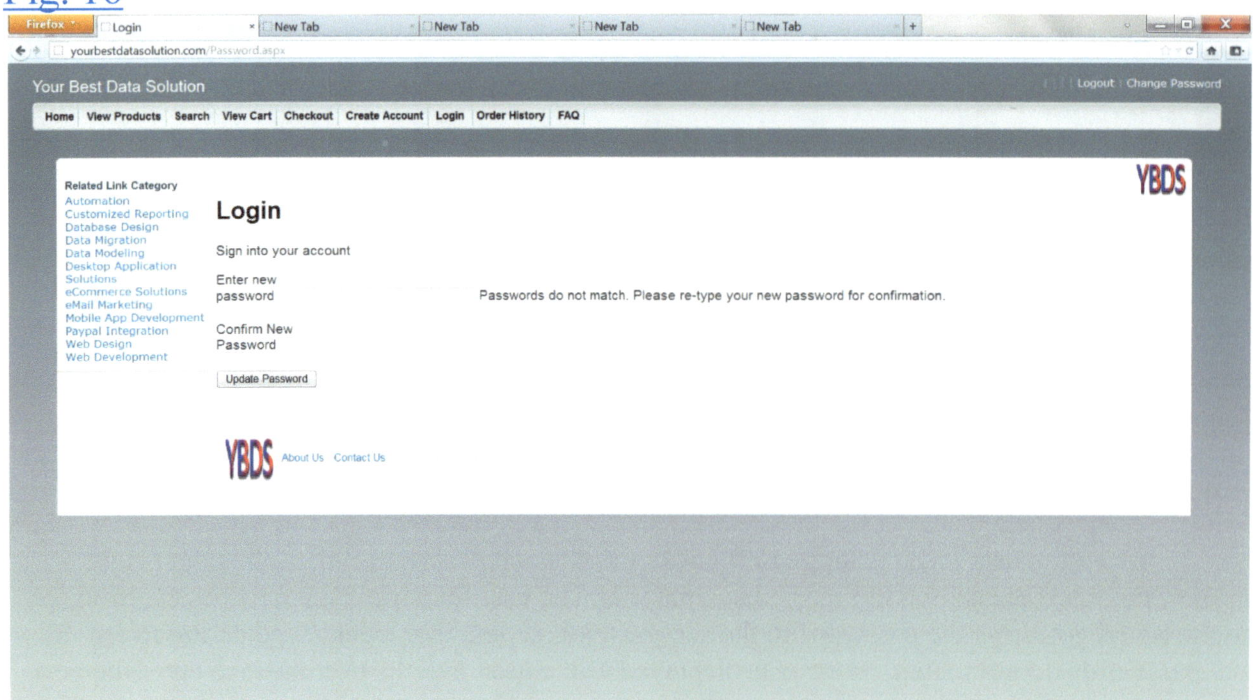

You may purchase a copy of our companion disk which contains all files for the project at http://www.amazon.com/gp/product/B00AOU76K8!

Fig. 17

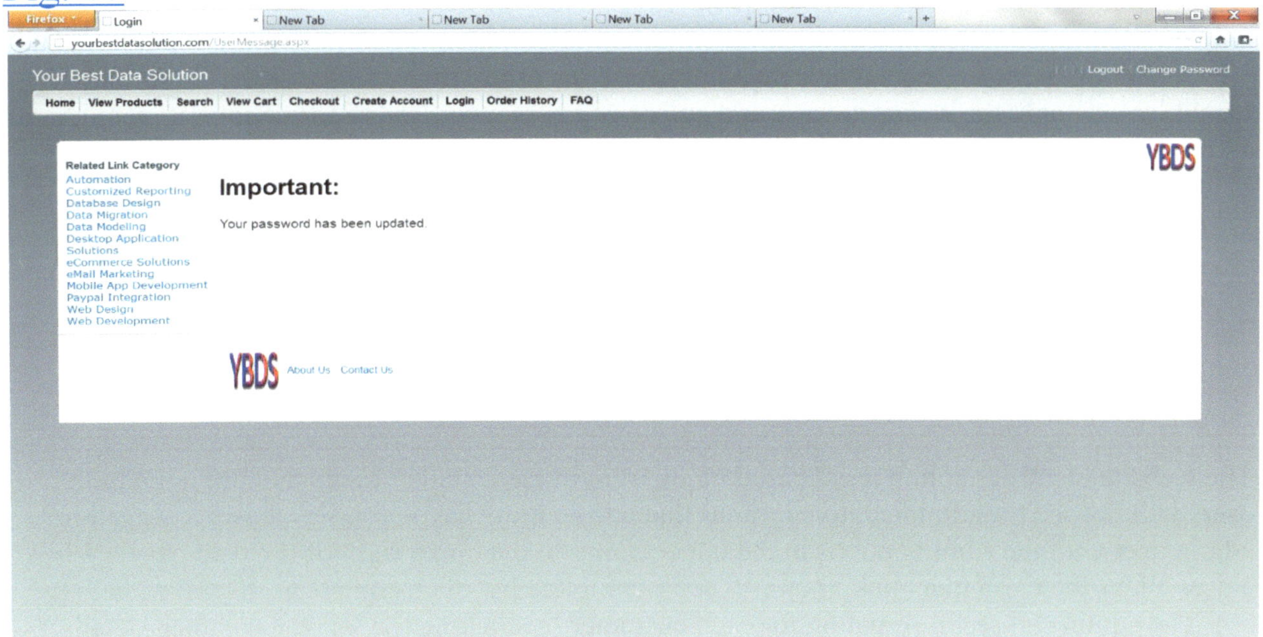

Logout

When the user clicks the Logout link, which is available on all pages once the user is logged in, the user is securely logged out and all features that require a login will only be available if the user logs back into the website. The user will see a logout confirmation page as depicted in Fig. 18.

Fig. 18

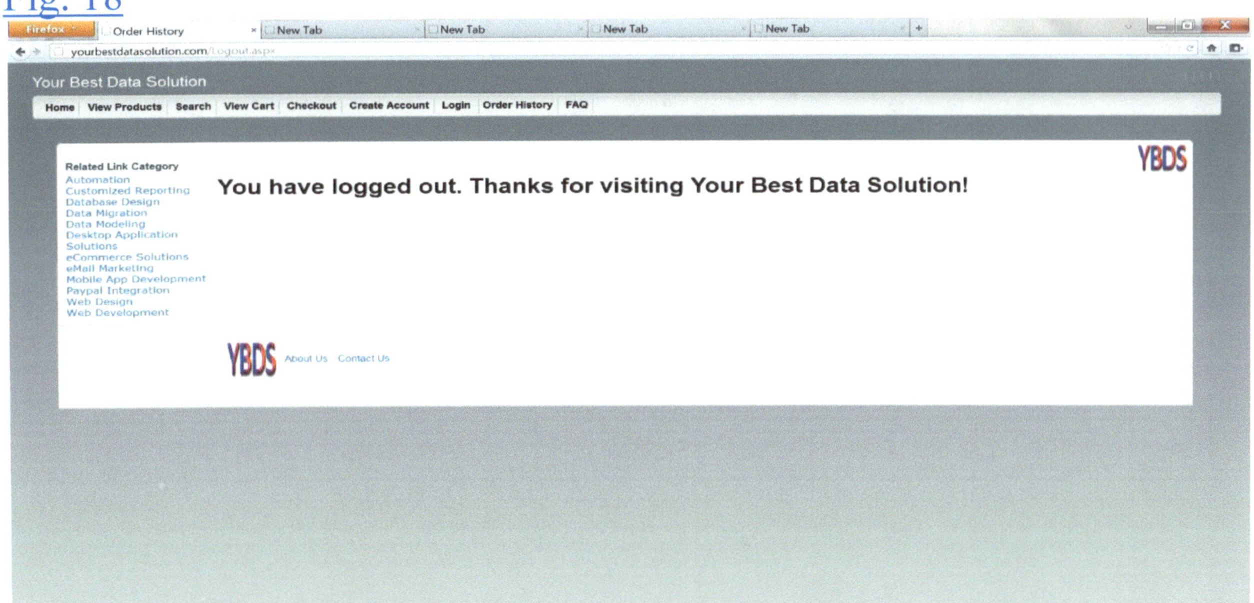

You may purchase a copy of our companion disk which contains all files for the project at http://www.amazon.com/gp/product/B00AOU76K8!

View Customers

Admin users are users that have administrative control over the website. These users would include only the website owner and authorized personnel. Admin functionality includes all customer functionality plus the following three areas of functionality:

- Ability to view entire customer list of information
- Ability to view all customer orders
- Ability to add new products to the site.

The website identifies admin users based on their login credentials. Users that are not admin users will not see the administrative options that admin users have. Fig. 19 shows a logged in admin user with the admin options in the upper center to the upper right of the web page. When a user clicks the Customers link, they will see a complete list of customers as displayed in Fig. 20. The admin can see information for each customer by clicking the View Customer Details link (Fig. 21).

Fig. 19

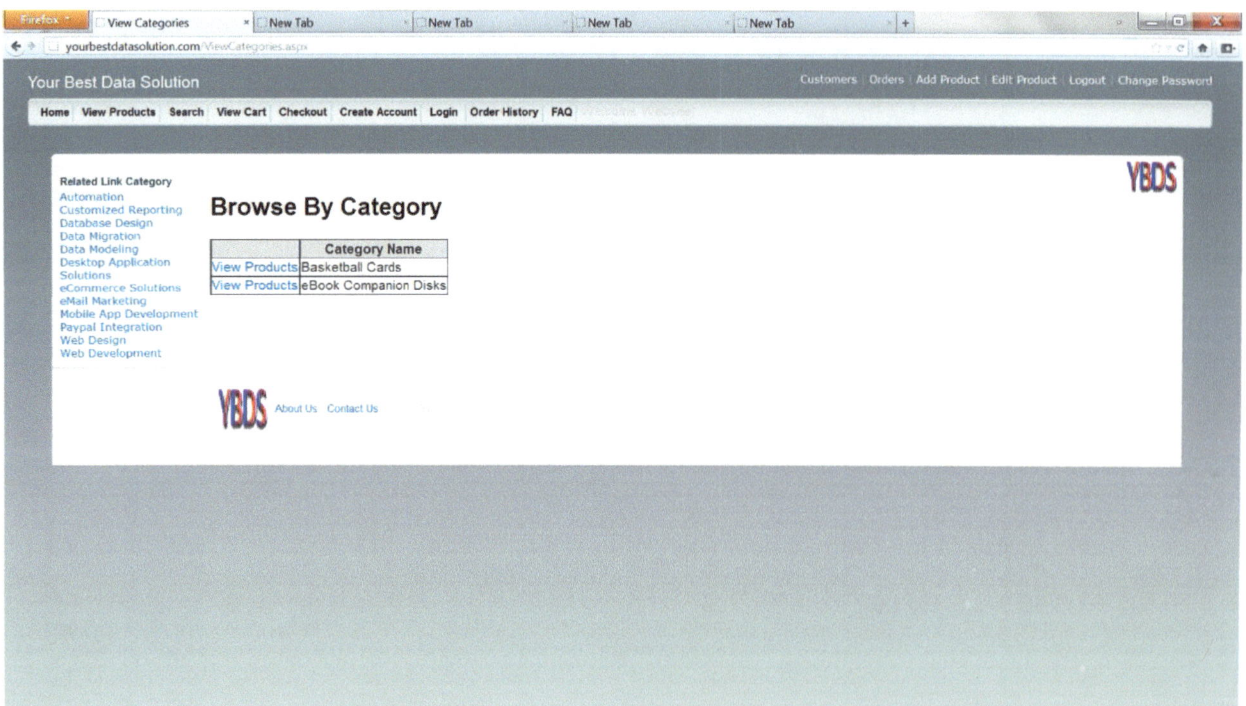

You may purchase a copy of our companion disk which contains all files for the project at http://www.amazon.com/gp/product/B00AOU76K8!

Fig. 20

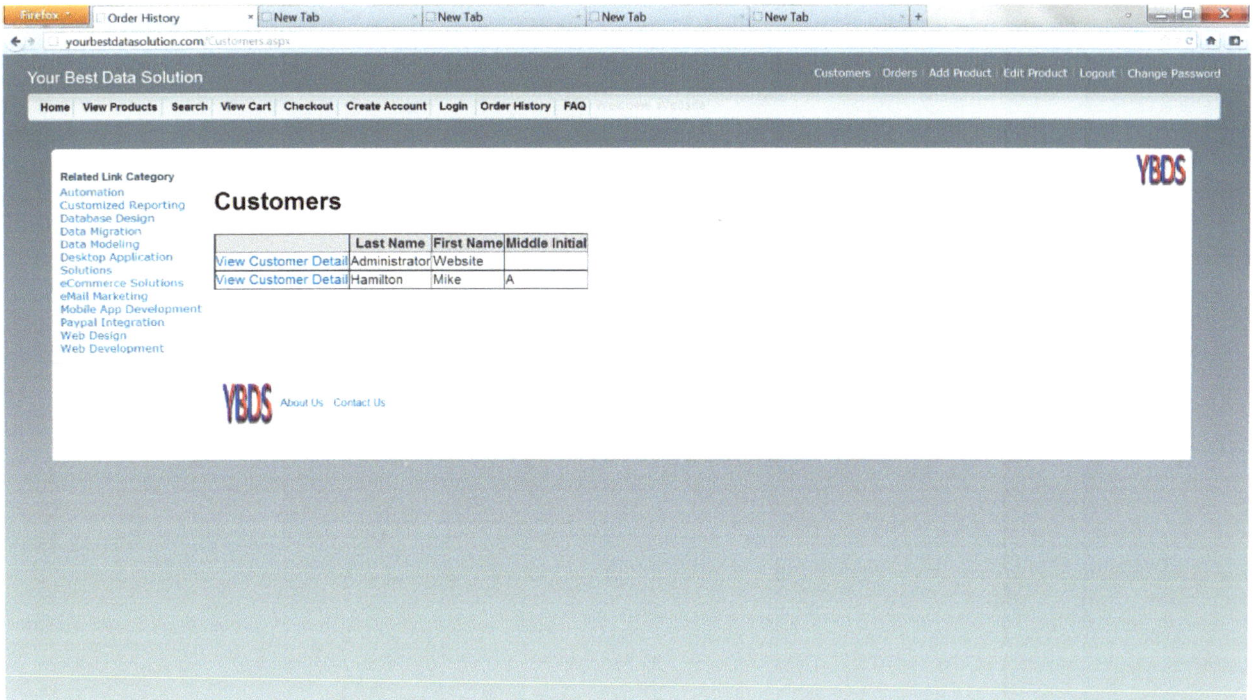

Fig. 21

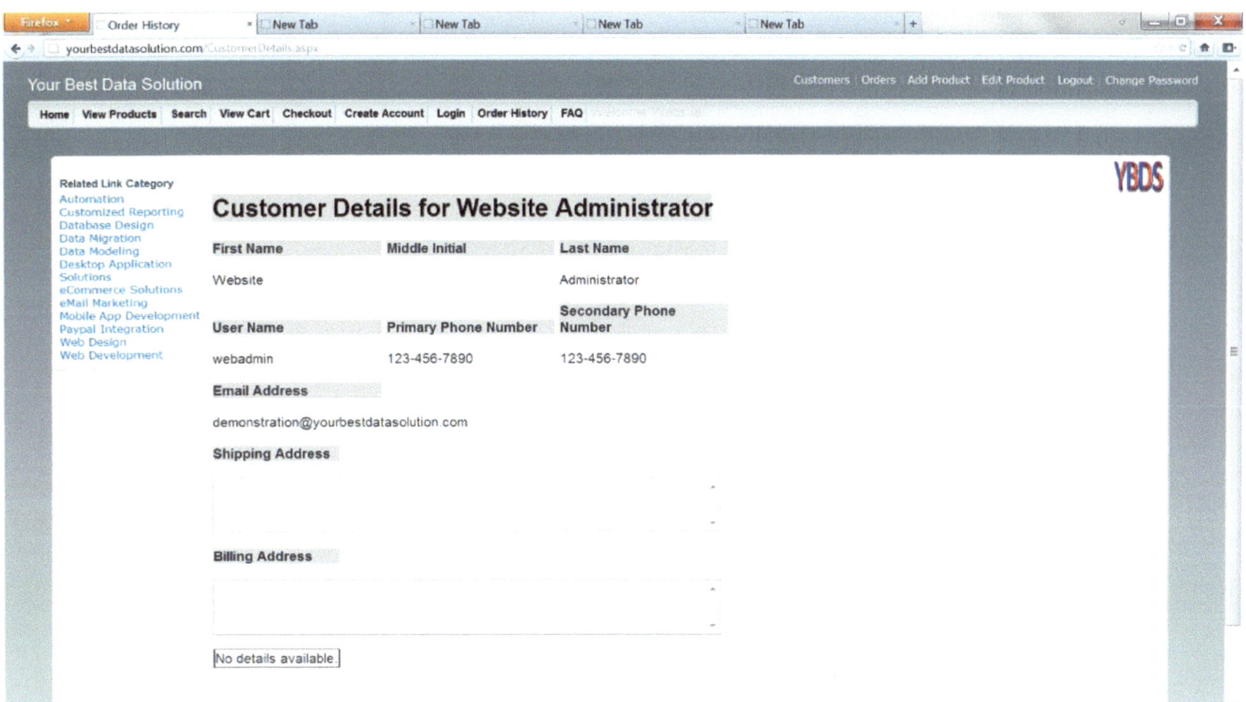

You may purchase a copy of our companion disk which contains all files for the project at http://www.amazon.com/gp/product/B00AOU76K8!

View Orders

When the admin clicks the View Orders link, a complete list of all orders is displayed as shown in Fig. 22. The admin can then view the order details by clicking the View Order Detail link (Fig. 23). The admin may also filter the order list by selecting Paid or Shipped in the dropdown box and clicking Filter by Order Status.

Fig. 22

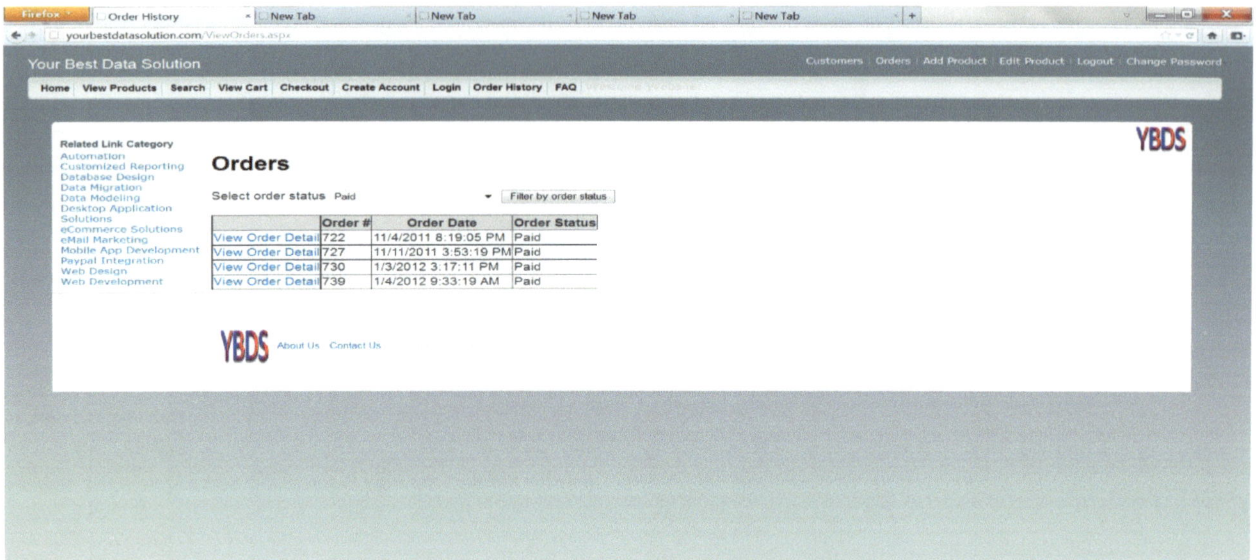

Fig. 23

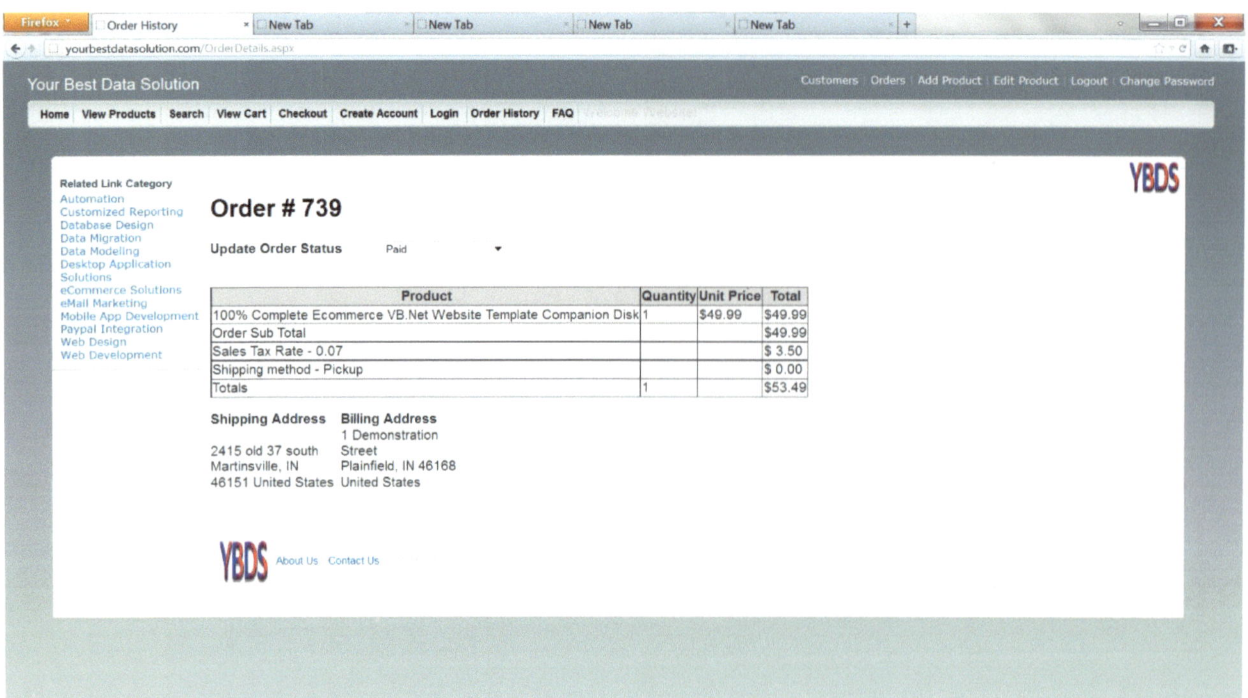

You may purchase a copy of our companion disk which contains all files for the project at http://www.amazon.com/gp/product/B00AOU76K8!

Add Product

Admin users may add products to the menu by clicking the Add Products link and completing the web form shown in Fig. 24 . Photos may be uploaded and related to the product entry by clicking the Browse button and selecting the desired file from the file dialog pop-up box (Fig. 25). The product is added when the user clicks Add Product. **It is not necessary to add a photo with the product; however, more extensive knowledge is required to add a photo to a product outside of the admin user interface.

Fig. 24

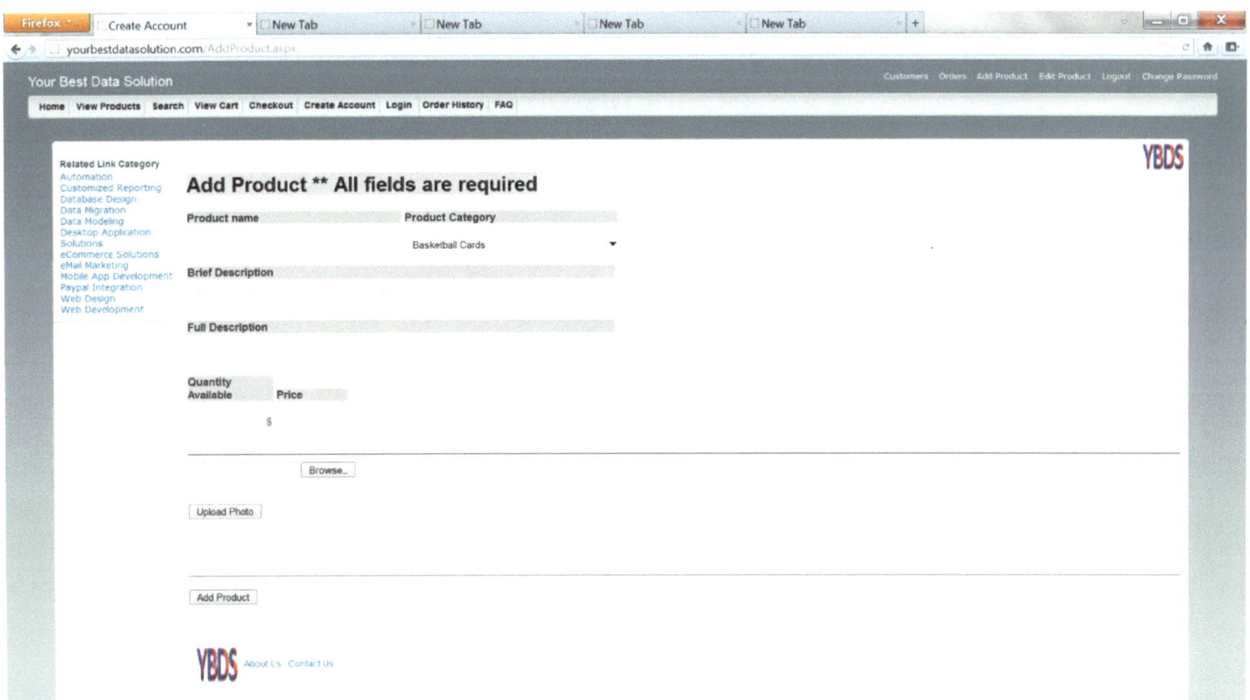

You may purchase a copy of our companion disk which contains all files for the project at http://www.amazon.com/gp/product/B00AOU76K8!

Fig. 25

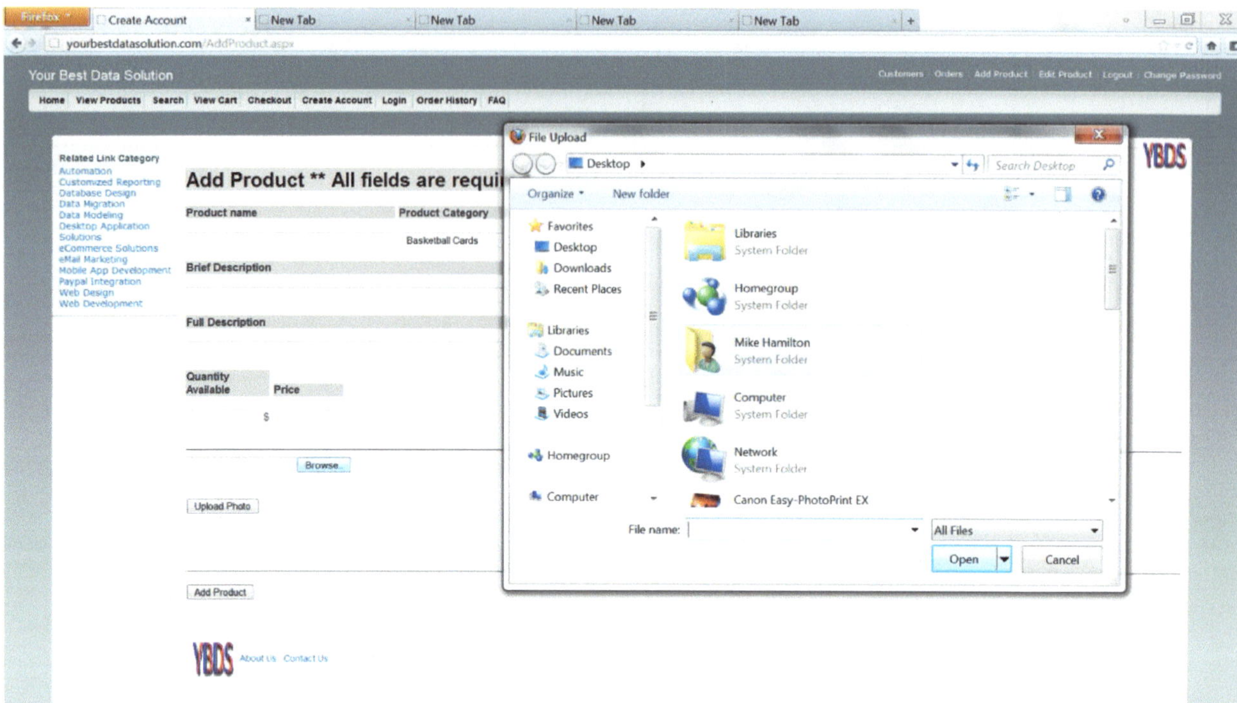

Conclusion

This online ordering system is designed to be user-friendly, while offering automation and reporting benefits to the business administrator of the website. It is the intent of YBDS, LLC to constantly improve existing products for its customers. All feedback regarding the functionality or ease of use of this site is welcomed and should be sent to mikehamilton@yourbestdatasolution.com. Thank you for choosing this product from YBDS, LLC!

You may purchase a copy of our companion disk which contains all files for the project at http://www.amazon.com/gp/product/B00AOU76K8!

About the Author

My IT journey began with a 1 1/2 year internship with the Center of Innovation in Assessment department of Indiana University in July of 2006. Since then, I have worked as an onsite consultant in the health care data industry for two years, and I was the principal programmer and database administrator for 2 1/2 years with OneAmerica, an insurance and financial services company in Indianapolis, IN. During my time at OneAmerica, I was

You may purchase a copy of our companion disk which contains all files for the project at http://www.amazon.com/gp/product/B00AOU76K8!

responsible for enhancing and maintaining desktop, database, and web applications which were utilized by over 400 users. Currently, I serve as Decision Support Analyst/Programmer in the Office of Research Administration at Indiana University. My approach to reporting projects, application development, and database development implements the Microsoft Best Practices approach.

Most of my work experience was achieved while obtaining my degrees. In 2008, I completed my Associates degree in Computer Science at Ivy Tech State College in Bloomington, IN. In 2012, I received my Bachelors Degree in Computer Science from the Purdue University School of Engineering. I will resume my education in 2013, as I pursue a Masters degree.

This book was written with the intent of expediting the development of the next generation of programmers. I also feel this book offers a low cost alternative to entrepreneurs and small business owners who do not currently utilize an ecommerce solution. I welcome your feedback. Please send any questions or comments to mikehamilton@yourbestdatasolution.com. Thank you and much success to your educational or entrepreneurial endeavors!

Works Cited

PayPal™. (2011, 01 08). *SDKs and Downloads.* Retrieved 01 16, 2011, from PayPal™ Web Site: www.paypal.com

www.ingramcontent.com/pod-product-compliance
Lightning Source LLC
LaVergne TN
LVHW070945210926
848482LV00002B/98

9780983417422